Dear Tom—

I thought you'd enjoy the latest thinking on corporate boards! It is a product of our KLI Conference held (for the first time!) in New York City last year.

My best wishes,

Jay A Conger

D1557758

Boardroom Realities

The Kravis Leadership Institute

The Kravis Leadership Institute plays an active role in the development of young leaders via educational programs, research and scholarship, and the development of technologies for enhancing leadership potential.

The Kravis-de Roulet Leadership Conferences

The Kravis-de Roulet Leadership conferences, which began in 1990, are annual leadership conferences funded jointly by an endowment from Henry R. Kravis and the de Roulet family. This perpetual funding, along with additional support from the Kravis Leadership Institute and Claremont McKenna College, enables us to attract the finest leadership scholars and practitioners as conference presenters and participants.

Boardroom Realities

Building Leaders Across Your Board

Jay A. Conger, Editor

Published by Jossey-Bass
A Wiley Imprint
989 Market Street, San Francisco, CA 94103-1741—www.josseybass.com

Jossey-Bass books and products are available through most bookstores. To contact Jossey-Bass directly call our Customer Care Department within the U.S. at 800-956-7739, outside the U.S. at 317-572-3986, or fax 317-572-4002.

Jossey-Bass also publishes its books in a variety of electronic formats. Some content that appears in print may not be available in electronic books.

Library of Congress Cataloging-in-Publication Data

Boardroom realities: building leaders across your board / Jay A. Conger, editor.
p. cm. — (The Jossey-Bass business & management series)
Includes bibliographical references and index.
ISBN 978-0-470-39178-5 (cloth)
1. Directors of corporations. 2. Chief executive officers. I. Conger, Jay Alden.
HD2745.B5954 2009
658.4'22—dc22

2008051602

Printed in the United States of America
FIRST EDITION
HB Printing 10 9 8 7 6 5 4 3 2 1

The Jossey-Bass
Business & Management Series

Contents

To my grandfather, John Jay Hopkins

About the Authors

Jay A. Conger holds the Henry Kravis Research Chair Professorship of Leadership at Claremont McKenna College. He is one of the world's experts on leadership. You'll see him quoted in the *Wall Street Journal* analyzing people and trends in the executive suite and in the boardroom. In recognition of his extensive work with companies, *BusinessWeek* named him "number five" on its list of the world's top ten management educators. *The Financial Times* described him as one of the "World's Top Educators," and *BusinessWeek* called him the best business school professor to teach leadership to executives.

Author of over ninety articles and book chapters and thirteen books, he researches leadership, organizational change, boards of directors, and the training and development of leaders and managers. His articles have appeared in the *Harvard Business Review, Organizational Dynamics, Business & Strategy, Leadership Quarterly, The Academy of Management Review,* and *The Journal of Organizational Behavior.* His most recent books include *The Practice of Leadership* (2006), *Growing Your Company's Leaders: How Organizations Use Succession Management for Competitive Advantage* (2003), *Shared Leadership* (2002), *Corporate Boards: New Strategies for Adding Value at the Top* (2001), *The Leader's Change Handbook* (1999), *Building Leaders* (1999), and *Winning*

'Em Over: A New Model for Management in the Age of Persuasion (1998). His book *Charismatic Leadership in Organizations* (1998) received the Choice book award. One of his earlier books, *Learning to Lead*, has been described by *Fortune* magazine as "the source" for understanding leadership development.

He has taught at the Harvard Business School, INSEAD (France), the London Business School, McGill University, and the University of Southern California. He received the highest teacher ratings in USC's first-year M.B.A. program. While at the Harvard Business School, he was ranked by first-year M.B.A. students in the top 10 percent of the school's faculty. He is also the recipient of teaching awards from the London Business School and McGill University. He has been awarded by the Center for Creative Leadership their prestigious H. Smith Richardson Fellowship for his research on leadership.

Outside of his work with universities, he consults with a worldwide list of private corporations and nonprofit organizations. His insights have been featured in *BusinessWeek*, *The Economist*, *The Financial Times*, *Forbes*, *Fortune*, *The Los Angeles Times*, *The New York Times*, *The San Francisco Chronicle*, *Training*, *The Wall Street Journal*, and *Working Woman*.

Joseph L. Bower, Baker Foundation Professor of Business Administration, has been a leader in general management at Harvard Business School for more than forty-five years. The faculty chair of "The Corporate Leader," until this year he served as the founding faculty chair of "The General Manager Program," both in Executive Education. An expert on corporate strategy, organization, and leadership, he has devoted much of his teaching and research to challenges confronting corporate leaders in today's rapidly changing, hypercompetitive global markets. Presently he is focusing on corporate value added—the contribution that corporate groups make to their operating divisions, as well as on the management of CEO succession. Bower is the author or coauthor of more than a dozen books. The newest, *The CEO Within: Why Inside-Outsiders Are the Key to Succession Planning*, was published in November 2007 by Harvard Business School Press. His previous book, *From Resource Allocation to Strategy* (with Clark Gilbert), was published in 2005 by Oxford University Press, and won the Best Book in 2006 award from *Strategy and Management*. His latest article is "Solve the Succession Crisis by Growing Inside-Outside Leaders," *Harvard Business Review*, November 2007. Others include "How Managers' Everyday Decisions Create—or Destroy—Your Company's Strategy" (with Clark Gilbert), *Harvard Business Review*, February 2007, "Not All M&As Are Alike—and That Matters," "Lead from the Center: How to Manage Divisions Dynamically," and the award-winning "Disruptive Change: When Trying Harder Is Part of the Problem," all published in the *Harvard Business Review*.

Bower is a member of several corporate boards and is a life trustee of the New England Conservatory of Music.

Dr. Ram Charan has captured his business insights in numerous books and articles. In the past five years, Dr. Charan's books have sold more than two million copies. These include the best-seller *Execution: The Discipline of Getting Things Done* and *Confronting Reality*, both coauthored with Larry Bossidy, *What the CEO Wants You to Know*, *Boards at Work*, *Every Business Is a Growth Business*, *Profitable Growth*, and *Boards That Deliver*. A frequent contributor to *Fortune*, Dr. Charan has written two cover stories, "Why CEOs Fail" and "Why Companies Fail." His other articles have appeared in the *Financial Times*, *Harvard Business Review*, *Director's Monthly*, and *Strategy and Business*.

Dr. Charan has served on the Blue Ribbon Commission on Corporate Governance and was elected a Distinguished Fellow of the National Academy of Human Resources. He is on the board of Austin Industries and Tyco Electronics.

He earned M.B.A. and doctorate degrees from Harvard Business School, where he graduated with high distinction and was a Baker Scholar. After receiving his doctorate degree, he served on the Harvard Business School faculty.

Catherine M. Dalton holds the David H. Jacobs Chair of Strategic Management in the Kelley School of Business, Indiana University. She also serves as editor of *Business Horizons*, as research director of the Institute for Corporate Governance, and as a fellow in the Randall L. Tobias Center for Leadership Excellence. She received her Ph.D. degree in Strategic Management from the Kelley School of Business, Indiana University. Professor Dalton's research, focusing largely on corporate governance and strategic leadership, has appeared in the *Academy of Management Journal*, *Academy of Management Review*, *Academy of Management Executive*, *Strategic Management Journal*, *Entrepreneurship Theory & Practice*, *Journal of Business Venturing*, *Journal of Management*, and *California Management Review*. She is a member of the Indiana University Alliance of Distinguished and Titled Professors.

Dan R. Dalton is the founding director of the Institute for Corporate Governance, dean emeritus, and the Harold A. Poling Chair of Strategic Management in the Kelley School of Business, Indiana University. Formerly with General Telephone & Electronics (GT&E), he received his Ph.D. degree from the University of California, Irvine. A fellow of the Academy of Management, Professor Dalton is widely published, with over three hundred articles in corporate governance, business strategy, law, and ethics. In addition, his work has been frequently featured in the business and financial press, including *The Wall Street Journal*, *BusinessWeek*, *Fortune*, *The Economist*, *The Financial Times*, *The Boston Globe*, *The Chicago Tribune*, *The Los Angeles Times*, *The Washington Post*, and *The New York Times*. Recognized by *BusinessWeek* as a "Governance Guru," Professor Dalton regularly addresses public, corporate, and industry groups on corporate governance issues. He is also a fellow of the Tobias Center for Leadership Excellence and a member of the Indiana University Alliance of Distinguished and Titled Professors.

Sydney Finkelstein is the Steven Roth Professor of Management at the Tuck School at Dartmouth College, where he teaches courses on leadership and strategy. He has taught executive education at the Tuck School (where he serves as faculty director of the flagship Tuck Executive Program) and has consulted to companies around the world. He holds degrees from Concordia University and the London School of Economics, as well as a Ph.D. degree from Columbia University in strategic management. He currently serves on the editorial review boards of the *Administrative Science Quarterly* and *Strategic Organization*. Professor Finkelstein has published eleven books and over sixty articles, including the number one bestseller in the United States and Japan, *Why Smart Executives Fail* (http:www.whysmartexecutivesfail.com). *The Wall Street Journal* called it "a marvel—a jargon-free business book based on serious research that offers genuine insights with clarity and sometimes even wit . . . It should be required reading not just for executives but for investors as well." His new book, titled *Think Again: Why Good Leaders Make Bad Decisions and How to Keep It From Happening to You*, will be published by Harvard Business School Press in 2009.

Edward E. Lawler III is Distinguished Professor of Business and director of the Center for Effective Organizations in the Marshall School of Business at the University of Southern California. He joined USC in 1978 and, during 1979, founded and became director of the University's Center for Effective Organizations. He has consulted with over one hundred organizations on employee involvement, organizational change, and compensation and has been honored as a top contributor to the fields of organizational development, organizational behavior, corporate governance, and human resource management. The author of over 350 articles and forty-three books, he has had articles appear in leading academic journals as well as *Fortune*, *Harvard Business Review*, and leading newspapers including *USA Today* and *The Financial Times*. His most recent books include *Rewarding Excellence* (2000), *Corporate Boards: New Strategies for Adding Value at the Top* (2001), *Organizing for High Performance* (2001), *Treat People Right* (2003), *Human Resources Business Process Outsourcing* (2004), *Achieving Strategic Excellence: An Assessment of Human Resource Organizations* (2006), *Built to Change* (2006), *America at Work* (2006), *The New American Workplace* (2006), and *Talent: Making People Your Competitive Advantage* (2008). For more information, visit http://www.edwardlawler.com.

Chosen as one of Canada's "Top 40 Under 40,"™ **Dr. Richard Leblanc** is an award-winning teacher and researcher, consultant, professor, lawyer, and specialist on boards of directors.

He has conducted over two hundred director interviews and has observed and assisted dozens of boards in action. He has served as an expert witness for underperforming boards, advised government regulators, and been an external adviser to boards that have won national awards and peer endorsement from institutional shareholders for their corporate governance practices.

Professor Leblanc's detailed advice helped shape the governance guidelines that are mandated for all Canadian companies. His empirical findings also have been of interest to boards of directors, shareholders, the media, professional advisers to boards, and industry associations. His Ph.D. degree was adjudicated as the winner of the Best Dissertation Award by the Administrative Sciences Association of Canada, and his book, coauthored with Professor James Gillies, is titled *Inside the Boardroom: How Boards Really Work and the Coming Revolution in Corporate Governance*, published by John Wiley & Sons.

Professor Leblanc has assessed the effectiveness of boards of directors; audit, compensation, nominating, and governance committees; chairs of boards; chairs of board committees; and CEOs; along with offering recommendations for improvement.

He may be reached by e-mail at rleblanc@yorku.ca.

Neng Liang is professor of management, associate dean, and director of the Executive M.B.A. Program at China Europe International Business School, and is a standing committee member of Shanghai Pudong Chinese People's Political Consultative Conference. Previously he was professor of management at Loyola College of Maryland and professor of management at the China Centre for Economic Research (CCER), Beijing University. He is the author of *Corporate Governance: American Experience and Chinese Practices* (Beijing: People's University Press, 2000). His articles have appeared in *Academy of Management Learning and Education*, *Journal of International Business Studies*, *The European Journal of Marketing*, *The International Executive*, *The Journal of Development Studies*, *Chief Executive China*, and elsewhere. He has served as a consultant to multinational firms including General Electric, Johnson & Johnson, and PepsiCo; as a vice president of the Chinese Economists Society (CES); and as chairman of the Baltimore-Xiamen Sister City Committee of the Municipal Government of Baltimore, United States. From 1998 to 2001, he served as the Chinese director of the Beijing International M.B.A. program at Peking University.

Jay W. Lorsch is the Louis Kirstein Professor of Human Relations at the Harvard Business School. He is an internationally recognized expert on corporate boards of directors and the author of two pathbreaking books about corporate boards: *Back to the Drawing Board: Designing Boards for a Complex World* (with Colin B. Carter, 2003) and *Pawns or Potentates: The Reality of America's Corporate Boards* (with Elizabeth MacIver, 1989). He has also served on the boards of many public companies in both the United States and Europe. He was elected to the American

Academy of Arts & Sciences on the basis of his work on corporate governance.

Mark B. Nadler is a partner at Oliver Wyman—Delta Organization & Leadership. He works with both public and private equity portfolio companies on improving leadership effectiveness at the board, CEO, and senior team levels. His clients include a broad range of *Fortune* 500 companies in health care, financial services, manufacturing, and consumer products, with a special emphasis on media and entertainment. Before joining Delta in 1995, Mark spent twenty-two years as a journalist and held senior management positions at newspapers including *The Wall Street Journal* and *The Chicago Sun-Times*, where he was vice president and executive editor. He has authored and contributed to numerous publications on topics involving leadership effectiveness and organization change, and was coeditor of *Building Better Boards: A Blueprint for Effective Governance*, published in 2006 by Jossey-Bass.

Katharina Pick is a visiting assistant professor at the Peter F. Drucker and Masatoshi Ito Graduate School of Management. Her research examines the internal group dynamics of corporate boards of directors, with a particular focus on the psychology of board membership, speaking-up behavior, and board process in decision making and conflict resolution. For her dissertation, *Around the Boardroom Table: Interactional Aspects of Governance*, she observed boardroom dynamics firsthand and conducted a qualitative analysis of group process. She is also the author of several case studies on boards of directors. Professor Pick's other research interests include gender and leadership, role negotiation and social identity in high-status groups, and the diffusion of deviant organizational behavior. She received a Ph.D. degree in organizational behavior from Harvard University.

Roger W. Raber is senior adviser and former CEO and president of the National Association of Corporate Directors (NACD).

Founded in 1977, NACD has ten thousand members and is the only nonprofit professional organization devoted exclusively to providing information, research, and education for corporate directors and boards. Dr. Raber has served on corporate boards and audit committees in the financial services industry. He also has served as a private college trustee and has chaired a public school district. Dr. Raber was appointed by the U.S. Secretary of Commerce to serve on the Board of Overseers of the Malcolm Baldrige Award Program. He speaks frequently to national and international groups, including the American Red Cross, Japanese Management Association, and the World Bank Group. He has been influential in shaping the founding of new governance institutes in a variety of regions, including Asia, Central Europe, and Latin America. Prior to his appointment to NACD in 1999, Dr. Raber was director of member services for America's Community Bankers (ACB) in Washington, D.C., and president of the ACB's Center for Financial Studies in Connecticut.

Sarah Smith Orr is the owner and principal in a management and planning consulting firm, Smith Orr & Associates, specializing in the nonprofit sector. She is also an adjunct professor at the Peter F. Drucker and Masatoshi Ito Graduate School of Management at Claremont Graduate University (CGU), teaching leadership and governance in the nonprofit sector. She is currently serving as the interim executive director of the Kravis Leadership Institute. She and colleague Ron Riggio, director of the Kravis Leadership Institute, coedited and published *Improving Leadership in Nonprofit Organizations* (Jossey-Bass, 2003), a text that includes chapters she authored or coauthored, one titled "Soul-Based Leadership" and the other "Transformational Leadership." Sarah is a certified trainer and a member of the Advisory Board for the Achieving Styles Institute. Due to her deep interest in the role of leaders and a commitment to support the advancement of women, she has been involved in the founding and startup of Leadership California, a statewide educational program for women leaders in California (founding executive director), Leadership Berks County, and Leadership Pasadena. She currently serves on the board of the National Women's Hall of Fame and as a founding member of the National Advisory Forum for The Women's Museum, an Institute for the Future. Sarah holds an executive M.B.A. from Claremont Graduate University and is currently completing her Ph.D. in Education at the same institution. Her dissertation research topic is "Older Women Making Meaning in Their Lives."

Jeffrey A. Sonnenfeld is the author of six leadership books, including the widely acclaimed *The Hero's Farewell,* along with hundreds of scholarly articles. Frequently cited in the media, he is the senior associate dean for executive programs at Yale University's School of Management, where he is the Lester Crown Professor of Management Practice as well as the founder and president of the Yale Chief Executive Leadership Institute. His A.B., M.B.A, and doctorate degrees are from Harvard University, where he was also a business professor for ten years. His consulting experience and public speaking are focused on CEO leadership, board governance, and leadership development. Sonnenfeld's commentaries on corporate leadership appear regularly in the media, with frequent appearances in *The New York Times*, *The Wall Street Journal*, *BusinessWeek*, *Forbes*, *Fortune*, the Associated Press, and Bloomberg, and on TV programs on CNBC, FoxNews, CNN, PBS, MSNBC, NBC, CBS, and ABC.

Michael Useem is William and Jacalyn Egan Professor of Management and director of the Center for Leadership and Change Management at the Wharton School, University of Pennsylvania. He has completed studies of corporate organization, ownership, governance, restructuring, and leadership. He is the author of several books, including *The Go Point: When It's Time to Decide* (Random House, 2006); *The Leadership Moment: Nine*

True Stories of Triumph and Disaster and Their Lessons for Us All (Random House, 1998); *Investor Capitalism: How Money Managers Are Changing the Face of Corporate America* (HarperCollins, 1996); and *Executive Defense: Shareholder Power and Corporate Reorganization* (Harvard University Press, 1993). His articles have appeared in *Administrative Science Quarterly*, *Academy of Management Learning and Education*, *American Sociological Review*, *Corporate Governance*, and elsewhere. He has presented programs on leadership and governance to organizations ranging from American Express and Citigroup to Intel, Toyota, and the World Economic Forum. He has consulted on governance with Fannie Mae, HealthSouth, Tyco International, and other companies.

Elise Walton is a consultant specializing in the practice areas of corporate governance, strategic change management, organization architecture, and executive leadership. Over the past twenty years, Elise has worked with clients such as AT&T, AXA-Equitable, Fannie Mae, Ford, Hewlett Packard, Merck, Tyco, TXU, Xerox, and Unilever. Her projects have included corporate center alignment and redesign, merger and acquisition due diligence and integration process support; business-driven leadership development and talent management programs; executive team effectiveness; CEO evaluation; and board assessment.

Elise received a B.A. from Bowdoin College, an M.A. from Columbia University Teachers College, and a Ph.D. jointly from Harvard University and Harvard Business School. She has taught in the executive M.B.A. programs of Columbia University and the NYU Stern School.

Andrew Ward is a member of the management faculty of the Terry College of Business of the University of Georgia, and author of *The Leadership Lifecycle: Matching Leaders to Evolving Organizations* (Palgrave Macmillan, 2003). Ward received his Ph.D. from The Wharton School of the University of

Pennsylvania. Ward's research centers on leadership, corporate governance, and the role and challenges of chief executive officers. His research has appeared in numerous academic journals, as well as publications including *BusinessWeek*, *The Financial Times*, *The Washington Post*, *Directorship*, *Directors & Boards*, *Corporate Board Member*, and *Investor's Business Daily*. He is frequently quoted in the media on leadership, governance, and CEO succession issues. Jeffrey Sonnenfeld and Andrew Ward are coauthors of *Firing Back: How Great Leaders Rebound After Career Disasters*, published by Harvard Business School Press, 2007.

Introduction

Leveraging Your Board's Leadership Capability

Jay A. Conger

I have been actively involved for a decade in studying boardroom governance and in consulting to boards. During that time, I have witnessed several waves of reforms. Practices that were relatively rare in the early 1990s such as lead directors and board evaluations are now commonplace. These were believed to preempt boardroom failures. They did not.

As you might guess, the spread of these reforms closely followed corporate scandals, downturns in the economy, and financial markets that negatively affected company fortunes. In other words, reforms often arrived as the byproducts of CEO and company failures. Eventually, the responsibility for these failures settled on the boards themselves. Each wave of reform promoted or accelerated the spread of a handful of boardroom governance practices. These were believed to provide greater safeguards against boardroom failures. Generally, they have not.

In the past few years, we have witnessed a rise in mandated governance structures, thanks to the Sarbanes-Oxley Act (SOX) and the post-SOX revisions in the guidelines of the listing exchanges. Although these provide some safeguards, they also have side effects. What I now see is that many boards are consumed by their mandated oversight and monitoring demands. Time for other critical board responsibilities has been minimized. Many boards have also slipped into a "check the box" mentality when it comes to governance practices. They have come to believe that assigning a lead director, holding annual board evaluations, ensuring director independence, and a set of other "governance best practices" will preempt boardroom failures. In the worst case, they feel that institutional investors and monitoring agencies demand such structures, and so they implement them.

What my colleagues in this book and I have learned is that simply having the "right" governance practices on your board is only a first step—at best. We actually know from research that there is little or no relationship between the presence or absence of most board governance practices and the performance of your organization. After all, Enron won acclaim for its many "best practice" boardroom governance structures.

The aim of this book is therefore twofold. One is to help you as a director or as a CEO or as a boardroom adviser to address the governance realities facing your boardroom today. It will organize the sea of opinions and research on boardroom governance into a coherent picture so that you and your board can make better choices about governance. It will critically evaluate the many practices that have become commonplace over the decade, from lead directors to non-executive chairs to board evaluations to director criteria for "independence."

The second aim of this book is to demonstrate that boardroom leadership and character make the primary difference in the performance of a board—not a set of governance practices. In other words, effective boards are more often the product of a leadership capacity shared across the board and a culture that encourages candid dialogue and inquiry. They are the combination of a CEO who earnestly shares his or her power with the board and directors who are able to lead in the unique setting of a boardroom. Effective boards possess a high-caliber directorate whose members are proactive, inquisitive, and highly responsible leaders. They operate as a team despite conditions that are not ideal for teamwork. The skills and backgrounds of directors complement one another powerfully and match the unique needs of the business. These are boards for which best practices are not window dressing but rather processes that enable an already empowered and informed directorship to act as both an outstanding source of counsel and a vigilant monitor. They are boards that advise their CEOs but also stretch them. They are high-performance boards.

The Organization of This Book

This book is organized into four sections covering some of the most critical topics facing your boardroom today—leadership, talent management, CEO succession, and general practices for improving the performance of your boardroom. A brief summary of each chapter follows so that you can pick and choose the topics of greatest interest to you as a reader.

Because the book is framed around the central issue of leadership in the boardroom, our first section dives deep into the challenge of effectively leading boards. As readers are well aware, boards have unique leadership challenges. In essence, boardroom leaders are leading peers rather than direct reports. Directors are accomplished individuals. Many are outstanding leaders in their own right. Leading a group of talented *peers* is like walking a tightwire. Authoritative styles are likely to be resisted; highly deferential and overly facilitative styles are likely to be seen as weak. There is also a serious imbalance of information on a board. The CEO is the most informed individual on the board today. As a result, many directors feel too uninformed to demonstrate strong leadership and therefore defer to the CEO's judgment. This outcome has produced catastrophic outcomes for some companies—Enron, Tyco, and WorldCom being some of the most pronounced examples. To counterbalance this possibility, we have witnessed the rise of two boardroom leadership roles over recent decades—the lead or presiding director and the non-executive chair. Whereas the majority of publicly traded boards today have a lead director, there is more controversy over the need for a non-executive chair. That said, this latter role is appearing with greater frequency on public boards. In some countries such as the United Kingdom, boards are actually required to have a chair's role that is not occupied by the company CEO.

In this first section, "Leadership in Your Boardroom," four chapters will help you address the issue of how your board can build strong leadership capability and achieve a healthy balance of power. The chapters in this section share a general concern for strengthening the leadership capacity of your board, but they do take differing perspectives on the topical issue of who should be the formal leader of the board—a non-executive director or the CEO. That said, all of the contributors in this section argue that directors themselves need to be proactive and vigilant and share in the leadership demands of running a boardroom.

In Chapter One, Jay Lorsch explores the critical issue of how leadership can and should be shared across the board. He helps us understand that becoming a boardroom leader is not just a matter of being given a title, whether it is board chair, lead director, or committee chair. Rather, gaining the mantle of leadership is a complex interaction between one's own actions and the perceptions of one's fellow directors around the board table. He notes that the most effective boards are those in which other directors emerge as active leaders. Quite simply: the more leaders that a board has, the better.

Lorsch also identifies critical leadership attributes that directors need to possess for boardrooms to be led well. These include a common attribute—the capacity to spot irregularities, to know when something may be not quite right, and to follow up. This is accompanied by a willingness on the part of directors to commit themselves to take the initiative to solve problems. The best also possess a strong sense that their responsibility is to do the right thing as directors. Their reason for board service is not the money they may receive, nor the status or prestige, but the sense of satisfaction they get in doing the job well. A related quality these leaders share is having or being willing to acquire the knowledge to act effectively. Sometimes the director has a reservoir of knowledge related to the issue at hand. But in many instances, the most effective directors spend a great deal of time and effort to understand facets of the business or the company that are new to them. Finally, they are thoughtful about the process of leading their fellow directors. If you are going to attempt to lead, you want to be as certain as possible that others will follow you. You are undertaking leadership, among peers, who are used to being leaders themselves and thus may not be enthusiastic followers. The best directors understand this dynamic and tailor their style and timing for best effect.

In the next chapter, "Why Your Board Needs a Non-Executive Chair," my colleague Ed Lawler and I argue that your board should seriously consider instituting a non-executive chair role. We take the point of view that there are enormous external pressures facing corporate boards to appoint a non-executive chair. We believe that these pressures are not likely to subside but rather intensify. Given this predicament, our objective is to help your board successfully meet the challenges of a dual leadership model in which authority is shared between the CEO and a non-executive chair. This is an inherently difficult position from which to lead any group, because "two heads" are more confusing than one. To succeed therefore, it is critical to define with immense clarity the chair's roles and responsibilities and to select candidates for the chair position very carefully. We will examine how best to divide the roles and responsibilities of the CEO versus those of the non-executive chair in leading a board. In terms of selecting candidates for non-executive chair roles, we strongly argue against appointing the retiring CEO of the company your board oversees. With a few rare exceptions, this appointment can seriously compromise the oversight role of a board. Rather, we feel that retired "outsider" CEOs are ideal candidates. In addition to this background, we will describe certain personal characteristics necessary to lead as a non-executive chair. For boards disinclined to go down the path of a non-executive chair, we discuss in some detail the alternative leadership models of a lead director and of committee leadership.

In sharp contrast to our point of view, authors Dan and Catherine Dalton will argue against a non-executive chair in their chapter, "The Joint CEO/Chairperson Leadership Issue in Sharp Relief." From their perspective, the CEO is the individual who should hold the board chair's role. The Daltons do not find the arguments in favor of separating the roles of the CEO and the chairperson of the board terribly compelling. They feel strongly that a single voice directing the enterprise at the board level is the optimal form of leadership. Under this model of "unitary command," there will be no parties and constituencies—internal or external—who will question who is in charge and who is accountable. In contrast, when the CEO and board chairperson roles are separated, the enterprise does not have a single presiding officer with the requisite authority to direct relevant personnel and other resources in pursuit of a unified purpose. The CEO and a non-executive chair structure simply does not provide for a single organizational voice. The Daltons argue that internal officers of the firm and a host of external constituencies such as shareholders need to know, definitively, who is in charge of the enterprise, whose voice is paramount, and most critically, who is accountable. The CEO is best positioned to be the "one in charge." When things go wrong, there is also clarity about who is "in charge." They do point out, however, that when the board confers substantial autonomy—as it should—on its combined CEO/board chairperson, the directors must still embrace vigilant oversight, fairly. Directors must not abdicate oversight responsibility with the CEO as their chair.

In the last chapter of Part One, "First Among Equals: Leading Your Fellow Directors as a Board Chair," Katharina Pick illustrates the profound impact of the board chair's leadership style. For example, she shows how chairs affect the way directors interact and work together through the manner in which they draw input from fellow board members. The chair influences how the board oversees management by shaping the relationship and communications that go on between these two groups. When chairs have the authority and legitimacy to lead, they have the ability to create a safe space for open dialogue in which management can receive both criticism and support from directors. Pick also highlights the ways in which leadership behavior by the chair can actually undermine these important aspects of board process. For example, board chairs, particularly *non-executive* chairs, walk a fine line between being too aggressive in their leadership and being too passive. In a group of high status and accomplished fellow directors, and with little *formal* authority, it is all too easy for a chair to overstep his or her position and lose the ability to lead. However, erring on the other side, a chair who is more passive can be equally ineffectual. Directors will be frustrated by a directionless discussion in which they do not have clarity regarding board tasks, or they will think the leader is weak vis-à-vis management.

Drawing upon rich case examples of both effective and ineffective leadership practices, Pick provides practical guidance for your board's chair. She identifies four broad leadership roles for the chair and explains how to successfully lead in each role. The four roles include (1) managing the "status dilemma" of leading a group of equals, (2) managing the "tension" between the various roles the board plays with senior management, (3) sustaining the cohesion of the director group while encouraging debate, and (4) managing the ambiguous nature of the board's role. Pick illustrates how to successfully lead fellow directors in each role.

Part Two of the book, "Talent Management Practices for Your Board," looks at critical boardroom talent issues. For example, does your board have the right skill and experience mix among the directors? Where and how can you find a sufficient number of talented directors? Does your board leverage diversity in meaningful ways? Does your board critically assess its own performance and that of its individual directors? Does your board take a transparent and rigorous approach for assessing your CEO's performance and pay? The four chapters in this section offer thoughtful insights to these questions along with best practice guidance. Specifically, they will examine the talent management topics of (1) how to effectively appraise your board's performance as well as evaluate your individual directors, (2) how to determine the right mix of director skills and competencies, (3) how to identify and build a critical mass of women directors, (4) how aspiring women can become board members and effective contributors as directors, and, finally, (5) how your board should approach the issue of evaluating your CEO's performance and in turn determining and communicating about his or her pay.

The opening chapter of this section, "Appraising Your Board's Performance," examines the three forms of boardroom appraisals—CEO assessments, full board assessments, and individual director assessments. As Ed Lawler and I illustrate, appraising a board's performance has many advantages. Formal, periodic board appraisals can help ensure that all the right processes, procedures, members, and relationships are in place and functioning well. For example, effective evaluations can clarify the individual and collective responsibilities of your directors and the CEO. With better knowledge of what is expected of them, directors are in turn likely to be stronger contributors. Formal evaluations can also identify areas needing greater attention by the board. Directors have told us that after they initiated board evaluations, their meetings went more smoothly, they made better decisions, they acquired greater influence, and they paid more attention to long-term corporate strategy. Formal appraisals of the board as a whole, and also of individual board members and the CEO, can help ensure a healthy balance of power between the board and the chief executive and improve the working relationship between the two. An institutionalized review process makes it harder for a new CEO to dominate a board or avoid being held accountable for poor performance. Finally, the clearest and most consistent benefit we have observed in those companies that have adopted effective board appraisal systems is a commitment by directors and the CEO to devote more time and attention to long-term strategy.

That said, many boardroom appraisals are poorly implemented. For example, feedback rarely reveals serious shortcomings or concerns. Appraisals are often simply a perfunctory exercise. In some boardrooms, an hour might be taken to review the results of the end-of-the-year appraisal but in a "checklist fashion." In our chapter, we will discuss how to avoid such outcomes. We will discuss why your board needs to consider both a rigorous board evaluation and individual director assessments. We will describe how best to implement each of the different evaluations providing practical guidance along the way.

In his chapter titled "Getting the Right Directors on Your Board," Richard Leblanc strongly argues that boards need to devote far more attention to competencies and behaviors in recruiting and assessing directors. The challenge he notes is to address these factors in a manner that is rigorous but at the same time highly pragmatic. As a starting point, your board needs to have a formal director-succession planning and renewal program in place. For example, your nominating committee should have a process for identifying and recruiting new directors, including (1) taking into account their character, ability, experience, behavior and ability to devote the time required; and (2) following an appropriate interview, background, reference check, and selection process. The nominating committee's mandate should also include recommending a director-succession planning process to the board that is objective, transparent, and rigorous. To assist in clarifying this information, the committee needs to create, maintain, and annually evaluate a director competency matrix. The matrix process should outline the competencies, skills, and experiences of the current directors and the key ones required for new directors, with an emphasis on critical gaps.

Following on Chapter Five's examination of board appraisals, Leblanc also explores the issue of director assessments with a special emphasis on individual director evaluations. He expresses the strong opinion that boards need to undertake rigorous individual director assessments. Many boards still avoid such evaluations or else assess by "going through the motions" using self-administered, nonrobust and painless—and ultimately ineffective—evaluations. As potential models for your own board, he offers examples of how companies that have received recognition for their corporate governance practices, and in particular their director peer-evaluation processes, conduct such evaluations with greater rigor.

Continuing on the theme of director selection and development, Sarah Smith Orr in Chapter Seven, "Women Directors in the Boardroom: Adding Value, Making a Difference," examines the issue of women in the boardroom. Despite the statistical evidence of the capabilities of women who are equipped with academic credentials and of extraordinary performance results, the representation of women on corporate boards remains surprisingly low. Yet nowhere is the influence of women as business leaders, investors, and consumers more crucial to decision making than in the corporate boardroom. Drawing on studies by the organization Catalyst, Smith Orr describes recent research showing that, with the exception of two sectors, *Fortune* 500 corporations that dominate in three business measures—return on equity, return on sales, and return on capital invested—were ones with boards including at least three women. Yet women hold just under 15 percent of the directorships on the boards of *Fortune* 500 companies. Why such a pronounced gap? Smith Orr explores the principal contributors to this dilemma, which range from the stereotyping of women's leadership effectiveness to a scarcity of women in the most common director pipeline (CEOs of large corporations) to a lack of a critical mass of women directors on individual boards.

Her chapter then explores how your board can create a conducive boardroom environment for women directors as well as how you can best approach recruiting and developing women directors for your own board. To women seeking directorships, Smith Orr offers invaluable advice on the work experiences, networks, and career planning approaches that will take you into the boardroom. Her chapter provides guidance for women directors on how to succeed in their role.

The last chapter in this section on talent management looks at the hot topic of the board's role in assessing CEO performance and setting and communicating CEO pay. In "Your Board's Crucial Role in Aligning CEO Pay and Performance," Roger Raber outlines five critical principles that must guide your boardroom actions and decisions in this regard. They are (1) independence among the directorship, (2) fair internal and external standards for pay decisions, (3) alignment to value producing performance, (4) an emphasis on achieving key metrics over the long term, and (5) clear and full disclosure of compensation arrangements. For example, the decision makers must be truly independent directors. They should have no material relationship with the company or no relationship that would interfere with independent judgment in carrying out the responsibilities of a director. The audit, compensation, and nominating committees must be composed entirely of independent directors. Fair internal standards for pay would imply that all employees of an organization should benefit when the company does well and share in sacrifices when necessary. A fair compensation policy also means that there will not be extremely wide gaps in pay at different levels (for example, between CEOs and senior managers, or executives and other employees) unless such gaps are justified and explained. Externally, executive pay should be judged according to an appropriate peer group, chosen by the compensation committee. Compensation committees must also strive to motivate not only short-term but long-term performance from CEOs and their teams. Therefore it is important to design pay packages that encourage long-term commitment to the organization's well-being. Tying bonuses, stock grants, or other compensation to an increase in the company's long-term value can help align a CEO's personal financial interests with those of shareholders. Your compensation committee should embrace a philosophy of transparency—meaning full and clear disclosure. In other words, compensation committee members should not only help guide the important facts about compensation arrangements but also let shareholders know these facts in a timely manner. These are several of the critical guidelines that Raber lays out for your board's actions regarding CEO pay.

The third part of the book, "CEO Succession: The Challenges and Opportunities Facing Your Board," offers several perspectives on what your board can and should do with regard to CEO succession. The authors of all three chapters voice their concerns that many boards have failed to engage their CEOs in a meaningful and rigorous succession-planning process—despite this being one of the primary areas of a board's responsibilities. Given the alarming failure rate of CEOs of publicly traded companies and the declining tenure of CEOs in general, it is clear that the process for replacing CEOs in many firms is to a large extent broken. Our contributors identify the reasons why CEO succession is often a flawed process and how your board can proactively preempt the most common breakdowns. They each paint a highly realistic picture of the challenges facing boards that wish to approach the succession challenge rigorously. They note that CEO succession is much more than finding the right replacement for a CEO. The process actually starts with the organization's long-term investment in leadership development across and down its management ranks. Without a long horizon and developmental perspective, it is hard to produce the handful of talented candidates who can fill the shoes of an outgoing CEO. Boards need to ensure that the executive team makes such investments. A critical difference between our authors in this section is the extent to which the board can and should directly influence succession versus provide oversight of the top team's activities.

In the opening chapter of this section, "Managing the CEO's Succession: The Challenge Facing Your Board," Joe Bower takes a position that may surprise you. He argues why your board's role in succession, though very important, must be distinctly subordinate to the role played by the incumbent chief executive. As important as CEO succession should be in the work of the board, the management of the succession process is one of the core responsibilities of the executive leadership team, not the board. Bower illustrates that boards are not constituted so that they can substitute for the CEO in the critical work of developing candidates or in making the final selection of who should be CEO. After describing the limited role of the board in succession, this chapter does clarify what then are the primary areas in which your board can contribute to CEO succession. For example, Bower feels strongly that your board must enquire regularly about the succession process, assess the CEO's and the company's investments in development, track the progress of candidates, and meet as many candidates as possible. At the same time, it cannot get into the details of organizational arrangements that ensure that talented executives have the opportunity to experience general management responsibility early in their careers. Most important, it cannot be present during the critical times when plans and budgets are developed and outcomes reviewed that turn out to be the most critical "teaching moments" for mentors. Rather, the keys rest in management's hands and involve the company's early attention to recruiting and developing talent. Board members must instead note whether management documents a sufficiently large pool of potential CEO candidates and whether the company promotes development that favors *inside-outsider* candidates when they can be found. Does the organization and executive team select its CEO candidates for future-oriented criteria and promote a period of transition that gives the new CEO a maximum chance to succeed? Finally, is there extensive exposure to leading candidates of those on the board who will make the final choice?

In Chapter Ten, titled "Beyond Best Practices: Revisiting the Board's Role in CEO Succession," Mark Nadler notes that the work behind the CEO succession process is much harder than it is often portrayed by governance experts or business journalists, who are quick to excoriate any board that suddenly finds itself with an empty CEO office and no obvious candidate in sight. Seeing an even more active role for your board in CEO succession than does Joe Bower, Nadler identifies a number of specific best practices for boards to implement to ensure a rigorous succession process. Specifically, ten best practices are discussed in this chapter, drawn from the seasoned insights and experience of directors at companies that have actually done succession well. Nadler not only illustrates each practice in detail, but, as important, highlights the challenges of implementing each practice. For example, one best practice of succession planning is for your board to begin the process three to five years before a CEO transition is actually expected to occur. Such a time frame is crucial, because companies are increasingly inclined to promote internally rather than recruit externally, and grooming inside talent takes time. A long succession process ensures the opportunity to fully develop the next CEO through a combination of assignments and activities. Directors need to spend three to five years identifying and monitoring the development of serious candidates and then selecting an heir apparent who spends the remaining time making the transitions through the roles of COO, CEO-designate, CEO, and, ultimately, CEO/chair. Nadler points out, however, that in reality only a minority of boards actually get involved three to five years before the moment of CEO succession. As a result, boards end up making poor choices or giving candidates insufficient time for development.

Nadler takes these succession best practices one step further by adding additional texture to the succession picture by overlaying what he has experienced as the three ever-present dimensions of the process—analytics, politics, and emotions. The best boardroom succession processes acknowledge and integrate all three elements. A powerful example of the interplay of one element in succession decisions occurs on the emotional level. Some CEOs actively avoid working on succession because they would rather not face up to all it implies about aging and mortality. This can be an enormous emotional stumbling block for many CEOs, and a good many will put it off interminably unless pressed into action by the board. Once the succession process is finally in place, the board must keep a sharp eye out for signs that the CEO is actually sabotaging the process, finding excuses to eliminate promising candidates and thereby starting the process all over again.

In the final chapter on CEO succession, "Ending the CEO Succession Crisis," Ram Charan argues that an outsized share of your board's attention has been captured by its governance and fiduciary duties. In other words, too many hours are devoted to monitoring accounting, Sarbanes-Oxley, risk, and financial performance and not enough to time planning for CEO succession and managing searches. Specifically, he recommends that your board should dedicate at minimum two sessions a year to hashing over at least five CEO candidates—devoting at least 15 percent of board time to succession. Directors should also personally get to know rising stars, by inviting them to board meetings and dinners, talking with them informally, and observing them in the natural habitats of their business operations. In addition, board members need to reach a highly refined but dynamic understanding of the CEO position and their options for it long before appointing a successor to the standing CEO. Promising candidates should be as well defined as puzzle pieces; their strengths and experiences must match the shape of their organizations' needs. Boards also need to specify, in terms as precise as possible, three or four aspects of talent, know-how, and experience that are nonnegotiable.

In agreement with Bower, Ram Charan feels strongly that the foundation for CEO succession rests on a strong internal leadership pipeline. Therefore the most important investment companies can make to improve succession is to bolster their leadership development and focus on those very rare people in their ranks who might one day become CEO. As noted by Nadler, they need to be thoughtful about assignments and experiences that cultivate an enterprise perspective and skills required by the future demands facing the company. Boards need to be proactive in encouraging such an investment by the executive team. As well, at the most senior level, functional leaders need to introduce the board to the top two or three most-promising heirs for their own positions, providing detailed analyses of those candidates' strengths and weaknesses. Emerging leaders should routinely take part in presentations to the board and meet informally with directors over lunch. Board members need to closely track the progress not of one or two people but of the top one hundred or two hundred, frequently discussing how each individual fits into the succession puzzle and what experiences or skills might improve that fit.

In the fourth part of the book, "Improving Your Board's Performance and Impact," we turn to three remaining topics. The first explores how your board can leverage team practices to enhance its performance. We know a great deal about superior team performance, and many of these insights and practices can be extrapolated to boardrooms. The second chapter looks at the research on executive derailment and its profound consequences on company performance. Drawing on this knowledge, advice is provided for your board to be better positioned to spot problems in the behavior and actions of the CEO or other executives that could in turn produce dire outcomes for the organization you are overseeing. The last chapter explores the impact of globalization on boards and their governance practices. Its insights are particularly helpful for boards of companies from emerging markets with ambitions to play on the world stage.

In her chapter, titled "How Your Board Can Leverage Team Practices for Better Performance," Elise Walton examines the unique and challenging circumstances a board faces in order to work effectively as a team. For example, its infrequent meetings and the ambiguity and complexity of the information it receives are serious barriers to teamwork. In the context of such challenges, Walton identifies what kinds of team practices can foster effective and appropriate teamwork in a boardroom. She describes the practices of developing a shared context: using tools to synthesize information, diversifying data sources, and anticipating the unexpected to ensure that the board is acting on an informed basis. Practices such as active learning, productive conflict, staying relevant, and versatility create a context in which your board, as a team, can approach issues objectively and with an open mind. Together, these practices vaccinate against unexamined CEO (or other) dependence, uninformed action, and groupthink by encouraging a thoughtful context for learning, insight, and action. Furthermore, by making use of the full capability and wisdom of the team, these practices promote team insight and action that allow the board to lead effectively. She also examines how current concepts of good governance support or undermine effective teamwork.

Chapter Thirteen, "What Your Board Needs to Know: Early Warning Signs That Provide Insights to What Is Really Going on in Companies," describes the critical role of directors in ensuring that the company's leaders are behaving in an ethical manner, are engaging in well-thought-out strategic initiatives, and are attuned to the changing landscape of business. Sydney Finkelstein argues there is virtually no level of acceptable risk that board directors can be willing to take on when it comes to the possibility of business breakdowns. The same challenge confronts individual directors contemplating invitations to join boards. What are the warning signs to look out for that might lead potential directors to say, "no thanks" when offered a board seat? There are some boards for which the potential for trouble will outweigh the opportunities associated with serving.

Finkelstein offers a set of specific questions that boards, and potential board members, should be asking on a regular basis about the companies for which they have critical oversight responsibility today, or potentially tomorrow. He outlines the common behaviors and mind-sets that will derail CEOs and ultimately their companies. Boards need to be on the outlook for such behaviors and characteristics of CEOs. For example, several key warning signs are apparent when it comes to character: Does the CEO believe that he or she is considerably smarter, or better, than other people? Does the CEO always seem to have the "answer" to problems, showing no sign of drawing on the strengths of his or her management team? Does the CEO rely on solutions to new problems that are no different from what he or she has done in the past? All of these questions need to be in the back of the minds of vigilant board members. Any one such attribute may be excused, but when a pattern starts to form the question of character comes to the fore.

Michael Useem and Neng Liang, in their chapter "Globalizing the Company Board: Lessons from China's Lenovo," explore how firms in China, India, and other major economies are reaching out beyond their national boundaries and what the implications are for their boardrooms. Equity owners are on much the same trajectory, with institutional investors, sovereign funds, private-equity firms, and hedge funds all allocating more of their portfolios to holdings outside their home markets. They in turn will be exporting expectations about the governance practices for the boards of the companies they invest in. Using Lenovo's experience as symptomatic of what other companies are likely to face as they globalize their operations and ownership, Useem and Neng foresee governance at globalizing firms moving toward greater engagement of directors in collaborative decision making with management. Executives and directors will ask, as one academic observer of Chinese enterprise has recently suggested, whether they "have a plan for corporate governance that will focus the firm on national competitive advantage and ultimately global advantage rather than short-term profitability in local markets." As they consider or adopt such a plan, that in turn will point toward an evolving skill set for directors, with greater emphasis on director capacity to work with executives at critical choice points. It will also point toward a changing skill set for executives, with a stronger ability to work with directors expected at major decision moments and less inclination to hold directors at arms' length. Institutional investors and other major holders will be more likely as well to look for directors and executives who can collaboratively engage in the firm's most important decisions. Although the norm that boardroom decisions stay in the boardroom has long prevailed, an emerging norm of transparency will encourage directors and executives to reveal more about their decision making behind closed doors. Useem and Neng offer a set of guidelines to help boardrooms successfully make the transition to the new demands faced by firms that are rapidly globalizing. For example, they may need to recruit board members to help address critical strategic priorities or to engage board directors as true decision-making partners with the executive team or to anticipate the governance norms of international investors.

Authors Jeffrey Sonnenfeld and Andrew Ward contend in the concluding chapter, "Conventional Wisdom, Conventional Mythology, and the True Character of Board Governance," that effective governance must go beyond simplistic indicators that can be put forward as mere window dressing or checklisting to the underlying character of the board and its members. Their chapter illustrates powerfully that conventional wisdom about good governance can actually undermine governance effectiveness. They examine certain tenets of conventional wisdom such as director independence, equity ownership, and age limits and expose the folly that exists in an overzealous pursuit of these characteristics. The authors conclude that much of the conventional wisdom about boardroom governance is actually folly.

Paradoxically, certain governance practices that are now frowned upon can actually enhance board effectiveness. Moreover, an obsessive focus on easily identifiable and measurable metrics can be as misguided as using placebos as panaceas for genuine physical ailments. In short, structural board governance metrics have become circular self-serving exercises that can erode the unique, honest entrepreneurial qualities of firms. The authors remind us that what is needed instead is a focus on the character and leadership of the board, both in terms of the individual directors themselves and the collective functioning of the board. There are genuine preventive tasks that boards can use which will enhance collective accountability and decision making, but they defy simplistic short-term measurement.

A Note of Appreciation

The genesis for this book was a conference held in New York City titled Leading Corporate Boardrooms: The New Realities, The New Rules, funded by the de Roulet family and Henry R. Kravis. I am deeply grateful to both benefactors. Henry R. Kravis has been especially generous with his ongoing support of the Kravis Leadership Institute and our conferences. His commitment has allowed us to bring together America's preeminent thought-leaders on board governance to assess the state of boardroom leadership today. Pamela Gann, the president of Claremont McKenna College, has been a wonderful supporter of the conference and of my own efforts to expand the "geographic" reach of the Kravis Leadership Institute. A special thanks goes to our board members of the Kravis Leadership Institute, who were so helpful with the planning of the conference. I would especially like to thank Michael Grindon, David Hetz, Jeff Klein, Duane Kurisu, Harry McMahon, Scott Miller, Ken Novack, Sarah Smith Orr, and

Peter Weinberg. Nancy Flores deserves very special thanks. She was my "right hand" and more in helping me to organize the conference and the early stages of this book. With a warm smile, she made it all work! Susan Murphy and Ron Riggio, my colleagues at the Kravis Leadership Institute, were incredibly helpful and supportive in coordinating the conference and in assisting me with some of the logistics behind this book. I am especially thankful for Kristin Dessie. She worked with me on the formatting of this book so that it would be ready for publication. She is a student at Claremont McKenna College and now the youngest well-informed individual on corporate boards. Kathe Sweeney, my editor at Jossey-Bass, was excited about the idea for this book from the very beginning. I have so appreciated her enthusiasm and guidance. Rob Brandt, editorial projects manager at Jossey-Bass, has played a very important role in the editing of this book, and I would like to thank him. Finally, I want to thank all the contributors to this book. They are the reason why this volume is a one-of-a-kind collection of the most current and informed thinking on boardroom leadership today. Thank you for your world-class contributions and for your patience with all of my editing on your chapters.

Jay A. Conger
Claremont, California

Part I

Leadership in Your Boardroom

1

Leadership: The Key to Effective Boards

Jay W. Lorsch

At a board meeting in 1993, the CEO and chairman of a mid-cap-listed company surprised his fellow board members by announcing that he had just agreed to sell the company to a larger competitor at the current share price. The announcement was stunning, not only because it was a complete surprise, but also because the CEO/chairman and his immediate family owned just over 50 percent of the company's shares. After the announcement, there was a shocked silence in the boardroom.

During this hiatus, the eyes of two of the six independent directors met. These two were not only the chairs of two of the board's committees (audit and governance) but also two of its most respected members—its leaders. On numerous previous occasions, they had earned the respect of the other directors by speaking out on issues that concerned them. Their interventions were usually thoughtful and well timed to affect the direction of the board's discussions. On this occasion, one after the other, they pointed out to their fellow directors that such a transaction, although it might appeal to the CEO/chairman, was not necessarily in the interests of the company's other shareholders. Using different language but making the same argument, they pointed out that the company's share price was near its low for the past two years, and that the company's strategic plan projected considerable growth in revenues and profits over the next few years.

The CEO/chairman responded that this was a deal that he and his family wanted done. They wanted to diversify their investments, and he believed the price was adequate. Besides he reasoned that as the majority shareholders, he and his family could do as they pleased.

One of the two vocal leaders, who was a lawyer, pointed out in response that the board's duty was to all the shareholders, not just the majority. The chairman responded heatedly that if the board did not approve the deal he could remove all of them and select directors who would. The other director, who had spoken earlier, rejoined by pointing out that the CEO/chairman was a bit like the Grand Poobah in Gilbert and Sullivan's operetta *The Mikado*. He did wear many hats. It was true that as the major shareholder he could remove the board, although that could lead to a nasty and public fight if the board members chose to resist. Moreover it was also true that as CEO, he was subject to the judgment of the majority of the board. If the directors did not like the actions he was taking, they could fire him!

At this juncture, other independent directors began to speak in support of their more outspoken colleagues. As the debate continued, it became evident that the CEO/chairman was very concerned that if the decision were not approved at this meeting the deal might fall through. Nevertheless the two board leaders, supported by their colleagues, persevered. The directors argued for a delay in any decision, while an independent investment banker evaluated the transaction and offered a "fairness opinion" to the board. Concerned about the negative impact any public spat would have on the company's share price, the CEO/chairman eventually agreed to this proposal.

On the basis of the independent assessment, and after a number of specially called board meetings, the CEO/chairman and his fellow directors reached an agreement that the company should remain independent. Three years later, the company was acquired by another larger company, at a substantial premium to its share price at the time of the original proposal.

This is one example from my twenty years of experience as a corporate director, scholar of, and consultant to corporate boards, which can be used to illustrate how I think about the leadership of boards. There are two related ways to consider the topic. First, boards can and should provide leadership of their managements and companies. As I have argued elsewhere recently, it is imperative that boards accept this aspect of their leadership role.[1] They cannot allow themselves to become totally absorbed in issues of regulatory and legal compliance, as important as they are. In this example, the directors prevented a "fire sale" of their company and eventually delivered much greater value to the company's shareholders.

The second aspect of board leadership that this example illustrates is who emerges as a board's leaders and why, as I have come to understand it. These two perspectives are interconnected. In this case, two directors proactively took on the company's CEO/chairman, and its major shareholder. In these discussions, they became the de facto leaders of the other board members. As I shall explain, becoming a boardroom leader is not just a matter of being given a title, whether it is board chair, lead director, or committee chair. Rather, gaining the mantle of leadership is a complex interaction between one's own actions and the perceptions of one's fellows around the board table. Certainly there are many boards in which the formally designated leaders are the only leaders. In my experience, however, the most effective boards are those in which other directors also emerge as active leaders. In fact, in my experience, the more leaders that a board has, the better.

How leadership emerges (and it is an emergent process) on a board has an impact on how well the board is able to exercise leadership over its management and company. If the board develops effective leaders, it will do better in interacting with its management and reaching decisions with them to move the company forward. For example, it will be able to work together in complicated discussions and decisions about the company's future capital structure, or future competitive direction.

The Importance of Board Leadership

Corporate governance and boards of directors have become a hot topic during the past two decades. This is because of the decline of many great American companies during this period as well as the corporate scandals at the turn of the century. The criticism has been that boards should have been more effective in preventing both types of problems. For example, directors at Disney, General Motors, and Morgan Stanley have been criticized for failing to halt the decline of their companies, and boards at Enron, Tyco, and WorldCom, among others, were accused of failing to spot and prevent the misdeeds that sank their companies.

Because of these failures in some of America's boardrooms, we have seen new legislation (Sarbanes-Oxley) and new regulations from the Securities Exchange Commission and the stock exchanges, all aimed at making boards better governors. Further, there has been pressure on companies from certain investors, especially government and union pension funds and their surrogates (such as Institutional Shareholder Services), to improve board practices and procedures. From all of this has come an emerging consensus of what are best boardroom practices (see Figure 1.1). Although I have been among those proposing and supporting such practices, what I find striking about them is the absence of much attention to the topic of board leadership. I define board leadership as the emergence of directors who are willing and capable to influence their fellow directors to take needed actions.

It is of course true that there is an ongoing debate about what is the best leadership structure for American companies and their boards—separate chairperson and CEO, or combining the jobs

- As many independent directors as possible (for example, only one or two management directors)
- As small a board as possible (for example, ten members or more)
- Regular executive sessions (independent directors without management)
- Three required committees and others as needed (audit, compensation, and governance)
- Six or more board meetings annually, including one multiday strategic retreat
- Approval and monitoring of company strategy
- Oversight of management development and management succession
- Selection of CEO and approval of his or her compensation
- Annual performance review of CEO related to his or her compensation
- Compliance with the Sarbanes-Oxley Act
- Established retirement age for directors
- Annual evaluation of board functioning
- New director selection to fit board and company needs

Figure 1.1 Board Best Practices.

with one person holding both. But what is missed in this discussion is an emphasis on the actual leadership behavior I am discussing here. With the exception of a white paper commissioned by the National Association of Corporate Directors and the book *Corporate Boards: New Strategies for Adding Value at the Top*, I am unaware of any attention to the topic.[2]

Yet my experience convinces me that the presence or absence of effective leaders is critical in determining how well boards can carry out their responsibilities. In fact, as I demonstrate in the balance of this chapter, it is the most critical determinant. As important as it is when boards are focused on their normal duties of ensuring the ongoing performance of their corporation, it is even more significant when they must deal with an unexpected crisis. Successfully conducting both responsibilities is the criteria by which boards should be judged, because both can and do have an impact on the health of the company and therefore on its value to its shareholders. In the balance of this chapter, I shall explore three topics: (1) the unique characteristics of boards that provide challenges for their leaders, (2) how these challenges differ under ordinary and extraordinary circumstances, and (3) the qualities effective board leaders must possess. I shall use several examples from my experience to illustrate these issues.

The Nature of Boards

Exercising leadership on a board is complicated by the very nature of boards. To start with, the directors come into the boardroom expecting to be treated as equals. This psychological expectation is rooted in a legal fact. In the laws of all fifty states, including Delaware (the state with the largest number of public incorporations), directors are jointly and severally responsible for all actions their board takes. Anyone who would exercise leadership—whether a formally designated leader or a director asserting himself to lead the board on a particular issue—who ignores the fact that directors expect to be treated as peers, does so at the risk of failing as a leader.

This belief in equality is reinforced by the fact that with very few exceptions independent directors (who constitute the vast majority on most U.S. boards) also have primary careers in which they are used to exercising leadership roles. They are, for example, CEOs or other senior business executives, or perhaps retired government officials. As a result, they enjoy high social status in their lives outside the boardroom, and they expect appropriate treatment within the inner sanctum of the board. As a consequence of these facts, it is not an exaggeration to draw a similarity between leading a board and leading a pack of alpha male dogs. I intend no insult to either species. It is just that this parallel exists and is one factor that makes boardroom leadership challenging. Because they have experience as leaders elsewhere, board members are also unlikely to be passive followers.

Due to this emphasis on equality, those with formal leadership roles have only limited power. In fact, they are usually chosen by a vote of the other directors, which further constrains their power. Certainly the chair, lead director, and the several committee chairs are assigned specific responsibilities, and are treated with respect and deference by their fellow board members. Yet the occupants of these positions, if they are to be effective, have to recognize the norms of equality that pervade the boardroom and that their fellow directors put them in their positions of leadership. For example, every board or committee chair that I have observed at work is very receptive to adding a suggestion by even the newest director for an item to be placed on the relevant agenda. Similarly, requests for more information are rarely, if ever, refused either by management or the board's formally designated leadership.

As I have argued earlier, small boards seem to work more effectively than larger ones.[3] In essence, it is a psychological fact that the fewer members a group has the easier it is for them to discuss issues and reach a consensus. But even a small board of say nine or ten independent directors, who expect to be treated as peers, can be difficult to lead. For example, a chair of such a board has the unenviable task of keeping the group focused on the topics listed on the agenda, and doing this in a specified and usually limited meeting time. It is not surprising that many chairs complain that they become so focused on the facilitation of the meeting that they find it hard to express their own views on the substance of issues.

The work of boards is characterized by two other factors that create leadership challenges. First is the timing of board meetings. For example, the typical American board holds six regular meetings a year, each of which usually starts late on an afternoon and continues for most of the next day. If there are matters that cannot be handled in the prescheduled meetings, or which arise between these meetings, special meetings are called to be held by telephone, or in person. It should also be noted that directors are very busy people, with complicated schedules, but the goal and expectation is to have all directors involved in every meeting.

Thus regular meetings are usually scheduled a year or more in advance, and special meetings are very difficult to arrange.

These time constraints create disjointed and truncated discussions. All directors, but especially those trying to assert leadership, face a challenge in remembering what has transpired in earlier discussions and therefore what actions they may wish to take in the next meeting. I have often seen management return at a board meeting to a complicated proposal that had been aired at the previous meeting, perhaps about a possible acquisition. Management is well versed in the details of the proposals. However, the non-executive directors, including the board's leaders, find themselves having to play catch-up on the details of the proposal, which can put them at a disadvantage both in leading their colleagues and in discussions with management.

The second complication confronting board leaders is even more daunting. Most board discussions do not take place just among the directors but also include members of management. A recent study by Katharina Pick reports that in the board meetings she observed, more than two-thirds of the interactions were between directors and managers rather than among the directors themselves.[4] Surprising as this may seem, it is not hard to explain. Most obviously independent directors depend on managers for information and knowledge about the company in general, and about the details of matters under discussion. Thus a significant purpose of many board meetings is to enable board members to understand their company better! Directors on well-functioning boards are provided with ample information in advance, but much of this relates to past company performance. Relying on it alone to make future-oriented decisions is like trying to drive a car by watching the rearview mirror. So it is not surprising that this much time in a typical board meeting is devoted to the directors learning about how management views the likely future of the company and the industry.

It is also true that a board must walk a fine line in its relationship with management. By now in most public companies, it is well accepted by the CEO and other senior executives that the board is the ultimate decision-making authority, legally and in reality. Yet management is the primary originator of most proposals that come before the board for discussion and decisions. After all, they have the knowledge and expertise to generate such ideas, and it is accepted that it is their task to do so. Further, it is the management team that will implement the decisions reached in the boardroom. Although directors may and do challenge management's proposals, they must do so in a manner that does not alienate senior executives. For those board leaders shaping the direction of the board's deliberation, this requires being sensitive to management's commitment to their proposals, even when the directors are critical of them. This is especially true because managers are so often in the boardroom during such discussions.

Even on the increasing number of occasions when directors hold such discussions in executive sessions, with no managers present, there is a need for sensitivity to management's feelings. Frank discussion among the directors alone is fine, but there is always the risk that openly critical remarks will get back to the management. Even if no such leaks occur, the board's leaders need to be mindful of how and by whom the board's conclusions will be communicated to their CEO and to other members of management. For example, I recall a board on which many directors were openly critical of the CEO in executive sessions. One or two directors took it upon themselves to talk to the CEO about these comments. These conversations were intended to be helpful, but they had the opposite result. The CEO became upset because he believed he had lost the confidence of the board.

All of the preceding characteristics of boards—a group of peers, leaders with limited power, time constraints, and a high dependence on management—shape the behavior required of those who would be effective leaders, whether they are formally designated or whether they emerge. Obviously, they make leading boards a challenging task!

Leadership in Ordinary and Extraordinary Circumstances

One of the challenges facing boards, which is especially important, is the delicate relationship that directors must maintain with their management. This is especially true in the normal course of business, when there is no crisis. In essence, it is management's responsibility to shape proposals for the company's strategic future and to operate the company toward this end in accordance with existing laws and regulations. Top management also has the responsibility to ensure a pool of future management talent. The board's responsibility is to ensure that management is performing these responsibilities well and to approve major decisions. As suggested earlier, the challenge for a board's leaders is to accomplish the board's role, while keeping manager's heads and hearts in the game! If there are no unexpected problems, this is the essence of the board's leadership goals.

However, when crisis occurs, the board's job changes dramatically—especially when the crisis, as it often does, involves members of senior management. Suddenly the board and especially its leaders have a very different purpose—they must resolve the crisis themselves. In my experience, this is the toughest challenge that a board and especially its leaders can confront. This is the time when a board's leadership capability becomes most apparent.

I have reached this conclusion from two perspectives. First as a director who has experienced a number of such events, and second from having read and reviewed reports about and the testimony of the directors on the boards of Enron[5] and WorldCom[6] at the time of the scandals at those companies. In both instances, the directors could and should have known that something was seriously wrong in their company. Yet no one on either board stepped up to take the lead in asking, Is something amiss? For example, the members of the audit committee of the Enron board were told by the Arthur Andersen auditors that the accounting methods being used, while acceptable, were "aggressive." Anderson suggested that the audit committee might seek a second opinion. None of the directors, including the committee's chair, who was a distinguished professor of accounting, chose to act on this advice. The only explanation for this failure that I can come to is that these directors had become so complacent because of their confidence in their top management that they believed management would do nothing improper.

In our recent book, my coauthor Colin Carter used the phrase "smell the smoke" to describe what directors must do to be certain that there is no fire underlying a whiff of something that seems not quite right.[7] What he was referring to was the need for directors to be alert to unusual events or data, and to maintain a certain skepticism about anything that seems amiss. Although I still believe this is an apt description of what directors must do under such circumstances, my own experience as a director involved with several different crises has led me to the conclusion that smelling the smoke is just the starting point for effective action in such situations. What is missing from too many boards is directors who are willing and able to take a leadership role when a whiff of smoke reveals that a conflagration has broken out.

Both in normal circumstances and in times of crisis, my definition of effective leadership is the same. As I have said, it entails having one or more directors who are willing to take the initiative to ensure that the board as a whole makes the right decisions and takes appropriate action. This means that board leaders must have the standing among their fellows as well as the will and ability to shape a consensus about the decisions and actions that need to be taken.

Examples of Boardroom Leadership in Crisis

I shall share a few examples of such leadership to provide a more thorough understanding of what effective board leadership involves. The first was described to my M.B.A. students by my former student and present colleague at Harvard Business School, Bill George, who when the events occurred in the 1990s was the chairman and CEO of Medtronic, Inc., a medical devices company. The second is derived from a teaching case about the American Express Company board in 1992.[8] The third is based on events at a company whose name and circumstances I have disguised.

In 1993, Bill George and his management team at Medtronic, Inc., brought a proposal to the board for the acquisition of a smaller medical devices company. This firm, like others Medtronic had acquired in the recent past, manufactured devices outside the company's original focus on cardiovascular medicine. Medtronic's strategy was to diversify the range of therapies for which it provided the health care industry medical devices.

The directors were well prepared for the discussion, which occurred at a regularly scheduled meeting, having reviewed a document prepared by management that described the transaction as well as the rationale for it. As the board discussion proceeded, various directors asked questions of George and his top managers present. In general the directors favored the proposal. There was one director, however, who expressed serious reservations about the acquisition. Even though he had a great deal of experience in health care and was articulate about his reservations, he was not successful in persuading any of the other directors about the validity of his arguments. To these other directors, management's argument seemed more compelling. After a couple of hours of discussion, the board gave the go ahead for the deal, with the one director abstaining. The board finished its other business, and the meeting was adjourned.

The next morning, George received a phone call from the dissident director, who lived several hundred miles from Medtronic headquarters in Minneapolis. He said he would like to fly back and spend some time talking with Bill about his concerns about the deal. Bill agreed, and they met a few days later. As a result of this discussion, George became convinced that the director had legitimate concerns, and agreed to reopen the discussion of the deal with the entire board. At a special meeting of the board, after reviewing the arguments for the deal and those presented by the lone director, it became clear to the other directors, as it had to Bill, that it was best to not move forward.

I have heard Bill describe these events to our students on several occasions. The lesson he draws from them is the importance of directors sticking with their beliefs, even if they are a minority of one. This is obviously one valid interpretation. However, for me, this is also an example of boardroom leadership. Too often I have watched a director, or even two or three, fold up their tent, and go along with the majority opinion, even though they had grave doubts about the merits of the proposed course of action. On this occasion, this director at Medtronic became a leader of the other board members, causing them to rethink what he considered a flawed decision. Incidentally, Bill says that had the original decision stood it could have cost the company many millions of dollars. So there can be real economic value to such leadership.

It is also interesting to reflect on how this director turned his concerns into proactive leadership. After losing the initial debate in the boardroom, he realized that he had to find support for his position. Recognizing that George was respected by the other directors, because of his successful leadership of the company, the director concluded that if he could convince the CEO, the other independent directors would be likely to follow. This illustrates well the point made earlier that management is almost always present in such board discussions. Directors who succeed as leaders need to be sensitive to this fact and to the nature of the relationship between the CEO and the directors. Directors who try to assert leadership without understanding this relationship can create chaos, as my next example illustrates. Clearly one lesson for directors from such an event is to be willing to stand up for your ideas even as a minority of one. However, this example also illustrates that effective leadership in such circumstances involves finding allies who can enhance your influence.

There was tension in the American Express boardroom in November 1992. The longest-serving independent director, Rollie Warner, who was retiring in a few months, had asked to address the board without the CEO/chairman James Robinson's presence.[9] Robinson had agreed to the request, and after the regular pre-meeting dinner, he departed. Warner than stood up and made a presentation that was a severe indictment of Robinson's leadership of the company. In essence, he argued that Robinson had presided over the decline of the company and was personally responsible for a long list of problems, including decisions to acquire or to attempt to acquire many other financial services companies, which had been ill advised. The failure of the company's "financial super market strategy" should be laid at Robinson's feet and he should be asked to resign immediately was Warner's argument.

There were two serious flaws in Warner's attempt to assert leadership. First, many of his facts were wrong and exaggerated Robinson's culpability. Further, the board and Robinson had agreed on steps to remedy the company's actual problems, and these plans had been communicated publicly. Objective observers, including security analysts, reported that the company was making progress toward these goals. Warner's second failure was not understanding Robinson's relationship with other board members. Warner had discussed his concerns with three other board members, who he knew were critical of Robinson. However, the American Express board was large—eighteen directors—and included prominent CEOs and former cabinet officers, most of whom were supportive of Robinson. After Warner delivered his diatribe, and the directors had absorbed the shock, a couple of Robinson's supporters were able to calm the waters sufficiently to work out a compromise. Robinson would stay for a few months and lead the search for his successor.

The lessons from this example seem clear. If you want to succeed as a leader in the boardroom, you better have your facts right and understand how your fellow directors will interpret them. Although this may seem obvious, it is more complicated than it seems. The facts underlying board discussions are often complex and subject to varying interpretations. Those who would lead also must count noses to understand how various directors interpret these facts. Because board members are usually so dependent on their CEO for their knowledge about the company, how they interpret these facts will obviously be related to how they feel about their chief executive and to their confidence in his performance. Successful board leaders need to understand these relationships! The implications for directors who want to be effective leaders are these. First, you need to stay focused on your director's role between board meetings. Even though you have a full time "day" job, you must continue to devote some of your attention to the boardroom issues between meetings. You cannot let the gaps between meetings dull your understanding of the company's issues. Second, you need to understand the company's CEO and other senior managers, and especially their capabilities, limitations, and biases. Finally, you need to understand the group dynamics of the board itself. Who are the other influential directors? What are their thoughts on the issues at hand? Who listens to them and to whom do they listen? In the end an important source of influences you have to become a board leader is the understanding that you demonstrate of the company's issues, and the alliances that you can establish with other directors to move the ball forward.

All of this is very well illustrated by the situation faced by the directors of a large diversified company at the beginning of this century. Their problems began with an outcry from some institutional shareholders that the CEO/chairman was given a huge compensation package as the company's performance was slipping. A few months later, there were allegations by class action plaintiffs that the company had engaged in improper accounting practices. These events cast a cloud over the company's board and governance, from the perspective of the media and some shareholders. The latter were also concerned because of the decline in the company's share price. The CEO publicly denied any wrongdoing and also privately to the board, and vowed to provide the company with world-class corporate governance. As one step in this effort, the CEO arranged for the board to add several directors who had financial and accounting experience, as well as a director who had worked in a regulatory agency.

In the next several months as the prior directors retired, other independent directors joined the board, including a retired CEO of a major consumer products company and the CEO of an aerospace company. Before deciding to join the board, the new directors each did their own due diligence to assure themselves that there was no foundation in fact about rumors and allegations of inappropriate accounting practices. They were assured by Wall Street lawyers and investment bankers familiar with the company that there was no substance to these allegations.

Thus as the new board began to take shape, there was a strong commitment among the directors to improving the company's corporate governance, and a belief that the CEO/chairman would lead in this effort. A major business publication ran an article at this time about the steps being taken to give the company "world-class corporate governance." In essence, the CEO presented himself as a strong advocate of good governance, and the board members, as well as many in the external world, believed him.

All of this underscores how essential, and yet how hard it is for directors in general, but especially those who would lead a board, to know their CEO deeply. In my experience directors are likely to give their CEO the benefit of the doubt, especially if the company is performing well. Most CEOs deserve such support, but directors need to be alert to even small signs of behavioral or character flaws.

But in this situation I am describing the directors were being duped! While they believed all was well, officials in the federal government thought otherwise. These officials were gathering evidence which indicated that company officers were involved in accounting fraud to inflate the company's revenue and profit figures and perhaps to enhance their own compensation. In meetings with the company's outside counsel, these government attorneys hinted that they had such evidence, but were not specific about it. The word that came back to the directors was that there was nothing of substance in these allegations. They were not to worry. There was smoke, but the board was told it was a false alarm, both by management and its outside counsel, who as it turned out was also being lied to by the CEO and other senior executives. According to these executives, what the government was hearing were rumors from disgruntled ex-employees.

This was where matters stood until the government announced that they were going to interview certain executives about these allegations. At this juncture, the board members concluded that they needed to understand better the government's position, since it was inconsistent with the constant reassurances they were getting from the CEO and other senior executives. A series of meetings were held between the government attorneys and the board's audit committee. At each session, the government lawyers, without revealing the evidence they had, became more insistent that they were building a case against company executives. They suggested strongly that the board needed to conduct its own investigation of these allegations. In retrospect, it appears that the government was unwilling to share specifics with the board's representatives so as not to jeopardize its cases.

As these events were unfolding the directors were beginning to wonder whether their favorable assessment of their top managers might be inaccurate. The problem the directors faced in adjusting their perceptions in such circumstances is what psychologists label "cognitive dissonance." In essence, individuals tend to interpret new evidence at least initially as being consistent with their strongly held prior believes, and therefore they are slow to accept new information inconsistent with these beliefs. Before they could decide to act, the board leaders in this company, like others I have observed under similar circumstances, had to grasp the reality that some top managers were dishonest. Yet they still clung to at least the hope their CEO wasn't involved.

Once they had finally accepted the conclusion that there was misconduct among their executives, other issues of board leadership came to the fore. A director who had earlier been elected lead director and was a member of the audit committee asserted himself, along with the audit committee's chair and the third member of the committee. All three argued that the board had no choice but to undertake a thorough investigation of its own. The other board members quickly agreed. Under the leadership of its chair, the audit committee engaged another law firm to undertake the investigation, because the original outside counsel had been compromised by apparent misinformation from management. Forensic accountants were also engaged. The investigation took nine months and cost the company $75 million. The board's investigation resulted in the termination of several senior executives but not the CEO. In essence, it became clear to the board, as it had to the government investigators, that these executives not only had been involved in accounting fraud but had lied to the company's outside council, its auditors, and the board.

Even though these directors still were unclear about their CEO's role in these misdeeds, they did not hesitate to put their time and effort into getting to the facts of the situation. While the actual work of the investigation was conducted by experts, the audit committee chair and his two members devoted many, many hours to the investigation; clearly this is something anyone who would lead in the boardroom must be willing to do.

As a result of this investigation and government indictments, all the named executives agreed to plead guilty, except for the CEO, who staunchly denied that he knew anything about all this criminal activity. If the government had any evidence implicating him, it was not sharing it with the board, and the audit committee's extensive investigation did not turn up any evidence indicating the CEO had been involved. The board faced a conundrum—their CEO seemed to be doing a good job of keeping the company performing in the marketplace in spite of these serious legal distractions. Furthermore, he denied knowledge of these illegal activities and had been an advocate of good governance at the company. There was no evidence of any wrongdoing by him. To remove him under these circumstances could damage the company and its value to its shareholders, a number of directors argued. Further, the board would be acting without evidence of any wrongdoing by their CEO. Other directors were more cynical. They could not believe that all this illicit activity could have been going on without their CEO's knowledge and consent. After all he was known as a "hands on" manager!

This was the tenor of the discussions that took place informally among the board's leaders, and at two specially called board meetings (without the CEO). At the same time the lead director, the audit committee chair, and other board leaders met with the CEO one on one. Instead of denying any knowledge about the illegal accounting practices, he "clarified" that he knew that theses practices were used, but that he thought this was being legally handled through an accounting reserve. Such a reserve had existed a few years earlier but had been eliminated by the company's former audit firm, a fact the CEO denied understanding.

This caused two of the more proactive directors to insist on another board meeting with the CEO present, so the entire board could ask him direct questions about whether he was involved and what he knew. As this meeting was being arranged, two other pieces of evidence emerged. First a former board member told one of the current directors that he had observed the CEO in meetings with accounting executives apparently discussing the practices in question. Even more damning, a memorandum was discovered which revealed that the CEO did know about the questionable accounting.

At the specially called board meeting, the directors asked the CEO about these facts and other matters. After he was asked to leave the meeting, the board's deliberations led by the lead director were conclusive. The CEO had to go! The discussion turned to how to ensure continuity in the company's leadership, and one of the independent directors was asked and agreed to serve as interim CEO.

This again illustrates the great difficulty that board leaders and other directors have dealing with dissonant information about their CEO. The board is dependent on its CEO for company success, and when it appears that he has been doing a sound job, directors—even those determined to do the right thing—find it difficult to reach a different conclusion.

In the weeks and months that followed these critical meetings, various board members stepped up to deal with various issues, under the chairman's overall guidance. The audit committee members continued discussions with the government officials and were able to arrange an agreement, under which the company would continue to operate but would pay a fine, and the board and management agreed to resolve the accounting and governance issues. Two other directors volunteered to serve on a search committee to find a new CEO. This process took six months, but a new permanent CEO was put in place. During this time the audit committee also had to ensure that the company was complying with the Sarbanes-Oxley Act.

It would be nice to report that all this went smoothly, but it did not. There was further turnover in senior management, because of problems in a significant European subsidiary. What the board members and the new management team learned together from all this was that when a company has suffered from such serious legal and ethical lapses there are also likely to be deeper flaws in the company's management practices and systems, and in its culture.

I introduced this example because it illustrates so well the relationship between board leaders' perceptions of their CEO and how they deal with and accept the new facts they are receiving. As long as board members have confidence in their CEO's integrity and his performance, it is difficult to challenge him. This explains one reason why boardroom leaders at other companies embroiled in similar scandals found it so hard to act decisively.

What is also impressive to me about the leadership on this board is how it stuck with the goal of saving its company. Today the company seems well on the road back! Certainly the company's management deserves much credit for this. But so does the board, especially the several directors who stepped up to take various leadership roles as the saga unfolded. Whenever there was a problem or an issue, there were always one or more directors willing to drop other commitments and to devote a large amount of their time to solving the problems in front of them.

Attributes of Effective Board Leadership

The preceding example along with the others I have described illustrate that one attribute of effective leaders is their willingness to commit themselves to take the initiative to solve problems. The directors in the first situation did not hesitate to step in and block the sale of their company. The board member at Medtronic stuck with his convictions, and certainly the leaders of the board I have just described demonstrated similar commitment on many occasions. And I have seen other directors on other boards do the same thing. Effective leaders are willing to devote extraordinary time and effort to solving problems. But as I have also indicated they have another common attribute—the capacity to spot irregularities, to know when something may be not quite right, and to follow up. The interesting question is why, what motivates these directors to demonstrate these leadership qualities?

I can only speculate based on my experience, but I believe that such leaders have a strong sense that their responsibility is to do the right thing as directors. Their reason for board service is not the money they may receive, nor the status or prestige, but the sense of satisfaction they get in doing the job well. In fact, I have never seen a director who takes on such leadership ask about extra compensation for themselves, even when they have spent many, many hours on an issue. Rather, what usually happens is another board member who has observed and appreciated this effort will suggest that some extra compensation be awarded.

A related quality these leaders share is having or being willing to acquire the knowledge to act effectively. In some instances, the director has a reservoir of knowledge related to the issue at hand. For example, this was true with the Medtronic director. But in many other instances I have seen directors spend a great deal of time and effort to understand facets of the business or the company that are new to them.

In sum, then, two aspects of effective board leaders are their willingness to take on the job and to be inquisitive about the business. But there is another aspect to being an effective leader in the boardroom setting. If you are going to attempt to lead, you want to be as certain as possible that others will follow you. You are undertaking leadership among peers who are used to being leaders themselves and thus may not be enthusiastic followers. So why do other directors accept the leadership of one of their peers? One reason, as I have just described, is because they believe the leader has the required knowledge, or at least will acquire it. This is akin to what sociologists would label influence based on competence. In some instances, this is based on specific knowledge, about a function or discipline-like accounting or a particular sector like the health care industry. But in many instances, the power granted to a board leader is based on perceptions of broader competence or experience in business. For example, sitting or retired CEOs often emerge as leaders when they join a board, simply because their fellow directors give them credit for having broad competence in business. In fact, it is not an exaggeration to say that when past or present CEOs join a board, the presumption of their peers is that they will emerge as board leaders, because of their experience. In contrast, a new director with a different background, for example in academics or government, has to demonstrate the relevance of his or her knowledge and competence to be accepted as a potential leader. It is for this reason that in a severe and dramatic crisis like that at the American Express board, it is usually a director with experience as a CEO who is accepted as the person to lead the board in solving the crisis.

There is yet another quality effective leaders demonstrate—sensitivity to interpersonal relationships and to group dynamics. An example from another board illustrates this well. This board's longest-serving director, who had become formally recognized as its lead director, was as strong on these qualities as any director I have observed. He was always sensitive to the feelings of managers in the room, as well as to those of other directors. He never dominated a discussion. Rather, he had an exquisite sense of when to speak in a discussion. For example, when the board was at an impasse he would intervene to clarify the issues, and to perhaps suggest a novel solution. If the managers in the room were becoming defensive, as directors asked questions and probed their reasoning, he might step in with a light-hearted comment that would relieve the tension and put the discussion on a more productive track. These attributes and his experience as the CEO of a major company clearly made him the board's leader even before he was formally elected the lead director. His style contributed greatly to the smooth functioning of the board.

Then he reached retirement age and was replaced as lead director by a person who, while he worked diligently at the job, was not as skillful at understanding the group's functioning. To make matters more complicated the director who was elected to replace the retiring director was a CEO of a major *Fortune* 500 company. Because he was a sitting CEO, he was immediately looked up to as one of the board's informal leaders. He relished this position and was not shy about expressing his opinions. After several meetings exhibiting this dominant behavior, which in essence was a violation of the board norms of equality, other directors retreated from the discussion. One even eventually resigned. What had been a very effective group had become dysfunctional largely because of one would-be leader's behavior.

In mentioning such qualities, I do not imply that all those who would be effective leaders have to have the sensitivity and skills of the first director I just mentioned. He seemed almost perfect. I have sat through many boardroom discussions in which directors expressed anger with each other, or were overly tough on the managers in the discussion. Emotion in the boardroom is not a bad thing, as long as there are leaders present who can monitor it and can act to control it. I have seen board meetings in which emotions became so high that two directors were standing on opposite sides of the table arguing with each other in angry voices! But what kept the board working well was a respected leader who said to both, "Come on guys, calm down!" After that meeting, the two angry directors headed to the bar for a drink together.

The fundamental condition for being a successful leader in the boardroom is the simple commitment to do the job. Directors who volunteer to step up to the plate are likely to be given the chance to lead. However, competence, knowledge, and sensitivity to the human relationships and dynamics in varying mixes are also of critical importance. Without them even the most committed director is unlikely to be able to establish himself as a leader among his fellow board members. Although directors are content to have others share leadership responsibility, they expect them to succeed, and these are the qualities which my experience indicates lead to success.

As I stated earlier, effective boards seem to have multiple leaders. In fact, one can argue the more the merrier. Remember, directors are part-timers whose time is always constrained, and they welcome others who will share the workload, including that of leading. Obviously the several leaders on each board have to work together, and there have to be complementary roles and coordination among the leaders. In my experience ensuring this outcome is the job of the chair.

Having boards with strong cadres of leaders, as I have also suggested, is the best assurance we can have that boards can and will live up to the increasing demands being placed upon them. This is not to downplay the importance of clear definitions of each board's role, nor the design of the board to accomplish this purpose. It is just that the practices and procedures in each board's architecture will only be effective if there is leadership to make them so.

So how do boards ensure themselves of a cadre of effective leaders? The answer to me is obvious! Directors must be selected who have the qualities I have just discussed in mind. In most boardrooms today, even those with active and responsible corporate governance committees managing the selection and nominating process, three criteria seem sufficient. First, does the director have the skills and experience the board needs to add, such as finance, or marketing, or technology? Second, is the director a person of integrity? Third, is the candidate someone who seems likeable and who is willing to engage constructively with other board members and will fit into the group that is the board? Although there is nothing particularly flawed about these criteria, I would argue that boards that want to assure themselves of an adequate pool of leaders need to examine potential directors more deeply:

1. Why does the candidate want to serve on the board? The answer I would seek is because he wants to see the company succeed from his efforts, and because he feels he will learn from and get satisfaction from the experience.
2. In addition to a particular competence or set of skills, does the candidate have an inquisitive nature? Does she seem interested in understanding how the company functions and why?
3. Given the person's main career (for example, CEO, CFO, academic, government), how will others perceive him, and what will be his likely reaction? Can he handle being looked up to because he has been or is a CEO, for example? Or can he handle the fact that a lack of business leadership experience may make it difficult to take leadership on issues?
4. Finally, how well does the candidate understand others and the dynamics of groups?

Getting answers to such questions will require not only interviewing the candidate but also getting input from others who have watched him in action. It will require more effort than is currently devoted to selecting directors by most boards. However, if boards want a plentiful supply of leaders around the table, and I believe they should, the effort will be well worth it.

2

Why Your Board Needs a Non-Executive Chair

Jay A. Conger and Edward E. Lawler III

We are in a period of experimentation and change when it comes to leadership in the boardroom. Largely gone are the days when the CEO "held court" as the board's sole leader. Today boards need multiple leaders and a shared leadership approach. Effective corporate governance simply cannot be achieved by relying on the CEO to lead the board. Boards need independent chairs who are effective leaders, and they need effective leaders to chair their committees. In the case of a crisis, they need the entire board to share in the leadership responsibilities.

There are two primary forms of board leadership today—non-executive chairpersons and lead directors—that are being used to counterbalance the CEO's authority. Each of these approaches, in effect, create dual leadership on a board. Our 2006 survey of the boards of the largest U.S. companies found that 75 percent of boards now have an independent lead or presiding director. To put this number in perspective, this is a dramatic increase from 48 percent of boards in 2003 and 32 percent in 2001. The same survey found that 30 percent of boards now have a non-executive chair, a similarly significant jump from 16 percent in 2003. Similarly, recent data from the Corporate Library show that over 30 percent of boards in U.S. companies have an outside chair, although about one-third of these are not considered to be independent chairs (often they are former executives of the company). In some European countries (Germany, Netherlands, United Kingdom), all or almost all companies have separated the roles of chair and CEO, although frequently the chair is not an independent outsider. In the United Kingdom, approximately 95 percent of the largest one hundred firms have a separate CEO and chairperson.

In this chapter, we will examine the different approaches to leadership in the boardroom, the fundamental dilemmas these alternatives pose, and a set of best practices for each. At the same time, we will argue that your board needs to appoint a non-executive chair. Although we agree with critics that there are important shortcomings to having an independent chair or lead director, we feel the non-executive chair is the best alternative.

Chapter Three by Dan and Catherine Dalton goes into great detail as to why two leaders on a board may be a serious mistake. The trade-offs that the authors identify are major ones for a board, and we are inclined to agree with their principle arguments. That said, we feel that there are enormous pressures on boards to appoint a non-executive chair, and these pressures are not likely to subside. We actually believe that they will intensify. In other words, your board will be pressured—largely by external forces—to adopt the non-executive chair model. Given this reality, our objective is to describe how your board can successfully meet the challenges of a dual leadership model.

We will explore the ideal selection criteria for non-executive chairs. We will also examine how best to divide the roles and responsibilities of the CEO versus the non-executive chair in leading a board. For boards disinclined to go down the path of a non-executive chair, we will discuss the alternative leadership models of a lead director and committee leadership. For readers wishing more concrete guidance on how board chairs can effectively lead their fellow board directors, Katharina Pick in Chapter Four offers specific guidance on leadership techniques.

The Board's Historic Leader: The Chief Executive Officer

In North America, the chief executive officer has been, and in many cases continues to be, the de facto leader of the board. This is due in large part to the many advantages of the CEO's position as well as the fact that until recently there has been no other designated leader of the board. For example, given their positions, CEOs have far greater access to current and comprehensive information about the state of the company. They also have been responsible for setting the agenda for the board. In contrast, given their part-time role and their "outsider" status (outsider in the sense that the vast majority of directors are not employees of the board's organization), the typical director's knowledge about company affairs is extremely limited. Most directors are all too aware of the gaps in their understanding and therefore concede authority to the CEO.

In addition, most directors see their first role as serving the CEO and their secondary role as providing oversight. Many directors are CEOs themselves, and they share in an etiquette that suggests restraint from aggressively challenging a fellow CEO or from probing too deeply into the details of someone else's business. These factors encourage directors under most circumstances to defer to the CEO's leadership in the boardroom.

From a CEO's vantage point, there are clear advantages to the CEO being the chair of the board (see Chapter Three). First, it puts board leadership clearly in his or her hands. There is no ambiguity about who leads the board. Second, it eliminates any possibility of a dysfunctional conflict between the CEO and a board chair. Rivalries between a CEO and a chair that might produce poor decisions or result in drawn-out decision-making processes simply do not occur. Third, it avoids the possibility of having two public spokespersons when it comes to addressing the organization's stakeholders. This is particularly important in the case of employees, shareholders, and the financial community. Fourth, certain efficiencies are achieved by having the most informed individual be the board chair. The CEO does not have to expend significant time and energy updating the chair on issues before every meeting and discussing the agenda. Not surprisingly then, most American CEOs strongly believe that the CEO should be the board's chair.

Despite the advantages associated with CEO "only" leadership, there is a compelling reason why combining the role of CEO and chair is not the best approach to corporate governance. The "CEO model" of board leadership does not provide an adequate system of checks, balances, and accountability. It simply puts too much power in the hands of the CEO. Moreover, investors, monitoring agencies, and governance activists are increasingly demanding that boards adopt a non-executive chair model. With this in mind, let's turn to the three alternatives to a CEO-only-led board—the non-executive chair, the lead director, and committee leadership.

The Non-Executive Chair

Though the idea of a separate or non-executive chair has been discussed for decades, only in recent years has it gained acceptance as a practice in U.S. corporations. Prominent companies such as Aon, Avaya, Avery Dennison, CBS, Intercontinental Hotels, Tenet Healthcare, Unisys, and Walt Disney Company today have non-executive chairs. The major stock exchanges, reports sponsored by some sixteen national governments, the National Association of Corporate Directors, and numerous academics have all recommended separating the board chair from the CEO role.

The main arguments in favor of a non-executive chair have to do with enhancing the ability of the board to monitor the CEO's performance and, if needed, operate independently of the CEO. With a separate chair, the board has a clear leader whose sole mandate is the effective functioning of the board itself. A non-executive chair increases the chance that directors will feel more at ease about raising challenges to the CEO. In addition, investors often prefer to have a separate chair, and as a result, having one may influence their willingness to invest in a company.

Whether accurate or not, many investors fear that the CEOs may first serve themselves and only secondarily serve shareholders. They believe a non-executive chair whose mandate is to enhance shareholder value is less likely to be compromised. As a result, they will be more willing to replace a poorly performing CEO. Moreover, a non-executive chair frees the CEO to focus on leadership of the company rather than the time-consuming demands of leading the board.

The Dilemmas with the Role

There are mixed feelings and data about the effectiveness of having a separate chair. For example, many American CEOs argue that it is cumbersome to have two leaders in the boardroom—themselves and the non-executive chair. The National Association of Corporate Directors recommends it as a device for transitions (new CEOs or crises) but not for a long-term arrangement. As we noted, Chapter Three goes into great detail about the serious complications this arrangement presents to effective leadership at the board level.

Research on the financial benefits of separating the roles of chair and CEO also does not strongly support the separation. For example, Yale Law professor Roberta Romano analyzed studies on the economic impact of separating the two roles in U.S. boardrooms and found that there was no statistically significant difference in terms of stock price or accounting income.[1] Institutional Shareholder Services (which has been supportive of the separation) found in an independent analysis that "attempts to correlate the separation of positions with market performance have been inconclusive."[2]

Similarly, a study of U.K. companies by Baruch College professor Jay Dahya in 2005 concluded that the separation of the two roles was not associated with an improvement in stock price or operating performance relative to benchmark companies.[3] Dan and Catherine Dalton have similarly found mixed empirical support for dual board leadership structures.

But the studies mentioned above have their limits. They have often not separated boards with non-executive chairs from boards with chairs who are former executives (most often the outgoing CEO). We feel strongly that promoting a former CEO into the chairperson role is a serious mistake, and a primary reason why performance may not improve under this model.

The "Insider" Chair—The Wrong Form of Board Leadership

Almost half of the separate chairs in the United States are former company employees, often a former CEO. This may explain why company performance in many cases is not higher with a separate chair. In these circumstances, there is no independent and objective counterbalance to the CEO, given that the chairperson is likely to have chosen the standing CEO him- or herself.

A CEO whose board chair is the company's former CEO describes the problems associated with outgoing CEOs making the transition to the chairperson role. "If he [the board chair] has been involved in selecting the new guy to be CEO as was true in my case, the chair is in a kind of funny position of not being able to be critical of the new guy for some time. He's got to preserve the honeymoon aspect of it. If a new guy comes in and wants to change anything, there is also the unavoidable explicit criticism of the old guy insofar as how he did things. There is an awkward tension set up between the new guy and the old guy which results in an awful lot of senatorial dancing around the issue of why these problems existed before and why the old guy didn't do anything about them. If the new guy comes in and wants to dramatically change direction, he has the old guy who is lurking there either biting his tongue or, heaven forbid, arguing with him about it. If the new guy wants to kill some of the pet projects of the old guy, it is an awkward situation. Personally, I believe the retiring CEO is 'in the way' in the simplest of terms and should exit gracefully. If the new CEO wants to call on the wisdom of the retired CEO, he is certainly free to do that without the old guy being on the board."

Interestingly, the rationale for promoting former CEOs into the board chair role is often not based on its impact on leadership. The most common argument is that the retiring CEO will assist the incoming CEO in making the transition to the new role. The thinking goes that this setup makes the predecessor available to be a coach, sharing wisdom and insight into company issues. To some extent, this might prove true, but critical leadership compromises are likely to occur. We will describe these shortly.

Other times, the chair role is bestowed on former CEOs out of a desire to reward or placate them. For example, many directors see the chairperson's role as a "reward" for the service of a CEO, especially in the case of long-tenured or highly successful CEOs or company founders.

In some cases, retiring CEOs simply do not want to let go. They maneuver the board to offer them the chairmanship post so that they can remain involved in the company during retirement. One chief executive officer candidly commented to us, "I think they [the board directors] would be very smart to have me stay on [as board chairperson] because I am the architect of the vision and the change that has occurred here, and I can be the coach of the next generation of managers. We've got a couple of guys coming up the ranks that I am very close to. I can help these people grow. I see myself in the next phase of my life as a kind of coach."

The desire of a retiring CEO to "stay involved" can set in motion a potential problem—the creation of a chairperson who doesn't step back and who becomes a meddlesome force that makes life difficult for the CEO. Reflecting on his own experiences, Denys Henderson, the former chairman and CEO of Imperial Chemical Industries, captured the dilemma: "In my own case [as a former CEO who becomes the board chair], it was difficult at first to give up day-to-day control because I was still very energetic, and it was clear that further change in the organization was required. I found it a considerable challenge to move from 'energy mode' to 'wisdom mode'."[4]

In summary, when boards create a separate chair position for a former CEO either to reward or placate him or her, they often damage the ability of the standing CEO to lead the company. Our advice is simple—don't make your retiring CEO or any other company executive the non-executive chair.

The Appropriate Board Chair—A Genuine "Outsider"

Who then should be your non-executive chair? An independent board member or some other individual who is independent of the CEO. That said, it must be an individual who is highly respected by the directors and who has the self-confidence and industry knowledge to take a leadership role, especially during times of trouble. This individual must also be someone who has the time to follow both the company and the industry closely.

In addition, it is very important that the non-executive chairperson should not hold a full-time job or a board directorship at any other company. The time demands of being a chair are so high that major responsibilities outside the board may seriously hamper the chair's commitment to the role. For example, researchers estimate that in large, diversified companies operating under normal conditions, a non-executive chair may need to spend up to one hundred days a year keeping abreast of the company.[5] In a crisis situation, however, this could easily be the minimum number of days required; indeed, being the chair might turn into a full-time job. As a result, CEOs of other companies are not appropriate candidates given the existing demands on their time. However, a recently retired CEO can make an ideal chairperson.

Because the board chair works closely with the CEO, the selection process itself should involve the CEO. Their relationship should be between a chair who is unafraid to challenge the CEO and a CEO with whom there is a strong positive chemistry. In the selection process therefore, the chemistry issue is best determined by the two individuals themselves. However, the chairperson's ability to challenge is best determined by the directors. They have to be sure that the non-executive chair has the skills necessary to run the board and the ability to act independently of the CEO. The ideal selection process is to have the board nominating committee choose from a roster of candidates that has been reviewed beforehand by the CEO.

In terms of specific selection criteria, the ideal chair candidate should be an individual who possesses a strategic perspective on the industry, the capacity to synthesize great quantities of information, deep curiosity about the company and the industry, a strong positive regard for fellow directors, mastery at coaching, a facilitative style in meetings (see Chapter Four), and the capability of providing strong leadership in a crisis. As might be imagined, this is a rare combination of attributes.

Helping Your Non-Executive Chair Succeed

The governance committee should take the lead in defining the very different, but complementary jobs of non-executive chair and CEO. One of the critical factors in determining the success of the independent chair approach is the creation of clear and negotiated expectations about each other's roles from the start.

Denys Henderson of ICI outlines what must happen at the very beginning of the relationship: "It's important that the chairman and the CEO agree from the beginning what each person's role will be. The last thing you want is a fight over turf. The agreement should be put down in writing and eventually approved by the board. But the process of understanding each other's viewpoint is more important than the final text."[6]

What should be the primary activities of a non-executive chair? (See Figure 2.1 for a detailed list.) First, the chair should set the agenda of board meetings. In consultation with the CEO, the chair should establish the topics to be discussed and the time allocated to each. The chair should also determine what kinds and the quantity of materials the directors receive for each meeting. Executive sessions of the board as well as the annual shareholders' meeting should be chaired by the non-executive chair. When needed, chairs should communicate with directors on issues that arise outside of board meetings. Perhaps their most difficult role is reviewing the performance of individual directors and giving them feedback. Because the chair is responsible for the board's performance, this is an activity that the chair and only the chair can perform. The chair should also ensure that the board annually reviews its performance. Last, but not least, the non-executive chair should organize and lead the evaluation of the CEO. When an organization is performing poorly, this is often the chair's most important role. The chair is in the best position to lead the evaluation, determine the CEO's compensation, and decide whether the CEO should be replaced. Chapters Four and Six provide additional perspectives on the responsibilities of a non-executive chair.

- Set board meeting agendas in collaboration with the CEO, board committee chairs, and the corporate secretary along with a yearly calendar of all scheduled meetings
- Govern the board's activities and assign tasks to the appropriate committees
- Act as a guide and mentor to the CEO
- Preside at the annual shareholders' meeting and at all board meetings
- Facilitate a candid and full deliberation of all key matters that come before the board
- Ensure that information flows openly between the committees, management, and the overall board
- Organize and preside annually at no less than two executive sessions comprising only outside directors to review the performance of the CEO, top management, and the company
- Brief the CEO on issues arising in executive sessions
- Review annually the governance practices of the board and the performance of the board itself
- Review annually the committee charters
- Serve as an ex-officio member of all board committees
- Review the performance of the board directors

Figure 2.1. Responsibilities of the Non-Executive Chairperson.

The Lead or Presiding Director

The most common alternative to the CEO-led form of board leadership is the lead or presiding director. As mentioned earlier, the majority of U.S. companies now have these positions. The "lead director" leads the independent directors, whereas a "presiding director" would lead or facilitate "executive sessions" (in which management is not in attendance) of the independent directors. These roles are typically used when the CEO is the board chair. If you take the concerns expressed in Chapter Three to heart, a lead director is a reasonable alternative to a non-executive chair, but presiding directors are not. Thus our discussion will focus on lead directors.

Lead directorships are almost always filled by someone who is an independent director. The lead director does not assume the role of chairperson; rather he or she is the directors' representative to the CEO. Lead directors are also both ombudsmen and facilitators of the governance process. Their role can include preparing the agenda for board meetings, chairing executive session meetings of the independent directors and raising controversial issues one-on-one with the CEO. In the case of a crisis, the lead director is likely to take over as the board's chair, replacing the CEO.

The role of the lead director is shaped by two realities. One, the CEO remains the boardroom leader. As such, the lead director participates in meetings like other directors. In contrast, the chair calls the board meetings, shapes the agenda in collaboration with the CEO and directors, and leads or facilitates the actual board meetings. The chair can also represent the organization to the external stakeholders and employees. A lead director typically has no such role unless there is a crisis situation. Second, the power of lead directors depends on their ability to influence and gain the support of other board members. Neither the lead director nor the chair has a role in company operations.

To succeed in the role, the lead director should be a highly respected member of the board who also serves in another board leadership capacity such as being chair of a board committee. By strength of personality and background, he or she should be able to effectively challenge the CEO when necessary. Similar to the non-executive chairperson model, the lead director should have significant executive experience. At the same time, he or she should not be chosen on the basis of seniority or loyalty. Sometimes boards honor long-standing members or "elder statesmen" with the lead director position, failing to recognize that the selection needs to be based on an individual's actual ability to lead.

The major responsibilities of the lead director involve how the board operates. His or her role is to ensure that the board approaches its responsibilities in a manner that guarantees the board's independence and ensures its effective operation. Following are a number of the things that a lead director can do in this regard:[7]

1. Setting the board's agenda in collaboration with the CEO, board committees, major shareholders, and other major stakeholders to ensure that multiple and independent perspectives are represented
2. Acting as an intermediary between the outside directors and the CEO, ensuring that sensitive issues or concerns are raised in a manner that provides a voice for directors who might not otherwise raise an issue or who might wish not to have a subject discussed publicly
3. Organizing and facilitating sessions of the independent members of the board to privately review company performance, management's effectiveness, and the CEO's performance
4. Briefing the CEO on issues arising in the executive sessions
5. Conducting exit interviews of executives who resign from the corporation to determine whether such resignations reflect

problems within the organization or with the CEO's style and approach

6. Meeting on occasion with major shareholders to ascertain their concerns and expectations
7. Ensuring that the discussion and decision processes in board meetings are open, clear, and effective

Leadership in the Board Committees

The chairs of board committees increasingly are playing a leadership role on their boards. In part, this has been driven by the growing importance of committees and the resulting need for committees to be led effectively. But a more important cause is the presence of a far greater number of outside directors on boards. They now sit on important board committees and often act in the capacity of committee chairpersons. One important by-product of governance reform is that committees now choose their chairpersons, unlike in the past when CEOs often hand-selected the committee chairs whom they "trusted." This usually means the committee chair is well positioned to lead the committee and to be a strong advocate for its decisions and suggestions.

In some ways, the shift in power on committees is not entirely surprising. CEOs rarely have the time to be active members of all of a board's committees. As a result, this is one boardroom activity in which CEOs feel they must play more of a consultative or advisory role. They almost have to allow the committees to be led by an independent director. Reinforcing this is the fact that the board governance movement has discouraged their playing a directive role in committees and has placed a strong emphasis on outside directors assuming key leadership roles.

There are, however, a number of steps that committees should proactively undertake to ensure they operate effectively. For example, in order for outsiders to take advantage of their majority position in committees, they often need to develop action plans and positions of their own rather than be guided by those of the CEO.

Because committee members usually do not have an opportunity to get together independent of their board activities, it is important that their board activities provide them with this opportunity. Meetings held without company executives during which committee members can discuss sensitive issues concerning executive succession and corporate performance need to become a norm. These may be the only opportunity a committee has to develop strong positions that are contrary to the stated preferences of senior management.

In addition, it is critical for committees to have the ability to meet when they feel that events call for it. They must be able to call meetings on short notice when they feel that a crisis or rapidly developing business condition calls for it. It is also critical that they have a vehicle for placing issues that they identify on the board's agenda without significant advance notice. Board committees must be in a position to hire outside specialists who can provide expertise and make objective assessments of the company's operations. They must be able to do this without management's prior permission.

The leadership and membership of committees is critical in determining the amount of influence that independent directors can have. To maximize influence, all or most committees should be chaired by independent directors. One committee that should be completely made up of outside directors is the compensation committee.

In addition to the compensation committee, whichever committee of the board (usually a nominating or corporate governance committee) selects new directors should also be predominantly, if not exclusively, made up of outside directors. The nominating committee should play a major role in the selection process and should establish specific criteria for filling any board vacancies. These criteria should be submitted to the full board for approval before a search is undertaken. Although the CEO should be consulted during the process, the committee should make the final judgment on who is nominated, and the nominations should be voted upon by the full board.

There is one potential problem associated with a nominating committee composed of outsiders. These directors can profoundly shape the makeup of the board itself. This might result in problems if this committee has very strong biases about "appropriate" directors. One relatively easy way to overcome this problem is to set term limits on committee memberships and to rotate the directors out of the committee on a regular basis.[8]

One final point: having strong independent leadership on board committees is not a substitute for having a non-executive chair. If a board lacks a non-executive chair, independent leadership is splintered among a number of individuals. No single independent director has overall responsibility for the board and ensuring that its range of activities is well-coordinated and meets high standards of corporate governance. Given their more narrow focus, committees can at best only shape portions of the overall agenda. Under a system reliant upon strong committee leadership, there may be no central ombudsman to give the full board a collective voice. Thus it is a good practice but only a partial solution to building truly effective board leadership.

In conclusion, strong committee leadership is where some of the greatest progress has been made in terms of corporate governance practices that correctly balance leadership and power. There is considerable reason to believe, however, that more progress is needed.

Conclusion

We have argued that the non-executive chair role will increasingly be the accepted form of boardroom leadership. Not without serious trade-offs, however, the success of this form of leadership depends heavily upon great clarity in the boardroom roles of the non-executive chair and the CEO. These must be negotiated at the very beginning of the chair's appointment with opportunities for later revisions given changing circumstances.

The chair must have the authority to provide leadership independent of the CEO. At the same time, candidates for the non-executive chair role must be chosen carefully. In addition to having ample time to devote to the role, candidates need to be individuals who can walk the fine line between being a partner and a judge of the CEO. They must be highly respected by the board members and possess the leadership skills required to successfully lead a group of accomplished peers (as described in Chapter Four).

Beyond the appointment of a non-executive chair, the foundation for effective leadership in boardrooms needs to include additional practices that provide the basis for a strong and independent board. The following are the characteristics that create the right foundation for effective leadership in board meetings as well as in the operation of committees:

- Independent directors (with no formal business or family ties to the firm prior to joining the board) constitute a clear majority (at least two-thirds) of all board members.
- The knowledge and abilities of directors are assessed regularly against the firm's changing market, business strategy, and technological demands to ensure that they have the skills necessary to effectively oversee the firm's actions and provide leadership.
- Independent directors chair and control all key committees—compensation, audit, and nominating or corporate governance. The compensation committee consists solely of outside directors.
- The board holds regular executive sessions in which no inside directors such as the CEO are present.

- Regular channels of information to the board that are independent of management are in place—for example, direct communication links with employees, customers, suppliers, and investors.
- The board has staff or resources so that it can conduct its own analysis of issues when it feels the need (for example, in benchmarking executive compensation).
- A regular executive succession-planning process is conducted that reaches down several levels of management.

In combination, these practices will produce an independent leadership capability on boards that should position directors to effectively govern today's complex organizations.

3

The Joint CEO/Chairperson Leadership Issue in Sharp Relief

Dan R. Dalton and Catherine M. Dalton

A recent issue of *Agenda*, a subscription newsletter for board members, featured an article titled "Calls to Split CEO, Chair Roles Heat Up." The concept of duality—when one person serves simultaneously as CEO and chairperson of the board—is a recurring theme in one of the most enduring debates in corporate governance. Such spirited discussions are based on the larger notion of the independence of boards of directors and the extent to which compromises in board independence are associated with poorer corporate financial performance.[1]

We provide a frank overview of this controversy. In the following sections, we briefly review the foundations of agency theory, the theoretical and conceptual basis on which the vast majority of research and commentary on duality is based. We would add that agency theory is also the basis for the many elements of independence as specified in the mandates of Sarbanes-Oxley (SOX) and the post-SOX revisions in the guidelines of the listing exchanges (such as the New York Stock Exchange [NYSE] and NASDAQ).

We also rigorously recount the disparate positions, diametrically opposed on virtually all aspects, of those who advocate the separation of the CEO and board chairperson roles and those who, by contrast, find the merging of these roles to be best practice. In addition, we address how this issue informs several other aspects of corporate governance, including executive committees of the board, CEO succession, emeritus directors, and the application of these principles for boards when the enterprise faces a crisis.

Agency Theory, Independence of the Board, and Board Duality

For at least four hundred years, observers of large-scale enterprises observed that boards of directors—or their equivalents—as the stewards of shareholders would not be effective monitors of management if these relationships were tainted by self-interest. Adam Smith, for example, in *An Inquiry into the Nature and Causes of the Wealth of Nations*, provided a prescient observation about independence and joint stock companies. He noted that managers of other people's money cannot be expected to "watch over it with the same anxious vigilance" as one would expect from owners and that "negligence and profusion, therefore, must always prevail, more or less, in the management of the affairs of such a company."[2]

In the United States, Chief Justice Layton in 1939 (*Guth* v. *Loft, Inc.*) has been credited with the "class articulation" of this perspective:

> Corporate officers and directors are not permitted to use their position of trust and confidence to further their private interests. . . . A public policy, existing through the years, and derived from a profound knowledge of human characteristics and motives, has established a rule that demands of a corporate officer or director, peremptorily and inexorably, the most scrupulous observance of this duty, not only affirmatively to protect the interests of the corporation committed to his charge. . . . *The rule that requires an undivided and unselfish loyalty to the corporation demands that there shall be no conflict between duty and self-interest* [emphasis added].[3]

Agency Theory

A more formal discussion of the notions of independence is a central element in agency theory, which is clearly the dominant foundation of corporate governance research and commentary.[4] The argument propelling agency theory is based on a fundamental change in the ownership of publicly-traded companies.[5] In the United States, through the 1920s and 1930s, owners of large-scale enterprises were increasingly less likely to manage their own enterprises. Instead, there was a growing reliance on professional managers to manage such enterprises. Professional managers during this period, however, owned very little equity in the firms they managed. The threat, then, from the perspective of agency theory is that these professional managers would have to be closely monitored to ensure that their interests as managers of the enterprise did not diverge substantially from the interests of owners of the enterprise.[6] In prior years, such alignment was not an issue because owners were both firms' managers and principal shareholders.

More recently, in the wake of a series of high profile-corporate scandals (for example, Adelphia Communications, Arthur Andersen, Enron, HealthSouth, Tyco, and Worldcom), this notion of independence was revisited and underscored once again. The Company Accounting Reform and Investor Protection Act of 2002 (also known as the Sarbanes-Oxley Act, Sarbox, SOX), for example, was passed by the U.S. Congress with an imposing (423-3 vote in the House of Representatives; 99-0 vote in the Senate) bipartisan and bicameral mandate.[7] Essentially in parallel with SOX legislation were the corporate governance guidelines set forth by the listing exchanges (such as NYSE and NASDAQ). These, too, comprised a host of requirements, but germane to our discussion are those addressing the independence of boards of directors. SOX and the listing exchange guidelines, in concert, provide guidelines for the composition of the overall board (a majority of which must be composed of independent members), and the composition of the auditing, compensation, and corporate governance and nominating committees (a minimum of three members each, all independent, and the chairpersons for which, derivatively, must be independent).

Notably, however, both SOX and the listing exchange guidelines are silent on the matter of duality of leadership roles—whether or not the CEO and chair roles should be separated. Indeed, there are no extant guidelines addressing the issue of duality. Publicly traded firms in the United States are at liberty to adopt the dual leadership structure or not, at the sole discretion of their respective boards of directors. Even so, the lines are clearly drawn—pro and con. We discuss each in turn beginning with the arguments favoring separation.

Why a Separate Leadership Structure Should be Embraced

The notion of a dual leadership structure was among the earliest applications of agency theory. Fama and Jensen cautioned against the combined board leadership structure, arguing that it would compromise the ability of the board to reasonably monitor the CEO.[8] More recently, Institutional Shareholder Services (ISS), the AFL-CIO, and other governance observers have argued that the CEO and board chairperson positions—the two most influential positions in a publicly traded firm—should be held by different individuals. Also, having an independent board chairperson has long been accepted practice on corporate boards in the United Kingdom. In fairness, it should also be noted that the campaign to separate the roles of CEO and board chairperson has been modestly successful. In 2000, the percentage of boards with the separate structure was 19 percent. Today, however, 29 percent of the firms that constitute the S&P 500 have a separate CEO and chairperson structure. In principle, then, one could argue that boards are, in fact, becoming more independent on this dimension. Chapter Two in this volume, by authors Conger and Lawler, asserts that this trend will only persist, and that therefore the discussion of whether to have a separate chair is a moot issue. They feel that boards will be pressured to adopt the non-executive chair model of leadership regardless of potential drawbacks.

The central argument that CEOs should not serve simultaneously as chairpersons of their respective boards is simply stated. Advocates for separating these leadership roles are adamant that directors are severely—if not perniciously—limited in their individual and collective ability to dispassionately evaluate the performance, policies, and practices of a firm's CEO if he or she also serves as chairperson of the board.[9] One observer has referred to this phenomenon as the functional equivalent of the "CEO grading his own homework."[10] Perhaps predictably, then, critics of the duality structure have suggested that a fundamental omission in the SOX legislation was its silence on a requirement to separate the CEO and chairperson roles.[11]

This argument is neither illogical nor imprudent. It is also, however, not dispositive. There are a host of factors to be considered when choosing whether the duality or the separate leadership structure is the more appropriate for the contemporary publicly traded company. From our perspective, however, the better choice is that a CEO should serve as the firm's chairperson of the board.

Why a Separate Leadership Structure Should Be Abandoned

Proponents of the duality leadership structure for boards of directors rely on several—and in some cases interdependent—arguments to support their position.[12] These include a rather serious misspecification issue, a dearth of empirical evidence for the alleged relationship between the separation of these roles and improved enterprise performance, unity of command, and a host of issues related to CEO succession. These elements singly or in concert may constitute the basis for a compelling rationale to retain the structure whereby the CEO serves simultaneously as chairperson of the board.

Separate Leadership Is *Not* Independent

At this point, it bears repeating that the central issue in the debate about duality is anchored in the notion of independence. The separate structure—one person as CEO and another as chairperson of the board—is intended to result in a *more independent* board leadership structure. This argument fails, however, because the notion of independence in this context is often utterly misspecified. In fact, for the vast majority of cases, when the positions of CEO and board chairperson are separated, the "independence" problem is actually exacerbated.[13]

A leadership structure with a separate CEO and board chairperson is *not* necessarily indicative of independence; indeed such a separation seldom results in an independent structure. In fact, in the clear majority of cases (67 percent), the person who is the "separate" board chairperson is the former CEO of the company.[14] Moreover, a closer examination substantiates that even the "67 percent" is grossly understated. In addition to these "independent" chairpersons who are former CEOs, other supposedly separate, independent chairpersons are also company founders, former CEOs of acquired or merged companies, or persons otherwise connected to their firms beyond their service as directors and members of the board.[15] As an illustration of the totality of the misspecification, 29 percent of S&P 500 firms had a nominally separate CEO and chairperson structure (two persons serving in these roles). Taking into account the independence issues we have noted, Spencer Stuart's *Annual Board Index* reported that "only 9% of the boards . . . have a truly independent chair."[16]

It should be noted, however, that there are some cases in which the chairperson of the board is independent and utterly unconnected from the CEO in the ways that we have described. Even in such cases, however, there are other reasons why we would still prefer the CEO to serve simultaneously as chairperson of the board. We will argue this position in the "Unity of Command" section.

Duality: Evidence of Poorer Financial Performance?

Proponents of duality assert that there is simply no evidence supporting the contention that either separating or combining the CEO and chairperson roles affects the financial performance of the firm. A distinguished tradition of multidisciplinary research, narrative reviews, and meta-analyses extending over many years and relying on multiple elements of corporate performance have not demonstrated a relationship between leadership structure and corporate financial performance.[17]

Unity of Command

From the earliest foundations of administrative and organizational theory, there is recognition of the principle of unity of command.[18] The basic notion is that any subordinate should have a single and unambiguous line of authority to his or her supervisor. Consider an early explication by McCallum: "All subordinates should be accountable to, and be directed by their immediate supervisor only. . . ."[19] The provenance for unity of command is impressive, varied, and long-standing. In a decidedly different context, for example, we find a similar exhortation: "No man can serve two masters" (Matthew 6:24). In the *Federalist*, Alexander Hamilton (1788), too, enthusiastically endorsed the notion of unity of command.[20] Consider also another example of more recent vintage. The *United States Marine Corps Officer Training Manual* notes that "Unity of command means that all the forces are under one responsible commander. It requires having a single commander with the requisite authority to direct all forces employed in pursuit of a unified purpose."[21]

Despite this ageless advocacy for unity of command, the often favored governance structure relying on a separate CEO and board chairperson simply does not have this character. When the

CEO and board chairperson roles are separated, the enterprise does not have a single presiding officer with the requisite authority to direct relevant personnel and other resources in pursuit of a unified purpose. The CEO and non-executive structure does not provide for a single organizational voice. There is not a single presiding officer, there are two.

This is a potentially serious issue. Internal officers of the firm and a host of external constituencies need to know, definitively, who is in charge of the enterprise, whose voice is paramount, and, most critically, who is accountable.[22]

Consider a recent—and regrettable—example. Affiliated Computer Services (ACS) had reached an agreement with Cerebus Capital to be acquired for $6.2 billion. A special committee of the ACS board insisted on a go-shop clause (that is, a contract provision enabling an acquisition target to seek other offers for a specified period even after an agreement is reached with the acquiring company) to enable a search for alternative buyers. In the meantime, Cerebus Capital withdrew the offer, citing the weakening of credit markets.

Mr. Darwin Deason, holder of some 40 percent of the equity in ACS, and ACS chairperson of the board, instead of appreciating the directors' fiduciary duty and efforts to solicit other offers, argued that these directors (including the firm's CEO) unnecessarily extended the process and thus sacrificed the transaction. In a hail of public recriminations, accusations of self-dealing, and allegations that law firms were working both sides of the transaction, the threats of lawsuits continue. This is a case in which the CEO of the firm and its chairperson evidently had a different perspective. This case provides a point in favor of unity of command.

What If We Have Neither? The Case with No Independence and No Unity of Command

Consider another distressingly common scenario. Suppose that the positions of CEO and board chairperson are, in fact, separated.

The "separate" chairperson is not, however, independent. The first irony of this regrettable outcome is the obvious one—the board chair is *not* independent; he or she, for example, is the outgoing CEO of the firm. And with this arrives a new set of potential agency problems for the board. With a CEO who is not independent (by rule, CEOs are not independent; they are officers of the firm) and a board chair who is not independent, Brickley, Coles, and Jarrell (with credit to Alchian and Demsetz) raise an interesting question: "Who monitors the monitor?"[23] Now the board must be concerned about CEOs' and separate chairpersons' leverage to extract inappropriate rents as a function of their positions. Dysfunctional tensions between CEOs and chairpersons of the board are not unusual—particularly when the chairperson is a former CEO. Consider a case that presents with a delectable irony. The CEO of a high-profile pharmaceutical company was dismissed, through the influence of the board chairperson (and former CEO), after just over a year of service. In due course, a new CEO was hired. And here is the irony. The new CEO accepted the position only on the condition that the current chairperson of the board be replaced.

As disquieting as incidents like this may be, they represent only a piece of the broken governance puzzle. Now, with the separate CEO and board chairperson, the—for us—eminently reasonable concept of unity of command is wholly compromised as well. We would argue that a separate CEO and board chair, neither of whom are independent, in concert with a clear violation of the unity of command, is a board leadership structure perilously close to the worst-case scenario.

Another Reality Check: Executive Committees of the Board

The executive committee (EC) of publicly traded companies provides an interesting series of issues under the broad rubric of corporate governance. As earlier noted, the guidelines promulgated by Sarbanes-Oxley and of the listing exchanges require that the audit, compensation, governance, and nominating committees must be totally composed of (and derivatively chaired by) independent directors. Such committees should also have written charters in which their mission or purpose, authority, and roles and responsibilities are set forth.

These guidelines, however, do not apply to other board committees, including the executive committee. This is notable because 46 percent of the *Fortune* 500 companies have ECs, but fewer than half of those (42 percent) provide a written charter.[24] ECs normally have a broad charter. The charter of the EC for Dow Chemical (2007), for example, notes that "the Executive Committee . . . shall possess and may exercise all of the powers of the Board of Directors in the management and direction of the business and affairs of the Company to the fullest extent allowed by the General Corporation Law of Delaware and other applicable regulations."

Now consider an enterprise with an EC and with a separate leadership structure. In that case both the CEO and the chairperson of the board would normally be among the EC's membership. In such a case, who is the voice of the EC? Who is in charge? Who is accountable for what is almost certainly the single most powerful committee for publicly traded firms?

In this scenario, too, there could be a textbook case in which there are actually multiple violations of best-in-class practices. Suppose there is a crisis, a pending SEC investigation. The company has just become aware of this action, and the chairperson of the EC has called an emergency meeting. Consider the issues. First, the chairperson of the board is the past CEO and is thus not independent. This person is, however, the chairperson of the EC. Consider, also, that the current CEO is a member of the EC. So on whose advice shall we rely?

CEO Succession and the Dual Leadership Structure

There are aspects of the contemporary corporate governance environment that will present boards of directors with difficult challenges with regard to CEO succession and its intersection with the leadership duality debate. An example is the escalation in CEO turnover rates. According to data available from Liberum Research (2007), 2,106 CEOs left their positions in 2006, an annual turnover rate of 16.2 percent, a rate unprecedented in U.S. corporate history. Also, Booz Allen reports that since 2000, 470 of the *Fortune* 1000 firms have new CEOs.[25] Understandably, a Booz Allen Hamilton study, commenting on the increasing turnover trend, referred to CEOs as "The World's Most Prominent Temp Workers."[26] Also, as noted in the *Harvard Business Review*, "The greatest challenge looming over corporate America [is] finding replacement CEOs."[27]

At the nexus of these historic CEO turnover rates and the debate about the separation of the CEO and board chairperson roles are several potential faultlines, most of which are directly attributable to the previously noted unity of command missteps. For the sake of discussion, assume that a firm's board decides to adopt the separation principle. The board names the former CEO as chairperson of the board and announces a separate CEO. This decision—one that would be embraced by proponents of separating these positions—could have a host of dire consequences. Consider several examples in the succeeding sections.

Transforming CEOs to Apprentices Is Ill-Advised Alchemy

First, recall that the vast majority of chairpersons of the board in firms with separate board leadership structures are not independent. We would argue that boards that appoint a CEO, presumably strongly enabled to lead the firm, who remains under the potential influence of the firm's founder(s) or past CEOs, are courting disaster. Such a structure effectively places the newly appointed CEO in an apprenticeship program, a point that is reinforced in Chapter Two.

Consider an illustrative case in which the prior CEO, now chairperson of the board, may have struggled with the transition. William Perez, former CEO of S.C. Johnson & Son, Inc., became CEO at Nike effective December 2004. Mr. Perez replaced Philip Knight, the company's high-profile co-founder and chairperson of the Nike board. From the onset, Mr. Knight reportedly continued to meet with senior officers of Nike who, not incidentally, were direct reports to Mr. Perez. Moreover, Mr. Knight scheduled weekly meetings with Mr. Perez. It was reported through company releases that Mr. Perez and Mr. Knight disagreed on the company's long-term growth strategy. Perhaps not surprisingly, Mr. Perez resigned as CEO of Nike in January 2006, just over a year after having assumed that responsibility.

Mr. Knight noted, in the wake of Mr. Perez's resignation, that "succession at any company is challenging. . . ."[28] Mr. Perez—in something of an understatement—explained that the situation "was confusing for the people and frustrating for me."[29]

This Knight-Perez CEO transition may have been doomed from the onset. Here were two strong individuals, each with world-class credentials, and apparently with some difference of opinion about who was "in charge." This case, although more public than most, is not unusual. Boards that make the decision to separate the CEO and board chairperson roles openly court such outcomes. Whatever else one may think about this particular case, its outcome, and its dynamics, we can probably agree that it does not engender faith in separating CEO and board chair roles, particularly when the outgoing CEO is to remain the board chairperson.

CEO Succession Planning

The model wherein a prior CEO is chairperson of the board and is nominally independent and there is a separate CEO also visits a substantial risk on the execution of best-practice CEO succession planning. Frankly, there may be a tendency for boards to overestimate the current structure's adequacy for succession exigencies. Chapters Nine, Ten, and Eleven strongly reinforce this point. An argument might unfold something on this order. The former CEO is now the board chairperson. If something should happen such that the current CEO is terminated, incapacitated, dies, or is otherwise removed from office, the prior CEO could easily step in and manage the enterprise through the crisis.

The financial community refers to this strategy as a reliance on the "boomerang CEO." This is not a compliment. Other observers are even less charitable when referring to changes of this sort as reliance on a "substitute teacher." Even as children in school, we realized that our substitute teachers were temporary, would be moving on soon. We probably—maybe unfairly—did not take them seriously. Pressing the metaphor, neither does the Street. Worse, it is a very poor substitute for a best-practice succession plan. In fact, a recent study on what the authors describe as a "comeback CEO" affirms that the value of firms' stock does fall on an announcement to rehire a former CEO.[30] In fairness, however, we should note that such hirings typically occur when the value of these shares has been in decline over the prior period.

The Market for a Replacement CEO Is Critically Compromised

This structure of a prior CEO as board chair may also compromise recruiting and severely constrict the market for potential candidates. This tendency will be in stark relief should the firm opt to recruit an external candidate. Consider an exceptional candidate with impeccable credentials. Such a person may have no interest in the position because he or she—with reasonable justification—is concerned that the prior CEO, now board chair, will interfere with the new CEO's discretion to lead this company.

Alternatively, this exceptional candidate may not accept the position because he or she simply prefers to serve simultaneously as CEO and chairperson of the firm he or she would join. The question is not whether a person can be identified who might accept the position. There will always be someone. The better question is whether the board can attract and retain the most able person, a person with the experience, expertise, and reputation to signal the market that the enterprise is guided by a strong leader and a single voice.

A Reality Check Regarding Emeritus Directors and CEO Succession

This tendency to moderate the leadership of CEOs is not limited to the separation of the CEO and board chairperson roles. The oversight of current CEOs by prior CEOs to which we have referred may actually extend over much longer periods.

"Emeritus" directors, for example, provide yet another vehicle to extend such influence well beyond a normal retirement cycle for a retiring CEO.[31] Boards of directors have the authority, at their sole discretion, to appoint emeritus directors. Although the duties and enablements of such a director may vary, his or her impact on a new CEO can have the same character that we have previously described. Consider, for example, a former CEO of the company who has reached mandatory retirement age. The board may appoint this person as a director emeritus. Accordingly, this person may have the right to attend all meetings of the board and may vote as would a "normal" director. Emeritus directors, however, will not likely ever stand for reelection, and their appointment may be "for life."

The point, of course, is that this special category of director could enable a prior CEO, prior chairperson of the board, or both to influence a new CEO for many, many years. In fairness, some emeritus directors will not have been invited to officially vote on matters of the board, but will, instead, be granted "voice" only. In that case, perhaps the potential influence would be mitigated. We would not subscribe to that view: we can imagine that the "voice" of a prior CEO/chairperson of the board could be a compelling factor in boards' deliberations.

Conclusion

We do not find the arguments in favor of separating the roles of the CEO and the chairperson of the board to be compelling. Moreover, for us this "independence" perspective is, beyond misspecified, largely unnecessary. We recognize the critical assessment that combining the CEO and board chairperson roles confers substantial autonomy and discretion on the CEO. Indeed it does and, in our view, therein lies its strength. We—with the timeless good counsel of the earliest foundations of organization theory—embrace the basic elements of unity of command. The CEO and board chairperson roles should be held by one individual. There is incalculable currency in one leader, supported by a seasoned top management team and an able board, with a single voice directing the enterprise. At its best, there will be no parties and constituencies—internal or external—who question who is in charge and who is accountable.

We do not, however, endorse maverick leadership. In the stewardship of a strong board, buttressed by the independence of its membership and, more important, by the independence of its judgment, well-executed unity of command guidelines actually attenuate unrestrained leadership. When the board confers substantial autonomy—as it should—on its combined CEO/chairperson, it must also embrace vigilant oversight, fairly administered and with finality, if the CEO/chairperson proves unsuitable for dual service.

There is a key principle that may underscore many of our concerns. Outstanding boards of directors, comprising members fairly characterized by expertise, experience, and reputation, may reach different decisions with regard to their choice of leadership structure—a CEO who serves simultaneously as board chair or a CEO and a non-executive chair. Under either circumstance, however, there is a principle that most observers can embrace. In the latter case, the dual structure, the board must be certain to establish the authority and responsibility of its dual leaders. Every effort must be made to reduce any uncertainty about those roles and responsibilities within as well as outside the enterprise.

We would add one additional thought, focused on the enterprise in crisis. The recent *Agenda* piece to which we earlier referred reports a trend in which investor groups and other outside observers are using recent corporate controversies (for example, extremely poor performance in the mortgage sector, scandals) as a wedge to encourage boards to separate the CEO and board chairperson roles.[32] With respect, we would argue that there is absolutely *no* worse time to make such a change. If there are scoundrels involved who are culpable for the mischief, then the relevant boards should remove these officers. Separating the leadership structure of the enduring enterprise as a reaction to these crises, however, is a potentially grave error.

When things are at their most trying, we advocate reliance on a single voice. Consider the leadership demands, for example, on a cardiac surgeon in the operating theater with the patient in extreme distress, a pilot with an aircraft floundering, a military officer challenged with a strategic position imperiled by opposing forces, a quarterback with fourth down and one yard to go and thirty-eight seconds left on the clock. In such circumstances, there is no need for two presiding doctors, two head pilots, two senior military officers, or two quarterbacks. Observers may press their own metaphors, but someone has to make the call and be accountable. Ultimately, there must be one voice, hopefully forged and honed in the crucible of experience. Several voices under such circumstances do not constitute a choir; they are a cacophony.

Certainly there will be less exigent circumstances, wherein a strong leader has the time and the resources to more broadly seek good counsel. Even so, *a* person must make the final call. With a successful call, that person will likely receive more credit than he or she is due; with failure, that person will likely receive more blame than he or she is due. So be it.

4

First Among Equals: Leading Your Fellow Directors as a Board Chair

Katharina Pick

As boards oversee increasingly complex global organizations and meet the rising governance expectations in the wake of Sarbanes-Oxley, the job of board chair is becoming more demanding and important. More than ever, boards are struggling to meet specific requirements, in a short period of time, and with limited information.[1] The leadership behavior of the board chair in this environment is critical to the performance of the board. In fulfilling his or her leadership role, the chair can both enable fellow directors and undermine them. This chapter draws upon real-time observation of board meetings to illustrate how board chairs can successfully lead inside the boardroom.[2]

The Duties of the Board Chair

Board chairs have several widely accepted duties that are spelled out in governance guidelines or best practices (see Chapters Two and Six). For example, they typically take the lead in developing the board meeting agenda. They are also the ones who communicate with directors between meetings; oversee the creation of premeeting reading materials; and act as the public spokesperson for the board with the press, analysts, and investors.[3] In addition to these relatively well-defined tasks, board chairs have the role of actually *leading* the group of directors and managing discussion among them.

Leaders of any workgroup or team have enormous influence over the performance of that group in the ways they manage the tasks of the group, structure discussions, lead the group through internal conflict, and display other more subtle leadership behaviors.[4] These latter forms of leadership are perhaps the most important roles of the board chair, yet they have received relatively little attention.

Why the neglect? First, discussions about board leadership turn almost invariably to the question of leadership *structure*—whether the chair and CEO positions ought to be combined or held separately. Although this is an important debate and one that is discussed in this book, it is only a portion of what produces effective board leadership. In recent years, boards under each type of structure have shown themselves to be both effective and ineffective. I will not address directly the structure debate, but it is noteworthy that the most directive, the most passive, the most respected, and the most criticized board leaders described in this chapter all were non-executive chairs. (Three of five leaders in this study were non-executive chairs.) In some instances, the separation of the two leadership roles worked extremely well. In others, it was meaningless for the board's work and in fact appeared to undermine the board's ability to be heard by management. As the debate about structure continues, most likely the answer will be a conditional one—meaning the circumstances of the board, the business, and the leadership situation will determine how successful one or the other structure can be.

There is a second reason, however, that the topic of strong leadership in the boardroom has not received a great amount of attention. On the basis of my observations and interviews, I believe that the notion of an influential and deliberate board chair who is a strong leader is somewhat unpalatable in the corporate governance arena. Board chairs themselves appear to be reluctant to take on this kind of responsibility. They instead wish to operate in a way that does not alienate or offend their compatriots, who are, after all, their equals. Holding no real formal authority over their fellow directors—in contrast to a CEO who has the authority to hire and fire his subordinates—board chairs know that it is too easy to overstep their assigned title and lose the respect or cooperation of the other directors.

Taking into account these biases in the discourse on board leadership, this chapter focuses specifically on the behaviors that help chairs become effective leaders of the boardroom.

Understanding the Process of Leadership on the Board

Studying firsthand the behavior of board chairs produces many different pictures of board leadership. It is difficult to draw conclusions about effective or ineffective styles, mainly because board functioning is hard to measure or to link to outcomes such as company performance or stock price.[5] In such situations, researchers often turn to understanding the *process* that is involved in producing an outcome and to identifying attributes of that process that are likely to produce better outcomes.[6] For example, scholars of decision making face the challenge of evaluating decision *quality*. Rather than debating what qualifies as a good decision outcome, they often turn to understanding the attributes and quality of the process that produced the decision.[7] Similarly, when we consider the elusive notion of board "effectiveness," we are better off identifying aspects of board *process* that are likely to produce better governance. This chapter relies on just such a process perspective, linking chair behavior to the kind of process that is desirable; a process that makes good use of directors and that is likely to set the stage for effective governance.

The academic research on groups provides a good starting point for identifying desirable attributes for board process. Good decision making and group functioning means *communication* and *information sharing*,[8] *positive relations* among group members, some degree of *perceived efficacy* on the part of the group, and the ability to *resolve conflict* and keep the group *working together in the future*.[9]

It is clear that the actions of the chair, whether intended or not, have consequences for all of these aspects of board process. For example, what tactics chairs deploy to solicit director input can shape the depth and honesty of the discussion that follows and who participates. How chairs facilitate communication between directors and senior management can shape what information is transmitted and how the two groups relate to one another. Finally, how chairs manage discussions can influence what directors think they should contribute, how productive they feel as a group, and how they feel about conflict in the boardroom.

Drawing on the experiences of both non-executive chairs and CEO/chairs, this chapter will illustrate how board leaders can have this kind of influence. Both observation and the chair's own reflections illuminate specific tactics used by board leaders and their consequences for board dynamics. I turn now to the key roles that board chairs have in leading their boards.

Four Key Roles for the Board Chair

In leading boardroom discussions, chairs must fill four broad roles. These are

1. Managing the "status dilemma" of leading a group of equals
2. Managing the "tension" between the various roles the board plays with senior management
3. Sustaining the cohesion of the director group while encouraging debate
4. Managing the ambiguous nature of the board's role

Each of these leadership roles relates to one or more of the process dimensions previously listed as being important to a board's work: communication, positive relations within the group, unfettered discussion, and conflict resolution. The four roles address challenges that any group or team leader would face, but, as will become clear, they also reflect some challenges that are unique to boards.

Introducing the Four Leadership Roles

The first leadership role of the board chair is to manage the inherent "status dilemma" that exists on boards. A status dilemma exists because one of the premises on boards is that everybody is equal. From a legal perspective this is true, but in reality we know this is not the case. Even when groups have no material information for determining who is better or worse at a task, they informally develop an internal hierarchy. They develop a sense of who is more powerful and who is more competent, often on the basis of the external status that group members have (such as age, gender, race, and so on).[10] We also know from social psychological research that group memberships are an important component of identity. As group members, people seek to get positive feedback that verifies their own self-view.[11] Similarly, directors attempt to find a niche in the group, a niche that affirms how they think about themselves and gives them a sense of competence and belonging to the director group. But boards have almost no formal hierarchy or individual role definitions. This inherent ambiguity and uncertainty can complicate group dynamics and lead to even greater reliance on the most visible status feature directors have: their external profession and expertise. This can lead to nonproductive contributions, posturing, and jockeying among the director group. It can also lead directors to be silent when they are unsure of how a particular comment would reflect on their status or identity within the group. The challenge for the board chair is to keep these status dynamics from hurting the quality of board discussion. Specifically, he or she must ensure that the board is using all the knowledge and experience that is assembled around the table—that individuals feel motivated and capable of sharing their ideas—but also that the board is working efficiently and without internal strife.

The second important job for the chair is "managing role tension": to help the board manage the multiple roles it plays with senior management. From a governance perspective, the board is expected to oversee and *monitor* senior management.[12] Along with this, a board must also *advise* management, offering experience and expertise to guide management toward a successful strategy. As boards get burdened with more and more compliance duties, they increasingly face a trade-off between their monitoring function and shaping strategy.[13] Monitoring and advising are, at least in passing phases, in conflict with one another,[14] and the tension between them must be managed continually. The behavior of the chair influences how this is done.

A third and related role of the board chair is to sustain group cohesion. Although cohesion can also have drawbacks for performance, the benefits for boards are notable.[15] Cohesive groups exhibit a collective motivation for the group to do well, greater ease in coordinating effort, and behavior aimed at keeping the group unified through its tasks.[16] One of the unique conditions that boards face is that they perform almost all of their work in the presence of and in interaction with senior management—the group they are meant to oversee! This dynamic makes cohesion both more important and more difficult. To be influential, boards must maintain a unified voice vis-à-vis management. This does not mean that directors should not disagree or that this disagreement cannot occur in front of management. But the board must be able to move past conflict and present management with a coherent message that comes from the whole board. The chair must sustain the kind of group cohesion that enables this.

Finally, the chair must help the director group understand its role as a board. Legally, the role of the board is only broadly defined, which can be confusing and frustrating.[17] The prescribed duties are contained in three statutes: "the duty of loyalty" (acting with no conflict of interest), "the duty of care" (using due diligence in the process), and, more recently, the "duty of good faith" (acting with a high level of care).[18] Boards are left to define for themselves how they will go about covering information or interacting with senior management. Some recent regulatory requirements, particularly for the audit committee, do specify more explicitly what materials the board must review and who should be involved. But for the most part, boards define for themselves how they govern.[19] A critical duty for the chair then is to ensure that the directors are operating with a common vision for the board's role. This role may change over time, but directors must share an understanding of what it is.

The Importance of Meetings: The Arenas for Leadership

The primary place where board chairs perform these critical *group leadership* roles is in and immediately around the board meeting. Certainly chairs also lead at other times, but there are at least two reasons why in-meeting leadership is critical. First, the board meeting is the primary setting in which the entire board is assembled and interacts as a group. It is where the directors develop norms about their process, their communication style, and their collective role. Group norms are shaped through interaction; by acting and responding to each other, directors learn what is accepted in the group, and they continually negotiate this together.

A second reason the board meeting is an important setting for leadership is because it is where the board as a whole interacts with senior management. It is where expectations between these two groups are negotiated. At board meetings, senior management comes to understand the role that the board is playing. Will the board be extremely critical during presentations? Are the directors primarily concerned with compliance or are they deeply interested in shaping the course of the business? These perceptions and interactions will shape how management brings information to the board in the future, and also how they will respond to input from the board.

I turn now to a more in-depth discussion of *how* board chairs actually perform or fail to perform each of the four group leadership roles inside of board meetings.

Managing the Status Dilemma: A Tightrope Walk

Because boards are theoretically a group of equals, individuals may struggle to understand their status, power, and identity relative to the other group members. Directors arrive with some notion of what their contribution might be. Perhaps they have financial expertise. Perhaps they have operational experience in the industry. However, without formal role definitions, directors learn what they can contribute primarily by speaking up and getting feedback from other directors and from management.

We often assume that directors—highly educated, powerful, and accomplished individuals—would have little trouble expressing their expertise in a board discussion. However, this overlooks two important factors. First, some directors simply are more reserved, and some are more dominant than others. Second, directors bring very visible external identities (such as professions or positions) for which they presumably were selected to join the board. Once inside the boardroom, they do not have a clear *role*, yet they must reflect for others and for themselves that their external identity gives them appropriate status and competence in the group. This makes speaking up in discussion a high-stakes and psychologically complicated act.

Group researchers have found that participation in groups is shaped not only by outside status indicators[20] but also by members seeking to contribute information that verifies how they see themselves.[21] In other words, a director who considers himself to be a "brilliant operations guy" may hesitate to say something that disconfirms this self-image. Ironically, he may be more inhibited speaking to an operational issue, where being wrong or naïve could harm his self-image and his status in the group, than he might be speaking to a regulatory issue. The ambiguity around how directors fit into the group or how their status compares to other directors only exacerbates this perceived risk.

At the other end of the spectrum, directors may contribute more aggressively, searching for affirmation, trying to establish an identity in the group, and proving that they belong alongside the other high-status people on the board. One accomplished director's comments reflect that status is not an insignificant factor: "This is the most senior board that I'm on. They're big hitters. Yes [it affects my experience.] Because I'm on some boards where I'm the most senior guy in the group, and I'm more comfortable there. And so the first board meeting here, I was a little more intimidated."

Many directors are familiar with this sensitivity. Most of those interviewed for this study were keenly aware of each other's status, experience, and reputations outside of the boardroom. They expressed deference to others based on tenure and professional differences and sometimes felt unsure about speaking on topics outside of their own professional background. Research on conformity shows that particularly when issues under discussion are highly ambiguous, group members are more apt to rely on each other's beliefs about those issues and are less confident in their own perceptions.[22] In other words, the ambiguity that typically characterizes complex discussion topics on boards further exacerbates the status dilemma in ways that lead directors to keep silent when they are unsure of their assessments or ideas.

The flip side, as mentioned earlier, is directors pushing too hard to establish their place in the group or in a discussion. Experienced board members often describe a tendency on boards for directors to posture in front of management or to speak simply "to hear themselves speak." Consider the comments of one director following a board meeting: "It's far more productive to discuss things outside the meeting. Nobody is posturing, and management isn't there. Posturing happens in the meetings because [director X] always has to make points. It's in his personality. He'll throw zingers. . . . He'll make a flip comment. In the meeting, he pursued that [discussion point] for far too long. He knew the answer. He was just trying to make a point. He made an, excuse me, [idiot] of himself. That was his choice. But he does that. [Trying to prove] that he has read whatever he was meant to read or something."

One critical role for the board chair then is to keep directors engaged and feeling valued, but not jockeying for position. To do this, he or she must ensure that directors know what others bring to the board and what they themselves bring to the board—to remove some of this status ambiguity. This is a tension, of course, and the chair must also make sure that directors' contributions do not become too narrowly specified. This would reduce the group to a set of experts who speak only on their individual topics. In such a case, some of the most important advantages of group process would be lost: the pooling of diverse and unshared information,[23] the expression of minority opinions,[24] and the group collective commitment to outcomes.[25] In other words, the chair must balance directors knowing their own and others' competencies with directors contributing on topics outside of their immediate area of expertise.

Active chairs use several techniques to do this. These include calling on directors, polling the board, and having premeeting conversations with directors.

Calling on Directors

Chairs can frequently "call on" directors in meetings to bring out a particular expertise or to express a concern they know is on a director's mind. This technique has two important consequences. First, it reminds directors of their unique contribution to the board. Being called on, directors learn where their expertise is needed and also have greater freedom to express their ideas.

Directors gain confidence in the board process knowing that their ideas will come to the table even if they do not assert themselves forcefully. Getting called on removes some of the risk of speaking up and creates a less threatening way to share information.

A second important benefit from calling on directors is that it enables them to understand each other better. Getting "called on" automatically frames the topic raised by a director within a context of professional expertise. As a result, other directors are less likely to personalize or dismiss whatever is expressed, but rather will seek to understand it within that director's experience and search for the potential value in it. When chairs periodically call on directors on the basis of their particular experience, it frames their contributions in a way that gives the whole board a clearer sense of what everyone has to offer.

Polling the Board

Another tactic used by chairs is to go around the room sequentially to get input from *all* directors on a particular issue. Most board leaders recognize that some of their directors are quieter than others and that the discussion on certain topics will be dominated by those who either are very vocal or are experts. Polling is one way in which active chairs ensure that, on occasion, all directors will hear from one another and each director will bring his perspective to bear on a certain issue. One CEO/chairman of a high-tech company was particularly articulate about the value of polling and the reasons why some directors' perspectives would be lost from discussion without it: "I have learned an important lesson of polling the board. Some board members are just more vocal than others. I don't think anybody's ever felt *uncomfortable* raising something, but I think some people aren't sure whether their opinion is strong enough to get it in there. So this is why I had to say 'really tell me what you think.' Some board members are just much more vocal than others. I learned, probably a couple of years ago, the importance of polling so that everyone speaks."

His approach contrasted with some of the other observed board chairs, who simply assumed that if directors had something to say they would say it. This later assumption did not always map onto reality for directors who at times would hold off from speaking despite having something to say. For example, one director noted, "I don't think anybody is *intimidated.* But sometimes I don't speak because I don't know enough to ask the right questions, probably the others are the same way."

The CEO/chairman quoted earlier had a more nuanced conception of "something to say" and argued that on occasion it is important to hear even comments about which directors are unsure or less passionate. This allows directors to hear others' viewpoints when they otherwise might simply assume agreement or disinterest.

A related benefit of polling is that when the entire group has spoken on something, the board as a whole is likely to feel greater ownership of the discussion outcome. In one instance of polling observed on a medical services board, a director's viewpoint was particularly influential, leading other directors after him to revise their own opinions. Whereas in another kind of discussion these directors might have remained silent, they expressed their prior and new opinions publicly to the group as part of the process of going around the table. Research on group behavior and conformity tells us that this kind of public statement of opinions creates buy-in from those individuals who revise their opinions.[26] It also gives directors the sense that they have contributed to the overall outcome despite being less influential than the more vocal director. In other words, polling creates a sense of collective effort and unity of voice as the board communicates the outcome of its discussion to the senior management team.

Of course it is not feasible or necessary to use this polling tactic for every issue under discussion. It could be divisive and could make directors uncomfortable in front of senior management. It could also frustrate busy directors sensitive about using board meeting time efficiently. Where polling was effective, the boards had strong norms about how much directors should speak and also had a trusting relationship with senior management. Directors on these boards cooperated with one another and were described as being very careful not to dominate discussion or to repeat points already expressed. A leader on a less integrated or low-trust board might not be able to risk opening the floor to this kind of polling discussion.

Premeeting Discussions

Both calling on directors and polling are facilitated by one other important tactic used by active board chairs: having premeeting conversations to understand the perspectives and concerns that directors are bringing into the meeting. Even brief exchanges before the meeting can give the chair enough information to call on a director (though not without warning) during discussion, to help him or her articulate an idea to the rest of the board.

The challenges in managing the status dilemma on boards are subtle but great. Chairs who manage it well are able to keep interactions professional, task-oriented, and efficient. They do this by soliciting input from directors and framing input within the director's professional background, and by getting directors to contribute beyond their own expertise. Directors are somewhat liberated from the difficulty of negotiating status and ambiguity within the group because they develop a broader sense of what each director can bring to the table. On boards where the chair did *not* actively manage director contributions, the perception of posturing and the accompanying frustration from board members appeared to be a common occurrence.

Even when the director group is contributing enthusiastically and productively, its members face a second challenge of how their contributions are being heard by senior management. The particular dilemma is that the directors must influence management with different aims at different times. This results in a tension between the various roles the board is trying to play. I turn next to the leadership challenge of managing this role tension at the board level.

Managing Role Tension: The Cop and the Adviser

One of the most difficult things a board has to do is to be an objective and independent critic of management, while also being supportive of management. In other words, directors must watch presentations with a critical eye, ask questions that will reveal potential errors, or even express disapproval. At the same time, they must keep management motivated and feeling supported. There is a more subtle aspect of this dilemma. Because the board is so reliant on management for essential information, it must sustain the kind of relationship that will keep senior managers bringing that information to the board. If the board is seen as overly critical or a nuisance that is best circumvented, then the board undermines itself. The board must sustain a nurturing relationship with management, but not at the expense of being conscientious.

This is difficult to do for individual directors, but even more so for the collective board. It requires first an awareness of the tension and then immense cooperation among the directors in resolving it. Most directors are intuitively aware of this tension in their governance role, but achieving the necessary responses at the group level is difficult. One director put it this way: "If you think about it, a board meets two or three hours every quarter and has three conference calls. There is only so much you can do and be effective in that room. It is all about building teams. You don't want some manager to come in and feel like they've got their knees knocked out of them. They could have been terrific managers, but it was just that they were sent a bad message."

This sensitivity was notable in the behavior of directors I studied. On some boards, directors deliberately interspersed criticism with outright cheerleading in an effort to preserve the balance between cop and supporter. In one board meeting, a director pushing senior managers to be more precise about a new venture critiqued their approach. After a few questions, another director chimed in enthusiastically to say, "It is *really* great that you are taking this on. Great stuff!" He went on to praise various features of their approach in a way that did not negate the prior director's critiques but rather complemented them. Several boards exhibited this pattern. Directors would hand off the cop and supporter roles to each other and cooperate to create an overall interaction that included both roles. In contrast, the tension on other boards manifested itself in directors turning on each other in the face of criticism. Here directors who criticized were dismissed and even overtly rebuked by the other board members. Directors were on edge about overstepping their monitoring role and damaging the relationship between the board and management.

On most boards, chairs represent the structural link between senior management and the board. As such, they drive the way these two groups interact and in turn manage the inherent tension between them. They help the board to balance the monitoring and advising roles. To do this, a chair must build and sustain trust between managers and directors but simultaneously encourage a certain objective distance and independence for the board. Skilled chairs employ several tactics to do this: building bridges, gathering information prior to the meeting, foreshadowing points of discussion, treating the meeting as a whole and integrated discussion, and modeling the relationship between the management and the board.

Building Bridges

The first observed tactic of active chairs was building bridges between senior management and the board during the course of the meeting. An example comes from a non-executive chair who knew that managers did not respond well to the somewhat aggressive style of one of his more vocal directors (Jim). To keep

Jim's important and insightful comments coming to the board and actually being heard by management, the chair spent extra effort framing the input that came from him. He asked rhetorical questions following Jim's comments and pointed out connections between the comment and other ideas being discussed. By doing so, he removed the pressure the other directors felt to keep Jim from alienating management and in turn created a safer space for them to hear his contributions.

The flip side of this helpful bridge-building behavior could be seen in the conduct of a CEO/chairman who actually exacerbated the tensions in the board-management relationship through his own behavior. Even when directors articulated seemingly innocuous points, this CEO/chairman construed input by the board to be an attack on management. During one board meeting, a director asked why a summary of the company performance on safety was no longer part of the board materials and asked if this was a reflection of a change in philosophy. Rather than engaging with the question, the CEO/chairman proceeded to tout the company's safety record, setting up his senior managers to cite comparative statistics as a defense. Rather than answer the director's question, he converted this opportunity for agreement into a distancing moment. The director who asked the question was villainized, and the other directors implicitly warned about future questions like this. Not only was this board constantly on edge during meetings, turning on each other and dismissing each other's comments, but it also wound up having very little constructive interaction with senior management in meetings.

Premeeting Information Gathering

As alluded to in the prior section, one of the ways in which board chairs prepare for bridge building is to talk to directors before meetings about the concerns and questions they have. This does not mean board leaders should begin "pre-cooking" important issues or using a "divide-and-conquer" mode of leading directors into discussions or key decisions. However, chairs who are effective at creating a productive dialogue between the board and senior management tend to know beforehand which concerns are likely to surface. For example, at one board meeting, the theme of which was specifically to discuss strategy, a director had a particular concern that he planned to raise regarding a business unit taking a new direction. Having spoken to the director before the meeting, the chairman was already aware of this director's perspective. He thus more easily played the role of incorporating the concern into the broader discussion. The chairman was then able to set up individual directors to make certain points. For example, a chair might say "Joe, you had mentioned that you had some experience with this. Can you share that right now?"

Done well, this tactic has two important consequences. First, the individual director is satisfied that he or she is valuable and has been heard. Second, and more important to the current discussion, this tactic takes the burden of speaking up off of the individual director. Instead, concerns appear to come from the board as a whole, meaning they immediately rise in importance to senior management. Individual directors are not easily cast as troublemakers or deviants, given that their points are more seamlessly incorporated into the contribution of the board as an entity. This in turn helps to remove some of the tension the director group feels around sustaining a good relationship with management while still giving critical input.

Foreshadowing Points of Discussion

A related tactic that is facilitated by knowledge gained in premeeting conversations is to foreshadow issues that chairs know will emerge over the course of the meeting. For example, a chair can frame anticipated points early in the meeting, alluding to them with regard to some larger issue. Later, when the point emerges in a more focused discussion, the groundwork for its importance has already been laid or at least entertained in the minds of the managers and other directors. In this way, the chair is able to shape how points from directors actually are heard by the group.

One non-executive chairman mentioned early on in a board meeting, seemingly as a side note, that he had recently spoken to an industry player who praised a new technology they were developing. He commented what a time-sensitive and terrific opportunity it provided. Later in the meeting, it became clear that directors were concerned that management was not doing enough with the new technology. Because this topic had been put on the table early on and in a positive way, the directors were better able to raise their own concerns about this legitimate issue. It now could be dealt with in a critical way.

Treating the Meeting Holistically

Chairs who actively manage role tension share an implicit idea about board meetings: that they are to be treated as a whole and integrated discussion. Throughout the meeting, these chairs will weave themes together, even across the various discussion topics. They create an overall purpose for the meeting around the big issues that are most urgent or relevant at that time. For example, one board was fundamentally concerned with being aggressive and acting on a current competitive advantage in a strategic way. This overall state of mind—the sense of urgency and the focus on long-term strategy—infused all topics of discussion. The chair was careful to tie every matter in front of the board back to this priority that currently was guiding the company. This broad sense of purpose also provided a context for directors' contributions. Both they and senior managers were better able to understand how criticism and new ideas were intended to help. Again, this served to create a more open and trusting dialogue between the directors and senior management. On other boards discussion was more haphazard and less integrated across a broad set of issues. On these boards, the relationship between management and the board tended to be more volatile and the interactions between them more strained.

Modeling the Relationship

Finally, effective board chairs model a relationship with senior management that shapes the culture of the meeting and of the board. The aforementioned CEO/chairman who always responded defensively to his directors was modeling a relationship that was adversarial, mistrusting, and distant. In contrast, another chairman modeled open and collegial interactions through his own communications inside the boardroom. He asked senior managers specific questions about the work they had done and indicated that he knew what unique challenges each person was facing. He took on a mentoring role with individual managers that created a culture one might see in a collegial working group.

Each of the tactics just described had the effect of easing the inherent tension in the roles that the board must play with management. It freed up directors to be more tolerant of each other and more influential with management. The next leadership role I will discuss addresses a challenge that is critical for all groups, but has even greater importance on boards: sustaining the unity of voice and cohesion of the director group through heated discussions and disagreements.

Sustaining Cohesion in the Face of Management: The United Front

To enjoy the benefits of being a group, boards must be able to balance open discussion and disagreement on the one hand with group cohesion, trust, and efficiency on the other.[27] One of the unique constraints that boards face as a group is that almost all of their work happens in the presence of another group: senior management. This makes sustaining cohesion all the more difficult and important. The board needs to work out its own process in a way that shows management that the board is not divided or confused but rather a strong and credible group.

The board chair, as the moderator of discussion, must encourage directors to be honest and contribute critically even if it engenders conflict. At the same time, he or she must ensure that disagreement does not paralyze the board, undermine the board's influence with management, or hinder the directors' ability to work together in the future.

Conflict was long considered to be almost categorically bad for groups.[28] Today, however, research suggests that certain *types* of conflict in groups are beneficial to the quality of discussion, decision making, and other group outcomes. Researchers make a distinction between *task conflict* and *relationship conflict;* task conflict being beneficial to the group and relationship conflict generally undermining the group.[29] One way in which the board can sustain cohesion in spite of the inevitable occurrence of conflict is to keep conflict at the task level. Task conflict means directors perceive themselves to be disagreeing about substantive issues (for example, distribution of resources, procedures and policies, and judgments and interpretations of facts related to the topic). Relationship conflict, in contrast, puts directors in conflict over their interpersonal styles or values.[30]

One way in which chairs can help to keep conflict at the task level is to frame director contributions in terms of directors' professional experience, as described earlier. This keeps the focus on the topic of discussion. Second, chairs must keep the board feeling effective even after conflict has occurred, showing the group that disagreement need not be destructive or divisive. Several leadership tactics enable boards to have meaningful discussion without getting torn apart by conflict: articulating discussion endpoints; treating discussions differently depending on their maturity, content, or depth of disagreement; and avoiding the tendency to become the hub through which all communication flows.

Framing and Articulating Discussion Endpoints

One tactic that enables board chairs to sustain group cohesion is to end discussions by articulating points of disagreement. This keeps the lines of debate open and legitimate. It reinforces the notion that disagreement is inevitable and acceptable. It is also a way of encouraging meaningful input from directors because it shows that disagreement will not derail discussions or the entire board meeting. A contrasting approach, exhibited by one non-executive chairman, is to avoid ending discussions while there is disagreement amongst the board members. Though well-intentioned, this chairman's inability to end debates began to undermine directors' participation because the lack of resolution frustrated them so much.

This leader's hesitancy to end discussion reflects a critical challenge faced by board chairs. They must lead, but must do it among equals—and among high-status, experienced, and often forceful individuals with big egos. This particular chairman was afraid to cut short people who had something important to say and who could easily get offended in a way that would undermine the board's ability to work together later. He expressed the difficulty of this position:

> I think the biggest challenge I have is giving all the board members the latitude they want in discussing items but then kind of reining it in and getting back to the subject at hand and going on with the meeting. We want [the CEO] to do this, we want this, we want that, and finally, I felt like I had given everybody an ample opportunity to express their opinions and I said, "now we have to let him do the job and quit trying to micromanage.". . . I certainly don't want to slight somebody by not giving them a chance to express their opinion, but a lot of times if somebody is going on and on and on, rather than cut them off, I just ask Joe, "well what

> do you think about it, Joe?" And that kind of diffuses the issue a little bit and lets someone else say something and then you can go on to other items.

This passive way of ending discussions, and the unwillingness to identify points of disagreement, translated to an inability actually to resolve the conflict. The result was an implicit understanding on the board that conflict was problematic. One director said, "I guess one of the things that I would be the least comfortable with at this point about the board, is that when we get to an ending point in our discussion we don't necessarily reach an agreement, whether it's unanimous or not. We seem to table the action and say we'll talk about it in the future. And nothing happens. I don't know how to solve it." In addition to frustrating directors, this dynamic also left senior management without any coherent messages from the board about what it should be doing.

Chairs who frame discussion endpoints and articulate rather than avoid points of disagreement are able to deal with conflict more productively. They allow disagreements to exist without sending the message that the board's work has been compromised as a result. One chairman described his approach this way:

> There's nothing wrong with having something that's not a unanimous vote. I mean there've been votes that have been, 8-1, or 7-2, or 6-3. It's OK. A lot of people feel uncomfortable doing that, but I think it's a healthy kind of environment. I don't necessarily subscribe to the idea that everyone then votes for what the majority is. I mean if I can't get consensus, and I go around and I let everybody chat, and I can see that there's not consensus, and yet it's an important issue that we have to decide, I just say, "OK, does anybody else have any other opinions? We obviously have two or three different points of view. Has everybody had a chance to articulate their viewpoint?" And then I'd say, "Listen, we need a vote.

> We need a resolution for such and such, and it looks like it's not going to be unanimous, but we need to decide something and the majority will rule. So we'll take a vote." And I will [call for a vote not knowing necessarily which way it will go.] And if the issue doesn't have to be decided, or there's more information that's needed, or there's something that came up where we need to investigate it before we can make the decision, we'll delay the vote. But if everybody's articulated their position and we've got everything that we need and we just have different viewpoints, then we'll call for a vote.

This chairman's board did not have less conflict than others. However, conflict was treated as a normal part of the group process. As a result, directors were less threatened by the prospect of it and did not experience it as some sort of group failure.

Treating Discussions Differently

Another more subtle tactic that enables chairs to keep conflict productive and maintain group cohesion is to treat discussion points differently. Chairs who did this recognized that not every discussion is the same and that not every kind of disagreement is the same. These leaders considered just how deep the disagreement ran, what the basis of disagreement was, and how directors would respond to having the discussion concluded. They considered the maturity of the discussion topic and how necessary it was even to resolve the conflict at the present moment. This idea is already reflected in the previous comment. It also comes through below, in this chair's description of a board discussion:

> At the previous board meeting there was encouragement from board members for management to [do A]. Then at the next meeting there was so much pushback from [director 1], which kind of surprised the management. And [director 2] and [director 3] said not to do it

> at all, which was 180 degrees from the previous meeting. So that's why I wanted to have an open dialogue. I was trying to get it resolved, but it was a little bit like corralling cats, if you will. People can change their mind, but there was some 180 [shift of position] on this issue. So I wanted to kind of do this [by polling]. And I started over at that end of the room because I knew those three personalities were going to be the most vocal about it.

During the process of polling, the directors came to agree on a compromise. Because they had *all* stated their opinions and found this compromise together, they were able to reach resolution and feel like a cohesive unit that had achieved the outcome together.

Avoiding Hub-and-Spoke Discussions

A final tactic chairs used to keep their boards cohesive is to encourage directors to speak directly to one another. Chairs who do not make an effort to keep this happening easily become the hub through which all board communications are conducted. The consequences of this were easily observable on one board for which the CEO/chairman was the node for all interactions. This individual was constantly pulling directors aside for conversation both inside and outside of the board meetings. Because directors on this board gave their input almost exclusively through him, they had very little direct exposure to each other's ideas or concerns. As a result, they could hardly understand each other's ideas in meetings and tended to know each other primarily as "personalities" rather than as contributors of professional expertise. The result was a board that was far from cohesive. It had no common understanding of its purpose, little cooperation or interaction, and no commitment to the group on the part of the directors.

Of course it should be noted that cohesion is a double-edge sword. Research shows that too much cohesion can lead to uncritical group process, conformity, and poor decision making with insufficient consideration of alternative viewpoints.[31] Directors and stakeholders might reasonably be concerned that a cohesive board could prevent individual directors from speaking up in dissent, particularly when the rest of the directors are in agreement with management. However, a distinction must be drawn between *social* cohesion and *task* cohesion. Social cohesion, "a general orientation toward developing and maintaining social relationships within the group," can undermine boards in precisely this way, as directors begin to operate on the basis of loyalty and a desire to belong.[32] This is the kind of cohesion that so often draws the ire of shareholders and media who note the strong uniformity and interconnectedness of the director population.[33] However, *task* cohesion, "an orientation toward achieving the group's goals and objectives," would mean that the board has a common understanding and commitment to what it is doing.[34] This kind of cohesion is essential to a board's ability to influence management.

The importance of task cohesion speaks to another challenge faced by boards: the fact that their collective role is so poorly and vaguely defined. Again, the board chair has a critical role to play in this challenge.

Managing Role Ambiguity at the Board Level: Critical Clarity

One of the most important jobs of the board leader is to ensure that the board understands its role, both generally and at specific times in the meeting. To operate cooperatively and efficiently, and to influence management, the board must have a common vision for what it is doing. This may change over time, of course, as the business goes through stages of establishing or exploiting its competitive position, or as the industry changes. However, at any given point in time, the directors need to have a sense of what the group's purpose is. This requires having discussions about governance, of course.[35] However, it also requires good leadership from the board chair.

As stated previously, the law regarding board duties is broad and vague. Most corporate governance principles also offer only generalized guidelines. Even when guidelines are specific, it is likely that the board must be flexible *within* them, to adopt different roles depending on what management has been doing. One director's comments reflect how boards can change their style and their focus depending on the state of the business:

> Since I have been on the board of [company], it's been a really nice-performing company. [The CEO] has been doing a great job, etc., etc. I think that if they were not meeting their business plan, if they were not doing as good a job as the board thought that they should be doing, you probably would have seen a very different dynamic and a different meeting. I think people would be more uptight, there would be a lot more probing and questioning, there would unfortunately be a lot more second guessing, there would not be the complete trust that exists today, there would be a lot of discussions about that we need to make some changes in the management team. It would be that kind of a meeting.

A non-executive chair similarly described how a particular aspect of the business was being prioritized and in turn shaped meetings and the role of the board at the current time:

> The most important item for us right now, the thing that will create the most shareholder value is our ability to leverage [new business]. And I think where I need to focus is to help [the CEO] to understand how important that is and how he has to step up strategically. And you could hear in the executive session some of the anxiety that some of the board members had about that. And one of the reasons for that . . . is that one of [the CEO's]

> strengths also highlights one of his weaknesses. He's a very, very strong operating guy. He's not quite as strong strategically. And what we really need now is for him to look at this from a strategic point of view and really leverage it. So, when you distill down everything at the board meeting, how I as the chairman could add value for our shareholders is to focus and drive on that [strategy point] for the next several months.

This board was in a phase of being very involved in strategy. At a different stage of the business, it may have focused more on operations, or on financial management, depending on the urgency of other issues.

In other words, how the directors conceive of their collective role in a particular discussion or during a certain year is shaped by the group itself, through interaction with each other and with senior management. The board leader must see to it that this negotiation of the board's role happens in a way that does not leave individual directors wandering off in different directions. This not only will result in unproductive discussions but also will produce frustration between the directors and management as they talk past each other and fail to meet each other's expectations. On one board, the directors knew the CEO/chairman was considering an acquisition but had not defined for themselves their role in this stage of the business. As a result, some were offering contacts. Others were in evaluation mode, and still others were simply cheering the process along. The result was meandering discussions, no clear understanding about what should happen next, frustration from the CEO/chairman that he was not getting what he needed from the board, mistrust among the directors, and little meaningful interaction between directors and senior managers. Neither the CEO/chairman nor any of the directors had taken it upon themselves to define a set of goals or an appropriate role for the board over this issue.

Active board chairs use several tactics to overcome this kind of role ambiguity: setting up and concluding meetings deliberately to articulate what would be and what had been done, modeling the role the board should be playing, and offering statements of philosophy.

Setting Up and Concluding Meetings

First, chairs who are good at managing the board's role ambiguity set up each discussion with a purpose, letting the board know what management is hoping to get from them in the discussion, what stage the discussion is in, its scope, and what has come before. The other component of course is to frame the conclusion of discussion: summarizing for the board what it has done and articulating what will come of the discussion going forward.

Of course, a board leader may not always frame this in a way that suits board members. For example, the chair may ask only for a certain kind of input regarding a piece of strategy, but the board may feel that its role is much greater and insist on having a different kind of input. Even when this happens, by articulating an expectation the chair forces some shared notion of how people should contribute and what influence they will have.

An extreme contrast to this style was observed on one board for which the CEO/chairman never framed discussion points. Directors on this board were unsure how to contribute and even asked on a few occasions, "What do you want us to do here? How can we help you?" Instead of framing discussions, this board leader ran meetings more like a self-help session, venting about concerns and problems without specific questions to directors. In one meeting, while getting the board up to speed on a merger negotiation, he described all of his frustrations to the board, telling story after story, with no structured openings for directors to offer advice. When they interjected ideas, he simply nodded and continued with his next story. Directors were patient and searched for ways to be constructive, but never knew how to help. Although this

CEO/chairman had very experienced and well-intentioned people sitting around the table, he was unable to create the kind of structure or clarity around expectations to get meaningful input from them.

Framing the purpose of a discussion can also occur at the meeting level. As stated before, several board leaders considered meetings from a holistic perspective, as integrated discussions. Some had an explicit theme for each meeting during the year, as described here:

> We set up ahead of time a theme for every board meeting. A year in advance. So we know that we're going to have five board meetings a year, and here are the things that the board is charged with from a governance point of view. We want to make sure that we focus on succession planning. We want to make sure that we focus on strategic planning. We want to make sure that we focus on operational issues. We want to make sure that we focus on governance issues. So there are five themes that we have. The CEO and general counsel and I sat back and said, "What is the board's responsibility?" If you stand at forty-thousand feet and say, "What is a board responsible for?" those would be four to five areas that I think most governance gurus would say are the overarching areas that boards should focus on. So we make sure that we plan our annual calendar to make sure that those get covered, because there are going to be a lot of perfunctory things that also have to get done, but each board meeting has a theme, and they're driven off of the major governance items, and then we fill in the rest with related issues or other things that need to get done.

By identifying themes for different meetings, this board could be clear about the kind of information it wanted and what sort of input it should give. It also did not have to relinquish the complexity and evolving nature of the board's role. In other words, directors could emphasize certain aspects of their governance duty, knowing that there would be space for others at later meetings.

Modeling the Role the Board Should Be Playing

A second important tactic for clarifying the board's role is for the chair to model this role for the other directors. This tactic may be easier for a non-executive chair to do simply because the other directors consider him or her to be one of their own. Modeling means interacting with management in a way that communicates what role a board member plays. All board chairs do this either intentionally or unintentionally. One deliberate and very influential style was exhibited by a non-executive chairman of a pharmaceutical company who, through his own interactions with management, was able to shape the way the entire board could interact with management. He took on a very tough but collegial governance role with management. He spoke directly to the senior management team, offering advice and feedback frankly. He knew which executives were responsible for what and often addressed them individually, turning physically to face them rather than articulating a general idea or speaking through the CEO. By doing this, he created a norm that directors could speak with individual executives and vice versa during board meetings. His mentoring created the atmosphere of a working group; the board as a resource rather than a formal and distant governing body.

Offering Statements of Philosophy

Finally, one important leadership tactic that helped boards negotiate their role was offering statements of philosophy during the course of the meeting. During one board discussion about a particular customer, the non-executive chairman relayed a story from his past. As a young salesman, he had learned that being honest about the limitations of his own product won him the trust and respect from a customer that was more valuable in the long run than if he had made the sale at a given point in time. In telling this story, he was taking a philosophical position on the importance of trust. He was encouraging the company and board to adopt a similar stance even while he was trying to argue why it might simply be good for business. These statements would at times be met with resistance from other directors, but they would, at the very least, force a debate and uncover assumptions about the goals of the board. Indeed, in this situation, a director pushed back on the chairman's opinion. The overall conversation allowed the board to entertain where it stood philosophically on these matters and to determine how much this should be transferred to the senior management team.

Another example of this leadership behavior occurred when one board was deciding whether or not to adopt a corporate governance practice proposed by the general counsel, the CEO, and the non-executive chairman. The board was hesitant about adopting the new corporate governance "best practice" because it seemed to be unnecessary. It also felt as though it was pandering to the corporate governance "gadflies." The chairman on this board took the extra effort to frame the discussion in terms of the goals the board had set for itself. Consider this excerpt from the meeting discussion: "When it comes to corporate governance we are right at the top, and we've said that's what we want to be. I guess I'm always sort of guided by the notion 'do the right thing.' And this issue, it's just good governance. So why not take a step if there is no downside?"

In this way he stepped out in front of the board and became a compass. The directors could overcome their hesitation and think about the issue in a different light. They could see the issue through a shared commitment from all the board members to corporate governance. The board wound up passing the resolution.

One reason this leadership role is potentially so difficult is that it edges into territory where some board chairs are uncomfortable: assuming a strong, visionary and directive leadership role. Board chairs cannot lead like CEOs who hold positional authority. They must cajole, cooperate, and herd. Moreover, it is not in the language of board leadership that a chair should determine the direction a board or company takes. It may be considered inappropriate, given the legal mandate of the board, for its leader to be too strong and persuasive. Yet leadership is a necessary aspect of group work. One non-executive chair put it this way: "You never start out if you don't know where you want to end. And my view of what a good chairman does is to understand what he or she thinks is the right direction for the company and to help guide the other members there. And that's called leadership. And that's what the other board members who are not as actively involved or intrinsically don't understand the subtleties of the business are looking for. So they exercise their own judgment but they're looking for leadership. So that's the role that somebody on the board has to play."

Considering this question of how much or what kind of leadership is appropriate to boards directs us to the question of authority. Most of the behaviors described here are befitting of any group leader. But boards are different. Directive leadership is extremely difficult, particularly for non-executive chairs, who walk a fine line between being too aggressive in their leadership style and being too passive. The main reason for this is that board leaders (either non-executive chairs or CEO/chairs) have no formal authority over the group.

The Sources of Authority for the Boardroom Chair

The concept of authority has been at the heart of discussions of leadership from the earliest philosophical texts to today. A leader cannot be a leader without permission to lead that is granted by the followers. Different kinds of authority exist, of course. Some leaders have charismatic authority over their followers. Others have authority based on tradition, or the belief that the leader deserves authority based on the sanctity of some tradition. Still others have a formal authority that stems from the acceptance of a system of hierarchy.[36]

The board chair, however, has no such formal authority. It is therefore critical that chairs have enough legitimacy by other means and that they understand how much power they actually have. Directors' conceptions of their chairs reveal three dimensions along which the legitimacy and authority of a board leader could rise or fall: (1) perceived professional competence, (2) perceived ability to govern independently, and (3) perceived legitimacy of the process by which they came to the position. I will examine each.

One way in which board leaders held legitimacy with their boards is through their professional competence, accomplishments, and affiliations. Some, like the non-executive chairman at the pharmaceutical company, are considered by their boards to be very experienced, successful, and highly reputable in an industry relevant to the board. This particular chairman had been a CEO of another important organization in the industry, had been a thought leader within the industry, and also had come into the industry at a young age and worked his way up. The directors had immense respect for his industry status, and this enabled him to lead with a directive style. Directors trusted his judgments and allowed his perspective to shape the direction of the company. In contrast, a non-executive chairman at another board came to that board through a family connection and had only limited relevant industry experience. Directors did not think he understood well the industry-related issues facing senior management, and his credibility as a leader was not bolstered by his professional background.

The governing styles of these two non-executive chairmen could not have been more different. One was directive, was hands-on, made tangible suggestions to managers, and framed directors' ideas in a way that made sense to managers. He also made directors feel like they had an important ally. The second chairman had the few tangible points he made dismissed or disregarded by his fellow directors, had difficulty speaking to management on *behalf* of the board, and also was not able to harness contributions from directors. Having industry and professional legitimacy was critical to how these chairmen were able to shape discussions and manage the relationship between the board and management.

A second way in which board leaders hold legitimacy is in the way they govern, and particularly the degree to which they show independence from management. Directors trust leaders they perceive to be strong, independent-minded, and skilled at mediating. One non-executive chairman, despite having a very close relationship with management, often used meeting time to articulate the board's expectations and to mix both supportive and critical comments in a way that asserted the board's authority. He also spent a lot of time between meetings talking to and trying to help management in the way they were bringing issues to the board. This allowed him to be a strong leader inside the boardroom even while showing respect to and gaining the trust of management. A contrast to this was a non-executive chairman who took a protective approach to managing the board's interaction with senior managers. He similarly spent a good deal of time between meetings helping and talking to management, but inside board meetings he was not able to demonstrate that he was independent from them. The other directors became frustrated that they, the board, did not have a real leader who was willing to protect the independence and power they needed to govern.

Finally, a third kind of legitimacy chairs have with their directors comes from the process through which they become chairs. Most board chairs are selected through a formal process that specifies the duties of the role and how the individual's background and skills will fit these duties. Others are selected through an informal process managed within the board. For example, one non-executive chairman was selected in a rather haphazard process that involved one-on-one conversations and lobbying with directors, and this ultimately affected his leadership role within the group. Directors believed he had become the leader not because he was most qualified but through passive acceptance on the part of other directors. His selection was the result of a laissez-faire process. His authority was undermined at every turn as directors pointed back to this process, and he was never able to assert any meaningful leadership of the group. In sum, one important component of the board chair's authority is a transparent and accepted process by which an individual becomes chair.

Answering the question of how a board leader gets the authority and power to lead is critical to producing effective board leadership. All of the behaviors described in this chapter are as much a function of the leadership "situation" as they are choices for a chair to make.

Concluding Thoughts

This chapter has provided a window on board leadership by discussing the various tactics used by board chairs in the context of board meetings. It draws attention to the ways in which leadership behavior can undermine or facilitate important aspects of board process. Chairs affect the way directors interact and work together by the ways in which they draw input from them. They influence how the board can oversee management by shaping the relationship and communications that go on between these two groups. They are critical to helping the board understand its role. When chairs have the authority and legitimacy to lead, they have the ability to create a safe space for open dialogue in which management can receive both criticism and support from directors.

This chapter suggests that board chairs, particularly *non-executive* chairs, walk a fine line between being too aggressive in their leadership and being too passive. In a group of high-status and accomplished fellow directors and with little *formal* authority, it is all too easy for a chair to overstep his or her position and lose the ability to lead. However, erring on the other side, being passive, can be equally ineffectual. Directors will be frustrated by a directionless discussion in which they do not have clarity around board tasks, or will think the leader is weak vis-à-vis management.

The diverse techniques employed by chairs show how varied and complex the task of the board leader is. They also reveal that the chair's job goes far beyond the task of fulfilling "governance" requirements, but includes the important and perhaps more difficult job of leading the board as a group. This kind of leadership is what enables boards to negotiate tensions with management and with each other, and ultimately to play a meaningful governance role.

Part II

Talent Management Practices for Your Board

5

Appraising Your Board's Performance

Jay A. Conger and Edward E. Lawler III

In recent years, formal performance evaluations have become commonplace at the board level. The most recent data from large U.S. corporations show that some 99 percent use a formal evaluation of the CEO, 98 percent evaluate the overall board's performance, 97 percent evaluate board committee performance, and 84 percent evaluate individual directors. These are remarkable numbers when compared to the state of affairs a decade ago. A survey of directors at *Fortune* 1000 companies conducted in 1996 by Korn/Ferry and the Center for Effective Organizations at USC indicated that although approximately 70 percent of the largest U.S. companies had adopted a formal process for evaluating their CEOs, only one-quarter evaluated their boards' performance. Evaluations of individual directors were even rarer, occurring in just 16 percent of the companies surveyed. Clearly, formal evaluations have gone from being conducted by a minority of boards to a standard practice in corporate America.

The critical question now is whether performance evaluations actually improve board performance. This question cannot be answered based on definitive data, but we believe that board appraisals can play a vital role in improving corporate governance. But like any management practice, how the practice is *implemented* is critical to its effectiveness. Our experience and that of others conducting research in this field suggest that many boards do not perform their assessments in a rigorous enough manner. Social norms of respect and mechanical evaluation processes get in the way of candid and constructive feedback that could actually improve a board's performance. We believe that although many boards conduct their board evaluations in a thoughtful manner they do not use the real power of such assessments to maximize the effectiveness of their boardroom dynamics. In this chapter, we will describe how to use board appraisal processes as well as identify common pitfalls in their implementation. But let's begin with why your board should conduct appraisals and how these can play a vital role in enhancing your board's effectiveness.

Why Conduct Appraisals

There are multiple reasons why companies should annually review the effectiveness of their boards, perhaps the most pressing of which is that influential investors—in particular, institutional investors—are demanding that boards improve their performance. Since the late 1990s, surveys have found that the quality of a company's board governance is an important evaluation factor for institutional investors. One visible measure of a board's governance effectiveness is the presence of key best practices. Appraisals are one practice that can bring a discipline to the board, its members, and the CEO and cause them to improve their effectiveness.

There are other important reasons. Appraising a board's performance can clarify the individual and collective responsibilities of directors and the CEO. With better knowledge of what is expected of them, directors are likely to be stronger contributors. Formal evaluations can also identify areas needing greater attention by the board. Directors have told us that after they initiated board evaluations, their meetings went more smoothly, they made better decisions, they acquired greater influence, and they paid more attention to long-term corporate strategy.

When done properly, board appraisals can also improve the working relationship between a company's board and its management—a powerful argument in itself for doing them. For example, directors have said to us that the evaluation process encouraged greater candor in their dealings with the CEO and other senior managers.

Formal appraisals of the board as a whole, and also of individual board members and the CEO, can help ensure a healthy balance of power between the board and the chief executive. Furthermore, once in place, the appraisal process is difficult to dismantle. An institutionalized review process makes it harder for a new CEO to dominate a board or avoid being held accountable for poor performance.

The changing role of corporate directors is another compelling reason to review board and director performance regularly. As greater attention has focused on corporate governance, directorships that were once relatively low paid and essentially honorary positions have become more demanding and well compensated. Investors understandably want to know what they are getting for the millions of dollars in stock options and cash their companies are paying to directors.

Finally, if the right evaluation process is in place, evaluation need not be an invalid evaluation. Nor need it be the kind of unpleasant, time-wasting event that makes performance appraisal nearly every manager's least favorite activity. In our research, we have interviewed and gathered written surveys from CEOs and board members at dozens of companies that are pioneers in performing and applying board appraisals. We have developed a set of best practices that represents a composite of the most effective techniques used by these organizations to appraise the performance of boards, individual board members, and CEOs. The discussion that follows highlights the lessons learned from these companies and their practices.

Assessing Performance

Any discussion of performance appraisals must cover three broad areas—what is to be appraised, the resources needed to perform the job, and the actual processes for evaluation. The issues to be appraised are determined by the board's ability first to define its own and then the CEO's responsibilities, to establish annual objectives for these responsibilities, and to create measures that indicate whether these objectives have been achieved. The resources and capabilities that a board requires are determined by a critical assessment of the knowledge, information, power, motivation, and time needs of the board versus what it currently has available. For example, a board may discover it is lacking in the critical knowledge it needs to reliably assess certain company initiatives. The appraisal process itself must be rigorous and dynamic; otherwise, perceptions can develop that it is a bureaucratic event deserving of little time and attention. In the sections that follow, we'll discuss each of these areas in depth.

What Your Board Needs to Be Assessing: Core Responsibilities and Activities

There is little argument about the modern board's responsibilities. First, it is responsible for oversight of business strategy development: not for the details of strategy implementation and definition—that job falls to the chief executive and senior management team—but for ensuring that a strategic planning process is in place, is used, and produces sound choices. Further, the board must monitor the implementation of strategic initiatives to assess whether they are on schedule, on budget, and producing the right results.

Second, a board is responsible for seeing that the company has the highest-caliber CEO and executive team possible and that certain senior managers are being groomed to assume the CEO's responsibilities in the future. Next, as the ultimate oversight body, the board must be certain that the company has adequate information, control, and audit systems in place to tell it and senior management whether the company is meeting its business objectives. It is also the board's responsibility to ensure that the company complies with the legal and ethical standards imposed by law and by the company's statement of values. Finally, the board has responsibilities for preventing and managing crises—that is, for risk management.

Before a board can even begin to evaluate its performance in these areas of responsibility, it must articulate the specific actions that each of them implies. In other words, boards must set objectives for themselves within those broad categories against which they can eventually measure their performance. The boards of most companies create a set of objectives annually—generally speaking, at the beginning of the fiscal year—that reflects the directors' collective judgment about which aspects of the board's overall responsibilities need particular attention in the coming year.

The nominating or governance committee may design an initial set of objectives that covers the essential responsibilities of an effective board. But it is vital that the full board and CEO take the time to discuss, debate, and agree to the final set of objectives and to establish priorities among them. Not until this is done can boards establish the criteria they will use to measure their performance and that of the CEO. For instance, as part of its role in developing business strategy, the board and the CEO may decide that the company wants to become the leader in Eastern Europe in its major product segments within three years. The board needs to specify the evaluation criteria it will use to assess whether the company has achieved that goal. Goals must be set that can be used to appraise the CEO's performance: revenue growth and market share. Boards also need to consider development objectives for themselves: for example, improving the board's knowledge of the region by adding a director who is knowledgeable about Eastern Europe, facilitating the establishment of a partnership with the Czech Republic government, holding a board meeting at the company's Prague headquarters in order to meet local managers.

Because of the many demands on a board's time, not every board responsibility can be evaluated each year. In a particular year, it is best for the board to pick four to seven areas that need attention. For example, a board might choose to focus one year on the following: improving its evaluation of senior management talent at the business unit level, identifying a system for tracking a particular strategic initiative, and enhancing the information that directors receive concerning environmental issues. The choice of issues should reflect the areas that the board feels are currently the most vital to the company and the board.

That said, all major areas of responsibility should be covered periodically. There is a clear advantage to assessing many of the same performance areas yearly. Directors are able to see trends. For example, one indicator might measure the extent to which directors have opportunities to observe senior managers. Over a three-to-five-year time frame, a board can assess whether it has indeed had a sufficient number of these opportunities. From a procedural standpoint, it is best if the board sets its developmental objectives in a meeting separate from the one at which the board appraises its own performance and rewards for the past year. This point is also applicable to the board's assessment of CEO performance. Development activities are best discussed at the time goals and objectives are set, not when rewards are discussed.

What Your Board Needs to Conduct an Effective Job of Appraising: The Critical Resources

A board is a team of knowledge workers, and to do its job, the board needs the same resources and capabilities that any other successful team of knowledge workers needs. Research indicates that to do their jobs effectively, such groups need *knowledge*, *information*, *power*, *motivation*, and *time*. We examine each of these in light of the unique needs of boards and their implications for evaluating performance.

Knowledge

The combined knowledge and experience of the board of directors must match the strategic and major operational demands facing the company (see also Chapter Six). Because today's business environments are so complex, it is nearly impossible for a single person or even a small group of individuals to understand all the issues that come before a board. Such complexity argues for assembling a group of directors whose skills and backgrounds are diverse and complement one another. Ideally, so that the board does not become unwieldy in size, each of its members should satisfy more than one need. Selecting directors for a single area of expertise or background characteristic can contribute to the creation of a board whose members focus only on their particular interests.

It is important that a board performance evaluation systematically assesses boardroom expertise and identifies current and future knowledge gaps to ensure that the right mix of knowledge is present on the board. This assessment should be used to evaluate existing members as well as possible new members. A leading aerospace company uses a simple matrix highlighting the capabilities of its directors, making it easy to see if individuals representing the right mix of knowledge are on both its board and its various committees (Chapter Six provides details on skill matrices). The required capabilities are derived directly from the company's long-term business strategy. They include competencies in such areas as developing new technologies, doing business in the Pacific Rim, dealing with governments, and creating shareholder value. The CEO explains the matrix's purpose: "We use it to evaluate the disciplines we want to have on the board, the capabilities we currently have, the capabilities that may rotate off the board because of retirement or other reasons, and the types of people we should be looking for. We do the same thing with the composition of our board's committees. We want to make sure those committees have the right kind of breadth and that there is continuity of experience. We try to move people around so that the capabilities we want to have on particular committees are covered. It's a chess game that gets played every year."

Information

To be effective in appraising its performance and that of the CEO, a board needs a broad range of information about the condition of its corporation. For example, it needs up-to-date information on the competition, on key strategic issues, on company operations, and on possible acquisition targets. And it needs that information presented clearly and concisely because time in meetings is limited. Furthermore, the board needs to get information from a broad range of sources such as key stakeholders, customers, employees, and the directors themselves.

An evaluation of board information must examine not only the kind of data a board gets but also their sources. Information derived solely from internal sources may have inherent biases that distort the reality of the company's competitive or financial position and performance. Outside data are particularly pertinent when assessing a board's performance relative to that of its competitors. Institutional investors, market analysts, regulatory bodies, the press, and academic journals are all potential sources of outside information. Recent surveys suggest that institutional investors, in particular, want to be asked for their views of board and company performance. Our research indicates that directors view the evaluation process as significantly more effective when boards receive information from a broad range of stakeholders.

Power

An effective board needs authority—the authority to act as a governing body to make key decisions. It also needs the power to see that senior management is accepting and implementing its decisions. One clear way to grant the board the independence it needs to exercise effective oversight of the CEO and the corporation is for the board's chair to be someone other than the CEO. It needs to be an individual who is not affiliated with management or the company.

Even when a single person is both the chair and the CEO, a company can take steps to achieve a balance of power between the board and chief executive. One step is to appoint a lead director, who represents the outside directors and who helps set the agenda for meetings and takes charge in a crisis. A formal evaluation of the CEO's performance also works to maintain a balance, as does making a portion of the CEO's compensation dependent on attaining targets agreed to by the board. Regular executive sessions at which only outside directors are present is another practice to ensure a balance of power. These meetings allow the board to discuss sensitive issues without raising alarms among senior managers.

It is also crucial that a majority of a company's directors be truly independent. Directors who have ties of business or family to the CEO and the company often have difficulty exercising independent judgment. They may be too easily swayed by the CEO's strong stance on an issue or by a fear of "upsetting" the CEO. Similarly, board members who sit on one another's boards have potential personal conflicts of interest.

It follows, then, that in a self-appraisal the board should ask questions such as, Do we have a healthy balance of power with our CEO? Is the board itself well led? Do we control the agenda of our meetings? Can we act quickly to replace the CEO if necessary?

Motivation

The right incentives must be in place to align directors' interests with those of the individuals they are meant to represent: the shareholders and other stakeholders in the corporation (employees, customers, and the community, in most cases). Together with the process by which directors are selected, the reward system is a lever that can be used to influence the motivation of board directors.

A growing number of companies require directors to own shares, paying them partially or wholly in stock rather than offering pension plans or other perks (see Chapter Fifteen for a thoughtful discussion of stock rewards for directors). According to David Golub, managing director at Corporate Partners, which specializes in taking large equity positions in publicly traded companies, "The most important factor in determining if a board is effective is whether there is a small group of directors—it doesn't need to be every one—that has a substantial ownership stake in the company, enough so that it hurts them personally if the company is underperforming." The board and individual director evaluation should take note of the degree to which individual directors own stock.

Time

To make effective decisions, directors need sufficient, well-organized periods of time together as a group. Board evaluations should note whether the frequency of meetings is adequate, whether there is sufficient time available to prepare for meetings and deliberate on important decisions, and whether the time spent in meetings is used efficiently. Board members should not devote time in meetings to getting information from management that could have been communicated earlier. Rather, they should spend meeting time engaged in substantive discussion and decision making. How effectively individual directors contribute to this discussion should be part of the appraisal of directors themselves.

The appraisal of board operations should consider whether board members are receiving the advance information they need in order to come to meetings well prepared to debate crucial issues. It should also consider whether the meetings themselves are devoted to the right issues. Evaluating the way the board operates will not necessarily lead to the conclusion that it needs to meet more often. On the contrary, after appraising its own performance, one board we studied reduced the number of regular board sessions and instead delegated more work to its committees and to telephone conferences.

Because even the most efficient boards can run short of time for an in-depth discussion of corporate strategy during regular meetings, more and more companies are scheduling annual multiple-day strategy retreats. In some cases—for instance, in high-technology industries in which product life cycles can be less than a year long, meeting annually to discuss strategy is not enough. So every board session has a few hours devoted to some part of the business that is going to affect the company's strategy. The board evaluation process should help boards decide whether they currently have enough time to discuss strategy and what the optimum forum for strategy discussions should be.

Getting Your Appraisal Process Right: The Best Practices

In the sections that follow, we will examine how to conduct appraisals. We have divided our discussion into three parts, one for CEO appraisals, one for board appraisals, and one for individual director appraisals. Given their differing aims, it is important to differentiate between each type of appraisal.

Evaluating Your CEO

The actual evaluation process of the CEO should involve three stages: establishing evaluation targets at the start of the fiscal year, reviewing performance at midyear, and assessing results and determining rewards at the end of the year.

Before the start of the company's fiscal year, the CEO and his or her direct reports should work with the board to develop the annual strategic plan establishing both the company's short-term and long-term objectives. Finding the right objectives and measures is a critical part of the process. Many companies build their CEO's objectives and compensation package around annual financial objectives and the performance of the company's stock. Although essential, such measures fail to take into account such important responsibilities as the CEO's plans for his or her own succession, lobbying efforts, involvement in trade associations, efforts at internal communications, leadership skills, and talent management. The most effective evaluations include both financial and nonfinancial objectives. That said, best-practice companies keep their lists to between six and ten objectives. In addition, it is a good idea to define carefully at least three levels of performance for each objective—poor, acceptable, and outstanding. These levels should be the benchmarks for differing pay packages.

A common problem that we have found is that boards rely too much on the CEO's self-evaluation. Although a self-evaluation is an essential part of an effective performance appraisal, it is by no means sufficient by itself. Clearly, individuals being judged on their performance may have many reasons to be biased in how they rate themselves and what they say to the board. For example, one CEO admitted to us that he purposely lowers his self-evaluation, preferring to be "pulled up" by his board's evaluation rather than be "put down." We suspect that he is not alone, but he is perhaps outnumbered by CEOs who overstate their performance. Self-assessment data must be balanced by other information. Ratings from customers and institutional investors, employee-attitude surveys, and comparisons of the CEO's performance with those of leaders inside and outside the company are all useful types of evaluation information.

Once the objectives are defined, the CEO must translate them into a set of personal performance targets and specify how his or her progress will be measured against each. The CEO then shares these targets and metrics with a committee of the board—normally, the compensation or board governance committee, which ideally consists solely of outside directors. This committee makes recommendations to the full board, resolving any differences between the perceptions of the CEO and the outside directors regarding what the objectives should be. This committee should also establish the financial rewards that will result from meeting the targets. Committee members must work with the CEO to ensure that targets are realistic but challenging. When the CEO and committee members agree on objectives and measures, the committee presents them to the full board for discussion and final approval.

The midyear review, like any midyear employee review, is a chance for the board to assess whether the CEO is on a course to meet or exceed objectives and, if not, to determine where the problems or challenges lie. The midyear review encourages directors to act before minor problems become major ones and ensures that the originally framed objectives are still relevant. In industries in which products and market conditions change rapidly, interim reviews may need to occur more frequently than once a year.

The final stage of the CEO's evaluation should take place at the end of the fiscal year, when the board's compensation committee compares the executive's actual performance against the targets. This comparison should determine the amount of compensation the committee will recommend to the full complement of outside directors. In most cases, this stage should also include the CEO completing a written self-evaluation that assesses his or her performance over the year. Individual outside board members should also complete a short questionnaire assessing the CEO's performance. We strongly recommend that the questionnaire combine open-ended questions with those that use a rating scale. Rating scales make it easier to compare different board members' evaluations and highlight clearly where perceptions vary. Open-ended questions allow people the flexibility to consider factors that fixed scales and targets may overlook. They also allow for very specific suggestions to be made.

The committee should also collect and consider pertinent outside information, such as perceptions of the CEO by the investment community and by the company's most valued customers. Using all this material as background, the committee should then prepare its evaluation, and the outside directors should meet to discuss and approve a final compensation package (without the CEO present). In many companies, 60 percent in our most recent survey of boards, the communication of this information from the outside directors to the CEO is oral. However, our research indicates that directors consider the evaluation process more effective when board members give the CEO written feedback as well. The act of committing thoughts to paper forces deeper reflection and greater clarity. In addition, it gives CEOs something concrete that they can review after the meeting. In addition, they don't have to remember what is said to them in what can be an emotional meeting. Written appraisals also ensure that every director is heard—not merely those who are the most vocal.

A critical part of the CEO evaluation process is finding the right objectives to measure and setting targets that reflect realistic levels of performance. Objective setting is critical because it determines what the board will focus on as well as the level of detail the board will be involved in. Objectives that are too focused on the content of day-to-day managing can encourage micromanaging by the board. For example, a specific advertising commercial is more of an operational issue that is best left to management. On the other hand, a multibillion-dollar gas pipeline project in Canada is a major strategic decision that needs to be evaluated and monitored.

The challenge in setting objectives is to assess and measure accurately the most salient aspects of corporate and CEO performance. An assumption behind many pay-for-performance plans is that the CEO's performance and the corporation's performance are synonymous. In reality, this is often not the case. An effective appraisal uses objectives that focus on behaviors and actions that the CEO can control directly. It should also employ measures that adjust for changes in the industry and economy. When setting objectives, it is important to set the right number. Too few, and performance is likely to be centered on financial indicators. Too many, and the CEO and his or her senior team risk losing a clear focus because the weight attached to each target is small.

It is important to ensure that objectives are not just financial ones. Many companies have built their CEO's compensation packages around annual financial objectives and stock market performance. They fail to capture important effectiveness measures that are not easily measured. For example, issues such as succession planning, lobbying efforts, trade association involvement, communications within the company, union relations, and leadership are all critical areas of CEO responsibility that need to be assessed. Targets focused solely on return on equity or company profitability can only very indirectly capture these important activities. In some cases, they may actually work against these activities by producing a focus on the short term. Chapter Eight, by Roger Raber, goes into great depth on the board's role in determining CEO compensation.

Evaluating Your Board

Our research suggests the approaches to board appraisal that are used by most companies are inadequate. Either they fail to gauge the adequacy of important board resources and capabilities or they fail to set clear performance objectives and collect data from all the organization's key stakeholders.

Self-evaluation is not an easy issue for any group to deal with. It is particularly difficult in the case of boards because it requires board members to make judgments and decisions about themselves and about the issues that affect their colleagues.

The effectiveness of the evaluation very much depends on how the board *structures* the evaluation process. Like the CEO evaluation, the board evaluation should consist of three phases. The first involves setting annual board objectives and measures at the beginning of the fiscal year. The process picks up again at the end of the year, when, in the second phase, the board secretary collects and disseminates information about the board's progress. The governance committee reviews the findings and presents them to the entire board. With that information in hand, in the third phase, board members can judge how close they came to meeting their objectives while also examining the adequacy of the resources available to them over the year. In this review, it is ideal to have the discussion guided by the chair of the governance committee or by the board's lead director. This individual should highlight progress made toward the objectives as well as areas needing more improvement.

The information used to measure board performance should come from both internal and external sources. It should include an analysis of how the board spent its time in meetings, breaking down the year's activities and accomplishments according to how they contributed to each area specifically set out for evaluation in the annual objectives. For instance, board members should be given a list of topics and issues that they addressed at meetings the previous year relating to business strategy development. The list should be organized by the dates of each meeting and the length of time spent on each topic. Wherever possible, this information should be linked to tangible benefits to the board or the company that may have resulted from these activities. For example, the record of a decision by the board to expand the company's markets in Brazil should be connected to the opening of the company's sales office in São Paulo some two months later and to sales figures in the region for the appropriate time period.

A careful examination of the topics covered at board meetings might show that certain of the board's objectives or portions of the company's business were largely overlooked. Such an analysis might reveal, for example, a failure to hear from a member of the senior management team who is a prime candidate to succeed the CEO, or perhaps it might reveal a failure to review the company's substantial real estate holdings.

One board that we studied defines its areas of responsibility at the start of every fiscal year (for instance, oversight of the company's financial health, ensuring adherence to corporate vision and values, planning for succession, and reviewing the CEO's performance) and lists, according to their priority, the objectives it creates for itself within each broad category. At the end of each year, the governance committee then analyzes the minutes of all board meetings to determine how the board allocated its time relative to those priorities. Board members receive this information as the basis for a discussion of the board's effectiveness. In this way, they use time spent on issues as a measure of the attention that issues received. We need to add, however, the caveat that time does not always accurately reflect the quality of attention and discussion on an issue.

Regular written attitude surveys of board members are a good way to assess how effectively the board is operating. They give every board member an equal voice in assessing the capabilities of the board to function well as a decision-making group. Board surveys can be used to gather data on a variety of issues including the effectiveness of the decision process, the quality of board leadership, and the willingness of board members to listen to each other.

As a general rule, it is useful to hold an open-ended discussion once every three or four years about the board appraisal process and the topic areas that are reviewed. Led by the chair of the governance committee or the lead director, the discussion should consider new dimensions that need to be added and ideas for improving the appraisal process itself.

In terms of what to measure for a board-level evaluation, some of the more critical board activities to assess could include (1) appropriate and proactive level of involvement in CEO succession; (2) rigor of processes to evaluate the CEO's performance; (3) effective use of the board by the CEO for advice and counsel; (4) quality of contingency plans in place for a corporate crisis; (5) appropriate structures and processes to review and comment on the company strategy and its implementation; (6) sufficient time for evaluating major initiatives and merger and acquisition proposals; (7) sufficient levels and diversity of information to make compensation, evaluation, and oversight decisions; (8) orientation and integration processes for new directors; (9) conducive discussion atmosphere at board meetings; (10) quality of mechanisms for employees to safely "whistle blow" and alert the board;

(11) nominating procedures to ensure independent directors; (12) sufficient input to the agenda of board meetings; (13) quality of information conveyed about committee deliberations; and (14) sufficient diversity in director representation.

Evaluating Your Directors as Individual Contributors

Perhaps the most controversial issue in the area of board appraisal is whether to evaluate individual directors. Although investors feel strongly that boards need to be more aggressive in weeding out underperforming directors, board members often express legitimate concerns about evaluating individual board members. The overriding concern is that turning a spotlight on individual members can undermine boardroom collegiality and lead to conflict. Directors worry that rigorous evaluations might drive away good board members who feel they have already proved themselves and should not be evaluated. In addition, evaluating a director in an objective and rigorous manner is not easy.

It is difficult to determine who should evaluate a director. Peers are one possibility, but they may lack the information needed to make an accurate appraisal of other directors' performance. Board members spend relatively little time together, and what occurs in the meetings may not be the best gauge of a director's contribution. Says one corporate secretary, "A lot of people are quiet [in board meetings], but they are very effective. They operate in different ways. It's what goes on in sidebar conversations, at dinners, during telephone calls between meetings, that kind of thing that may really matter."

Because each board member brings a different set of competencies to the board, it can be dangerous to establish blanket evaluation criteria, which might, for example, overlook the different ways members contribute. And, finally, research on team effectiveness clearly supports the idea that when individuals are interdependent, as they are on a board, it is important to place the main emphasis on evaluating and rewarding the effectiveness of the group as a whole. Otherwise, people tend to optimize their individual performance rather than contribute to the effectiveness of the team.

Despite the potential problems with an appraisal of board members, we believe there is a definite role for individual director appraisals as one component of an overall board-evaluation process. Certain issues relating to the effectiveness of boards simply cannot be addressed without evaluating individuals. Although underperforming directors are relatively rare, it is a sound practice to identify them through formal assessments and to act quickly either to improve their performance or to remove them. Richard Leblanc shares our concern and in Chapter Six explores several models from his research for conducting individual director evaluations.

As the average size of a boardroom decreases and the demands and rewards for serving on a board increase, companies need more from directors than good attendance and perfunctory questions. Individual evaluations are an effective means to make performance expectations clear. Support for this view comes from our research, which shows that directors rate the overall effectiveness of their boards significantly higher when they evaluate individual directors. However, it is important to note that evaluating the CEO and evaluating the entire board seems to have a stronger impact on how effective boards are.

The easiest place to begin a board member evaluation program is with self-evaluations. These ask about the member's behavior or contribution in key areas. They are for the individual director's private use only, and the results are not shared with any committee or other board member. They serve as a simple discipline and structure that directors can use to reflect on their performance and can also be used to start the transition to a peer-based evaluation.

Although they may be a good place to start, we don't believe that self-appraisals are enough. The individual biases reflected in self-appraisals need to be balanced by the perceptions of others.

One option is for the chair, the CEO, and the head of the board's governance committee to meet periodically to assess each director according to criteria they have established. They should use objective criteria, such as specific contributions to projects or committee work, ability to bring outside resources of value to the board, and the number of meetings the director has attended.

A more balanced approach is to combine anonymous peer evaluations with individual self-assessments and evaluations by the CEO, board chair, and head of the governance or human resources committee. The peer evaluations should be conducted by a lead director, a trusted adviser, or an outsider who can provide board members with a summary of the comments and ratings of their peers. This individual sets the standard in terms of the quality of information that is collected and how it is used for constructive and developmental feedback. He or she must be adept at interviewing and at obtaining concrete examples of contributions to make credible assessments, and must be able to "translate" this information into actions that individual directors can undertake to improve their contributions. Keeping the sources of all information anonymous is an imperative. The full results should be presented to the committee charged with nominating directors to help it identify underperforming directors. The results of individual appraisals can be used as the basis for tying the pay of board members to their performance and as a basis for continuing membership and committee assignments. In most cases, however, it is not advisable to link appraisal results to director pay, as this poses too great a threat to board teamwork. What often is desirable is to use individual performance appraisals as the basis for individuals continuing to be board members.

Among the possible dimensions for assessing individual performance, the following should be considered: (1) level of contribution to boardroom discussions in the individual's area of expertise, (2) depth of understanding of the company's critical and overall strategic issues, (3) quality of preparation for full board and committee meetings, (4) willingness to take constructive stands at board or committee meetings, (5) constructiveness in addressing and managing conflict in meetings, (6) discretion and confidentiality with board information, (7) value as a resource in fulfilling the accountabilities of the board, (8) willingness to encourage the contributions of other directors, (9) effectiveness in communicating, and (10) ability to ensure that the board makes decisions. Several actual company examples are provided in Chapter Six.

Conclusion

When done correctly, appraisals create a way for the board and the CEO to hold each other accountable and to clearly define performance expectations while avoiding the dangers of getting the board involved in day-to-day management. Evaluations can also improve the operations of the board, clarify the respective roles of the board and the CEO, and ensure that both consistently focus on their responsibilities. Perhaps the clearest and most consistent benefit we've observed in those companies that have adopted effective board appraisal systems is a commitment by directors and the CEO to devote more time and attention to long-term strategy—and that by itself is an outcome significant enough to justify their implementation.

In a way, boards are like fire departments: they aren't needed every day, but they have to perform effectively when called upon. Performing effectively requires good planning preparation and systems. One board chair observed that in good times corporate governance is largely irrelevant, but in bad times it is crucial. Formal, periodic board appraisals can help ensure that when the board is needed, all the right processes, procedures, members, and relationships are in place and ready to go.

That said, board appraisals require a high level of effort. In some boardrooms, an hour or even less is taken to review in a "checklist fashion" the results of the appraisal. In these boards, there is little chance the results will justify the efforts. It is not easy to do them well, and in fact it is probably better not to do them at all when a board is not willing to invest the time and effort it takes to make them effective. Appraisals become simply a perfunctory exercise. In addition, there are important legal issues. As Chapter Six will explain, written assessment comments can be used in cases of shareholder litigation. Board reviews done in the normal course of business are discoverable evidence that can be shared in trials.

We prefer to think of appraisals as creating a forum for disciplined reviews of the board's and CEO's performance. Rather than simply confirm a board's importance, they should be seen as an opportunity to critique and improve upon how the board operates. We also believe that every few years the board should step back and reassess its appraisal processes and the dimensions it assesses. Evaluating the same dimensions over years may, at best, yield merely incremental improvements and can discourage challenges to established boardroom procedures and the introduction of new practices. Using the same dimensions over and over again can also cause the board to overlook areas it needs to review. Our advice is that boards should set aside a block of time every two or three years to review their appraisal processes and to evaluate their effectiveness. Ideally, a board's governance committee would conduct a thorough review and critique of the board evaluation procedures, actively seeking input from all board members. Given the importance of board performance, spending time to improve its performance is easy to justify.

6

Getting the Right Directors on Your Board

Richard Leblanc

We have been led to believe that a set of external metrics examining the presence or absence of certain corporate governance practices can result in better financial performance. This notion is reinforced by rating agencies and others. But we know that in reality there is not necessarily a causal relationship. So what does make a difference? In this chapter, it is argued that boards need to look beyond external metrics and internally at the directors themselves and their competencies. The focus must shift to *selecting* and *assessing* the right directors for your board. These are the critical variables in your board's performance.

"Check the Box" Governance and Corporate Performance: Is There a Relationship?

For years, researchers have been asking the question, "What is board effectiveness and what impact does an effective board have on corporate financial performance for shareholders?" Despite the intuitive appeal of the concept that better governance practices lead to better corporate performance, researchers cannot provide a definitive view of this, which is not to say that a causal link does not necessarily exist. There is ongoing debate among academics concerning the correlation between governance measures and future stock market performance and the causal relationship between better corporate governance and firm performance.

Quantitative governance researchers write the following: "[T]he empirical evidence . . . supports the findings that firms with good governance changes do not have better performance than firms with bad governance changes"[1] and "[C]ontrary to claims in GIM [Gompers, Ishii, and Metrick[2]] and BCF [Bebchuck, Cohen, and Ferrell[3]], none of the governance measures are correlated with future stock market performance."[4]

In addition to the unsettled debate over the relationship between governance and financial performance, there is also dissatisfaction among academics with common measurements of board effectiveness. In particular, criticism has been leveled at commercial agencies that rate boards using externally measurable criteria. As Jeffrey Sonnenfeld wrote in 2004:

> ISS [Institutional Shareholder Services, now part of RiskMetrics Group] and GMI [GovernanceMetrics International] look at public records to score firms on their governance effectiveness by using similar checklists of standards or metrics based heavily upon clichés and myths, rather than on genuine research. . . . They perpetuate unfounded myths and clichés by downgrading firms for such reasons as failing to have a retirement age for directors and failing to separate the chairman and CEO roles. . . . Other reasons for poor ratings are failing to require that managers and directors have a formally set amount of equity holdings; prior history of service on boards suffering financial distress; failure to have a formal retirement age, board size and code of conduct; allowing a former CEO to serve on the firm's board; failing to have a separate chairman and CEO; and failing to have a supermajority of outside, independent directors.[5]

Since this seminal article, other academics have further critiqued so-called "good governance metrics" and the rigid "check the box" and "homogenized" board evaluation measures employed by governance rating firms. For example, Professors Daines, Pfeffer, and Rose write:

> We find that these governance ratings have either limited or no success in predicting firm performance or other outcomes of interest to shareholders. . . . Moreover, even when there is a statistical association with future outcomes, the economic or substantive effect seems small.[6]

> ISS has some 65 rules and guidelines. . . . Yet there is almost no evidence that ISS's prescribed practices are actually related to outcomes such as higher rates of return for shareholders or improved company performance. . . . The rating of board management practices should be based on empirical evidence, not on guidelines seemingly plucked from thin air.[7]

> Additionally, governance firms may be overstepping their expertise in proxy voting decisions and in governance rating, in part because of their reliance on "good governance metrics" for which there is little evidentiary support. Finally, erroneous governance metrics (and indeed, a reliance on one-size-fits-all governance checklists) . . . may have a more general, harmful effect on corporate governance regulation.[8]

However, it is not enough simply to critique the conventional approach to examining and rating boards. If there is no definitive causal relationship between governance and financial performance, and if the metrics currently in use are neither predictive nor empirically based, corporate governance researchers must demonstrate, with considerably greater clarity than they have to date, what contributes to board and individual director effectiveness. This chapter aims to provide some direction on that front.

Board Effectiveness Cannot Be Assessed from the Outside

Rating agencies themselves acknowledge the disconnect between boards with high scores *on paper* and boards *in reality*. In a communication to the author, an individual associated with an entity that uses external metrics to rate boards remarked that "our . . . scoring indicated [company X] was good [the company has since been sued by shareholders for alleged governance failure]" and suggested there exists a need "to get beyond the scores into reality." A *BusinessWeek* article titled "Building an Exceptional Board" reads:

> "It is difficult to identify the best boards," says Patrick McGurn, executive vice president and special counsel at the ISS unit of RiskMetrics. "You can have a board that looks great on paper and then you see the work product and how they react when a problem emerges and it's another story," he says. There are boards that have all of their governance best practices checked off . . . but there is no guarantee they will perform at a high level.[9]

> "You have to observe them in action," [Ira Millstein] says. "A board might look terrible to an outside observer because they don't have enough independent directors, but when you get in the boardroom, you find that they work great together."[10]

The commentary above suggests that externally measurable governance scores do not reflect the leadership, chemistry, decisions, information, reporting, and competencies and behavior of boards and individual directors. The Corporate Library acknowledges this defect:

> Ric Marshall, chief analyst and co-founder of The Corporate Library . . . says that governance ratings . . . don't necessarily identify the best boards. "A great board is magic. It's human chemistry and the right kind of experience. . . ." In fact, a board that takes a check-the-box mentality and lives by the letter of the law is unlikely destined for greatness, he says.[11]

What the Corporate Library, however, does not acknowledge is that great boards do not work together by accident, "magic," or happenstance. Great boards are deliberately designed to go beyond simplistic structural metrics and involve careful thought by directors, who know the board best, on the recruitment, assessment, development, and, when necessary, removal of fellow directors. The best arbiters of requisite director competencies and leadership skills are directors themselves, and, in particular, the nominating committee of a board. The problem, therefore, is not with corporate boards *per se*, but with the scoring metrics themselves and empirical studies used to underscore and measure a very complex and dynamic reality: these governance scoring methodologies appear to be incomplete at best, and deeply flawed at worst.

Checking the Box of "Usual Suspects" Versus Focusing on Director Competencies and Leadership

As stated earlier, it is not enough simply to critique the status quo approach to examining and rating boards. In this chapter, it is suggested that there are other factors more important than structural demographic factors, such as formal or definitional director independence; whether the chair is non-executive; the size of the board; the chronological age, tenure, or share ownership of the director; or other externally measured metrics. These factors emerge from asking fundamental questions such as the following:

1. Does the board have the complement of required competencies and skills in its directors to ensure optimal decision making, strategic direction, and oversight of management in shareholders' interests?
2. Are the board and its committees effectively led by able board and committee chairs?

Director competencies and leadership, however, are difficult to measure from outside of a boardroom.

Selecting Director Competencies and Leadership Capability

As Kenneth Daly, president and CEO of the National Association of Corporate Directors (NACD), put it, "The key to effective boards is to get the right skill set on the board. However that happens—and it ought to happen through the nominating committee selection—the priority is getting the right skills on the board."[12] The following sections will explain in detail the role and responsibilities of the nominating committee in getting the right skill sets and directors on the board, by adopting best practices and tools such as a competency skills matrix. Examples from leading listed companies and chairs the author has researched or advised will also be provided.

Responsibilities of the Nominating Committee: Transparency and Rigor in Director Selection, Appointment, and Retirement

Each board should have a formal director succession planning and renewal program in place. The nominating committee should have a process for identifying and recruiting new directors, including taking into account their character, ability, experience, behavior and ability to devote the time required and an appropriate interview, background, reference check, and selection process. The nominating committee's mandate should include recommending a director-succession planning process to the board that is objective, transparent, and rigorous. Sufficient detail of this process should be disclosed to shareholders so as to ensure robustness and effectiveness.

Board and committee chair-succession planning should also occur, as part of the nominating committee's mandate. Succession planning should exist for all committees, including identifying gaps between current committee member competencies and skills that are aligned with committee requirements and having a pool of directors possessing desirable qualifications to serve on and chair each committee. Board renewal and effective succession planning should address director underperformance issues, as necessary or appropriate, for example, once directors' competencies and skills are no longer relevant or suited for the company, or directors are unable or unwilling to fulfill the requirements of the position. The objective assessment of individual director competencies and skills is difficult to accomplish without some sort of director self- or peer evaluation, which will be discussed later in this chapter and was also covered in Chapter Five.

Next, there should be a position description developed for board leadership roles, including (1) the chair of the board; (2) the chair of each board committee, for example, the audit, compensation, and nominating committees, or their equivalents; and (3) the CEO. There should in addition be a position description for individual directors. Strong examples of these position descriptions for the board chair, committee chairs, and individual directors are included in Exhibits 6.1 through 6.4, which appear at the end of this chapter.

These board leadership position descriptions should inform the following: (1) the recruitment of new directors; (2) the appointment of incumbent directors to occupy certain leadership roles within the boardroom; and (3) the assessment of board and committee chairs, annually and directly by individual members, against the achievement of their applicable position description. The position descriptions for board and committee chairs, individual directors, and the CEO should be complete, accurate, detailed, clear, reviewed annually, benchmarked against regulatory requirements and best practices, published in all appropriate public documents, and posted on the company's Website. Board and committee chair position descriptions should include leadership roles and responsibilities. Chair responsibilities should include the setting of agendas; ensuring that appropriate information is made available to the board; the marshalling of resources, expertise, and advice; the establishment of performance expectations and oversight of management; the chairing of *in camera* or executive sessions; coordination among committees; and making appropriate reports and recommendations to the board. Appropriate action should be taken if a board or committee chair's performance or commitment is determined to be inadequate, such as developmental suggestions, peer remediation, and so on, and taking timely, corrective action when necessary, such as chair succession, member rotation, or retirement.

Skills Matrix Gap Analysis and Developing the Candidate Director Profile

The most important step when recruiting directors is for the nominating committee to learn precisely what competencies, skills, and experiences are needed on the board, and which ones, if any, are missing. To assist in clarifying this information, the committee should create, maintain, and annually evaluate a director competency matrix. The matrix process should outline the competencies, skills, and experiences of the current directors and the key ones required for new directors.

Following is a summary of how nominating committees should effectively execute a director competency matrix, reflecting the views of nominating committee and board chairs, regulation, and a literature review by the author.

1. Assess what competencies and skills the board deems necessary for it to possess as a whole (not the competencies and skills the board currently possesses), given the requirements of the business; the future strategic needs of the company; and the requirements (including strengths and weaknesses) of the CEO and management team.

Management should be requested to suggest the knowledge, skills, background, diversity, and experience they believe would be useful on the board. Some are basic and common to all boards—for example, every board wants a financial expert (usually a C.A.) for the audit committee. Some are specific to the company—for example, a mining company will want several directors with varied mining experience.

The nominating committee reviews this list and suggests changes if appropriate. The final matrix is approved by the board.

2. Assess what competencies and skills each existing director possesses, keeping in mind planned or unplanned director retirements and competency and skill loss to the board, and possible overreliance on the expertise of any one particular director.

Best practice here is that current board members are asked to self-assess themselves relative to the matrix, with an opportunity for verbal or qualitative feedback. The nominating committee may lack full information and not be aware of a director's skills or experiences in a particular sector or industry. The self-assessment should be annual, as experience and exposure of a director may change from time to time.

3. Assess the gap between steps 1 and 2, that is, deficiencies identified in particular competencies and skills. The nominating committee chair then reviews directors' self-assessments against the matrix and modifies them as appropriate, as some board members tend to be excessively modest and some the opposite.

The nominating committee chair may consult with directors' self-evaluation or developmental plans, as needed or appropriate, in reviewing the competencies and skills of each director.

4. Assess the competencies and skills each new director nominee will bring to the boardroom; in other words develop a candidate profile or specification and demonstrate how a prospective candidate director will fill it. The desired competency set for a new director may be multifaceted. For example, a board may wish to recruit a chartered accountant who is a challenger.

A board should maintain an "evergreen" list of candidate directors to match the required competency gaps for its board, with noted availability of candidate directors for planned or unplanned board vacancies.

Telus Corporation provides a pictorial view of the process it undertakes in its director recruitment program, shown in Figure 6.1. By adopting this process, the nominating committee makes it objectively easier to determine which competencies, skills, or experiences are lacking in the existing set of directors. For example, in commenting on the advantages and ease of use of a skills matrix, a board chair of a large publicly listed company writes

> [T]he "skills" matrix in my opinion has been the BEST tool for helping our Governance and Nominating Committee seek out and screen new Board members [emphasis in original]. Quite simply the process starts with an understanding of the business the company is in and outlining the top eight to ten "skill and knowledge sets" that would be desirable to have on the Board to provide the required oversight that is needed. In general I would think that three or four of the skill sets required would be common to any publicly traded company. The most obvious ones are: financial competency (would rise to expertise if the Board didn't have depth in financial

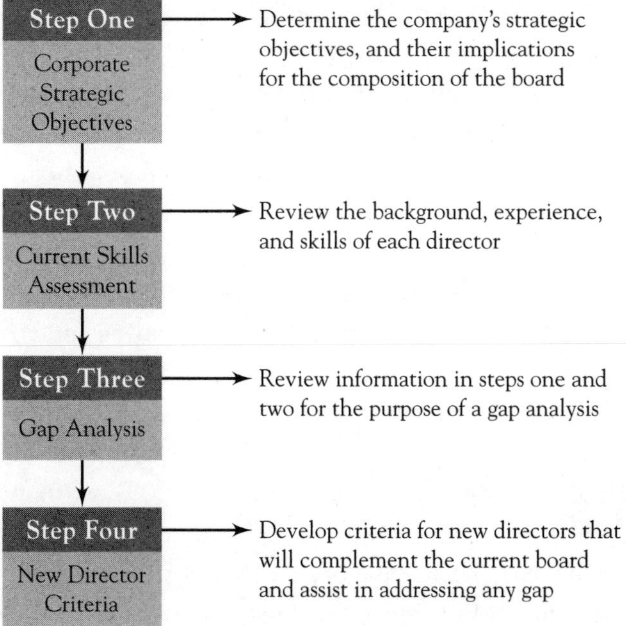

Figure 6.1. Example of Director Recruitment Assessment Steps: Telus Corp., Inc.

Source: Telus Corp., Inc., Board Policy Manual, "Appendix J—Director Criteria and Search Process." Available at http://about.telus.com/governance/policy_manual_appendix_J.html; last amended August 2007.

> and accounting skills), business experience and acumen, human resource and compensation knowledge, and environment and safety knowledge. From that starting point a company looks to their own situation and what skills are required. For example if you are in [our] business an understanding of how [our industry] work[s] is essential on the Board. Also if the company is operating internationally some experience with international businesses and associated risks is crucial. . . .

> It is easy to put a matrix together for a company. However it is more difficult to have a template as there is so much variation amongst businesses. Most companies would find it easy to identify those eight to ten skills that are crucial to have represented on a Board. (Board chair communication to the author, 2008)

The outcomes of the matrix analysis then determine the search for a pool of candidate directors. As an example of how this process helps to find directors that a board needs, the chair of a large company board writes the following:

> When we did our annual review in early 2003, we found some gaps including: not enough women (within the Designated Group category); a lack of CEOs as directors (within Enterprise Leadership category); further Industrial industry experience within Market Knowledge category; few younger directors (*i.e.*, not in their 60s). We shared these gaps with our director search firm (. . . at that time) and they found a number of candidates including a young woman who was CEO of a . . . company who was approached and subsequently joined the board in 2004. (Board chair communication to the author, 2008)

This is a real example of how implementing a competency matrix served the board well.

In building an effective board, therefore, it is essential that board selection be competency-based, as opposed to solely interest- or representation-based. The process should not default to the personal networks of directors, management, or others (including director search firms). This is not to suggest, however, that recommendations from directors or management (or others, including shareholders) should not be actively pursued as part of the candidate pool search.

This would be permissible when the suggested candidate's competencies and skills, in the judgment of the nominating committee, match the requirements and candidate profile emanating from the nominating committee's analysis. The nominating committee, led by an effective chair, must unambiguously own this process, invest the time, and be accountable for it.

Defining and Assessing Director Competencies and Skills

The National Association of Corporate Directors has set out a "Sample Board Expertise Matrix" in its *Report of the Blue Ribbon Commission* (Figure 6.2). The competencies and skills on the left side of the director competency matrix should be collectively exhaustive and mutually exclusive to the extent possible. That is, it is important that each competency and skill, financial acumen and so on, be well defined, so as to avoid confusion and misperception when the nominating committee assesses (or directors

	Smith	Jones	Davis	etc.	Total
E-Commerce	4	3	6		13
Acquisition Experience	8	7	7		22
International Marketing	2	3	1		6
etc.	6	7	8		21

Figure 6.2. Sample Board Expertise Matrix (NACD).

Legend: Names of current directors are on the horizontal axis and the skills considered important over the next five years on the vertical axis. Directors are rated on a scale of 1 to 10, where 1 indicates low expertise and 10 denotes extraordinarily high expertise, for each area. In this example, the board is weak on International Marketing and might consider seeking candidates with that expertise.

Source: National Association of Corporate Directors, *Report of the Blue Ribbon Commission—The Governance Committee: Driving Board Performance* (Washington, D.C.: NACD, 2007).

self-assess) each director's level of competency or skill acquisition. The rating of each director on his or her level of competency, skill, or expertise (the cells within the matrix) should also be well defined and objective. Note that the NACD has suggested rating directors on a scale of 1 to 10, "where 1 indicates low expertise and 10 denotes extraordinarily high expertise." An advantage in using a ten-point scale is that a spread of ratings is more likely. Other scales are possible, for example, 1 to 4; Low/Medium/High, and so on. For example, if a three-level scale is used, each level should be defined, such as "outstanding," "fully satisfactory," and "improvement required" (example used by a financial institution). Ideally, performance outputs and examples should accompany each skill level, to ease directors' assessment accuracy and enable the process to be as objective and transparent as possible. Terms such as *needs improvement* should be avoided as an indicator of a low level of expertise, particularly for behavioral competencies, which can be sensitive matters. Better language would be "opportunity for development," or similar positive language. If a director is rated as low on a particular competency or skill, tactful verbal feedback should also accompany that rating to assist in providing context and proactive advice.

When the nominating committee is instituting a competency gap analysis, adopting these practices will lead to a more objective and transparent process, endorsed by directors and avoiding potential misunderstanding or resentment.

Implementing the Skills Matrix: A Practical Example

Increasingly, companies with leading practices will disclose to their shareholders the precise competencies, skills, and experiences used in selecting new directors and assessing current directors, together with appropriately disclosed results of its skills assessment. An example in this regard is Nexen Inc., which discloses the number of Nexen directors possessing "skilled or expert application" in each of the skills and experiences within its own skills matrix (Figure 6.3).

Areas of Expertise

Nexen maintains a skills matrix, and each director indicates his or her level of expertise in each area according to:

1. No or limited application
2. Basic application
3. Skilled application—significant operational experience and knowledge in the area, but not at a senior executive level
4. Expert application—senior executive experience in the area from a function, role and knowledge perspective

The areas of expertise set out in the directors' bibliographies are those areas in which they are most skilled.

Skill / Experience Description	**Number of Directors with Skilled or Expert Application**
Managing / Leading Growth—Senior Executive experience driving strategic insight and direction to encourage innovation and conceptualize key trends to continuously challenge the organization to sharpen its vision while achieving significant organic growth.	12
International—Senior Executive experience working in a global organization where Nexen is or may be active. Has a thorough understanding of different cultural, political and regulatory requirements.	10
CEO / Senior Officer—Experience working as a CEO or Senior Officer for a major organization with international operations.	10
Exploration—Experience as a Senior Executive or top functional authority leading an exploration department in a major upstream or integrated exploration and production company. May have formal education in geology, geophysics, or engineering.	5

(Continued)

Figure 6.3. Example of a Directors Skills Matrix: Nexen Inc.

Source: Adapted from Nexen Inc., 2008 Management Proxy Circular, "Board of Directors—Areas of Expertise," March 21, 2008, p. 23. Available at http://www.nexeninc.com/Governance/Board/AreasofExpertise.asp

Skill / Experience Description	Number of Directors with Skilled or Expert Application
Compensation—Senior Executive experience or Board Human Resources Committee participation with a thorough understanding of compensation, benefit and pension programs, legislation and agreements. This includes specific expertise in executive compensation programs, including base pay, incentives, equity and perquisites.	10
Oil and Gas—Senior Executive experience in the oil and gas industry combined with a strong knowledge of Nexen's strategy, markets, competitors, financials, operational issues, regulatory concerns and technology.	7
Governance / Board—Prior or current experience as a Board member for a major Canadian organization (public, private or non-private sectors) with international operations.	11
Financial Acumen—Senior Executive experience in financial accounting and reporting, and corporate finance, especially with respect to debt and equity markets. Familiarity with internal financial controls.	9
Health, Safety, Environment and Social Responsibility (HSE & SR)—Thorough understanding of industry regulations and public policy related to workplace safety, environment and social responsibility. May have had an active leadership role in the shaping of public policy in Canada and abroad. Demonstrated commitment to Nexen's HSE & SR values.	10
Diversity—Contributes to the Board in a way that enhances perspectives through diversity in gender, ethnic background, geographic origin, experience (industry and public, private and non-profit sectors), etc.	8
Marketing Expertise—Senior Executive experience in the energy marketing industry combined with a strong knowledge of Nexen's strategy, markets, competitors, financials, operational issues and regulatory concerns.	5

Figure 6.3. Example of a Directors Skills Matrix: Nexen Inc. (Cont'd)

The Behavioral Dimension of Director Effectiveness

Once a company has adopted a skills and competency matrix process, the behavioral dimension of director effectiveness comes into greater focus. What is frequently missing in the selection of directors, however, is the concept of director behavior.

The principal work of a board of directors revolves around complex decision making. Because people make decisions, it is the people on the board—plus the manner in which they are led and interact among themselves and with management—that determine the decision-making process. The leadership and mix of director behaviors is crucial in creating the board's chemistry (or lack thereof) and in influencing its decision-making process. There is frequently the temptation, however, to obtain the most qualified or high-profile director, perhaps focusing exclusively on narrow expertise or past accomplishments. Such recruitment efforts, undertaken without due regard to the board as a group decision-making body, with each director making his or her own contribution that affects the whole, may be missing a key consideration. We have all seen examples of sports teams that have recruited star athletes only to fail due to lack of chemistry:

> [T]here is no guarantee that top talent will make for an outstanding board. Sometimes a dream team of stellar individuals doesn't click, like the 2004 U.S. men's Olympic basketball team [or the 2006 Canadian men's hockey team] that, by all accounts, had the best players in the world but finished with a bronze medal because they couldn't play as a team. "One thing that boards do wrong is to go for the biggest name or the best athlete available, to steal a sports cliché, instead of filling the specific need they have. . . ."[13]

It is the author's contention that great boards pay close attention to the dynamics of the board as a team (see also

Chapter Twelve). The team decision-making processes of the board, in the final analysis, determine the fate of the corporation. A body of literature exists to document how and why groups fail at decision making (see Chapter Twelve). Like any other group, boards of directors suffer from cognitive and decision-making infirmities and biases, including, in particular, groupthink; obedience to authority or expertise; fear of lack of knowledge or embarrassment; diffusion of responsibility; self-censorship; illusion of unanimity; time pressure; incomplete information; and failure to welcome dissent or seek out alternative courses or disconfirming opinion. And so, like any other group, a board's behavioral characteristics are also worthy of exploration.

There is no shortage of formally independent and financially qualified directors sitting on boards, and yet many decision-making failures have come on boards with just such an abundance of individuals on those boards. Therefore, it makes sense that because these boards failed in their decision making and oversight of management and the risks to which the corporation was exposed, the identification of director and chair competencies and skills should be expanded to include behavioral and interpersonal dimensions of performance. This examination would include how directors lead, relate to one another and management, and understand and appropriately manage cognitive and decision-making biases. This would allow board effectiveness to be explored to its fullest extent. Postmortem decision failure analysis may reveal, for example, that there was a person on the inside that people did not want to hear, not that there was a shortage of expertise on the board. That poor boards do not pay sufficient attention to director behavior to the extent they can is cause for concern. That good boards do so (through a variety of means) demonstrates that there are empirical data and best practices that can be learned from and advanced.

It is suggested, therefore, that if an effective board is to be maintained or developed, nominating committees should engage in a reasonable behavioral analysis of prospective candidates. Nominating committees (and search firms advising them) should determine (and provide reasonable assurance as expert third parties) that the candidate director has the personal and interpersonal qualities that will contribute to the boardroom process, culture, and chemistry of existing members (particularly if that person is not known to existing directors and is being recommended by the director search firm). This means that the behavioral qualities of incumbent directors must also be assessed in some reasonable fashion and addressed and remedied as appropriate.

Defining and measuring behavioral dimensions of individual director performance and chair leadership, however, are inherently more subjective tasks. Personal and judgmental qualities do not lend themselves as readily to transparent, accepted, or objective quantification. This in large measure has been why boards have tended to shy away from behavioral and competency dimensions of individual performance. As noted in the introduction, academics cannot definitively prove a relationship between board effectiveness and corporate financial performance. This does not mean that a relationship between the two does not exist. In the same vein, the challenge of measuring behavioral dimensions of director performance does not mean that such dimensions do not matter or that they should not be pursued. The most complex phenomenon is often the most difficult to study and measure. And, as noted above, with respect to the governance rating agencies, what is readily measurable (external metrics) may matter far less than what is not readily measurable (director competencies and behaviors). It is incumbent on academics to research what may be uncomfortable or unpopular, to advance knowledge.

With this goal in mind, the author has developed a framework grouping for the experiences, knowledge, competencies, and skills that individual directors and chairs of the board and committees are expected to bring to a board on which they serve, or chair. It can be found in Figure 6.4. It is not expected that all directors

Experience-oriented: skills, abilities, and resources resulting from the director's enterprise leadership and other past and current experience

CEO/enterprise leadership (CEO/senior officer/business unit leadership; former/active plus company/unit size, scope)

Industry/relevant business (senior executive/top functional plus training/education/knowledge)

Value enhancement (managing/leading growth/value creation; senior executive plus track record)

Geographical (senior executive in region/community where company is/may be active plus understanding/linkages)

Governance (years, performance, size/type of boards plus specific leadership role)

Linkages to resources (human, financial, markets, other)

Diversity (such as leadership, perspective, background, other)

Other (for example, distress/crisis, government/regulatory, operating/manufacturing, issue/transaction)

Knowledge-oriented: literacy, expertise, and functional capabilities acquired through learning, training, and experiences of the director

Understanding of the organization/strategy (business model/value drivers, industry, board, executives, products/services and communities)

Financial acumen (literacy, expertise; plus senior executive/professional experience/designation)

HR and compensation literacy (plus senior executive/board/HR committee experience/understanding)

Risk management competence (plus senior executive/professional/assurance experience)

Information-seeking, knowledge-building, and learning appetite (for example, knowledge acquisition/enhancement plus current, relevant)

Other (such as sustainability/environmental; marketing/consumer; legal/compliance; technical/specialist; R&D; plus experience/understanding)

Individual-oriented: personal characteristics, qualities, and commitment of the director

Independence of thought and action (plus lack of conflicts)

Probity, trust, and confidentiality

Thinking and reasoning (inductive, deductive)
Reputation and earned peer respect
Fortitude and willingness to act
Initiative and commitment to follow through (for example, leadership of particular topic)
Achievement orientation and individual accountability

Group-oriented: interpersonal, relationship and decision-making skills, and style of the director

Advisory temperament
Listening and communication
Self-management and interpersonal sensitivity
Tolerance for ambiguity, change, and dissent
Cognitive and decision-making bias awareness
Analysis and judgment (plus early warning/pattern recognition)
Candid/constructive engagement and relationship resilience
Impact, persuasiveness, and influence

Figure 6.4. Individual Director Experience, Knowledge, Competency, and Skills Framework.

Source: Author's empirical data, modified by a literature review.

would perform at high levels exhibiting most or even many of the competencies and skills set out in the framework in Figure 6.4. What is important is that the board, collectively, has the majority of the requisite competencies and skills sufficiently represented, given the needs of the company and its strategic goals.

In addition to the competencies, skills, and experiences in Figure 6.4, which individual directors would possess to varying degrees, the chair of the board or chair of a committee should possess each of the skills, competencies, and experiences shown in Figure 6.5.

Over time, as these competencies, skills, and experiences of individual directors are further studied, this framework will develop, including defining behavioral director competencies and associating them with performance outputs and tasks.

Governance Leadership
Conducting of meetings, group decision-making process
Fluid understanding of portfolio of director roles (for example, past CEO, committee chair, other)
Mentoring, coaching, and development (CEO, board members plus no personal agenda)
Consensus/relationship-building and conflict resolution
Results orientation and holding to account

Figure 6.5. Board or Committee Chair Skills, Competency, and Experience Framework.
Source: Author's empirical data, modified by a literature review.

There is a growing body of literature (but still rather nascent) addressing specific competencies and skills that effective individual directors are expected to possess. The thrust of this literature largely centers on technical competencies, such as financial literacy and expertise, compensation literacy, and so on, as well as the experience base that the director possesses, for example, current or former CEO or other executive experience. Various performance levels of expertise for these types of competencies and experiences in some cases are well developed and becoming easier to measure and quantify. This development bodes well for the identification and measurement (and ultimately acceptance) of behavioral competencies of individual directors.

Assessing Director Competencies and Leadership

Perhaps the most qualified individuals to evaluate the effectiveness of a board, its committees, and individual directors are the respective directors or committee members themselves. Shareholders, regulators, rating agencies, or academics, many or most of whom remain outside the boardroom, are hard-pressed to understand, know, or observe the board in action.

A rigorous system of internal governance self-review and accountability has been missing for some time. The evidence indicates that boards are just beginning to develop models of self-assessment and a level of psychological comfort in assessing their own performance and that of their colleagues. Boards, comprising some of the most respected and qualified individuals in business, need to exercise leadership and adopt this self-assessment initiative to a far greater extent than they have to date. If boards instead choose to wait for the public, shareholders, creditors, consumers, the media, and other stakeholders to impose a level of accountability from these external perspectives, the result may be a misguided, incongruent effort with unintentional consequences. Some of the difficulties boards are presently grappling with, as they struggle with assessment processes, are outlined in the following sections.

Board Evaluations Are Currently Defective

Despite the NYSE Governance Rules having been approved by the SEC in 2003—including the requirement of boards of directors to conduct an annual self-evaluation to determine whether they, as well as their committees, are functioning effectively—in 2008, Kenneth Daly, president and CEO of the National Association of Corporate Directors, stated,

> Some of the board evaluations I've seen don't even rise to the level of awful. Essentially, they don't even evaluate the board member. Because of collegiality, you don't want to go to somebody and say, "Look, you're no longer productive. You're a dud." So what happens is you evaluate the whole board. I don't know what good that does for figuring out problems for particular individuals.[14]

Other commentators, such as Ray Troubh and Charles Elson, have similarly remarked on the current state of board evaluations:

> As Ken Daly said, the present effectiveness of the evaluation system is terrible. But that's our fault. We get these standardized forms—10 or 12 pages, and you check, check, check and off it goes to an independent agency to be counted. They come back and say, "The board is OK on these six points." Then you destroy the documents because you are worried about lawsuits—you don't want anyone to see what you really wrote. There are a few comments, which are anonymous. You may say, "He's a jerk," but you don't sign it. We have got to do something about the evaluation process. They have to be better. They have to be tougher. That's going to take a long while.[15]

> The difficulty that I found with board evaluations has been the reluctance to pull the trigger on a nonperforming director.[16]

Nevertheless, despite these defects in current board evaluations, there is support for robust board assessments to take place. Governance commentators such as Ira Millstein, Patrick McGurn, and others (Ram Charan, Roger Raber) have all called for "robust board evaluations." Clearly, there is an opportunity for improvement that presents itself.

Boards Do Not Assess Individual Directors

When you look to boards themselves and whether they engage in rigorous review, including at the individual director level, the results are not particularly encouraging. Academic Paul Graf recently canvassed a subset of large American corporations on director evaluations, and the results are interesting to say the least (Table 6.1).

Table 6.1. Data on Individual and Peer Director Evaluations.

Board Evaluation—Who Does What?					
Even Top Companies Are Shy on Individual Evaluation					
		Director Evaluation			
Dow Jones Industrials	**Continuing Education**	**Board**	**Committee**	**Individual**	**Peer**
3M		x	x		
AIG		x	x		
Alcoa	x	x	x		
Altria Group		x	x		
AT&T	x	x	x		
Boeing	x	x*			
Caterpillar		x	x		
Citigroup		x	x		
Coca-Cola	x	x			
Disney		x			
DuPont	x	x	x		
ExxonMobil	x	x			
General Electric		x	x		
General Motors	x	x			
Hewlett-Packard	x	x	x		
Home Depot	x	x			
Honeywell		x			
IBM	x	x	x		
Intel	x	x	x	x	
Johnson & Johnson		x	x		
JPMorgan Chase	x	x**			
McDonald's		x*	x		
Merck		x			
Microsoft		x*	x		
Pfizer		x			

(Continued)

Table 6.1. Data on Individual and Peer Director Evaluations. (Cont'd)

Dow Jones Industrials	Continuing Education	Director Evaluation			
		Board	Committee	Individual	Peer
Procter & Gamble	x	x***			
United Technologies		x	x		
Verizon	x	x			
Wal-Mart Stores					

* The board evaluation also includes an evaluation of each individual director.
** The evaluation is made by the Governance Committee.
*** The board evaluation is performed with the use of an outside facilitator.

Source: P. Graf, "Myths About Director Evaluation," The Corporate Board 28, no. 166 (2007): 19.

Reluctance to Assess Individual Directors Explained

Some directors, management, and professional service advisers may have vested interests in not asking individual director review questions and ensuring that robust director assessment takes place. Further, it is easier to deal with structural factors, for example, whether the chair is non-executive or independent, rather than whether he or she is truly effective. Such structural inquiries offer a path of least resistance compared to inquiries on measures of individual performance, be they competencies or behavior. For examples of individual director leadership, competency, or performance-related standards, see Figure 6.6.

Garbage In, Garbage Out

Rigorous board and individual director performance metrics require careful thought and will ultimately lead to dealing with candid feedback and discussions on matters such as board leadership and dynamics. Therefore, it is often for reasons of ego, reputation, fear, risk, discomfort, or sheer laziness that it simply becomes easier for many boards to ask diluted, structural-based questions,

The board chair has an effective personal leadership style (sets a good example; is courteous, inclusive, sensitive, yet decisive; establishes high standards and holds directors and management accountable to them, and so on)

The board chair carries out the role well (sets agendas; ensures that appropriate information is available; marshals resources and expertise; and ensures that the boundaries between board and management responsibilities are clearly understood and respected and that relationships between the board and management are conducted in a professional and constructive manner)

The board chair has a constructive working relationship with the CEO (supportive and collaborative, yet independent)

The board chair conducts an effective decision-making process (ensures that, for crucial decisions, alternatives are generated, a thorough discussion and analysis ensues, relevant perspectives are brought to bear, the best decision is made, and the decision is supported)

The board chair builds healthy boardroom dynamics (relates well with directors and management, deals effectively with dissent, and works constructively toward consensus)

The competencies (financial literacy, experience, skills, knowledge of the business, and so on) **of all members of the Audit Committee are appropriately matched with the requirements of the committee** (for example, all members, at a minimum, have a full understanding of how the company earns income and how these transactions affect the accounting judgments management makes)

The financial expertise on the Audit Committee (for example, recent, relevant, and meets regulatory requirement criteria—in other words, at the level of financial expert), **as a whole, matches the future financial oversight needs of the company** (capital and balance sheet management, accounting, financial control and assurance, financial markets, treasury, funds management, investment banking, taxation, risk management, and so on, as required)

Inadequate performance (including commitment) **by directors is promptly addressed through the board chair taking appropriate action** (for example, developmental suggestions, peer remediation, and taking timely, corrective action as required, such as member rotation or retirement, with leadership provided from the board chair)

Figure 6.6. Sample Standards for Assessing Director Leadership, Competencies, and Effectiveness.

Source: Board, committee, and director evaluation research and assessment conducted by the author.

Rigorous succession planning occurs for all members of the committee (includes, with due consideration by the Nominations Committee, a formal and transparent process, identifying gaps between current member competencies and skills and committee requirements, a pool of directors possessing desirable qualifications to serve on and chair the committee and, where appropriate, retaining a search firm to identify such a director(s))

Qualitative question: **What candid and constructive suggestions would you provide to the board chair, if any, to enhance his or her effectiveness?**

Figure 6.6. Sample Standards for Assessing Director Leadership, Competencies, and Effectiveness. (Cont'd)

not unlike external governance rating firms. This leads to a process of "going through the motions" with a self-administered, non-robust, and painless—but ultimately ineffective—evaluation. Because boards may be reluctant to solicit the input of professional service advisers to advise them on an effective process for individual director evaluation, for reasons of liability, confidentiality, and data sensitivity, new and independent knowledge may not permeate and become embedded within the evaluation tools themselves. What therefore occurs in many cases is the proliferation, photocopying, and passing off of substandard, paper-based board and director evaluation questionnaires, as Mr. Troubh has mentioned. In other words, garbage in, garbage out.

If a board does retain a professional service firm to assist with the evaluation, for example in the fields of law, accounting, employee searching, or consulting, there are many issues that those firms face that may affect their ability to assist with board and director evaluations. It is often the case that these firms may be concurrently retained in another ongoing professional capacity by the board or committee (or management). The professional firm may therefore be disinclined commercially to engage in rigorous, in-depth reviews, including those of individual directors.

Advising on the board or director evaluation could raise the perception of a conflict of interest or could actually constitute a direct conflict of interest for some firms. For example, a director search firm providing a negative review when it would benefit from the search for a new director would be an example of the latter. When firms branch out and attempt to expand their advice across multiple director competencies beyond their disciplinary "silos," this carries risk for the firm's credibility and market permission. Further, director evaluation may not be viewed as particularly remunerative or worth such risk, given more lucrative work being done for management. More important, however, the cost to a professional firm in facilitating a negative review of an individual director or board, and providing negative data of this nature to the director or to the chair, may well be that the firm may not be retained for future work. Professional relations may be disrupted, given the unavoidable human dynamics. There is a real risk in the governance space of delivering negative feedback; in other words, the messenger getting "shot." Simply put, the downside risk for professional firms of providing meaningful advice on the assessment of individual directors may be too great.

The reality seems to be, therefore, that if reform is to occur in the evaluation of individual directors, it must come from four groups: academics, shareholders, regulators (the least preferred), and, most important, boards themselves.

Effective Director Assessments

Let's consider what an effective assessment regime would include (see also Chapter Five). Under the direction and supervision of the corporate governance and nominating committee, or its equivalent, the assessment of the performance and contribution of board leaders and all other directors should consider the applicable position description(s) and the competencies and skills each individual director is expected to possess and apply in the discharge of his or her duties. This committee's oversight of the director-assessment process should include mandatory feedback provided to each assessed individual, and be followed where applicable by timely, corrective action. The results of the assessment of individual directors should inform the continued tenure or renomination of that director. In other words, director evaluation should be an important tool for determining who should be on the board (recruitment and retirement), rather than relying exclusively on bright line independence tests, retirement age, or tenure limits. The results of the board evaluation should be discussed in executive session and action planning and setting of priorities and accountabilities should occur. The results of individual director evaluations should be discussed with the chair of the board. And the chair's assessment should, in turn, be discussed with the chair of the governance and nominating committee (or its equivalent). If the board chair's performance is in question, and a confidential tap on the shoulder or otherwise is warranted, independent directors should be able to approach another director—for example, the lead director or a committee chair—and this performance feedback route should be understood and documented within a position description or committee mandate.

In essence, as steps toward addressing and improving board effectiveness, shareholders should consider asking the following four important questions of the boards of the companies in which they invest:

1. Are there position descriptions for individual director performance, including director leadership positions?
2. Is director effectiveness assessed and if so by what criteria and process?
3. Are the results acted upon and if so how?
4. Are the results of a director's assessment linked to that director's continued tenure on the board?

In this manner, a self-accountability regime within the board system may be implemented and reinforced by shareholder interest, inquiry, or formal mechanism. Shareholders may therefore not need to rely primarily on majority voting standards and director elections, which have procedural impediments. Moreover they are expensive and time consuming, and lack systemwide effects.

Companies are beginning to disclose to shareholders their evaluation processes for key director roles, including the assessment of the board chair by members of the board, the assessment of committee chairs by committee members, and the assessment of individual directors via a chair-led peer-review process. See Figure 6.7 for an example from a leading company in this regard.

Annual Assessment of the Board Chair by Members of the Board
Each year members of the board are asked to assess and comment on the discharge, by the board chair, of his duties. Individual responses are received by the chair of the CG&N Committee. A summary report is then provided to the board chair and the full board, with no attribution of comments to individual directors without their consent. As part of the annual board chair assessment, the board reviews and considers any proposed changes to the board chair position description.

Annual Assessment of Each Committee Chair by Members of Each Committee
Each year, members of each committee are asked to assess and comment on the discharge, by each committee chair, of his or her duties. Responses are received by the corporate secretary and the committee chair under review. A summary report is then provided to the appropriate committee and to the full board, with no attribution of comments to individual directors without their consent. As part of the annual committee chair assessment, the board reviews and considers any proposed changes to the committee chair position descriptions.

(Continued)

Figure 6.7. Example of Evaluation Processes of Individual Directors: Potash Corp. of Saskatchewan, Inc.

Source: Adapted from Potash Corporation of Saskatchewan, Inc., Notice of Annual and Special Meeting of Shareholders and Management Proxy Circular, May 8, 2008, p. 68. Available at http://www.potashcorp.com/investor_relations/stock_information/proxy_circulars_archive/?year=2008.

Annual Assessment of Individual Directors
Each year during the period from May to September, the board chair (and, as in the opinion of the board chair is desirable, the chair of the CG&N committee) formally meets with each director individually to engage in full and frank two-way discussion of any and all issues that either wish to raise, with a focus on maximizing the contribution of each director to the board and committees. In completing the review, the Board Chair will employ a checklist, discuss both short-term and long-term goals, and establish action items to allow individual directors to enhance both his or her personal contributions and overall board effectiveness. The board chair will share peer feedback with each director as appropriate and will review progress and action taken. Each director, during such formal review, shall be prepared to discuss with the board chair how the directors, both individually and collectively, could operate more effectively. The board chair will discuss the results of the individual evaluations with the chair of the CG&N committee and report summary findings to both that committee and to the full board at the November meeting.

Figure 6.7. Example of Evaluation Processes of Individual Directors: Potash Corp. of Saskatchewan, Inc. (Cont'd)

"Litigation Chill" of Director Assessment and Lack of Regulatory Impetus

From a policymaking perspective, it should not be the case that boards engage in nonrigorous evaluations (for example, superficial questionnaires, perfunctory oral discussions) with a view to avoiding legal liability by not producing data that would accompany a rigorous review, such as a skills matrix or peer review. General agreement among lawyers is that board reviews done in the normal course of business are discoverable. This further explains the reluctance of boards to self-assess at both the board and director levels. Ideally, there perhaps should be a safe harbor or zone of confidentiality to promote boards' undertaking a thorough review, with the work product protected from plaintiffs' counsel as appropriate. Just as lawyer-client privilege promotes full disclosure by the client, in order to obtain the best advice, board and director reviews might be afforded similar legislative protection with appropriate safeguards. An individual director evaluation should not be viewed as a "smoking gun" but should be undertaken with the primary objective of development and improvement.

Further, it must be noted that there is no regulatory requirement within the United States to evaluate the effectiveness and contribution of individual directors. This is not the case in Canada, where regulatory guidance is provided to achieve this end. Comparisons are made in Table 6.2 concerning how Canadian and American regulators treat the recruitment and assessment of individual directors: the Canadian Securities Administrators' "National Policy 58-201" and the New York Stock Exchange "Corporate Governance Rules," respectively.

It is arguable that the result of the NYSE rules has been to require a level of granularity and prescription that makes it more challenging for nominating committees and boards to appear in their disclosures to be complying in letter and spirit with the regulatory guidance when in practice they are really engaging in superficial, pro forma compliance.

Reluctance to Address Underperforming Directors

Perhaps the greatest locus of opposition to the assessment of individual directors comes from boards and individual directors themselves. Interestingly, many underperforming directors are becoming known as such by fellow directors and members of management. Yet these underperformers may have external reputations as seemingly strong individuals and leaders (or former leaders) in their chosen field. The cost to such directors in admitting that their performance is defective in some manner (independence, competence, or behavior), both within the boardroom and outside it, is typically very high. This makes it even more difficult to solicit support from such directors for a director performance assessment regime.

Underperforming directors do not wish to be seen by their peers as being less than effective. Therefore they are likely to

Table 6.2. American Versus Canadian Regulations Regarding Director Recruitment and Assessment.

Regulation	New York Stock Exchange Corporate Governance Rules[17]	Canadian Securities Administrators National Policy 58-201[18]
Director nomination requirements	Moderate: board guidelines must address "director qualification standards" and Nominating Committee must identify individuals qualified to become board members, consistent with criteria approved by the Board	Yes: a detailed two-step individual director competency and skills gap analysis (incumbent and prospective directors) undertaken by the Nominating Committee, advising the board
Board leadership position descriptions?	No	Yes: for chair of board and chair of each board committee, in writing
Assessment of board and committees?	Yes: annual performance evaluation for each	Yes: regular assessment for each, considering respective mandate or charter
Assessment of individual directors?	No	Yes: considering applicable position description(s), as well as competencies and skills each individual director is expected to bring to the board

Source: Adapted from R. Leblanc, "External Disclosure of Leading Governance Assessment Practices: What Shareholders Should Be Asking and Companies Should Be Disclosing." *International Journal of Disclosure and Governance* 4, no. 3 (2007): 169.

resist, in tactful, diplomatically smooth but unambiguous manners, the notion of director performance scrutiny. This problem is especially acute if it is the board chair who is reluctant and underperforming. Enabling underperforming directors to continue to serve evidences a lack of courageous leadership and director initiative. The cost to such enabling may be tacit resentment by other directors, the resignation of performing directors, impairment of the board's ability to attract strong directors, and an overall decline in board effectiveness.

If underperformers refuse to improve or are incapable of it, for whatever reason, then they need to be asked to step down and not seek reelection. This requires intervention by the chair of the board, the governance committee chair, or both; in other words, effective board leadership. Counseling underperformers off of the board is easier to achieve if a neutral, even-handed director self- or peer assessment is part of the overall board evaluation process.

Implementing a Director Peer-Review Process

As Conger and Lawler in Chapter Five and as Daly and Elson earlier have stated, a primary defect in board evaluations is the lack of attention paid to evaluating individual director performance. To devise director performance criteria and to implement an objective and fair process for regularly assessing individual director contribution requires thought and tailoring to the board, circumstances, and personalities involved. It may be said that different directors contribute in different ways, and that a "standard" evaluation may not capture such performance nuances. Director "X," for example, may not say a lot during meetings but is instrumental in building bridges between positions outside of meetings. This observation, however simple, acknowledges that the methodology used (a survey, an interview, or both) should reflect multiple director performance dimensions, including within committees and outside of meetings, and differential exposure directors may have in observing one another. Performance criteria need not be overly quantitative, rigid, or formulaic, but it should reflect multiple competencies and performance outputs expected of directors. Expectations should be managed and guidance provided to ensure the focus remains on director contribution to the board's effectiveness. During a peer review, there should be sufficient opportunity for directors to provide constructive feedback, context, and qualitative perspectives in their remarks, whether they are oral, written, or both.

Concern About Collegiality

The main resistance to assessing individual directors on a peer-to-peer basis—in other words, going beyond the self-review to include all directors assessing one another—is the process of the review, providing feedback, and the consequences. There is perennially a strong concern that peer assessment will disrupt overall board collegiality. The assumption is that directors have already proven themselves in their lifetime or in their other career experiences and should therefore be immune from further review on the grounds of disrupting collegiality. Yet numerous other professional occupations engage in constructive peer review, and there are those boards that have devised systems of successful collegial review.

A respondent from a company widely regarded for its governance practices and, in particular, its director performance evaluation (including peer review), offered the following instructive commentary on maintaining board collegiality throughout the context of peer reviews:

> Peer reviews have only recently been in my view "accepted" as a best practice, and so directors are still struggling with the concept. However, a collegial peer review I would suggest is one that has several elements to it. Firstly, the review starts with how the "team" is functioning—this removes personalities to some extent

as it is a question of whether the team is good. . . . It is important to remember that in the team context not everyone is a star—and that while some board members may be stronger than others, it is the mix and the fact that everyone contributes at the appropriate time—that is, the analogy is the third line center chips in a goal when it's important to do so—which makes it effective. I think my analogy of a director being on the "third line" may be hearsay—because they are all accomplished or have had "hall of fame" type careers—but . . . you cannot have everyone leading all the time. It is the mix of perspectives that can be and are raised for consideration, which drives the best outcomes or decisions.

Second—I would suggest that the ability of the board chair (working with the Corporate Governance Committee chair) to have the open dialogue or "crucial conversation" with the board as a whole and directors individually about why things are working or not working that will direct the ultimate effectiveness of the board as a whole and board members individually. Directors . . . are generally (except in egregious circumstances) reluctant to comment on other directors directly. . . . Except for a disruptive board member, it is the team and team systems, and the ability of the team members to have their game raised through the system, that needs to be tweaked—and that is the board chair's responsibility. Unless a board member clearly does not fit, the chair needs to create the environment that draws out the best from the board. The difficulty with peer reviews in the context of a board and even in the business context of "hiring" a senior employee—it is a situation that one wants to create the environment for success. Much is vested in the education and

> training and emotion of bringing someone into a quasi-family—and so the concept of evaluating one's "brother or sister" is different from making a trade in the sports analogy to upgrade one's team. Therefore—the peer review needs to be focused on how a director can best contribute to the effective functioning of the board. For instance, the chair may advise a board member that they would really like to hear his or her view on various topics because the board needs that input—or conversely that the board member needs to be better prepared or have a better perspective on the company or industry and what can be done to provide that education.
>
> Third—the board needs feedback from management on how it interacts within itself and with management. This is also an important consideration that needs to form part of the chair's data or information to be analyzed and responded to. . . . (Communication to the author, 2008)

How the Director Peer Review Occurs

An impediment in the director peer-review process is how to provide an effective mechanism for data collection and feedback. This need not occur in survey form, but could involve the board chair having one-on-one annual meetings with each director to discuss his or her performance as well as that of their colleagues, in contributing to overall board effectiveness. The governance committee chair could meet with the board chair to discuss the board chair's performance, in the context of leading board effectiveness. If, however, some sort of written or electronic feedback is solicited as part of the peer review, providing anonymity to directors by not attributing comments to any one director assists in candor and improves feedback sensitivities for individual directors. The written or electronic feedback should not be shared with all directors unless directors consent to this disclosure. The results of each director's peer review should be shared only with that individual director, preferably via the chair, in a constructive and tactful manner. Again, it is worth emphasizing that it is important that the focus of the review be developmental and not judgmental.

Practical Examples: Three Models of Effective Director Peer Review

The examples of peer-review processes described in this section involve real companies that have all received recognition for their corporate governance practices, and in particular their director peer-evaluation process.

Model One: Chair-Director Interview (No Survey)

The first model of director peer review involves personal one-on-one interviews between the chair and each director. Alternatively, it is possible to have director interviews using a two-on-one approach, with the chair of the corporate governance and nominating committee, or its equivalent, also included in the interview along with the board chair and individual director.

In the words of one director involved with such an interview process:

> The key question to each director in that context is, "Do you have specific constructive advice for any of your fellow directors?" This generally cuts right to the chase in an interview setting and elicits the kind of feedback you need while still keeping the collegiality. Also, it's a good system for supporting board renewal and succession. If you do it regularly, you then have a robust system that enables you to deal with succession and renewal as a matter of course (changing business needs of the company and hence the board; less engaged or noncontributing

> directors, and so on). (Director communication to the author, 2008)

This model would work well for a high-functioning board whose chair is performing and effective. The chief defect in this approach is that relying solely on the chair to solicit oral feedback from directors might inhibit candor, lack supporting objective data, and invite assertions of subjectivity or bias from underperformers. In addition, there is the risk for potential "slippage" to occur, in that an oral process may be less rigorous than a written procedure (depending). A chief advantage of this model is that a skilled chair can invite and deliver negative feedback in a very collegial manner.

Model Two: Third-Party Survey, Shared on a Volunteer Basis with the Chair for the Chair-Director Interview

One company, well regarded for its peer review, uses a third party who collects and analyzes the data and provides assessments back to individual directors, on a director-by-director basis. In the words of one director involved with this process:

> The individual can, if he or she wishes, contact the third-party collator or adviser for a review. And, as we do in one-on-one chair-director interviews, the director might bring up a matter that comes from the survey. . . . most people are pretty open about their shortcomings if it comes from a broad base of observations. (Director communication to the author, 2008)

This company's proxy circular indicates that the chair meets with each director to discuss his or her peer assessment.

The author recently completed a research project for a government that was interested in how to improve director peer review. The chairs of several boards interviewed indicated that the shortcoming in the peer review, when it is conducted by a third party, is that the feedback on each director is not shared with or seen by the chair of the board for developmental purposes, as part of the one-on-one debriefing after the peer survey between the chair and the director.

To remedy this identified defect in a "third party only" model of director peer review, it appears that there needs to be a viewing and follow-up by the individual director and the chair of the board in order to integrate the survey data into development of that director. One would also require, of course, a skilled expert third party with governance experience in providing constructive feedback.

Model Three: Hybrid of Third-Party Survey Informing the Chair-Director Interview

The third model is a hybrid involving a third-party survey assessment informing one-on-one interviews between the governance committee chair and directors. One leading governed company uses this model, as follows:

1. The third-party adviser's report, which is based on the questionnaire exploring director views on performance components (including peer assessment), is provided to the governance committee and board chairs;
2. After receiving and reviewing the third-party report and other inputs, the governance committee chair has formal, confidential interviews with each director regarding, among other matters, individual director performance; and
3. The discussion includes, as appropriate, matters raised in the third-party report or results of other questionnaires or interviews.

As the company itself explains:

> Directors complete a detailed questionnaire that explores their views on each of the six performance components [including peer assessments]. . . . The responses are received confidentially, tabulated and analyzed by our independent third-party consultant, Dr. Richard Leblanc, who also provides expert advice. Confidentiality encourages candid and constructive commentary. Dr. Leblanc provides an executive summary to the Governance Committee Chair and the Board Chair, together with a tabulation of the quantitative scores and all qualitative commentary, without individual directors being identified. . . . After receiving and reviewing Dr. Leblanc's report . . . the Governance Committee Chair has a formal confidential interview with each director. . . . The discussion includes, as appropriate, matters indicated in the executive report from Dr. Leblanc or the results of management questionnaires and interviews. The Board Chair is provided a report on the director interviews and conducts a similar confidential interview with the Governance Committee Chair. . . . A full report on the evaluation is presented by the Board Chair and the Governance Committee Chair to the Governance Committee and the board. . . .[19]

In this manner, one obtains the objective, independent expertise of a third party combined with the board chair leading the process and ensuring collegiality. Another leading governed company also uses this model (the survey report informing the chair one-on-one director interview), except that the "collating of results of the survey" is done by the corporate secretary and forwarded to the respective chair. For the most part, directors may be more candid in providing feedback to an independent, objective third party, rather than a member of management (or the board), particularly for individual director performance assessment, although this would also depend on the skills (and trust) of the member of management (or the board).

Conclusion

Boards are complex, closed social systems. The central argument this chapter has advanced is that certain structural-based factors may be necessary inputs to board effectiveness, but they are not sufficient. Attention to competencies and behaviors in recruiting and assessing directors, while more difficult to measure, are necessary in order to address and improve board effectiveness and firm performance. The challenge for the field, including scholars and practitioners, is to address these factors in a manner that is rigorous but at the same time highly pragmatic, using examples and learning from leading companies who have undergone governance improvements. This chapter has attempted to accomplish both of these goals.

Selected Excerpts of Effective Position Descriptions

Note that the following exhibits contain *excerpts* from position descriptions selected by the author to emphasize certain strengths. Because these partial transcripts of position descriptions are not reproduced in their entirety, they should be read as illustrations of what certain companies do well, in the context of the position description. They are not intended to serve as stand-alone, comprehensive position descriptions.

In Exhibit 6.1, CIBC effectively sets out the major areas for which its chair of the board is responsible, including board management, relations with the CEO, chair succession, strategy, shareholder communication, and reporting to the board.

In Exhibit 6.2, SNC-Lavalin's performance review standards for the chair of its board include a dual committee oversight process. This process consists of the following: one board committee,

Exhibit 6.1: Chair of the Board: Canadian Imperial Bank of Commerce (CIBC)

Accountabilities and Responsibilities

Board Management

(a) Board Meetings and the Annual General Meeting—The Chair shall chair Board meetings and all shareholder meetings. The Chair may vote at a Board meeting on any matter requiring a vote and shall provide a second vote in the case of a tie vote.

(b) Board Meetings—In consultation with the Chief Executive Officer of CIBC, the Chair shall set the agenda for each Board meeting. Each Board meeting agenda shall include reviews of appropriate operating and strategic issues, plus any other matters requiring approval of, or consideration by, the Board.

(c) Director Appointments and Nominations—The Chair shall provide input to the Corporate Governance Committee on its recommendation to the Board for approval of (i) candidates for nomination or appointment to the Board; and (ii) members and chairs of Board committees.

(d) Director Development—The Chair shall lead CIBC's director development program. At least annually, the Chair shall report to the Board on the status of CIBC's director development program and shall recommend changes he or she considers appropriate.

(e) Access to Management and Outside Advisors—On an ongoing basis, the Chair shall assess whether the Board and its committees have appropriate administrative support, access to senior management and access to outside advisors for the purposes of the Board fulfilling its mandate.

(f) Regulatory Matters—On an ongoing basis, the Chair shall create opportunity for the Board to review and provide feedback on CIBC's response to material regulatory recommendations and requests.

(g) Organization Structure—The Chair shall create opportunity for a Board Committee and/or the Board to review and, if advisable, approve any proposed changes to CIBC's organization structure which have a significant effect on a strategic business unit reporting lines or the independence of key control groups such as internal audit, finance, legal, compliance and risk management.

Advisory Matters Relating to the Chief Executive Officer

(a) Input on Chief Executive Officer Matters—The Chair shall provide input to the Corporate Governance Committee and the Management Resources and Compensation Committee of the Board on the appointment, removal, evaluation, compensation and succession, as applicable, of the Chief Executive Officer.

(b) Meeting with Chief Executive Officer—At least monthly, the Chair shall meet with the Chief Executive Officer to provide feedback and advice on behalf of the Board. On an ongoing basis, the Chair shall communicate with the Chief Executive Officer, on behalf of the Board regarding concerns or comments of the Board, shareholders or other stakeholders.

Succession—The Chair shall participate and provide input, as required, to the Corporate Governance Committee on succession plans for the Chair position.

(Continued)

Exhibit 6.1 : Chair of the Board: Canadian Imperial Bank of Commerce (CIBC) (Cont'd)

Strategic Planning—At least annually, the Chair shall ensure the Board reviews management's strategic planning initiatives, including the outcome of management's annual strategy meeting.

Communication with Shareholders—At least annually, in conjunction with the Board and the Chief Executive Officer, the Chair shall review CIBC's communication strategy and measures for receiving feedback from CIBC shareholders.

Reporting to the Board

The Chair shall report to the Board on material matters arising in undertaking his or her functions and responsibilities under this mandate and, if necessary, shall make recommendations to the Board for its approval on these matters.

Currency of the Chair's mandate

This mandate was last revised and approved by the Board on May 29, 2008.

Source: Adapted from Canadian Imperial Bank of Commerce, "Mandate of the Chair of the Board of Directors," May 29, 2008. Available at http://www.cibc.com/ca/inside-cibc/governance/board-of-directors/mandates.html (under "View Mandate").

the Human Resources Committee, meets to review the chair's performance. A second board committee, the Governance Committee, establishes rolling special performance objectives, in conjunction with the chair. The chair is responsible for these in addition to the chair's regular functions and responsibilities.

In Exhibit 6.3, Nexen effectively sets out the major areas for which the chair of its Health, Safety, Environment and Social

Exhibit 6.2: Chair of the Board: SNC-Lavalin Group Inc. (SNC-Lavalin)

3. Performance Review

(a) In December of each year, the Human Resources Committee shall meet to review the performance of the Chairman of the Board.

(b) The information which is used as a basis for discussion will include:

(i) the foregoing description of the basic functions and responsibilities of the Chairman of the Board;

(ii) the list of special objectives that were established at the last performance discussion; and

(iii) input gathered from the Board concerning the Chairman's performance and special objectives for the ensuing year.

(c) The other members of the Governance Committee shall meet with the Chairman of the Board and, with input and comments from the Chairman of the Board, establish a list of special objectives for the next twelve (12) months.

Source: Adapted from SNC-Lavalin Group Inc., "Chairman of the Board: Duties and Performance Review," Corporate Governance Handbook, December 9, 2005. Available at http://www.snclavalin.com/en/6_0/6_4_1.aspx.

Responsibility Committee (one of six Nexen board committees) is responsible, including the following roles and responsibilities: leadership; ethics; committee governance; committee meetings; committee reporting; committee-management relationships; evaluations; advisers; and resources, together with sub-components of

Exhibit 6.3: Chair of the Health, Safety, Environment and Social Responsibility Committee: Nexen Inc. (Nexen)

Committee Meetings

7. Ensure that the Committee meets at least five times annually and as many additional times as necessary to carry out its duties effectively.
8. With the Board Chair, other Committee members, the Secretary, members of Management and outside advisors, as appropriate, establish the agenda for each Committee meeting.
9. Chair all meetings of the Committee, including closed sessions and in camera sessions. If the Committee Chair is not present at a meeting, the Committee members present will choose an independent Committee member to chair the meeting.
10. Ensure sufficient time during Committee meetings to fully discuss agenda items.
11. Encourage Committee members to ask questions and express viewpoints during meetings.
12. Deal effectively with dissent and work constructively towards arriving at decisions and achieving consensus.
13. Ensure that the Committee meets in separate, non-management, closed sessions with internal personnel or outside advisors, as needed or appropriate.
14. Ensure that the Committee meets in separate, regularly scheduled, non-management, in camera sessions.

Committee Reporting

15. Following each meeting of the Committee, report to the Board on the activities, findings and any recommendations of the Committee.

16. Ensure that Committee materials are available to any Director on request.

Committee / Management Relationships

17. Take all reasonable steps to ensure that Committee members receive written information and are exposed to presentations from Management to fulfill the Committee Mandate.
18. Facilitate effective communication between Committee members and Management, both inside and outside of Committee meetings.
19. Have an effective working relationship with members of Management.

Evaluations

20. Ensure that an annual performance evaluation of the Committee and the Committee Chair is conducted, soliciting input from all Committee members, other Directors and appropriate members of Management.

Source: Adapted from Nexen Inc., "Health, Safety, Environment and Social Responsibility Committee Chair Position Description," December 3, 2007. Available at http://www.nexeninc.com/Governance/Committees/Safety_Env_And_Social_Responsibility.asp.

each. Note the attention paid to behavioral competencies within certain items and the scope of the committee's "360 degree" evaluation within the final item.

In Exhibit 6.4, Agrium effectively sets out the major areas for which each of its directors is responsible. Note the attention paid to director competencies and behaviors within items relating to communication (5), committee work and process (6), knowledge facets (7), and personal characteristics (8).

Exhibit 6.4: Individual Director: Agrium Inc. (Agrium)

5. Responsibilities of Effective Communication

Each Director has the responsibility to:

(a) participate fully and frankly in the deliberations and discussions of the Board;

(b) encourage free and open discussion of the Corporation's affairs by the Board;

(c) establish an effective, independent and respected presence and a collegial relationship with other Directors;

(d) focus inquiries on issues related to strategy, policy, and results;

(e) respect the Chief Executive Officer's role as the chief spokesperson for the Corporation and participate in external communications only at the request of, with the approval of, and in coordination with, the Chief Executive Officer; and

(f) indicate where appropriate, when conveying personal views in public, that his or her views are personal and do not represent the views of the Corporation or the Board.

6. Responsibilities of Committee Work

Each Director has the responsibility to:

(a) participate on Committees and become knowledgeable about the purpose and goals of each Committee; and

(b) understand the process of committee work, and the role of management and staff supporting the Committee.

7. Responsibilities of Knowledge Acquisition

Each Director has the responsibility to:

(a) become generally knowledgeable of the Corporation's business and its industry;

(b) participate in Director orientation and continuing education initiatives developed by the Corporation from time to time;

(c) maintain an understanding of the regulatory, legislative, business, social and political environments within which the Corporation operates; and

(d) become acquainted with the senior managers and high potential candidates of the Corporation, including by visiting them in their workplace.

8. Personal Characteristics

Each Director should possess the following personal characteristics and competencies in order to be considered for initial and continuing Board membership:

(a) demonstrated integrity and high ethical standards and an established reputation for honesty and ethical conduct;

(b) career experience, business knowledge, and sound judgment relevant to the Corporation's business purpose, financial responsibilities, and risk profile;

(c) understanding of fiduciary duty;

(d) communication, advocacy, and consensus-building skills;

(e) experience and abilities that complement those of other Board members so as to enhance the Board's effectiveness and performance; and

(f) willingness to devote sufficient time and energies to the work of the Board and its Committees.

Source: Adapted from Agrium Inc., "Individual Director Terms of Reference," February 22, 2006. Available at http://www.agrium.com/investor_information/5751.jsp.

7

Women Directors in the Boardroom: Adding Value, Making a Difference

Sarah Smith Orr

Despite the ever-expanding statistical evidence of the capabilities of women who are equipped with academic credentials and extraordinary performance results, their representation on corporate boards and in officer suites remains low. Their influence, needed skill sets, and buying power have been translated only marginally into the boardroom and executive suite. Yet nowhere is the influence of women as business leaders, investors, and consumers more crucial to decision making than in the corporate boardroom and officer ranks.

The position taken in this chapter will not be disguised. Tokenism is not representation. Representation is not a numbers game, although tracking through numbers is critical to measure progress. The representation of women needs to be more than tokenism or a numbers game. By creating a progressive and inclusive culture promoting gender diversity, businesses can enhance performance.

Numerous organizations are studying the impact of gender diversity in the boardroom, of which Catalyst, a New York City–based organization, is the most prominent. Catalyst has illustrated and affirmed many benefits of gender diversity through special studies and annual reports. This research-based organization has found a means to measure a correlation between gender diversity and the bottom line, with the conclusion that women board directors add value, and the bottom line is improved when their expertise and voice are part of corporate boardroom and executive suite decision making.

Consider PAX World's means of demonstrating the impact of women's intellectual capital. PAX World is a $2.5 billion socially responsible mutual fund that comprises eight funds, including the Women's Equity Fund, which outperformed the market, weathering an overall decline better than most in the first quarter of 2008 and performing better than the S&P 500 and the Russell 3000. Sujatha Avutu, the director of Women's Equity Fund, which has $34 million total net assets,[1] asserts that companies must use different tools at their disposal to outperform competitors; companies that include the perspectives and intellectual capital of women at all levels perform better.

Numbers reflected in bottom-line results speak to the success of a company. Numbers, in the case of leadership diversity, speak to the commitment of a corporation to involve the changing faces of leadership, in particular qualified women as leading executives and board directors.

This chapter will briefly examine the "numbers," statistically rooted progress reports covering gender diversification results for *Fortune* 500 boards and corporate board initiatives to evolve from the historical all-white male CEO profile. It will also include perspectives and experiences provided by a selected group of women board directors who make the case for diversity as a means of delivering better business results. Gender bias will be discussed, with recommended measures for eliminating invisible organizational barriers. Finally, boardroom practices designed to achieve gender diversity will be outlined along with best practices for the workplace, the corporate board, and the individual woman leader seeking her place in the executive suite and, in addition, a board director appointment.

Your Boardroom Needs Diversity: The Compelling Case

As external factors such as globalization and heightened competitiveness affect the marketplace, a diverse board signals independence, creative thought, opportunities for breakout strategies, and an open-mindedness on the part of the company.[2] A 2007 Catalyst study of corporate performance and women's representation on boards statistically shows an alignment between women board directors and strong performance at *Fortune* 500 companies. Catalyst presents the results in graph format, revealing the following:

- Return on equity—Companies with more women board directors outperform those with the least [women board directors] by 53 percent.
- Return on sales—Companies with more women board directors outperform those with the least [women board directors] by 42 percent.
- Return on invested capital—Companies with more women board directors outperform those with the least [women board directors] by 66 percent.[3]

The findings in the study were based on the four-year average (2001–2004) of these three financial measures. Seven different business sectors were included in the study, and although financial performance measures vary by industry, the evidence showed that the companies that dominate in all three business measures were ones with boards that included at least three women, with the exception of the "financial" and "materials" sectors.

To demonstrate to businesses that engaging talented women is to their benefit in a dollars and cents way, a cadre of researchers are assessing performance, relating companies' financial success to the diversity of their executives and boards of directors.

One study examined the effect that having women on top management teams of initial public offering (IPO) firms has on these organizations' short- and long-term financial performance.[4] The researchers used data from 534 IPO firms, with results suggesting that IPO firms are gaining in the number of women they employ in their top management teams. Further, women in top management appear to have "a positive association with the firms' short-term performance (Tobin's Q), 3-year stock price growth, and growth in earnings per share."[5] The researchers consider possible reasons for the positive effect of women on performance and conclude that women on the IPO top management teams are higher performers than men on the same teams, bringing better innovation and more effective problem solving. They speculate, on the basis of reports in popular press articles, that highly talented women are leaving larger firms due to glass-ceiling types of barriers, engaging their talents in smaller entrepreneurial firms and helping these organizations in both the short and long terms. The research indicates that the percentage of women in IPO top management teams is growing, resulting in more opportunities for skilled women executives and better bottom-line performance at IPOs.[6]

Two other studies looked specifically at board of director diversity and firm financial value. In both, the broader definition of board diversity was used: the percentage of women, African Americans, Asians, and Hispanics on the board of directors. One study found "statistically significant positive relationships between the presence of women or minorities on the board and firm value, as measured by Tobin's Q."[7] The other report focused on both return on investment and return on assets as the researchers investigated the relationship of executive board of director diversity and the two organizational performance measures.[8] The findings of both support the hypothesis that diversity within boards of directors appears to have an impact on overall organizational performance.

In summary, the inclusion of women in corporate executive suites and on boards of directors is associated with stronger firm value. What organization in today's economy *is not* affected, at varied levels, by its service to women as clients, as customers, and as employees? When women hold leadership positions, either in the executive suite or on boards of directors, organizations can have better relationships with these groups, plus gain perspectives and points of view on a wide variety of business issues critically important to product selection, advertising, public relations, and labor relations. Through gender diversity an organization's public image may be more favorable, in addition to the organization gaining important and desirable leadership styles. The referenced research demonstrates that diversity, specifically gender diversity, is linked to business success and positive bottom-line results when it becomes a primary business strategy and an organizational competency.

Women in the Boardroom Today: Progress Has Gone Flat

In an article published in *Directorship* titled "Women on Corporate Boards: The Challenge of Change," Sheila Wellington, then president of Catalyst, revealed the results of Catalyst's first annual census of women on corporate boards.[9] "There were 46 women on corporate boards of the top U.S. businesses in 1977. Now [1994] the number has reached 570 [9.6 percent], and for the first time in history, more than half of the *Fortune* 500 companies have at least one woman on their boards." The percentage of women directors (9.6 percent) was reported to be an increase of 11 percent over 1993.

Fast forward to the 2005 census, the tenth anniversary of Catalyst's profiling of women board directors of the *Fortune* 500.

The title of the report? "Ten Years Later: Limited Progress, Challenges Persist." Statistically, in 2005, women held 14.7 percent of board seats at *Fortune* 500 companies, an average increase of 0.5 percentage points per year. Catalyst reported that almost 90 percent of companies had at least one woman board director, up 0.2 percentage points from 2003, and further, that sixty-four companies had 25 percent or more women directors, compared with fifty-four companies in 2003.[10]

Ilene Lang, president of Catalyst, summarized the findings:

> "Progress has been steady despite a decrease in average board size. In addition, the number of individual women board directors has grown more quickly than the overall number of seats. Nevertheless, ten years ago, we would not have predicted that progress would come so slowly—at the current growth rate, parity [50% of director seats] won't come for 70 years."[11]

For the first time, the Catalyst 2007 Census gave an accounting of the women directors who served as chair of a top decision-making committee—audit, compensation, nominating, or governance—disclosing some positive news. Women gained board committee chairs in the *Fortune* 500, with women's share of governance and nominating committee chairs (15.1 percent) surpassing their 14.8 percent share of all board positions. Uncloaked via the report, however, is *that little or no change* occurred in the following areas:

- The percentage of women board directors—from 14.6 percent in 2006 to 14.8 percent in 2007.
- The number of companies with zero, one, two, and three or more women board directors.
- The percentage of women of color board directors.[12]

So why aren't there more women directors? Especially in the face of the evidence pointing to the added value of diversity, and in this instance, gender diversity? And when Catalyst data concur with all data sources—women constitute a growing percentage of the educated and managerial labor force?

> "Since 1991, women have earned the majority of college degrees. In 2004, women earned more than 57% of all four-year college degrees, 41% of master of business degrees, and 32% of M.B.A. degrees. Women currently account for 50.6% of the managerial and professional workforce."[13]

Denise Morrison, president, Campbell USA, Catalyst Advisory Board chair, and board director at the Goodyear Tire & Rubber Company, referenced recent (2008) Catalyst census results, revealing that at the middle- and entry-level management positions, 50 percent of the workforce is women, yet women make up only 15.4 percent of corporate executives, the pipeline to a board directorship. The issue is further complicated by the fact that only 2 percent of *Fortune* 500 CEOs are women—retired *Fortune* 500 CEOs being most in demand for corporate directorships.

The underrepresentation of women at the top is clear. Stereotyping of women as leaders is one contributing factor. Frequently women's styles of leadership are still identified as special or different from the presumed leadership norm—the norm that says men possess "inherent" leadership tendencies, that they are the presumptive leaders. Catalyst research finds that gender stereotypes are a consistent barrier to advancement. *The Double-Bind Dilemma for Women in Leadership* is the third in a series of Catalyst reports examining broad-based stereotypes about gender, which create challenging situations for women leaders in the workplace. Catalyst findings reveal that because of stereotypical biases, the skill sets and talents of women are often undervalued and underutilized, talents necessary for organizations to achieve the highest levels of success. In the report three specific "double-bind dilemmas" are examined and "unraveled":

- Extreme perceptions: women are too soft, too tough, and never just right.
- The high-competence threshold: women leaders face higher standards and lower rewards than men leaders.
- Competent but disliked: women leaders are perceived as competent or likable, but rarely both.[14]

The Catalyst analysis shows that when leadership behaviors are considered, stereotypes limit what are perceived as effective behaviors that are acceptable for *both* women and men.[15]

Stereotypes affect how leaders are liked and how they are evaluated for leadership effectiveness, according to findings in a recently published study by Johnson, Murphy, Zewdie, and Reichard. The study found no differences between males and females in "non-gendered prototype dimensions" such as intelligence, dedication, charisma, and attractiveness.[16]

Their findings did affirm, however, that gender-specific leadership prototypes are held and suggest that although unconscious, the prototypes can result in subtle discrimination against female leaders. Their research also suggests that male versus female leadership differences are not necessarily behavioral, but rather the interpretation of behaviors. If female leaders were seen as strong but lacking sensitivity, their behavior was evaluated less favorably. Looking through the perceptual lens of followers, women need to exhibit the masculine behavior of strength coupled with the feminine behavior, sensitivity, as they respond to the needs of followers to be evaluated as an effective leader. "Female leaders were seen as *ineffective* when they failed to exhibit either strength or sensitivity, whereas male leaders were *only seen as ineffective* when they failed to exhibit strength."[17]

In alignment with other research, the study revealed the effects of perceptual, stereotypical biases that are reflected in selection, promotion, and performance management functions:

> "[W]hen all else is equal, male leaders are generally perceived as more effective than female leaders. The fact that male leaders were generally perceived as more effective, coupled with the added demands that female leaders have in terms of their behavior, may explain why fewer women reach top leadership positions."[18]

The research findings above coincide with Catalyst findings that when women use the same behaviors men use to get the job done, they are often viewed with disfavor.[19] Hence, the double-bind dilemma becomes a reality. Catalyst refers to it as a "damned if you do, doomed if you don't" situation for women leaders.

Proposed strategies for organizations to address "double-bind dilemmas" that reflect a commitment from the organization to tackle stereotypes in their workplace include the following:

1. Provide women leaders and other employees tools and resources to increase awareness of women leaders' skills and of the effects of stereotypic perceptions.
2. Assess their work environment to identify in what ways they are at risk of stereotypic bias.
3. Create and implement innovative work practices that target stereotypic bias. These practices can be particularly effective when they address specific areas of risk.[20]

Only when an organization takes an inclusive, problem-solving, comprehensive approach are the efforts successful to maximize the value of a workforce for men and for women. Catalyst has annually presented an award to organizations that have taken innovative approaches with proven results to address the recruitment, development, and advancement of all managerial women, including women of color. The evaluation criteria utilized, as each submitted initiative is considered, includes business rationale, senior leadership support, accountability, communication, replicability, originality, and measurable results. Since its inception, sixty-six corporate initiatives have been honored.

Finding Women Directors: Where and Who

To paraphrase a character in an old advertisement for a fast-food restaurant ("Where's the beef?"), the inquiry most frequently voiced may sound like "Where're the qualified women?" In addition to addressing the "where" and "who" questions of finding women directors, this section will challenge prevailing biases that (1) candidates must have previous board experience, (2) each board candidate must be a sitting *Fortune* 1000 CEO or one who is retired, and (3) there are not a sufficient number of qualified women in general. In addition to refuting the aforementioned, options will be offered for nominating or governance committees seeking gender diversity in their board.

In a 2007 special supplement of *Corporate Board Member*, *What Directors Think*, 57 percent of board director respondents had no reservations about recruiting a new director without previous board experience. Two reasons were cited: board education and orientation are more readily available to support new directors, and there is a growing awareness that boards need new members who will bring fresh perspectives and needed skills to assist the board in overseeing the company.[21] This area of gender bias appears to be changing in a positive direction.

Historically and to a large extent presently, boards seek retired executives as candidates. Korn/Ferry International's 33rd Annual Board of Directors study included a table identifying composition characteristics for corporate boards. The table showed that the percentage of retired executives (from other companies) in board seats increased from 75 percent in 1995 to 95 percent in 2006.[22] Given the profile of retired executives typically selected (*Fortune* 1000 CEOs), it is not as likely that this category of representation will include many women.

Kramer, Konrad, and Erkut challenge the premise that being a CEO, and in particular a *Fortune* 1000 CEO, is crucial for all board members. "In fact," the authors purport, "many white men on these boards don't meet that qualification." Pressing further, the authors maintain that boards need to look further into senior-management ranks to identify women candidates, successful business women in corporate America who have eminent qualifications to contribute to corporate boards. They also suggest that successful women entrepreneurs, lawyers, nonprofit executives, consultants, and academics be considered as well.[23]

Betsy Berkhemer-Credaire, president, Berkhemer Clayton, Inc., a Retained Executive Search firm based in Los Angeles, maintains that a sufficiently large pool of qualified board candidates does exist, in particular successful women COOs and CFOs. She argues that if a company's values include a strong commitment to diversity as a key business strategy, the nominating committee will no longer rely on its own limited networks, requiring that a search firm dig deeper—"the talent is there." Nominating committee members should consider the large nonprofit boards they and their CEO serve on, where fellow women board members (with corporate experience) have managed large budgets, and demonstrated strategic leadership and collegial spirit. Berkhemer-Credaire has found many qualified women with the talent and experience, especially in very large corporations, who are just a level or two under the CEO.

Denise Morrison reinforced the reality that many highly educated top women are performing in corporations across America, stating that a great divide must be bridged between corporate nominating committees and the talent pool. Nominating committees, she emphasized, must elevate gender diversity as an integral part of their business strategy. Nominating committees must challenge a search firm to give them a diverse slate, and insist that the search present a database that includes female talent from the executive suite and top management levels.

Alison Winter, retired president and CEO of Personal Financial Services-Northeast, Northern Trust Corporation; co-founder of *WomenCorporateDirectors*, a national organization of women serving on corporate boards; and a Nordstrom, Inc. director, respects the preference of boards to have people actively engaged in business rather than retired. She firmly holds, however, that just as there are retired male CEOs, there are very successful women CEOs and top executives retired from a primary career who are excellent candidates—who possess the business acumen and the operational experience required for board service. Winter also suggests consideration be given to seasoned senior women entrepreneurs who understand the full operational scope of a business as well as have specialized talent and experience to bring to a board.

Considering the bigger picture, Winter's position is that the pool of talented women has not shrunk. She sees a rise of women in the executive suite and upper division ranks in corporate America.

An oft-stated reason for eliminating candidates coming from an academic, nonprofit, or entrepreneurial background is their lack of experience dealing with the financials of a publicly owned business versus a private organization. Although those experiences may be seen as specialized and out of the realm of corporate leadership, consider the number of women presidents at large universities, Harvard University for example—complex organizations with an equally complex financial mix. Although these are organizations that don't have stockholders, managing a broad range of academic issues along with an equally complex package of donors requires exceptional leadership skills, financial management expertise, and good judgment, skills transferable to the corporate boardroom.

Endowments and foundations, as a *New York Times* article describes, are places where the "glass ceiling is edging lower" with an increase of women chief investment officers who handle billions of dollars for big university endowments and private foundations. The article notes that of the fifty largest endowments and foundations, women now manage ten, overseeing a combined $60.6 billion.[24]

Conger, Lawler, and Finegold contend that diversity, in a best-case scenario, occurs as part of the selection process; a process of identifying the knowledge areas and stakeholder groups the board needs to represent, which will naturally lead to the appointment of a diverse board. "It is likely to be a logical consequence of creating a board that can truly understand the environment and the marketplace within which the corporation operates."[25] Disappointingly, instead of a logical consequence when the subject of gender diversity is raised, research and anecdotal evidence reveal it is frequently viewed as a "woman's question" rather than a business strategy to improve board performance and corporate results.

What Your Board Can Do—Best Practices for Boards

The strategies for the recruitment, development, and advancement of women in leadership identified in prior sections can and must be applied not only in the workplace as a whole but through a cultural assessment of the boardroom in order to create a highly effective and productive climate for decision making.

Best practices for business leaders to advance gender diversity in the boardroom are outlined in this section.

- *Make a leadership commitment* to create a work environment that values diversity (confronting and eliminating stereotypical bias). The role of the CEO in promoting women is key to creating a culture valuing the intellectual capital of women. Leadership must increase opportunities for women and minorities to perform as leaders in their rise to the executive suite, thereby contributing to an increased number of women and minority leaders in the pool of qualified leaders for the boardroom. "It does start with the tone at the top, with me saying over and over again that diversity is important in the organization because it does deliver better business results at the end of the day. Diverse leadership and diverse points of view contribute to better decision making," observes Maggie Wilderotter, chairman and CEO of Frontier Communications Corporation.

- *Commit to a selection process* that identifies areas of expertise, experience, and stakeholder representation (corporate environments and markets)—voices and perspectives the board needs represented in the boardroom. Diverse leadership and diverse points of view in the boardroom can deliver better business results, as described in the Catalyst Census Report.[26]
- *Frame diversity for your board* as a source for competitive advantage. When Wilderotter became president and CEO in 2004 of Citizens Communications Company (which through a July 2008 name change is now Frontier Communications Corporation), executive and board-level diversity was lacking. After studying the company's customer demographics, she initiated a companywide commitment to identify the talent mix, new and existing, to create a richer, more diverse decision-making environment. This was not an exercise in meeting quotas but about finding great people with diverse opinions, points of view, experience, and backgrounds.
- *Use the services of a search firm that understands and is committed to the value of "digging deep"* into senior management ranks within a company to recruit women leadership talent to the board. Confirm the search firm's level of commitment to diversity demonstrated through the composition of its own governing board. In an April 2008 issue of *Portfolio.com*, a featured article examined the "baffling" halt to progress for women's gains at work. During an interview with a search firm head, it was revealed that the

firm had only one woman on its nine-person board. When asked "why," the response was "that's a good question." This is not an acceptable response. One needs to ask what the recruiting firm's gender diversity priorities are and why one should do business with the firm when five of the ten top professional recruiters for the firm are female.[27]

- *Consider and search for successful women who are retired from a primary career* who have the business acumen and the operational experience required for board service. Include in that search seasoned senior entrepreneurs who understand the full operational scope of a business as well as have specialized talent and experience to bring to a board.
- *Talk to women about possible service.* Later in this chapter, one of the recommendations made to women who aspire to serve on corporate boards is to become involved and visible in professional and community organizations as a means of developing business expertise and leadership skills, as well as expanding their social and professional networks. A 2007 survey found that women executives are very active in a wide variety of governance and leadership positions, especially in the nonprofit sector. Members of large for-profit boards need only network with their counterparts on smaller corporate or nonprofit boards to find qualified women.[28]
- *Charge the nominating or governance committee with recruiting and seating three or more women*—the appointment of three or more women to the board can cause a fundamental change in the boardroom and enhance corporate governance. Including women directors on the nominating or governance committee will ensure a high-level focus on diversity. A key governance and gender diversity issue is the effect on board dynamics when there is only one woman on a board. Women directors are typically the only woman on a board once a board decides to embrace the value of gender diversity. "Serving in such small numbers [that is, solo] may reduce women's effectiveness as leaders, as they lack

the critical mass necessary to make change. Women serving 'solo' may also face increased scrutiny that can hinder their leadership opportunities and performance."[29]

Research has revealed that as the number of women serving on the board increased, so did the likelihood that the board had a woman chairing the audit, compensation, nominating, or governance committees.[30] Women directors interviewed through Catalyst research agreed with the critical mass theory not only "to make a statement" but also to reflect society. Further, from the perspective of employees and other stakeholders, "solo" women directors can be viewed as tokens or can represent a paucity of convincing evidence that the company is committed to diversity.

The critical mass theory was the focus of a study carried out by Kramer, Konrad, and Erkut through which these questions were explored: If it matters whether women serve on a board, does it make a difference how many women serve? and Is there a critical mass that can bring significant change to the boardroom and improve corporate governance?

> "Based upon interviews and discussions with 50 women directors, 12 CEOs, and seven corporate secretaries from *Fortune* 1000 companies, we show that a critical mass of three or more women can cause a fundamental change in the boardroom and enhance corporate governance."[31]

Kramer, Konrad, and Erkut found that women who have served alone experience "not being listened to, being excluded from socializing and even from decision-making discussions, being made to feel their views represent a 'woman's point of view,' and even being subject to inappropriate behaviors that indicate male directors notice their gender more than their individual contributions."[32]

An invitation to serve as the first woman on a board presents a dilemma for many women. Although there is a desire to serve, a potential board member must determine whether or not it will be a fit for her with the board and organization. Jeri Finard, former executive vice president and chief marketing officer of Kraft Foods, Inc., currently a director on the Frontier Communications Corporation board, posits that being solo doesn't represent a credible corporate commitment to diversity. Real diversity, according to Finard, is about encouraging everyone to bring their diverse skills to the table. "My team at Kraft heard me say, repeatedly, if there are ten people sitting around the table and they all think alike, nine are redundant; different viewpoints are needed in order to attack problems and address issues and opportunities creatively." When Finard made the decision to serve on the Frontier Communications Corporation board, it was due in large part to the CEO's expressed values and the values of the company that promoted diversity; she considered who else was on the board, and the board's commitment to diversity.

Kramer, Konrad, and Erkut list three ways having a critical mass of women directors is good for corporate governance:

- The content of boardroom discussion is more likely to include the perspectives of the multiple stakeholders who affect and are affected by company performance; not only shareholders, but also employees, customers, suppliers, and the community at large.
- Difficult issues and problems are considerably less likely to be ignored or brushed aside, which results in better decision making.
- The boardroom dynamic is more open and collaborative, which helps management hear the board's concerns and take them to heart without defensiveness.[33]

Maggie Wilderotter has served on sixteen boards of publicly held companies in her career, and during that period of time, she was the first woman on all but two boards. Although she may have been the only woman initially, there were at least two and sometimes three women on the board by the time she left a board (usually resulting from an acquisition, merger, and so on). She realized early in her board service that one of the ways she could affect change in board composition was to serve on the governance and nominating committee, where she could influence change and the identification of the skill sets and background for new directors.

Advice to Women—Building a Career Path to the Boardroom

The women featured in this article have taken full responsibility for their paths to leadership; nevertheless, they each have benefited from the support and professional respect provided by men and women with whom they interacted throughout their careers. Through the recounting of lessons learned from these women and sorting through the primary lessons revealed in cited research, the following have emerged as best practices for women aspiring to lead from the executive suite and ultimately the corporate boardroom.

- *Consider your career as a journey, more labyrinthine in nature.* Early in this chapter a reference was made to the "glass ceiling" metaphor introduced by the *Wall Street Journal* twenty-plus years ago. Frequently it is asserted that the glass ceiling metaphor is no longer as apt, because top positions of leadership are no longer the exclusive domain of men. Although that is true to some extent, the data and reports of Catalyst and other research organizations referenced thus far indicate that invisible barriers (glass ceiling, cultural walls, or gender bias) continue to be present and do impede the development and progress of women.

A convincing alternative argument uses the labyrinth as the metaphor most applicable in today's workplace environment.

The labyrinth provides an image reflective of the complexities of women's careers, with various twists and turns seen and unseen, not an invisible barrier (glass ceiling). Despite various impediments, many women are successful in confronting obstacles, overcoming challenges, discovering and navigating multiple paths to achieve their goals.

> "Contemporary women still face many challenges, especially in relation to male-dominated leadership roles. They must be brave, resourceful, creative, and smart to be successful, because they can face the most elaborate of labyrinths on their path to leadership. The women who find their way are pathbreakers of social change, and they usually have figured out how to negotiate the labyrinth more or less on their own."[34]

From Berkemer-Credaire's perspective, a woman's career is like working through a web of ten-year strategies in addition to a network of relationships. Aspiring women leaders, she contends, must be willing to start small, to move up (and possibly out), and through a personal strategic plan.

Morrison feels that the labyrinth concept fits and concedes that her journey has been labyrinthine in nature. Nevertheless, it has been one with clear goals and a strong sense of her credentials, along with a working plan, all of which enabled her to navigate twists and turns, overcoming unseen and palpable barriers.

- *Experience in line positions is key*. Line, not staff, positions provide necessary experience to move into top senior management positions. "Line experience is necessary for advancement into CEO and top leadership positions, and Catalyst's annual censuses show that women are historically underrepresented in these roles."[35] Although outstanding performance in specialty staff roles is important, P & L responsibilities are vital in order to get into the executive suite. Gaining experience in business operations is a must—the earlier in one's career, the better. The reality is that women who rise to senior positions from staff jobs are not as likely to be considered for a director's seat unless, for example, the woman has been head of human resources of a major corporation known for their talent pool, a point emphasized by Winter.

For example, Wilderotter's start was with a software company the founder of which was a strong supporter of women and their advancement. In her twelve years at the company, she held fourteen different jobs. A strategic opportunity for her was developing regional offices when she was twenty-two years old, providing her with basic general management expertise that she continues to utilize as the chairman and CEO of a *Fortune* 1000 company. Wilderotter strongly encourages women managers to take general management roles, which enable them to see and lead a business in a holistic way.

- *Be willing to move and create new product or business lines*. Twenty years after Morrison's career launch, when serving as the top sales manager for Nabisco, she became a general manager in charge of a new business venture launched through her creative initiative, the Down the Street division, now run by Kraft Foods. Later, when Morrison was recruited as Campbell Soups head of global sales, she would not sign on until the leadership assured her she would be in line to lead a large division.
- *Develop extensive and powerful networks*. Take a strategic approach to your career to build social capital. Bonding with people through networks both within and outside of your organization in the industry or in the community nonprofit sector can help in countless ways. Good relationships build opportunities to tap into new areas of knowledge and support, including the sponsorship of career advancement. Research has shown that the more contacts individuals establish at high organizational levels (both

within and outside of an organization) the more they gain from career sponsorship. Having multiple mentors reaps greater career benefits. Network benefits provide access to information, access to resources, and career sponsorship.[36]

Wilderotter became an expert at developing and growing a business network that resulted in her first corporate director appointment at the age of twenty-eight. When the post for president of Citizen's Communications opened, her network went into action. She knew five Citizens' directors with whom she had served on another company board ten years earlier; they were part of the corporate leader network she had developed over the years who, when considering a new CEO, saw Wilderotter as the lead candidate.

The women featured in this chapter emphasize the importance of being involved in networks outside organizational walls. Morrison has held various leadership roles in industry activities, nonprofit boards, and corporate boards, building her social capital and enabling career opportunities. Winter was elected the first woman chair of the Los Angeles Chamber of Commerce, her ascent to which resulted from her active involvement, leadership, and skilled performance in the business community outside her organizational employer, knowing that the relationships developed would not only help build business but expand her professional network.

- *Take a strategic approach to career planning.* Begin early in your career, strategically defining career intentions and values, setting your sights on the executive suite and a future board directorship as a means of developing your potential and experience base.

For example, Morrison's fundamental career strategy was grounded in sales, where she began her career soon after her college graduation. An additional strategy was her decision to remain in the consumer products industry, developing her sales expertise and management prowess while preferring the expanse and opportunity of larger corporations. Her commitment to support family—her husband's interests and children's needs—was a strategic lens through which she discerned the paths to take.

How did those strategies play out for her? Early on, when her husband's New York City job required a move, she asked her employer for a transfer; when she was told she'd have to take a lower-level position even though she was leading her division's top sales team, she secured a higher-level position at another company, saying good-bye to the organization unwilling to offer her a viable option to remain. When her husband wanted to run a fruit farm in Bakersfield, California, Morrison, who was then with Nestlé, told her boss she wanted to stay with the company, but she needed to move to Bakersfield. So with her boss's support, she made a Bakersfield ice cream plant Nestlé's national sales office for frozen and chilled foods. Later, when she joined Nabisco, her husband followed her and became the primary family link with their children's school and after-school activities.

- *Take control of your career.* All agreed that the primary responsibility for moving on a career path lies with the individual—staying focused on life and career priorities.

Early in Morrison's journey, for example, she learned to manage her career maintaining a chart of her career moves, recording her tenure in each job, financial budget and performance responsibilities, number of people supervised, and her accomplishments. Finard feels that just as a marathon runner has to be in charge of her run, pacing herself, striving for personal best, so must each individual be in charge of her own career, collecting as many skills and successes as she can on the way to the executive suite.

Finard saw her professional work, her family, and her husband's career as a cohesive whole. She kept in perspective that her career was about her agenda, not someone else's agenda. Relocation was not an option in Finard's life plan, for example, a commitment for which she did not deviate, although some pressured her to take another path. Through it all she had many growth opportunities that took her from an entry marketing position at General Foods (acquired later by Kraft) to the executive vice president position at Kraft Foods and then to a board seat at Frontier Communications Corporation.

Arrival in the Boardroom—Performance in the Director's Role

Scandals and subsequent reforms in the past few years have driven corporate boards' heightened commitment to be above reproach in their ethical behavior and to achieve boardroom independence. They employ the tools to ensure accountability, good decision making, and effective oversight. Greater emphasis is being placed on board education, on equipping board members with the knowledge they need to fulfill their fiduciary responsibilities and overall corporate governance. Looking to the women leaders interviewed, a few suggestions can be found for women board directors to consider as they fulfill their roles.

- *Deliver leadership in the boardroom.* The myth that women aren't competent enough still exists, so a consistent high level of competence is necessary to dispel that myth and achieve equality. Women bring a new perspective that enhances the discussion and decision-making quality of the boardroom as they represent different insights, strategic ideas, and past business experiences, which add value to a company. Exceptional performance, advises Wilderotter, is a given; if serving as the first woman director on a board, exceptional performance is mandatory to give credence and access to more women directors to follow.
- *Educate yourself in all aspects of the business: market position, success record, trends, critical strategic issues, and competencies (existing and those to develop). Actively participate.* Women who are

selected for board service have demonstrated substantial education and tenure in their occupations. Prepare to use the capabilities you bring in conjunction with what you've learned about the organization. Give your opinion, speak, be heard, be bold—don't get put into a box as a token board member. According to Finard, women worry that what they say must be brilliant, but from her perspective it is more important to make sure they are in the decision-making mix demonstrating their expertise and the validity of their contributions.

- *Understand the culture of the board—in other words, how the board operates*. Different boards are at different points in the continuum of being fully engaged, disengaged, or overly engaged. You need to understand a board's social culture, how much you need to join in and how much you need to push back against, and transform.[37] Be self-confident, but be sensitive to stereotypical perceptions that may impede your ability to perform effectively or adapt appropriately. Research shows effective board membership involves the ability to engage in a process of building shared values and attitudes, a process that significantly reduces uncertainty about women's role and contributions to a board. Being alert to communication styles and effective means of interaction and deriving self-esteem from group membership will eliminate many potential barriers for women serving on boards.[38]
- *Be an advocate for other women qualified for board directorships*. Build your network to include other women executives to support them in their careers. Wilderotter moves beyond organizational walls helping women leaders get board appointments, exemplifying a role she feels all women CEOs should fill. Morrison mentors women leaders, supporting their advancement in professional positions and to board director seats.

Conclusion

In *Making Boards Work*, authors David Leighton and Donald Thain profile the current state of corporate boardrooms with a focus on the "glacial" pace of change in the number of women boards of directors. They quote from a 1995 article from the Spring 1995 issue of *Directors & Boards*, written by John H. Bryan, then chairman and CEO of Sara Lee Corporation:

> "It is clear to me that a group of generally older, white male executives of the same nationality—men who have usually reached the same status in various companies—represents a dangerously narrow profile of exposure for a board in a world changing as rapidly and dramatically as ours is today. It is a world demanding aggressively creative approaches to business, and it is through diversity that much of that creativity can be found. Diversity is a major source, if not an imperative, for creativity in the future."[39]

Sara Lee walks their talk. Bryan's quote was first published thirteen years ago. In the 2007 Catalyst census,[40] Sara Lee topped the list, with women directors representing 45.5 percent of their board. The words and actions of leaders such as Bryan need to echo across Corporate America to prompt new initiatives to ensure gender parity according to the demographics of the customer, investor and stockholder profile, and the composition of the workforce. CEOs need to take responsibility to address diversity for the boards on which they serve—to call the question and lead change. Women do need to use their investor and consumer clout through their various networks to influence change.

In an early segment of this chapter, Catalyst CEO Ilene Lang was quoted as she described the slow incremental progress made in women's representation on *Fortune* 500 corporate boards since Catalyst's annual census began in late 1993. Reflecting on the growth rate of women's representation up to 2005, she revealed that if history were our guide, parity [50 percent of director seats] wouldn't come for seventy years. Unfortunately, 2005 was a benchmark year but not a positive one. Since that report year, growth has essentially flattened or stalled in the representation of women on *Fortune* 500 boards.[41]

A *New York Times* article described women's gains in board appointments in Europe.[42] Norway, "a homeland of strong females," led in gains. Norway recently met a goal set through national legislation adopted in 2003, requiring companies to fill 40 percent of publicly held corporate board seats with women by 2008.

The reality of such action in the United States seems far more remote, as it requires a critical mass of leaders in alignment with the goal of parity for women. Further, legislation should not be the driver for gender equity. Leadership for change must emerge from corporate boardrooms.

The roadmap has been created. Corporate and boardroom best practices for diversity exist and have been described herein. The talent pool continues to expand and is ready to perform. The case for women adding value to the boardroom and improving the bottom line has been made. The evidence is compelling. What is needed is a deeply rooted commitment along with dedicated action to achieve gender parity in Corporate America for its executive and boardroom leadership.

We are a nation founded on values of freedom, equality, and opportunity for all. It shouldn't require legislative action to change the profile of the corporate boardroom and executive suite. Look to and listen to customers, stockholders, and workplace constituents. As a governing board it's time to look like them—it's time to achieve gender diversity across Corporate America.

Distinguished Contributors

The first three distinguished women contributors participated in the 18th Annual Kravis-de Roulet Conference held in late January, 2008, during which various issues and questions related to leadership in the corporate boardroom were examined. The final two distinguished women contributors were selected on the basis of their expertise and their work with women board directors. All contributed valued perspectives augmenting the author's work and research results. The author extends gratitude for their time and contributions.

Jeri B. Finard, director, Frontier Communications Corporation. Formerly executive vice president and chief marketing officer of Kraft Foods, Inc. Other positions with Kraft Foods, Inc. included executive vice president, global category development and group vice president and president, U.S. beverages sector. She was responsible for managing some of Kraft's most successful and fastest-growing businesses, including Jell-O gelatin, Altoids mints, Toblerone chocolate, and Balance energy bars. She joined General Foods Corporation in 1986, which later merged with Kraft. While at General Foods, she was responsible for strategy and new product development for the Maxwell House Coffee Division and for Post Cereals.

Denise Morrison, senior vice president and president, North America Soup, Sauces and Beverages, where she is responsible for leading the Campbell USA, North America Foodservice & StockPot, and Campbell Canada businesses. Prior to this position, she was president, Campbell USA (2005) and president-global sales and chief customer officer (2003). Previously she served as executive vice president and general manager of Kraft Foods' Snacks and Confections divisions. Prior to moving to Kraft, she worked for Nabisco Inc., where she served as senior vice president. She began her career in sales at Procter & Gamble, later joining Pepsi-Cola, and then went to Nestlé, Inc. prior to going to Nabisco. She serves on various boards, including that of The Goodyear Tire & Rubber Company, and is a former director of Ballard Power Systems, Inc. She is actively involved in various nonprofit boards and professional organizations. Morrison has been named one of *Wall Street Journal*'s fifty Women to Watch, 2007.[43]

Maggie Wilderotter, chairman and chief executive officer, Frontier Communications Corporation. Prior to joining Frontier Communications (formerly Citizens Communications), she was senior vice president of Worldwide Public Sector at Microsoft; president and chief executive officer of Wink Communications, Inc.; executive vice president of National Operations for AT&T Wireless Services, Inc.; and chief executive officer of AT&T's Aviation Communications Division. She also served as senior vice president of McCaw Cellular Communications, Inc. She currently serves on the boards of Yahoo! Inc., Xerox Corporation, and Tribune Company. She also serves on the boards of a number of nonprofit organizations. Her corporate board service began when she was twenty-eight, and at this point in her career she has served on sixteen publicly held company boards.

Betsy Berkhemer-Credaire, president of Berkhemer Clayton, Inc., retained executive search, leads the corporate communications and board development specialty practices. Betsy has three decades of management experience as a woman business owner. Prior to establishing Berkhemer Clayton, she launched and built one of the largest independent public relations agencies in Los Angeles, Berkhemer & Kline, which was acquired by national PR firm Golin/Harris. Active in community service, she serves on the boards of the Los Angeles Chamber of Commerce and the Southern California Leadership Network. She is the statewide president of the National Association of Women Business Owners—California. Betsy serves on the California Utilities Diversity Council, a consortium of public utility companies seeking to enhance diversity in their business operations. She cochairs the Southern California Chapter of *WomenCorporateDirectors*, a national organization of women serving on corporate boards. She is a member of numerous other organizations based in the Los Angeles area.

Alison Winter, president and chief executive officer (ret.), Personal Financial Services-Northeast, Northern Trust Corporation. Alison recently retired from Northern Trust Corporation, completing a highly successful thirty-five-year career. When she retired, Winter was serving as the founding president and CEO of Personal Financial Services-Northeast, charged with establishing the Northern Trust presence in that highly attractive market, based in New York. She opened four offices during that time, bringing to twenty the new markets she entered to expand the Northern Trust franchise as a leader in managing the wealth of the affluent. Alison joined The Northern Trust Company in 1971, starting as a portfolio manager; she went on to serve as department head of the Investment Management Group in 1982; as senior vice president and head of marketing and sales for personal financial services in Illinois in 1986; and as founding president and CEO of Northern Trust of California in 1987. Over the ensuing eleven years, she and her team opened eleven offices in California, becoming one of the largest trust companies in that state. Currently she serves as a director of Nordstrom, Inc.; is co-founder of *WomenCorporateDirectors*, an international organization of women serving on corporate boards; is a member of the National Association of Corporate Directors; is on the board of Chief Executives' Organization; and is a member of World Presidents' Organization.

8

Your Board's Crucial Role in Aligning CEO Pay and Performance

Roger W. Raber

Dr. Alexandra R. Lajoux, NACD Chief Knowledge Officer, contributed key research to this chapter.

During the meltdown of the subprime mortgage market in early 2008, the American public was treated to a "morality play" of lasting significance. In March 2008, members of the House Oversight and Government Reform committee grilled the CEOs and compensation committee chairs of several leading financial institutions that had succumbed to the meltdown in the subprime mortgage crisis. The congressional representatives were asking, each in his or her own way, "How could you award or accept such high pay when the companies have done so poorly? What went wrong?"

In response, some of the CEOs and compensation committee chairs explained that much of the compensation was in the form of deferred compensation, severance compensation, and retirement pay that was not supposed to be correlated with company performance. This part of the pay, they said, was owed to the CEOs by reason and law. The combination of rising stock values and these contractually owed incentives created the perception of "awarding failure," but they did not in fact prove a fundamental disconnection between pay and performance per se.

For example, Angelo Mozilo, former CEO of Countrywide Mortgage, now merged with Bank of America, called reports about his nine-figure severance pay ($115 million) grossly exaggerated. The Countrywide founder and forty-year veteran pointed out that he never even took his golden parachute, turning down $37.5 million in potential severance pay. As for his other post-departure compensation, he explained that the Countrywide stock price had gone up more than 23,000 percent during his tenure. Because a substantial percentage of his pay was awarded in the form of stock, and because he had deferred payment of much of his pay until after retirement, he did receive what seemed like a windfall, but the pay was earned over time. Also, his four decades of service had caused him to accrue retirement benefits. The combined total, being in the scores of millions, only seemed excessive; in fact it was fair.

But the question still remains, was Mr. Mozilo's pay, deferred or not, too high to begin with?

Morality plays are dramas that elucidate basic articles of belief about what is right and wrong. So in this story, who is right? Those who attack high executive pay or those who defend it? In fact, neither group has true reason on its side. The first group sees the forest, but not the trees. The second group sees the trees, but fails to peer into the forest. One must see both, and that is the board's role. That is, the board bears unique responsibility for understanding both the mechanics of a compensation package and its meaning to the organization and to society.

The answers given by the CEOs and board members at the Congressional hearings made good sense. The problem is that they were pointing at details, and most members of Congress, most reporters in the media, and most non-executive employees care more about the big picture. Although in a court of law, specific fact patterns and details are of immense importance, in the court of public opinion they matter far less.

True enough, the details (trees) do show that the official "performance-based pay" CEOs received was in fact correlated with performance as defined in the performance-based pay plans—generally based on the price of company shares. But when you add it all up and look at the big picture (the forest), something very big is very wrong. Given the fundamental structure of CEO pay today, large-company CEOs such as Mr. Mozilo and hundreds of others can accumulate generous pay during times of rising stock prices and then, because of deferment or retirement, may not always share in the general pain when stock prices then go down. What can boards do to rectify this situation?

The Board's Vital Perspective—and Five Principles

It's been said that the board's most important role is to find and keep a good CEO. Compensation plays an essential role here, and board perspective is urgently required.

The current reality is that CEO pay is high and rising. Equilar, a major compensation consulting firm, publishes average total pay for S&P 500 CEOs every year. Although there have been some dips annually, the general trend has been upward. The 2008 study reported $8.83 million in average annual pay, compared to $7.06 million in 2003.[1]

In the very largest firms, pay can run into eight figures. Clearly, compensation committees of very large companies are faced with major financial decisions. The reported signing bonus of John A. Thain, who took the top office at Merrill Lynch this year, was valued at almost $83.8 million, the highest compensation reported so far in 2008. The real cash involved was the promised annual salary of $750,000, as well as a cash bonus of $15 million for fiscal 2007, to make up for the bonus he forfeited when leaving the New York Stock Exchange (NYSE). The rest of the pay was awarded in the form of options subject to market risk. In compensation for the forfeiture of unvested equity awards from the NYSE, he received Merrill Lynch stock options with a Black Scholes value and vesting, expiration, and other terms identical to the forfeited options, as well as Merrill restricted stock units with the same value and vesting terms as the NYSE restricted stock units he forfeited. The pay also included sign-on equity awards made up of 500,000 restricted stock units and 1.8 million Merrill stock options. Two-thirds of the stock options are subject to performance vesting requirements. The agreement did not provide for any guaranteed bonus payments for future years. Any future bonus compensation will be determined annually by Merrill Lynch's management development and compensation committee.

To maintain perspective on compensation in such an environment, boards can follow a few important guidelines. The following five principles come from the *Report of the NACD Blue Ribbon Commission on Executive Compensation*, published five years ago and still full of timely guidance.[2] The principles are (1) independence among the directorship, (2) fair internal and external standards for pay decisions, (3) alignment to value-producing performance, (4) an emphasis on long-term value for shareholders, by achieving key metrics, and (5) full and clear disclosure of compensation arrangements.

Principle 1: Independence

One of the most overused words in governance has to be *independence*. Yet the "I" word needs emphasis and attention anyway, because it is actually a very complex issue. Yes, it is obvious that family ties and pay can compromise independence, but what about subtler forces of compromise? Boards and compensation committees must strive for independence in *all facets* of their operations.

For example, board and committee members should resist the tendency to "go along" for the sake of harmony or to simply rely on the precedents set by others. An effective group dynamic encourages members to speak their minds, examine assumptions, thoroughly discuss the issues, and arrive at appropriate decisions. To have such an environment, boards need to make a conscious effort to achieve diversity in as many ways as are possible.

Having candidates with skills that match the strategy is only the beginning. Boards need to ask themselves, Are we "all alike" in any obvious way? Diversity should not just end with profession, it should extend to other categories such as gender, race, and personality type—perhaps even educational background. There is no rule that says everyone in the boardroom needs to have an Ivy League education. Some boards just may need some street smarts! If boards are going to break the spell of overcompensation, they must try some new solutions.

Meanwhile, the standard means to achieving independence still hold. The New York Stock Exchange (NYSE) and NASDAQ governance listing standards say, respectively, that an independent director has no material relationship with the company (NYSE) or has no relationship that would interfere with independent judgment in carrying out the responsibilities of a director (NASDAQ).

The NYSE rules require that every listed company have independent committees for oversight of audit, compensation, and director nomination, and that these committees be composed entirely of independent directors. Companies may allocate the functions of compensation, nominating, and corporate governance committees to committees of their own denomination, provided that the committees are composed entirely of independent directors. NASDAQ rules also require independent oversight of audit, compensation, and nominating functions. Compensation in NASDAQ-listed companies must be overseen by an entirely independent committee or by a majority of independent directors, with some exceptions. On both the NYSE and NASDAQ, the CEO may not be present during compensation committee voting or deliberations on the CEO's compensation.

The governance and nominating committee and the board should take account of personal friendships, prior business relationships, and ties created by philanthropic activities between the CEO and the prospective committee members. It may be tempting to make exceptions, but these connections really can interfere with objectivity and resolve in evaluating CEO performance and setting executive pay.

Independence increases the likelihood that committee members will be objective in their consideration of compensation matters. But independence alone is not enough; compensation committee members also need diligence, understanding, and resolve to act on convictions. They should ensure that committee membership, processes, and approach are entirely independent from the CEO and management. Also, they should strive to make sure that the dynamics of groupthink do not compromise the independence of mind of each individual director.

A truly independent compensation committee will be better prepared to engage in negotiations, an increasingly critical part of recruitment process. Through questioning and an informed exchange of ideas, an independent committee will be able to engage in objective negotiations, while also showing confidence in the organization's leadership.

Committees can work more effectively with the help of qualified professionals who are independent of management. The compensation committee should consider engaging an independent compensation consultant to assist in the development of both its compensation philosophy and specific pay packages. The consultant should be hired by and report directly to the committee, and should not be retained by the company in any other capacity. To be effective, the consultant should be afforded full access to management, in-house counsel, the human resources staff, and any compensation consultant hired by management. To avoid "dueling consultants," any consultant hired by management should not be engaged in assignments involving CEO or senior executive pay.

Principle 2: Fairness

Fairness is not readily defined or measured. Different companies may define fair pay in different ways. Nonetheless, each compensation committee should try to create pay packages that will pass the test of scrutiny for fairness both internally and externally.

Pay systems must look and actually *be* fair both internally and externally. At DuPont, the compensation committee has made a concerted effort to align CEO and senior management pay, and to avoid a large gap between senior management and worker pay.

DuPont's 2004 proxy statement explained how the company addresses the pay gap as follows. "Over the past decade, the position of DuPont's Executive Vice President has been used as a benchmark tie to the peer group, in addition to the CEO. Total annual cash compensation for the CEO is currently targeted at twice that of the Executive Vice President." The company explained that it pursued this practice to address "concerns over the upward spiral of CEO pay and the widening divergence in CEO compensation compared to the average employee." At DuPont, total annual compensation for the CEO is approximately double that of the EVP.[3]

Internally, all members of an organization should benefit when the company does well and share in sacrifices when necessary. A fair compensation policy also means that there will not be extremely wide gaps in pay at different levels (for example, between CEOs and senior managers, or executives and other employees) unless such gaps are justified and explained. The average CEO of a *Fortune* 500 U.S. public company made $10.8 million in 2007, or 364 times that of U.S. full-time and part-time workers, who made an average of $29,544, according to a joint analysis from the Institute for Policy Studies, a liberal think tank, and United for a Fair Economy, a labor group.[4] This average multiple is actually lower than a few years ago, when it surpassed 500, but it is still well above the famed rule of thumb of 20 widely attributed to John Pierpont Morgan a century ago. Modern-day legislative efforts to mandate a ratio have been in the two-digit realm. (Rep. Barbara Lee, D-CA, has proposed a cap on deductions for any compensation paid at greater than twenty-five times the earnings of a company's lowest-paid workers.)

The retail industry has seen two good examples of internal fairness at work. Whole Foods Market CEO John Mackey's pay is limited to no more than fourteen times the pay of the company's average employee. To help reduce pay disparity at Best Buy, CEO Brad Anderson gave two hundred thousand stock options to outstanding non-executive employees in 2003.

Externally, executive pay should be judged according to an appropriate peer group, chosen by the compensation committee. This is in fact a requirement of the Securities and Exchange Commission, following new disclosure rules passed in 2006. But in 2007, the SEC sent out letters to companies asking for more data. In some letters, the SEC asked the companies to identify the names of the peer companies selected. In other letters, the SEC asked the companies to disclose exactly how each element of compensation (for example, base salary, bonus, and so on) related to peer group compensation for that same element.

The NACD Blue Ribbon Commission not only flagged the peer group issue but also raised a related question about the relevant "compensation marketplace." Is it a myth? Sometimes it is. Compensation committees and boards sometimes have failed to question market analyses presented to them, or to explore alternative models.

Take, for example, the situation of a board wanting to retain the CEO of an oil or automobile company who has been there for twenty years. Is it really meaningful to say there is a "market value" for CEOs in a highly concentrated industry, in which a movement of a CEO from one company to a competitor is highly unlikely? Market values should reflect the specific financial circumstances and business strategies of a given company. All this requires seasoned perspective.

The compensation committee should also strive to understand the survey methodology used by their consultant. When judging peer companies for appropriateness, committees should use multiple criteria (such as number of employees, market capitalization, revenues), not just one of those elements. World at Work has posted a useful set of compensation-related questions on its Website, www.worldatwork.org. They include

- What are market pay practices?
- How reliable and accurate are compensation market data for programs of this type?
- Do you need to develop alternative sources of data?
- To what extent do you want to match or differ from market pay practices?
- Do you need to pay a premium for a particular skill set or expertise?
- If new or unusual, will it help create a competitive advantage for your company in attracting or retaining human capital?

Principle 3: Link to Performance

In selecting performance measures, committees should link pay to desired outcomes that the individual can affect through value-producing performance, rather than to stock price or reported profits alone. If pay is linked only to stock price or reported profits, this can incentivize manipulation of financial results, which was one of the problems that contributed to the downfall of Enron.

As a good example of a general compensation philosophy, consider this one from Comarco, Inc.

> Our executive compensation philosophy is to provide our executives with appropriate and competitive individual pay opportunities with actual pay outcomes heavily influenced by the attainment of corporate and individual performance objectives. The objectives of our compensation program are to attract, retain, focus and reward top quality executives to achieve performance

> aligned with our business goals and the creation of shareholder value.[5]

Companies have used metrics for years, but now they are a matter of public record. Today, each public company must disclose the criteria for evaluation of the performance of the five most highly compensated managers, unless the disclosure would release confidential information to competitors. Some companies do keep details to themselves, saying that disclosure would indeed reveal confidential competitive information, but these are becoming the exception rather than the rule. In a study of 2007 proxy filings, Watson Wyatt found that more than two-thirds (68 percent) of the seventy-five large, publicly traded companies studied disclosed the actual goals on which they based rewards under their 2007 annual incentive plans, up from 54 percent that disclosed goals last year. In addition, 57 percent included the goals for long-term incentive plans, compared with 45 percent in 2006. Of those that did not disclose actual goals, only 19 percent stated affirmatively that disclosing them would result in competitive harm.[6]

This reasonably detailed disclosure from Comarco, Inc. is illustrative of the trend in disclosure:

> The Compensation Committee benchmarks total compensation, as well as annual cash and long-term performance compensation, to that of executive officers performing similar job functions at comparable companies, adjusted to reflect various factors including relative company size, complexity of operations, performance and geographic location. Because of the diverse nature of the Company's business units, it is difficult to establish a peer group based on industry sectors, so other than a broad grouping in the technology area, the Compensation Committee uses other factors, principally company size and geographic location to establish a comparable

> group of companies for comparison. However, the Company's policy is to endeavor to attract and retain the best talent among its senior management team. Therefore, the Compensation Committee may approve total compensation packages for senior management that vary from the benchmarks noted above based on several principal factors. Specifically, executives with relatively less overall experience, less demanding or complex operational responsibilities, less tenure with the Company and/or lower performance ratings over several years will have total compensation set at or below the median for our executive group.[7]

Or consider this example from Torchmark describing the company's compensation principles:

> The business philosophy of the Company focuses on maintenance and improvement of insurance operating margins and other operating margins through the efficient management of assets and control of costs. The Company's executive compensation program is based on principles which align compensation with this business philosophy, company values and management initiative. The program also takes into consideration competitive remuneration practices in the insurance and financial services sectors. Torchmark's executive compensation program seeks to attract and retain key executives necessary to the long-term success of the Company, to mesh compensation with both annual and long-term strategic plans and goals and to reward executives for their efforts in the continued growth and success of the Company.
>
> Annual goals for executive compensation, whether paid under the Section 162(m) Plan or outside that Plan,

> *focus on a number of factors, including growth in net operating income per share, pre-tax operating income and/or return on equity for holding company executives and on growth in insurance operating income, underwriting income and/or premium growth for the executives of the Company's insurance subsidiaries* [emphasis added].[8]

Some companies such as 3M wisely leave themselves flexibility for discretion in setting the criteria:

> In its discretion, the Committee or subcommittee will determine the performance criteria upon which the award will be based and the specific targets upon which the face value of the performance units will be based. The criteria *may* be based upon the *Company's return on capital employed, sales growth, or general performance comparisons with other peer companies*. However, the Committee or subcommittee will have no discretion to alter or amend the performance criteria or the specific targets of the awards under the Plan after they have been communicated to participants or after the commencement of the respective performance period, whichever shall occur first [emphasis added].[9]

Most companies will probably not disclose all their performance criteria for senior managers, because those criteria may be linked to aspects of strategy that the company does not wish to disclose to competitors. But in general, it is a good idea to give shareholders a sense of the kinds of criteria a company may (emphasizing *may*) set. A useful list from the Blue Ribbon Commission follows:

Financial Metrics

- Revenue growth
- Increase in cash flow

- Increased earnings
- Increase in earnings per share
- Higher margins
- Reduced debt

Nonfinancial Metrics

- Improved customer satisfaction
- Higher market share
- Improved product quality
- Improved ethics and compliance
- Greater workforce diversity
- Strong succession planning
- Prepared crisis management plans
- Strong team building
- Positive community relations[10]

Disclosure of possible performance metrics will do much to correct the impression that compensation committees are not striving to link pay to performance. This is the common perception. For example, NACD's recent *2007 Public Company Governance Survey* showed that 59 percent of the participants believe that when CEO compensation is out of sync with performance, the fault lies in the board's lack of genuine performance metrics.[11] If boards are in fact aligning CEO pay to accepted metrics, they need to set the record straight.

It is also important to define compensation peers with care. Certainly a company should stay within its industry. Factors such as size and complexity must also be considered. A report by the Compensation Committee Leadership Network (CCLN), published in *Directors Monthly* (July 2007), emphasized the challenge of finding the right peer groups when setting compensation. The group—compensation committee chairs from some of the largest and most respected companies in North America—recommends making compensation decisions based on a variety of data and using benchmarking figures as a final check on internal calculations. The CCLN suggested three important steps:

- Using multiple peer groups
- Removing outliers
- Calibrating by performance, size, and complexity[12]

Although a part of executive pay should be based on nonfinancial metrics such as ethics, diversity achievements, leadership, and other important metrics, when it comes to the selection of a peer group, common sense would indicate that such metrics should not apply. A peer by definition is a company that is similar in ways that are easily verifiable by objective outside parties.

Allowing a company to go outside its basic industry and size to consider intangible factors when determining a peer group makes the peer group choice subject to manipulation. To use an extreme example, suppose the compensation committee of a $2.5 million consulting company declared that the peer group it would select for compensating its CEO would be a $25 billion energy company, because both companies were committed to excellent values, high quality, and so forth. Through this extreme example, the absurdity of going outside the scope of size and industry becomes quickly apparent. For example, Ford was roundly criticized in 2007 for including non-automobile companies and nontraditional metrics in its peer group.

In selecting a peer group for size, it is best to use a combination of market capitalization and revenues, as each can change over time. Between the two, market cap may be more volatile, as the financial crisis of the fall of 2008 showed.

Principle 4: Long-Term Value for Shareholders

Compensation committees should strive to motivate not only short-term but also—and more important—long-term performance from CEOs and their teams. Therefore it is important to design pay packages that encourage long-term commitment to the organization's well-being. Tying bonuses, stock grants, or other compensation to an increase in the company's long-term value can help align a CEO's personal financial interests with those of shareholders. Although executives do need to meet short-term targets and should be rewarded for doing so, these rewards should not amount to a large percentage of total compensation. Compensation committees should focus primarily on awards for achieving key metrics over an extended period of time. A commitment to long-term stock ownership by management is the best way to align executives' interest with the owners of the business. Long-term generally means anything more than three years and can extend into two digits (ten or more years) in some plans.

For CEOs and other senior executives, salary is usually only one part of a compensation package that includes bonuses, stock grants or options, deferred compensation, pension payments, insurance, and non-monetary perquisites. Recruitment incentives such as a signing bonus, "make whole" provisions to compensate for forfeited benefits from a previous employer, and severance and change-of-control agreements add further complexity and increase the cost of each package.

The compensation committee needs to understand the role of each pay element in motivating both short-term and long-term performance, the true cost of each element, and the total cost of all elements combined in each package. In assessing costs, the committee should consider not only the current but also the future financial cost of the element, including "soft" costs such as reputational harm. Consider, for example, the impact on brand value if overly generous perquisites to senior executives offend other employees and the general public.

To ensure that managers have a stake in the long-term performance of the company, compensation packages should also include incentives to buy or own stock and disincentives to sell it. Figure 8.1 shows the different ways equity can be awarded, and notes advantages and disadvantages of each. To achieve this goal, committees should consider using the following practices:

- Require executives to purchase at least some stock on their own, rather than receiving all their stock awards as pay over and above their base salary. For example, when ImClone hired John Johnson in 2007, it stipulated that he had to buy $500,000 of company shares within ninety days of the effective date of his employment agreement and hold them for at least one year after the end of his four-year employment agreement. (The shares went up shortly thereafter, and when Johnson was falsely accused of insider trading the board pointed to its stock purchase requirement.) Set guidelines for minimal executive ownership of stock as some multiple of salary. About 77.6 percent of *Fortune* 250 companies have this requirement, according to a study by Equilar, the most typical multiple being five for the CEO (and lower multiples for lower-level executives and for directors).[13]
- Require directors to own stock. The 2007 NACD corporate governance survey found that 58 percent of respondents had this requirement, which was most typically expressed as a multiple of the retainer (typically three).[14]
- Put longer holding periods on stock acquired on exercise of options or received via grants (less sales necessary to fund exercises and tax payments).

Stock Options Advantages
* Is a simple equity instrument, widely used and easily understood
* Aligns perfectly with shareholders' interests in stock price growth (no growth, no gain)
* Provides more upside leverage than a grant of equivalent value in restricted stock
* Provides significant flexibility to individuals in timing of gains after vesting

Stock Options Disadvantages
* Is capricious in rewarding performance; gain depends more on timing of exercises and sales than on long-term performance
* Works effectively only in rising markets; no retention or incentive power when options go "underwater"
* Is not an effective device for building ownership when executives can "cash in"; aligns interests of executives more with short-term speculators than with long-term investors
* Lacks a downside risk
* Poses risk of controversial practices such as backdating, repricing, and spring-loading

Restricted Stock Advantages
* Provides stronger retention vehicle than options, particularly in volatile markets
* Provides real ownership and sharing of value changes, up and down, with shareholders (options are only potential ownership)
* Is simpler for employee: no need to make exercise decisions or engage brokers in cashless-exercise transactions
* Uses fewer shares than options in "overhang" calculations; makes shareholder-authorized equity pools last longer
* Is currently favored by investors over options, if the restricted stock has performance requirements

Restricted Stock Disadvantages
* Limits individual's flexibility in timing of gains (taxes due at set vesting dates)
* Less risk or reward for future performance than a grant of equivalent value in options
* Not deductible under IRS Section 162(m) unless subject to performance vesting requirement
* Without performance requirements, restricted stock is a "giveaway"; rewards executives even if stock price declines

Figure 8.1. Advantages and Disadvantages of Stock Options and Restricted Stock as Long-Term Equity-Incentive Vehicles for Executives.

Source: Report of the NACD Blue Ribbon Commission on Executive Compensation and the Role of the Compensation Committee (Washington, DC, NACD: 2003/2007 Edition)

- Consider restricting executives' ability to exercise the options, to sell the stock, or both in less than a twelve-month period (with the exception of exercising stock options and selling shares to pay for the exercise price and the withholding tax). Also consider requiring executives to preannounce stock sales at least thirty days in advance or to engage in a preannounced program sale in compliance with federal securities laws.
- Consider requiring top executives to hold stock at least six months after leaving the company.
- Set sensible limits on the amount of stock and stock options awarded to executives in order to reduce the risk of dilution and overhang. The old rule of thumb for companies was 10 percent of shares outstanding to be used for pay, but that has changed to 20 percent, given the increasing importance of compensation in pay.

In addition to these practices, compensation committees should monitor dilution and overhang carefully—NYSE and NASDAQ require shareholder approval of all new compensation plans that include equity. The compensation committee should regularly calculate how much the CEO and others stand to gain if goals are met or exceeded. In particular, the committee should know the value of stock options already granted, both exercised and unexercised. New grants should be calculated at various stock prices to make certain that these results would be acceptable to the committee.

Compensation committees should consider the wisdom of requiring recapture of funds that are not merited. Sometimes companies make incentive payments to executives who appear to meet certain financial targets. Later, however, a restatement of accounts shows that the executives did not actually meet the targets. In such cases, compensation committees should consider recapturing the payments. Recapture is now required under Sarbanes-Oxley Section 304 in cases of restatement following misconduct.

No discussion of long-term compensation would be complete without mention of the Aspen Institute's landmark manifesto, *Long-Term Value Creation: Guiding Principles for Corporations and Investors.*[15] Despite its broad and almost bland title, this document is actually a sparingly focused look at one topic: compensation. Crafted by a group of CEOs, business organizations, institutional investors, labor unions, corporate lawyers, and accountants, the document was prompted by concerns about the growing "corrosiveness" that short-term pressures are having on publicly traded companies and rising public sentiment against executive compensation. Nicknamed "The Aspen Principles," the four-page document now bears signatures from a variety of organizations, including the AFL-CIO, the Business Roundtable, the Council of Institutional Investors, and the National Association of Corporate Directors. The Aspen Principles call for corporate boards to communicate with "long-term-oriented investors" on senior executive compensation. Among other recommendations, the Principles call on boards to

- Require senior executives to hold stock they are given for at least some period beyond their tenure with the company, thus tying them to the long-term growth of the company. A one-year minimum would seem wise.
- Ban senior executives from hedging the risk of stock options of long-term-oriented compensation.
- Provide for "clawbacks," which involve recouping senior executive compensation that was awarded on the basis of achievement of performance targets that were subsequently slashed or wiped out by corporate financial restatements. Compensation expert James Reda recently noted that some compensation committees are now including these in their charters.

Boards should consider following these practices as a good way to build long-term shareholder value.

Principle 5: Transparency

Compensation committees should embrace a philosophy of transparency—meaning full and clear disclosure. Not only should compensation committee members help to guide the important facts about compensation arrangements, they should also let shareholders know these facts in a timely manner. In this way, a philosophy of transparency can both inspire and enable the highest degree of care in approving packages. SEC regulations require inclusion of a committee report in the annual proxy statement, signed by the committee. The report should include

- A discussion of the relationship of executive and CEO compensation to company performance
- The compensation committee's compensation philosophy
- The basis for determining CEO compensation

In addition to fulfilling reporting requirements, compensation committees should oversee the other compensation disclosures in the company's SEC filings.

Boards should also design plans that are as simple as possible and spell them out in a brief summary that describes company goals, executive performance objectives, and potential payouts under various scenarios. Simplicity of design and communication will ensure that executives, compensation committees, boards, and investors understand the plan. Under most circumstances, one page should be sufficient. Using "plain English" in all public disclosure statements will help build better relations with both shareholders and regulators.

The compensation committee should strive to give accurate and thorough reports to the full board. No director should be embarrassed because he or she did not know what the compensation committee has done, particularly with regard to employment contracts.

Full and prompt disclosure is one clear way to allay public concern about compensation. This was the great lesson of the SEC's disclosure requirements passed in 2006. As a result of those requirements, companies are now disclosing full details on compensation, including deferred compensation, retirement plans, and supplemental executive retirement plans (SERPs). The NACD Blue Ribbon Commission recommended that compensation committee reports identify the specific metrics used to determine performance, and report on executive performance as measured by these metrics.

When the SEC went on to require this, some companies protested that they did not want to give away competitive secrets. The use of the word *may* (as used in the 3M example earlier) has helped companies share their plans without feeling bound by them, and without disclosing too much.

When people talk about transparency, they often talk about the details (or, back to the metaphor at the start of this chapter, the "trees.") But it is important to also have transparency about the overarching values that motivate the compensation—or, in a word, the philosophy behind the compensation.

The SEC requires companies to include their philosophy in the report in the annual proxy statement. Directors should use this requirement as an opportunity to discuss the relative merits of each element of compensation and to actively decide which ones help promote the board's vision for the company. The philosophical framework should express the fundamental principles guiding the board and the compensation committee in awarding pay, as illustrated in Figure 8.2, taken from Unionbancal's 2007 proxy statement.

All compensation committees should ensure that their boards have such a guide. Just as the compensation committee needs a written charter to describe its work and responsibilities, so the committee also needs a thoughtful and comprehensive philosophical framework to guide its decision-making process.

Our Philosophy on Executive Compensation

It is our philosophy to compensate executive officers in a manner that promotes the recruitment, motivation and retention of exceptional employees who will help us achieve our strategic business objectives and increase stockholder value. Our executive compensation philosophy is implemented through compensation programs based upon the following principles:

- Targeted total compensation (salary, bonus, and long-term incentives) and benefits package for executives should be positioned around median competitive levels, taking into account the relative responsibilities of the executive officers involved. Actual total compensation in any given year may be above or below the target level based on individual and corporate performance.
- Our total compensation package should provide an appropriate mix of fixed and variable compensation to support a meaningful pay-for-performancer elationship for our executive officers.
- Performance-based compensation should be tied to performance measures believed to influence heavily stockholder value and which can be influenced by our executive officers.
- Our long-term incentive program should be designed to encourage executive retention and link executive compensation directly to long-term stockholder interests.
- Compensation plans should be easy to understand and communicate.

Figure 8.2. Excerpt from 2007 Proxy Statement of Unionbancal.

Source: Unionbancal Proxy Statement, 2007.

Compensation committees that base compensation on approved performance goals, as required for deductions under the tax code, will benefit from an articulated philosophy.

Articulating a philosophy can bring many benefits. First, having a well-articulated philosophy can help a board assess whether or not pay is appropriate. Furthermore, having a clear philosophy can also help companies meet the requirements of the tax code, at Section 162(m), which say that any amounts paid over $1 million cannot be deducted unless they are awarded for achieving performance goals that have been approved by an independent committee of the board. It can also counteract—and even prevent—criticism of generous pay that is, in fact, linked to outstanding individual and company performance.

Last but not least, developing a clear statement of philosophy and carefully choosing the criteria for financial rewards can enable a compensation committee to underscore the values of a corporation and to help a company attract and keep the leaders it needs to fulfill its strategy for building long-term shareholder value.

Conclusion: The Burning Questions

The principles advocated here—independence, fairness, link to performance, long-term value, and transparency—are all valuable, yet they are not enough. Action is required. Independent-minded and engaged directors need to study the elements of compensation, learn the facts of specific pay packages, and ask the tough questions about the big picture—what it all means.

President George W. Bush, speaking before a Wall Street group shortly before the end of his second term as president, gave out a challenge. "The salaries and bonuses of CEOs should be based on their success at improving their companies and bringing value to their shareholders," he said in a speech at Federal Hall in January 2007 to the Association for a Better New York. "America's corporate boardrooms must step up to their responsibilities," he said. "You need to pay attention to the executive compensation packages that you approve."

As one committed to boardroom excellence, I would heartily agree. Now is the time to take a good look at the big picture—the compensation forest throughout this country and the world. Although the vast majority of companies are doing the right thing, it takes careless giveaways by a handful of boards to cause overcompensation rumors to spread like a wildfire—turning valuable company reputations into ashes. It will take perspective—and courage—to keep those fires in check, but I for one believe directors are up to the task.

Part III

CEO Succession: The Challenges and Opportunities Facing Your Board

9

Managing the CEO's Succession: The Challenge Facing Your Board

Joseph L. Bower

In most major industrial countries of the world, corporate law assigns the job of selecting the chief executive officer of a company to the board of directors. This legal responsibility is mirrored in much recent discussion by leading commentators on corporate governance such as Jay Lorsch.[1] Indeed, it has become common in circles devoted to "good governance" to hear arguments that the management of CEO succession is the board's prerogative.

The objective of this chapter is to explain why the board's role in succession, though very important, must be distinctly subordinate to the role played by the incumbent chief executive if the board is to be effective. As important as CEO succession should be in the work of the board, the management of the succession process is one of the core responsibilities of the *incumbent top leadership*. The board is not constituted so that it can substitute for the CEO in the critical work of developing candidates or in making the final selection. In the case of large publicly held corporations, if the board is actually and not just formally choosing the CEO, it is usually a sign that the succession process has failed. The CEO did not do his or her job. Beyond describing the board's role, this chapter makes clear both how a constructive succession process can be managed and what the positive contribution is that the board can make to that process.

To make this argument, I draw upon my research on CEO succession, on case studies that illustrate that process, and on my own experience as a board member taking part in the succession process.[2]

Before beginning a discussion of the role of the board, a little context is useful. A capsule summary of recent research on the management and performance of major companies includes the following points.

- With few exceptions, the economic performance of publicly held corporations rarely exceeds the mean for long periods of time. Only a handful of companies has maintained performance that has kept them in the top quartile for more than a decade. Generally high performers regress to the mean. A study of eighty-seven high performers in the 1976–1993 period showed a decline in spread above the S&P average from 21 percent to 2 percent (see Table 9.1).[3] Low performers rise toward the mean or disappear. The implication of these numbers is daunting. If performance prior to your CEO's arrival was above average, he or she will have to do something special to avoid a decline. If it was below average, your successor CEO will have a lot of problems to find and fix. Either way, the CEO has a very demanding job.
- If anything, the job has become more difficult. Accelerating technological change and globalizing markets have intensified competition. Growing, vast, and liquid capital markets have led to the emergence of an active market for corporate control. Companies that do not perform well are often gobbled up by strategic competitors or private equity funds. Top managements operate under enormous pressure.[4]
- Moreover, increasingly competitive global markets mean that world-class efficiency, capability for innovation,

and customer focus are needed for sustained success. To achieve these capabilities, continuity in CEO leadership is critical.[5]

- One constant factor in the mix of attributes associated with those companies that sustain high performance over time is that they manage succession well. More often than not they pick insiders to succeed incumbents.[6]
- My research shows that from a sample of eighteen hundred transitions, CEOs chosen from inside the organization perform better than outsiders whether or not the company has been doing well. The difference is less dramatic when performance prior to succession has been good.
- Careful case-by-case analysis of succession suggests that the reasons for this difference in performance have to do with the insider CEO's knowledge of the company's technologies, operations, and competitors as well as his or her knowledge of company capabilities and culture.[7]
- Despite the apparent superior performance of CEOs appointed from the inside and the importance of continuity, and in the face of the growing demands on leadership and the complexity of modern companies, CEO turnover is higher in this decade than in earlier times, as is the number of outsiders chosen as new CEOs.[8]

Table 9.1. Median Market Adjusted Stock Returns Three Years After the CEO Change.

New Ceo Was An	Prior Company Performance Was	
	Better than S&P 500	Worse than S&P 500
Insider	-3.4%	4.5%
Outsider	-5.0%	-1.3%

Source: Joseph L. Bower, *The CEO Within*, Boston: Harvard Business School Press, 2007, page 13.

> Data from Booz&Co's most recent study show *outsiders* replacing incumbents around 20 percent of the time even though performance is consistently poorer and tenure shorter.[9]

Taken together, the preceding points suggest that we are in a CEO succession crisis. Why? How could it be that the succession process is not working well when so many companies say that people are their most important asset and when succession is highlighted as a key board responsibility?

The Challenges of CEO Succession

The answer has three parts, one touched on in the preceding section. These three parts provide the basis for understanding what role the board can and should play in CEO succession. To begin, the job of the CEO is very hard and probably has become harder in the last couple of decades. Second, the process of developing great candidates for leadership is demanding and time intensive, especially for the CEO. And third, the board is under a great deal of pressure to make a defensible choice of candidate. The chapter deals with each of these challenges in turn.

The Job of CEO

Probably the most elegant and concise description of the CEO's job was provided by Ken Andrews in the opening chapter of his seminal work, *The Concept of Corporate Strategy*.[10] He parses the job into four basic tasks.

> Chief executives, presidents,. . . are first and probably least pleasantly persons who are responsible for the results attained in the present as designated by plans made previously. Nothing that we will say . . . can gainsay this immediate truth. (p. 5)

This is why, as a rule, CEOs are thought of as doing a good job during times of economic prosperity and performing badly during recessions. Executives have to own their results. Continuing, he suggests that

> [CEOs] see as their second principal function the creative maintenance and development of organizational capability that makes achievement possible. (pp. 5–6)

In other words, they have to deploy the organization's resources in such a way that this builds the organization's capacities. The business of enterprise software provider SAP, for example, consists largely of building integrated reporting systems so that the many parts of large companies can be coordinated in a global strategic effort. Without such systems, global competitors are doomed to regionally fragmented activity. This activity leads in turn to a third key function:

> The integration of the specialist functions which enable their organizations to perform the technical tasks in marketing, finance,... which proliferate as technology develops and tends to lead the company in all directions. If this coordination is successful... , general managers will probably have performed the task of getting organizations to accept and order priorities in accordance with the company's objectives. Securing commitment to purpose is a central function of the president as organizational leader. (p. 6)

This is "General Management 101." Nonetheless, it is still normal to find functional divisions of a company pursuing their own objectives. Thus a country manager of a commercial operation works to keep capacity employed and local customers satisfied, often at the expense of the programmatic needs of global customers of strategic importance as viewed from headquarters.

Finally, and most critical to the long-term future of the company, Andrews turns to the question of corporate purpose, the motivation for the entire idea of corporate strategy.

> The most difficult role . . . of the chief executive of any organization is the one in which he serves as the custodian of corporate objectives. . . . The presidential functions involved include establishing or presiding over the goal-setting and resource allocation processes of the company, making or ratifying choices among strategic alternatives, and clarifying and defending the goals of the company against external attack or internal erosion. (p. 12)

To recap, regardless of who planned the action and who made the decisions leading to the present results, the CEO is responsible for current operations. That is why we ceremonially dispatch CEOs for the sins of their predecessors. Charles Prince was the general counsel of Citicorp. Because of a series of ethical lapses that led to large fines and the near shutdown of some important Citicorp operations in Europe and Japan, Prince was asked to succeed Sandy Weill and clean up the company. Three years later, he was fired for the severe consequences to Citicorp of their large subprime mortgage portfolio. Was it Prince's fault? It really doesn't matter. It happened on his watch. Unless a crisis is clearly pinned to the coattails of the previous CEO, its consequences belong to the incumbent.

In turn, the CEO has to build the organizational capabilities required to move forward. This will always require integrating the functional and strategic capabilities of the company. It is very clear that Prince was focused on compliance in his early moves. It is less clear that he focused on risk management. A fascinating positive example is provided by Sam Palmisano's work at IBM in transforming the company into a fast-moving, technologically creative provider of advanced IT solutions. The knitting together of IBM's global technological and commercial capabilities is remarkable.[11]

Finally, the CEO must preside over the crafting of corporate strategy, always a difficult task but now even harder because of the rapid change in market and environmental conditions. The CEO of Nokia, Olli-Pekka Kallasvuo, recently remarked, "Who would have thought eighteen months ago that our most important challenge would come from Apple?"[12]

As this comment suggests, today's CEO has to operate, build organizational capability, and craft strategy in a world in which markets are global, new competitors based in a variety of economies—some state sponsored—emerge regularly, and technologies are evolving rapidly, thereby changing the basis of competitive advantage. And should the financial markets' judgment as to the company's prospects turn sour, a pool of close to two trillion dollars of liquid capital exists populated by fund managers ready to exploit a low share price with a contest for corporate control.

But the job of the successor CEO is even harder. The entire question of corporate objectives needs to be rethought, taking into account the circumstances of markets and technologies to come—not just the ones that the incumbent has been considering. Jack Welch most famously sold off the major acquisition of his predecessor, restructured the company so as to eliminate large staffs that the predecessor had built, and reoriented GE away from its industrial heritage in the United States and instead built major foreign operations and a financial services group of formidable strength. The results were remarkable. In contrast, Sir Richard Greenbury improved the efficiency of Marks & Spencer but made no fundamental change in its sourcing operation, so that the company was vulnerable to new kinds of mid-market retailing. The eventual result was a significant decline in financial performance. Under these circumstances, filling the shoes of CEO is no easy task. Where does one find such an unusual person?

Developing CEO Candidates

I have already suggested that the best place to look is inside. This is such an obvious answer that one immediately is forced to ask, "Sure, but then why are there so many outsider CEO candidates?" In my study of over eighteen hundred transitions, a third of the new CEOs were outsiders.[13]

Again there are two parts to the answer. First, for a surprising but understandable set of reasons, many companies do a poor job of developing insiders who might arguably do an effective job of leading the company. Companies (more specifically the CEO and board of the company) are often forced to go outside. The basic reason is that they do not invest systematically in the development of leaders. One survey showed that 60 percent of respondents to a survey of 1,800 human resource managers of large companies do not even have a succession planning process in place.[14] This number is so startling that it is often challenged when I speak to groups of managers. Yet when I poll the group, the number who think their company has a CEO succession planning process in place has never exceeded 40 percent and is often lower.

Many companies think a horse race among potential candidates is all you need to pick a winner, without worrying whether the horses are fast enough for the decade to come. These are companies that pride themselves on being obsessive about managing for performance, on paying and promoting those who deliver while firing those who don't. They deliver on plans without fail. But often they turn out to be companies that think investing resources to develop general managers is a waste of time, that Human Resources is a routine administrative function to be delegated and then ignored, and that CEO succession is something that you begin to worry about the year before the CEO retires. After describing to me the extensive arrangements that his high-performing company made for developing leaders at all levels, its CEO noted, "These are the expenses a financial buyer would strip out in an instant." In my discussions with the customers for executive programs at Harvard Business School, I am often told that our seven- and eight-week comprehensive general management programs take too much time. The customer then asks, "Can't you provide a transforming experience that takes three days?" When I reported this in a conversation with past GE CEO Jack Welch, he replied, "Joe, you've hit the nail on the head. That is exactly what I hear as I go around the country."[15]

But second, when many CEOs and their boards finally turn to succession, they may have a bias against the insiders. If there has been great success, it is easy for a view to develop that "the demands of our scale and scope are more than any of our people can handle. They haven't grown with the company." Of course this suggests that the company has not invested in that growth. In a similar vein, an "imperial" CEO may believe that "none of my people are up to my standard." Many CEOs who think that way have created a self-fulfilling prophecy. Most problematic, the insiders that have posted good performance sometimes seem to lack strategic vision. Unless they have been properly challenged with strategic assignments, they are "inside the box" operators. They do not understand the need for change.

My guess is that this weakness of insiders is the primary reason that performance of top-quartile companies regresses to the mean following succession. The new CEO does not really understand how much change is needed.

There are also more human reasons for picking outsiders. Some CEOs find the prospect of succession downright depressing. For them, succession implies a kind of "death" for them. Their life is their job. They love the job; it is their identity. They are dead without it. They think of building a cohort of potential leaders not as the path to growth and prosperity but as a sure route to lame-duck status. Even among those who plan for succession, some manage in such an imperial fashion that the potential successor leaders wither in their shade. Sadly, some sitting CEOs in their heart of hearts fear being surpassed. A symptom of this problem is the CEO that values loyalty above competence. One of the executives I interviewed for my study put it this way:

> I've seen situations where people with the title CEO are insecure in their position. And, sometimes, times are difficult. The company isn't doing well. News of problems for the CEO usually comes from below, so the CEO may focus on loyalty, rather than who is the best candidate for the job. They want to know "who's watching my back?"... But the organization sees it. . . . And they start thinking, "Maybe this *isn't* a meritocracy."[16]

When the Board Makes the Succession Choice

We can begin to understand the problem the board faces when it does put succession on its agenda. Let's summarize the problematic behaviors described earlier:

- Attention to short-term performance has been all that counted for promotions.
- The organization has been designed so that general management jobs are broken up into functional assignments and candidates have never had the experience of running a whole business.
- General managers have not been developed with strategic assignments.
- CEO succession has been treated as an event, and discussion of that event has been awkward or postponed.
- The incumbent CEO has managed in an imperial fashion so that the top management cohort has never really developed their capabilities.

Where several of these behaviors are the norm, the board will find a cohort of operators as opposed to leaders when they turn to consider CEO succession. The men and women who have been described as performing at a high level are found to be lacking when measured against the criteria developed for the company's next leader. In particular, they do not see the need for real strategic change.

It is not surprising that when talent development has not been a priority of the company and its board, the board turns to outsiders. If performance has been poor, a natural reaction is that the insiders are part of the problem, not a source of the solution. It may be true. Unless the company's organization permits several managers to have the experience of running business units, it is hard to sort out the insiders who have not been unsuccessful. Outsiders bring a fresh view and an attractive track record.

Where performance has been good, it is not unusual for the incumbent CEO to frame the problem of succession as a choice among some number of his or her direct reports. Unless the board has been actively engaged in monitoring a talent development process, it is quite natural for the board to accept this assessment and discuss how the baton should be passed to the best of the candidates, or as a horse race managed among them. That is what happened at Marks & Spencer, where the winner of a horse race turned out to be considerably less than the job required. Faced with a very difficult retail environment, the new CEO Peter Salsbury panicked and made a series of poor moves that worsened the financial squeeze on the company. The board then brought in an outsider who managed a temporary turnaround. When that turned sour, the board finally brought in Stuart Rose, an insider who had left the company in frustration a decade earlier. Rose was able to rebuild Marks &Spencer's fundamental capabilities.

Let us consider the problem from the board's perspective. What happens when a board has been able to get involved and decides that the candidates are not up to the challenge? What if performance has not been good, and there is not a lot of faith in the recommendation of the incumbent? The problem, of course, is that a board, even a diligent board, is made up of part-timers whose knowledge of the company is based on what they have been presented at board meetings and whatever else they are able to gather from outside sources. Especially when performance has been problematic, there will be skepticism toward insiders.

To begin, it takes time to decide to act. If succession has not been a priority of the board for a period of time, the board will be reluctant to move unless there is a crisis. The 2007 study of succession by Booz Allen Hamilton found that CEOs who had experienced an absolute loss of shareholder value over two years of 25 percent or more and underperformed their regional peers by 45 percent were most likely to be removed. But the likelihood was only 5.7 percent. In discussion with the authors, we observed that boards without choices find it very hard to make a move![17] (See Figure 9.1.)

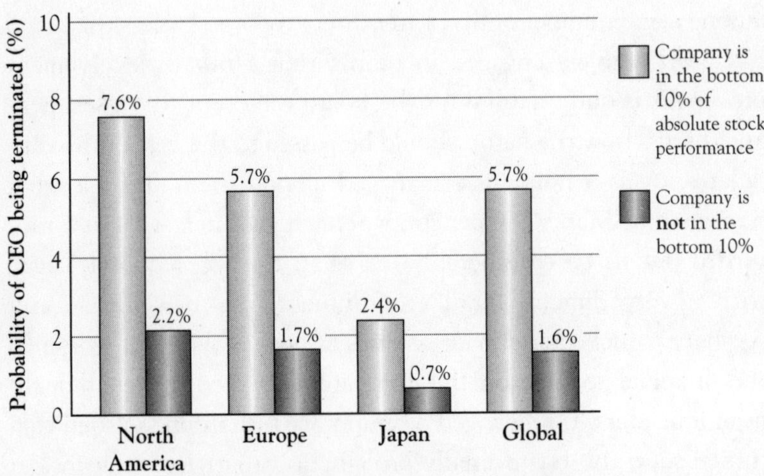

Figure 9.1. Termination and Extreme Performance.

Note: Data do not include interim CEOs or merger-related departures.
Source: P.-O. Karlsson, G. L. Neilson, and J. C. Webster, "CEO Succession: The Performance Paradox," *strategy + business* no. 51 (Summer 2008).

It is hard for directors to remove a CEO if they are not confident that inside successors are qualified. Inevitably, a board will turn to a search firm for assistance in assessing inside candidates and finding outsiders. Known colloquially as "headhunters," search firms play a crucial role in helping boards find new outsider CEOs. An important asset that these executive recruiters bring to the task is a database of executives who might be appropriate and available for the new job. Because search firms are a third party, they are able to begin a process of exploration under conditions of confidentiality, important both to the company and the candidates—because candidates are usually employed somewhere else.

The forces at work as a board seeks an outsider have been well described by the sociologist Rakesh Khurana.[18] Central to what happens is concern for the credibility of the candidate and the due care taken by the board in the process. The members of a board seek to work collegially. As well, they are concerned that their decisions are defensible. The recommendation of a leading search firm of a candidate with a record of success at a well-known company counts for a great deal. It makes it easier for the board both to coalesce behind a candidate and to justify its decision.

Often the desire by a superficially informed board for credentials leads their search firm to find a celebrity CEO, a star from one of the "people factories" such as GE or Proctor & Gamble.[19] For a board worried about declining performance or facing a crisis, celebrity CEOs provide the same kind of comfort that used to reassure purchasers of mainframe computers when they bought IBM. Unfortunately, it is not unusual for these very capable recruits to lack critical understanding of the companies' industries and markets. Examples of this sort would include PepsiCo's John Sculley, who moved from a stellar performance in the Cola Wars to Apple Computer, where he could not cope with Microsoft and Intel, and GE's Larry Johnson, who went from running GE's Home Appliance group well to running the Canadian retailer Albertson's poorly. But even when the outside recruit has the requisite knowledge of the business to lead the development of new strategy, he or she very often lacks the understanding of the company's culture and people needed to drive change. That would appear to have been the problem at 3M, where the brilliant James McNerney appears to have been unable to build on the firm's culture of creative innovation.

There is a second aspect to the outsider's problem. Many outsider CEOs who are brought in to turn around or reenergize a company are generalists who know how to drive efficiency but are fundamentally unequipped with the industry or market knowledge necessary to craft and implement an innovative strategy. They can cut costs but cannot drive growth. When they leave (the 2006 Booz Allen Hamilton succession study says three years is the reported average tenure for turnaround artists), profits may be better but the company is strategically weaker.[20] And their turnaround has not involved investment in leaders for the future. As a result, there are no potential CEOs within the organization. Of more concern, the same Booz Allen Hamilton study reveals that one-third of the time, the outsider CEO sells the company. Indeed there are CEOs who have made a serial business of such short turnarounds followed by a sale.

My research suggests that the answer to the dilemma posed by the problems of insiders and outsiders is what I call the *inside-outsiders*. These are men and women who have performed well and risen high but have maintained their objectivity. Blessed with independent minds and high integrity, they have also been nurtured by executives who valued their capabilities and helped them learn to use them. They are aware of how much change is needed to sustain success or turn around a failure, but they also know the organization, its culture, and its people. They have learned to deliver on their commitments, so their track record is solid, but they have also been given the opportunity to drive strategic growth. They can do more than bring in consultants or make across-the-board cuts. Beyond getting short-term profits, they can build for future growth.

These unusual folk are often found at the periphery of the organization managing new businesses or new markets. Among the well-known versions of this type are GE's Jack Welch, who rose to CEO from his role as maverick president of GE's Plastics group and transformed GE's culture and systems; his successor, Jeff Immelt, the first GE leader to come from sales, who dramatically increased the scale and potential of GE's medical system business (far from the core engine and turbine businesses); Proctor & Gamble's A. G. Lafley, who came up in the personal care business and spent years building a very successful Far Eastern business (far from laundry and Cincinnati); and IBM's Sam Palmisano, who in a company known for closed systems and hardware championed open systems and software.

Managing the Succession Process

Although I have argued the importance of building a cohort of inside-outsiders, it is obvious that much of the time boards are not faced with that prospect. We need, therefore, to consider both succession circumstances: incumbent to insider and incumbent to outsider.

Incumbent to Insider

Well-managed succession is a process that meets at least three tests. Through their assignments, their evaluations, and their mentoring, executives grow to be effective leaders so that there is a pool of candidates for CEO to consider. That work is done by senior management. All the board can do is to make sure it is happening. In the process of pruning the pool, as discussed earlier, the CEO and board need to have established criteria that reflect the needs of the company going ahead. In making their selection, they focus on values, intellectual integrity, and fit with future needs, as well as past performance. In today's fast-changing world, the past is not necessarily prologue.

Building a pool of leaders begins with recruitment to the company. It continues with a pattern of assignments that permits development of real expertise in a line of business and development of managerial skills. For that to happen, staffing needs to balance the needs of the businesses with the needs of the managers. A strong HR staff led by an executive that has the complete trust and commitment of the CEO is what it takes to make that happen. Evaluation and compensation are critical as well. Finally, planning and budgeting have to be managed with care so that it is a process in which managers grow, not a game of "gotcha" in which they succeed or fail on the basis of meeting short-term performance targets.

This takes time and discussion, often one-on-one coaching by trusted mentors. Managers have to learn that accountability for one's commitments is critical to success in an organization. But because the future is uncertain, they have to learn that fast action in response to changed circumstances is an important aspect of producing on commitments. Finally, when proposing projects that involve new and innovative elements, managers need to learn the importance of careful planning of both the substance and the story that is told to sell their idea. They must learn to listen to feedback that is critical both as a way to learn but also as a way to discover how arguments can be made more effective.

By way of example, let us consider the career of Jeff Immelt at GE. It is well documented and fascinating, although his strategy of growing GE through a focus on infrastructure development, water and clean energy, and health care delivery has attracted criticism from those who want the stable earnings growth provided by Welch's financial services businesses. In addition, a badly handled earnings forecast has further irritated the critics. Nonetheless, Immelt remains the choice of GE's board.

Figure 9.2 charts Jeff Immelt's career at GE. Certain features stand out. To begin, he spent an initial period being introduced to the company and trained in the sales function. He then spent five years in positions of increasing responsibility in the sales function of the Plastics group. A period of still greater responsibility followed in Home Appliances, followed by more assignments in Plastics and finally the top job in Medical Systems, a role in which Immelt distinguished himself by driving dramatic growth.

1982	Enters GE on Commercial Leadership Program
1983	Manager—Business Development/GTX Product Management, GE Plastics
1984	Manager—Dallas District Sales, GE Plastics
1986	General Manager—Western Region Sales, GE Plastics
1987	General Manager—New Business Development & Marketing Development, GE Plastics
1989	Vice President of Consumer Service, GE Appliances
1991	Vice President of Worldwide Marketing and Product Management, GE Appliances
1992	Vice President Commercial Division, GE Plastics Americas
1993	Vice President and General Manager, GE Plastics Americas
1997	President and CEO, GE Medical Systems
November 2000	President and Chairman-elect, GE; Elected to Board of Directors
September 2001	Chairman and CEO, General Electric Company

Figure 9.2. Career Timeline for Jeff Immelt at General Electric Company.
Source: General Electric Company documents.

What is not apparent is the attention he received, from recruitment by one of GE's strong young line executives to an early presentation to GE's CEO, Jack Welch. The first assignment as a sales manager provided him with regular tough feedback on the importance of making the numbers, the foundation of accountability. Throughout his progress, he was mentored by the president of GE Plastics and tracked by the executive who recruited him, now a high-ranking member of GE's leadership team. Mentoring was complemented by annual feedback in GE's Session C, a robust process of detailed assessment and counseling. Having succeeded in driving growth in the Plastics business, Immelt next went to Home Appliances, a move chosen by Welch to provide Immelt with an ordeal by fire—the management of a huge product recall. Success with that problem was rewarded with promotion in Appliances. And progress there was followed by another stint in Plastics and then another promotion to a position in which inflation in raw material prices confronted Immelt with a brutal challenge to profitability. The resolution of that problem took time and involved weekly contact with Welch and the man who had recruited him, now GE's CFO. Immelt's eventual success led to the Medical Systems assignment, and a brilliant performance success.[21]

The case study from which this example is drawn makes clear that Immelt was tracked by the very top managers of GE and mentored on a regular basis from the moment he was recruited. Later, during trying periods, he received regular calls from Jack Welch tracking events and from GE's vice-chairman providing guidance. For *inside-outsiders* to flourish, mentoring is vital. The kind of personal detailed attention that Immelt received is key. No staff system can by itself cope with the idiosyncrasies of strong-minded folk as they learn to work in the context of teams and large organizations. They need to be called up short immediately when they have violated important norms and *told how they can make amends* so that the damage does not linger. They need to be protected from impatient elders, and their individuality nurtured and matured. That is how their ability to see the need for change is transformed from a nuisance into an asset. It is not easy, but when it happens, it is a delight.

Where the leadership of a company has supported the development of a cohort of inside-outsiders, the board's role is relatively simple to describe. Directors have to get to know the candidates, work with the CEO to frame criteria for choosing among them, and manage that process over its final months. Getting to know the candidates is a problem. Unless the board or its compensation committee have had independent access to the candidates, the board is really processing information provided by the CEO. Directors have heard about these people for years, but the information is provided by the company. To go beyond that, it is necessary to have a program of visits, and the CEO has to agree to stay out of the way. That is a very unusual set of arrangements.

The second challenge is to reach consensus in the board as to the nature of the strategic challenges facing the company over the next five to ten years and *the implication of that judgment* for the choice of a leader. Interestingly, this may be a very different discussion from the one the board has been having with the incumbent CEO. The new ingredient is extreme focus on those aspects of the world ahead that will require new capabilities from the company and hence new attributes for the leader. This is an aspect of the process in which the board may have an advantage. If its members have knowledge relevant to the business, their judgments may well complement those of management.

Other issues of importance in this circumstance involve attempts to retain the "losers" in the company if that is the desire of the board, the structuring of new assignments of top officers during the transition, and determining the role of the departing CEO.

The Challenges of Succession: Bringing an Outsider In

For an outsider, the transition to leadership is a brutal learning process in which their *industry knowledge*, *organizational knowledge*, and *leadership skills appropriate to the culture* are engaged with the company's challenges. It is certainly possible that the first and third criteria can be met by an outsider, although it is easy to misunderstand important subtle differences between industries. A great marketer of branded power tools from Black & Decker can have a hard time with nonbranded housewares. This was the problem when Joseph Galli moved from Black & Decker to Newell. Similarly, leadership skills that worked well in one culture may be quite inappropriate to another. That would appear to be the problem when Juergen Schremp's team from Daimler moved to Chrysler.[22] Organizational knowledge is a huge barrier to the outsider that can only be overcome with time and early success.

Lack of any of the three forms of knowledge and skills raises the probability of failure. The fact that knowledge of industry, organization, and culture are company-specific makes taking over especially daunting for an outsider.[23] The importance of these factors certainly suggests the lines of questioning that the search committee of the board should follow. But if board members are not deeply familiar with the industry, organization, and culture—not improbable if they have chosen to look for an outsider—they may be in a poor position to make the necessary judgments.

Unless the board has found a new leader that meets the three criteria, the best they will get is a period of improved earnings. But it will be a miracle if major strategic issues that influence longer-term growth will be faced and resolved. It does happen—Lou Gerstner kept IBM integrated; Charlotte Bears restored the advertising agency Ogilvy & Mather's client base and renewed the firm's culture. But it is far more typical for the new CEO to leave after a few years—or sell the company. The 2007 study of CEO succession by Booz&Co reports that "outsiders tend to have shorter tenures than insiders. For outgoing CEOs in 2007, the mean outsider tenure was 4.8 years, compared to 6.4 years for insiders."[24]

The Role of the Board of Directors in CEO Succession

The foregoing arguments make for a dismal recitation. How can a board help avoid a negative succession outcome? The first step is to understand how much work has to be done by the CEO and his or her top team, how early they have to start, and how extensively all key aspects of the way the company is run must be involved to support leadership development. Succession is not an event. Most of this chapter has described a *process* by which over the years talent is recruited to the company and developed, a pool of high-potential candidates is identified, assignments are chosen to develop those candidate's talents further, and opportunities are provided to prove their mettle. Only management can do that work—not the board.

The next step is to help the CEO focus on that challenge. It isn't easy. If a company does not have a tradition of building talent, and if it is not organized so that talent can develop without turning the process into a wrestling contest, it takes time to build the human resources organization—starting with a first-class chief talent officer. It may take time just to persuade the CEO that this is a marvelous opportunity, not a threat, which may be difficult for an insecure CEO, or an imperial CEO, or a CEO preoccupied with poor current performance.

If the succession question and a clear program of leadership development are not on the table five years before the incumbent CEO might leave, then there is an issue. A CEO who provides thoughtful leadership of the process for the board will pick an early time to initiate discussion of the topic or respond with alacrity when it is first raised by the board. The head of HR will be trusted and capable of staffing the process. In the opposite case, if the CEO is reluctant, the lead board director or functional equivalent has to force the issue. In other words, the job of the board is to get the CEO to do the job. The board cannot do the job itself.

The next step is to establish a process in which a pool of CEO candidates is identified and developed. Identifying the pool is very important. The pool should be as large as possible. The mavericks who might be inside-outsiders need to be on the list. Who built a new business? Who led the exit from a core business? Who has transformed the core so that what was once in decline is now a platform for future growth? These are the kind of achievements one should be seeking.

The subsequent steps are more obvious. The pool is pruned, the candidates are selected, a final choice made, and the transition managed. The board needs to spend time on each of these steps. It should be the preoccupation of the governance and nominating committee. In particular, the board or the committee should meet the candidates and get to know their strengths and weaknesses.

The process need not be a horse race among candidates. Although a leader must be chosen, the entire team is an asset. One company I recently studied was able to keep a cohort of five leading next-generation executives, promoting all to take over the company working for a collectively chosen leader. I had never before seen this trick accomplished, but it suggests that a great deal can be achieved when the CEO and board start early and work together. When a board is passive, none of this may happen. Reassurance that "we have several good candidates" or "I have a 'name in the envelope' that I have discussed with the lead director" are no substitute for careful extended discussions as part of the succession process outlined earlier. When the board intrudes and tries to manage the process directly, its interference with the operations of the company can lead to a crisis of governance. The board can insist that there be a succession development process. But because the process is a central aspect of the way the company is managed, it cannot be carried out by the board.

The board can—indeed must—inquire regularly about the process, track the progress of candidates, and meet as many as possible—but it cannot do the recruiting and talent development required. It cannot get into the details of organizational arrangements that ensure that talented executives have the opportunity to experience general management responsibility early in their careers. Most important, it cannot be present during the critical times when plans and budgets are developed and outcomes reviewed that turn out to be the most critical "teaching moments" for mentors.

As long as the steps in the succession process are accomplished, there is no formula for how management and the board accomplish their task. Once again, the keys are early attention to recruiting and developing talent; a large pool of candidates; further development that favors *inside-outsiders* where they can be found; careful pruning and then selection against future-oriented criteria; a period of transition that gives the new CEO a maximum chance to succeed; and, finally, extensive exposure of those on the board who will make the final choice at every step of the way.

If a board can check off each of these steps, the chances are very good that the next CEO will succeed.

10

Beyond Best Practices: Revisiting the Board's Role in CEO Succession

Mark B. Nadler

Of all the ways in which boards have been taking a stronger hand in corporate oversight, few hold as much potential for so much impact over such an extended period of time as the board's active participation in the development of future leaders and the selection of CEOs. So how successfully have boards wielded that powerful tool?

Consider the stark difference between two big-company succession announcements that came on the same day, but involved dramatically different succession scenarios.

The date was November 5, 2007. As the year drew to a tumultuous close, Wall Street had become enmeshed in the subprime lending meltdown, in which billions of dollars in bad loans and shareholder value evaporated within a matter of weeks. One of the companies hardest hit was Citigroup, which eventually was forced to write off more than $18 billion in decimated assets in early 2008. Embattled CEO Charles Prince, under fire throughout much of his four-year tenure from shareholders disappointed with the company's performance, announced his resignation on November 5.

What followed was the highly public spectacle of the nation's largest bank suddenly caught up in a frantic search for a new CEO. As some observers noted at the time, the succession plan at Citibank had basically consisted of asking former Secretary of the Treasury Robert Rubin, a top adviser at the company, to temporarily hold down the CEO job until a permanent replacement could be found. And that's exactly what happened. But in the interim, the company was subjected to an absolute media circus with endless speculation about who had been offered the job, who had turned it down, and who might be next on the list. In the end, the board selected Vikram Pandit, a former Morgan Stanley executive whose small hedge fund had been purchased by Citigroup earlier that same year.

Contrast that with the situation at Time Warner. On the same day that Chuck Prince announced his resignation from Citigroup, Time Warner was announcing that Dick Parsons would be succeeded as CEO by Jeffrey Bewkes effective January 1, 2008. The announcement, which came as absolutely no surprise to anyone, was made by Robert C. Clark, chairman of the Time Warner board's governance and nominating committee. The transition was the culmination of an orderly, structured, two-year process in which the board and management worked together to create a fully articulated view of the job requirements for the next CEO and then monitored Bewkes's readiness to meet those requirements and make the move from president to CEO.

Obviously, when it comes to evaluating boards' roles in CEO succession, the scorecard is mixed. A few boards have made excellent progress on this front, and some have made a decent start. But for many, the game is barely under way, which is a little surprising. Research by our firm (together with the Center for Board Leadership) and others indicates that as recently as 2006 and 2007, at least half of large U.S. companies, both public and private, had no explicit CEO succession plan in place.[1] We continue to watch with dismay as world-famed corporations scramble to find a new CEO to replace the one the board has just forced out. For every Coca-Cola, Target, Microsoft, and McDonald's that selected a new CEO from the inside using an orderly process, you could easily find a Boeing, Ford, or Merrill Lynch that had no well-groomed candidate waiting in the wings. It's still common practice at some companies for the emergency succession plan to exist exclusively in a sealed envelope locked in the CEO's desk drawer, with the designated successor's name remaining a total mystery to the board until a crisis hits. What's more, you don't have to talk with too many directors before it becomes evident that the death notices for the imperial CEO were somewhat exaggerated and the birth announcements for the activist board were a bit premature, particularly when it comes to planning for the transition in the corner office.

Perhaps our expectations were too high. Compared with other governance practices that have significantly changed the way boards and CEOs work together—a focus on board composition and leadership, the appointment of lead directors and the regular use of executive sessions, periodic CEO performance evaluations and board assessments—the widespread emergence of a new approach to CEO succession is still in its early stages.

Let's begin by stipulating that successful CEO succession is a lot tougher than it looks. Why? Because succession planning, unlike many other governance reforms, has less to do with legal requirements and formal procedures and everything to do with the emotional, political, and occasionally irrational behavior of a set of powerful players caught up in the most personal of all professional dramas. No matter how you shuffle this deck, the human wild card keeps showing up when you least expect it. Any succession plan—no matter how detailed, elegant, and deliberate—is destined for trouble if its underlying model is a chessboard instead of a playground. Succession at the CEO level is messy—sometimes beyond description or belief—precisely because it involves so many individual players, each with his or her own set of needs.

This is not to suggest that succession planning is pointless. To the contrary, planning is essential, as long as it takes into account the full complexity of the process rather than focusing unrealistically upon a mechanistic approach that ignores the inherent messiness of such an essentially human process.

To that end, our firm (then known as Mercer Delta Consulting) collaborated in 2006 with the National Association of Corporate Directors (NACD) on a comprehensive study of the role of the board in CEO succession. As part of that project, we identified a list of ten "best practices," based on our interviews with twenty-three directors of *Fortune* 500 companies where the board had an active role in CEO succession planning, where there was a robust succession planning process, and where there had fairly recently been a smooth and orderly hand-off from one CEO to another. The companies involved in the study represented a broad spectrum of industries, including airlines, aerospace, technology, retail, pharmaceuticals, and consumer goods, and included such well-known corporations as McDonald's, Microsoft, and Starbucks.[2]

By and large, the best practices that emerged from those interviews still make sense. But for the great number of U.S. companies where this approach to succession continues to be more aspirational than actual, there is value in revisiting the best practices with an eye toward highlighting some specific ways to make them more realistic and actionable. The key is to bring these best practices to life by taking into account the full range of personal and organizational dynamics that inevitably come into play whenever the top job is at stake.

Exploring the Three Dimensions of Succession

The selection of senior managers in general, and of CEOs in particular, always involves three critical dimensions: the analytical assessment of a candidate's readiness for the job, the emotional considerations that influence the decision, and the political dynamics that surround the organization's transition from one CEO to another.

These dimensions are always present in one form or another, but they are magnified in unique ways when it comes to identifying CEO candidates, developing them, and then selecting the next leader.

Analytical

The *analytical perspective* views selection as a rational process, strongly guided by the collection and analysis of objective data through an explicit and defined work process. It is all about gathering dispassionate, hopefully quantifiable, data about each candidate's strengths and weaknesses and then matching those profiles against the explicit requirements of the job. Ideally, the process clarifies the trade-offs raised by each alternative, thus leading to a final selection decision based on objective evaluation of the best available data.

For example, not long ago we assisted a communications company in assessing members of the senior team and rating each as a potential CEO prospect. Each assessment involved a variety of tools—personal interviews; psychometric instruments; 360-degree feedback surveys; and a rating of each executive, by both the chair and the CEO, on seventeen key dimensions that the two of them had selected as the most important attributes for the next CEO. Taken together, that variety of data provided ways to very literally compare and rank each candidate's level of "fit" with the articulated CEO role criteria.

As it turned out, one internal candidate clearly emerged from the initial evaluation as the most serious prospect, by far. Over the next eighteen months the board nominating committee used the same CEO job profile—the seventeen dimensions used in the initial assessment—to evaluate external candidates and to monitor the progress the internal candidate was making. Ultimately, the board decided that the internal candidate's development had progressed to the point where they were comfortable in formally designating him as the CEO's successor.

Emotional

The analytical assessment of candidates is in sharp contrast to the *emotional perspective*. There is usually some emotional component present in any promotion decision. But it absolutely permeates the CEO succession process from start to finish.

- Some CEOs actively avoid working on succession because they would rather not face up to all it implies about aging and mortality. That can be an enormous emotional stumbling block for many CEOs, and a good many will put it off interminably unless pressed into action by the board. Once the succession process is finally in place, the board must keep a sharp eye out for signs that the CEO is actually sabotaging the process, finding excuses to eliminate promising candidates and thereby starting the process all over again.
- Because the choice of a successor is so critical, some CEOs obsess over making the right decision. That plays out in a variety of ways. The CEO might be hypercritical of all potential candidates, subjecting them to endless scrutiny. Or something resembling paralysis sets in; the CEO is simply incapable of settling on any candidate. The decision can also become clouded by unrealistic comparisons: in other words, the experienced CEO compares candidates to himself at this moment, rather than stepping back and remembering what he was like at the moment he was selected as a novice CEO. Consequently, he sets the bar so unrealistically high that any candidate who doesn't have some CEO experience can't possibly hope to pass muster.
- When it comes to internal candidate selection, it's impossible to ignore the emotional overtones. Typically, both the incumbent and the candidates have known and worked with each other for years, possibly decades. There might well be strong friendships, or bonds of loyalty, or feelings of obligation, or all of the

above. CEOs often find themselves torn, weighing a candidate who has been loyal, steadfast, conscientious, and competent against someone with whom they share little history but has the potential to become a superstar. Beyond that, the stakes are incredibly high for the candidates, and the CEO knows that. When people vie for any other job, there is usually an assumption that if this promotion doesn't work out, other opportunities will come along. Not so with the CEO position; candidates usually get one serious shot at the job, and if they lose out, odds are they won't get another chance to become a CEO unless they give up and go somewhere else. That is a heavy emotional burden for some CEOs to deal with as they think about a pool of candidates they have long-term relationships with.

- CEOs, like the rest of us, often experience an unconscious impulse to clone themselves. Even in the face of overwhelming evidence that the company's situation calls for an entirely different kind of leader, CEOs find it hard to resist the natural tendency to gravitate toward people they perceive as similar to themselves. Perhaps more important, CEOs are often drawn to like-minded successors whose appointment will be viewed symbolically as a continuation of their own tenure, much as the first President Bush's election was generally viewed as an extension of the Reagan presidency.

Political

Finally, there is an intensely *political perspective* to CEO succession. Individuals and groups, both inside and outside the organization, care about the selection of a CEO in ways that far surpass any other appointments. For some stakeholders, support for a particular candidate is grounded in strategic, philosophical, or ideological beliefs about how the company should be run, what businesses and markets it should be in, and what sort of financial performance is expected. For others, it's all about power, and the expectations that a particular choice will have direct implications on who will benefit in terms of position, influence, resources, and career opportunities.

There are four major groupings of stakeholders who figure into the political mix. Clearly, the board has emerged as the most important group of players, a situation that has dramatically changed over the past decade. During the same period, we have also seen a significant increase in the role of outside stakeholders—activist shareholders, potential investors, analysts, the business press, unions, major customers, suppliers, regulators, and various political and social interest groups. For the most part, succession used to be an in-house activity, with occasional lobbying from the outside; today, outside influence has become a huge factor. In an increasing number of situations, the search for a new CEO is being spearheaded by activist shareholders, and their efforts are accelerated and amplified by a business press that is infinitely more excited by the drama surrounding a change in the corner office than by covering the nuts and bolts of routine business news. The third political force includes the candidates themselves. Some adhere to the rule that the best way to win the new job is to steer clear of politics and let performance speak for itself. But others will take matters into their own hands by actively lobbying for their candidacy or trying to sabotage others. Finally, there are various internal constituencies who search for ways to either support their favorite candidate or undercut the competition—office politics at its most destructive and dysfunctional.

Revisiting the Best Practices

With this framework of the three succession dimensions in mind, let's now take a closer look at the ten "best practices" identified in our 2006 study. It is not our intention to go through the list and discuss how each of the three dimensions of succession applies to each of the best practices. Instead, our goal is to revisit the ten—focusing specifically on several that merit particularly closer attention—and to apply a realistic, integrated perspective to some practices that even the most successful boards espoused more in theory than in practice.

1. Plan Three to Five Years Out

Board and CEO discussions on long-term succession planning should begin three to five years before a CEO transition is expected.

No question about it: this is the ideal scenario. And it's a best practice followed by such respected companies as Microsoft, McDonald's, Pepsi, and Wyeth. It makes perfect sense; companies are increasingly inclined to promote internally rather than recruit externally, and grooming inside talent takes time. The benefit of a long succession process is the opportunity to fully develop the next CEO through a combination of assignments and activities. More specifically, the directors interviewed for the study described a multiyear process in which the board spends the first two to three years identifying and monitoring the development of serious candidates, then selects an heir apparent who spends the remaining time making the transition through the roles of COO, CEO-designate, CEO, and, ultimately, CEO/chair.

That sounds great. The only problem is that only one-third of those interviewed—and remember, these are the directors whose companies had recently been through successful CEO successions—said their boards actually got involved three years or more in advance of the event. In fact, over half said their boards actually got involved less than two years before the CEO was scheduled to leave (see Figure 10.1).

The other problem with this best practice is the implication that a single candidate should be identified two to three years

Question: How many years before a planned CEO transition (that is, long-term succession planning for a CEO's retirement):
A. Does the board *typically* get involved in the succession planning process (current state)?
B. *Should* the board get involved in the succession planning process (desired state)?

	Less Than Two Years	Three to Five Years	More Than Five Years	Not Applicable/ Don't Know
Current state	56%	22%	11%	0%
Desired state	6%	61%	22%	0%

Figure 10.1. Time Frame for the CEO Succession Process.

in advance. That can be awfully risky, if not impractical. As already noted, a CEO who is fundamentally ambivalent about giving up the job may become a serial "candidate killer," allowing a succession of candidates to advance to a certain point before he sours on them and decides to search for a replacement. Disney's Michael Eisner, for example, became famous for anointing successors and then concluding they were totally unfit to replace him as CEO. In other cases, there is a real risk in putting all your eggs in one basket too far in advance because that single candidate might suddenly find another opportunity outside the firm. Talented, ambitious CEO candidates get restless. Their sudden departure in search of more immediate gratification can erase years of planning and leave the succession plan back at square one. One of the most sensational examples of that happened in 1996 when Alex Mandl, the president and CEO of AT&T, got tired of waiting for CEO Robert Allen to retire, and went off to lead a wireless startup, leaving AT&T without an obvious successor. But that was far from an isolated example. Ed Breen, the apparent successor to Chris Galvin at Motorola, left in 2002 to become CEO of Tyco only seven months after being promoted to president/COO of Motorola. History repeated itself in late 2007 when Charles Giancarlo, the heir-apparent to Cisco CEO John Chambers, decided upon turning fifty that he wasn't willing to wait another five years for Chambers to step aside and went off to join Silver Lake, a leading Silicon Valley investment group.

The point is that involving the board in a well-thought-out succession plan three to five years in advance is great, if you can do it—as long as the board fulfills its responsibility by dissuading the CEO from placing all his succession eggs in a single basket. A few years ago, the CEO of a *Fortune* 500 health care company hired a new COO with the explicit intention of grooming him as a successor. In almost every way, their five years together literally became a textbook case of how succession should be done; the transition was written up in business magazines and professional management journals as an example of succession planning and execution at its best. And it was, with just one caveat; if the heir apparent, at some point in the five years, had been hired away by another company, or become physically incapacitated, or involved in a scandal, or just decided to go live in the mountains and write poetry, all bets would have been off. There was no other internal candidate; there was no Plan B.

The moral of the story? By all means, start early, get the board involved, provide plenty of lead time—but be sure to spend time developing the entire pool of executive talent, rather than prematurely placing all your bets on a single candidate.

2. Ensure Full Board Involvement

The full board should be involved in CEO succession planning; the process should not be relegated to a committee.

Directors in the NACD study stressed the importance of involving all board members at critical stages in the succession process: setting the criteria for the CEO role, evaluating candidates, and making the final decision. That marks a dramatic departure from the traditional practice in which the CEO owned the process and the board's involvement was often limited to a few members of a board committee.

Indeed, our firm's research and experience clearly indicate the gradual emergence of a new model of CEO succession.[3] Until the 1990s, the prevalent approach was basically a "concurrence model," which can still be found today. In this model, the process begins when the CEO decides that it is time to start thinking about succession. He identifies potential candidates, provides them with some development opportunities, tests them, and possibly offers further development. Periodically—at times of his choosing—he informs the board, or, more often, a few of its members, how the candidates are coming along. As he nears the end of his term—usually, sometime in the final two years—the CEO chooses a successor and takes his selection to the board for an up or down vote. And they usually concur—hence, the "concurrence model."

More recently, we have seen two new and very different models showing up in boardrooms—the "collaborative" and the "crisis" models. The "collaborative model," which seems to be emerging as the dominant approach, still positions the CEO as the major player in the succession process, in terms of identifying and developing candidates, but includes the board as a full participant in terms of overseeing the process and making the final selection. The entire board is involved, but the lead director or a committee chair is usually designated to work as the CEO's primary partner throughout the process.

Of course, the "collaborative model" assumes there is someone for the board to collaborate with—presumably, an incumbent CEO who is performing reasonably well and has substantial credibility with the board. Yet, more and more, that isn't the case; in 2006, nearly one-third of CEO departures at large companies were involuntary, compared with one in eight in 1995, according to Booz Allen Hamilton's 2007 study of CEO turnover.[4] With increasing frequency, boards are employing a "crisis model" of CEO succession, in which the lead director or the chair of one of the key committees drives an accelerated succession process, often involving an outside search, within a tightly compressed time frame.

The numbers from our 2006 study with NACD demonstrate that the collaborative model was quickly growing in popularity during the middle years of the decade. Only 11 percent of the directors in the survey said their boards were still using the "concurrence model," whereas 39 percent said their boards had adopted a collaborative model. And the momentum is clearly building; half the directors, in fact, said they would prefer to go beyond the collaborative model and give the board primary responsibility for running the succession process, with the CEO in a secondary role—providing input only as requested. Again, that is more aspirational than actual; only 28 percent said that was how their board actually operated (see Figure 10.2).

The role of the board vis-à-vis the CEO is only one aspect of this issue. The other is the importance of involving the entire board, rather than a small number of board leaders or members of a particular committee. As mentioned earlier, there are some board members who are happy to abdicate any active role in succession until it's time for a final vote. In our view, the time for that kind of passive role is over. Every director should be required to take part in the process, have a say when CEO selection criteria are developed, and be expected to personally interact with candidates so that when the time comes for a vote, they can make an informed decision rather than following the lead of the CEO or a committee chair. At the other end of the spectrum, there tend to be a few board members who would love to dominate the process, if given the opportunity, which can leave candidates with a skewed sense of the board, its members, and their opinions. Active involvement by all directors should be the standard in every boardroom.

Question: How do CEOs collaborate with boards on CEO succession planning?
Current state: How they typically work together
Desired state: How they should work together

CEO Responsibility ←	No Board Engagement	Low Board Engagement	Moderate Board Engagement	High Board Engagement	Exclusive Board Engagement	→ Board Responsibility
	CEO has primary responsibility and keeps the board informed.	CEO has primary responsibility and asks the board for input.	CEO and board are jointly responsible and work together.	Board has primary responsibility and asks the CEO for input.	Board has primary responsibility and keeps the CEO informed.	
Current state	11%	17%	39%	28%	0%	
Desired state	0%	6%	39%	50%	6%	

Figure 10.2. CEO and Board Collaboration.

As a best practice, it makes sense for a key committee—most often, the governance and nominating committee—to oversee and work closely with management on the process for identifying, developing, and vetting potential candidates, and to periodically report to the full board on where things stand in terms of the development and readiness of potential candidates. The role of the full board is to provide input to the committee, to avail itself of appropriate opportunities, to become familiar with potential candidates, and, of course, to make the final selection decision.

3. Establish an Open and Ongoing Dialogue and an Annual Review

The board and the CEO should maintain an open and ongoing dialogue on succession planning and should devote substantial time to discussing the topic.

If the ultimate goal is to make succession a process rather than an event, then this is an essential best practice. One of the more positive signs we're seeing is that periodic reviews of the succession plan and the progress of potential candidates have become fairly routine items on board agendas, showing up at least once a year and frequently more often.

Companies have devised various ways to accomplish the same goal. Some boards devote half a day, once or twice a year, to a thorough review of how candidates are progressing toward the goals of their respective development plans. Others spend a full day reviewing the succession plans not only for the CEO but for all his direct reports as well. Some boards also view these reviews as a logical opportunity to revisit the effectiveness of the company's overall leadership development processes.

These discussions provide the greatest value when positioned within the larger context of talent development. Not long ago, we were given a dual assignment by the compensation committee of a mid-sized media company: first, to determine whether any of the

CEO's direct reports should be considered serious candidates for the top job, either near-term or at some point farther down the road; and second, to assess each executive's overall strengths and weaknesses and to help them put together a personal development plan to discuss with the CEO.

It turned out to be a valuable exercise for everyone involved. It revealed, among other things, that although the number two executive was certainly capable of keeping the company up and running during a crisis, no one (except for him) thought he was a viable candidate to become CEO on a permanent basis. At the same time, it became clear that three younger members of the senior team had tremendous potential, which would require providing each with different development opportunities over the next five years or so. The implication was clear: someone new had to be brought in very soon, at a very senior level, to be groomed as a bona fide near-term successor. As a result, a very capable, highly experienced executive was recruited from the outside to join the senior team, and development plans were put in place for the three younger executives with an eye toward long-term succession.

What was particularly interesting about the process was the conversation it prompted among board members. After hearing us explain why one executive was on our list of long-term CEO candidates, a board member mused, "She's been with the company for eleven years. If she's so good, why is this the first time I've ever heard her name?" The answer, clearly, was that up to that point the board and the CEO's predecessors had never engaged in any regular discussions of succession plans or of any but the most obvious CEO candidates.

The cadence of these discussions has a lot to do with how far in the future the transition is likely to be. As the CEO's planned departure draws closer, it is only natural for the conversations to become more frequent and more detailed. However, there is an element of risk involved here. Taken to extremes, you can find yourself with a nonstop assessment process in which it becomes all too easy for the board to get hung up on isolated and relatively unimportant episodes. A few years ago, we worked with a private-equity-owned firm in which the president was being trained as quickly as possible to become CEO. As with most PE-portfolio companies, the board met monthly, and at each meeting, the president took on an increasingly prominent role. After meetings, the directors would compare notes on the president's performance. Because the conversations were held so frequently, the board sometimes became fixated on a particular slip-up or an uncharacteristically weak performance and had to be reminded to take the long view and focus on the president's overall progress and performance.

The issue is one of balance. There is enormous value in regularly scheduled, substantive conversations between the board and the CEO to review the progress of CEO candidates and of the overall talent development program. The board's challenge: knowing how deeply to dig into details without getting so hands-on that they start to act like super-HR directors.

4. Develop and Agree on Selection Criteria

Criteria for the new CEO should be developed with the company's future strategic needs in mind.

Let me be candid: my personal belief is that this "best practice" from the 2006 report is unquestionably valid, yet somewhat limited.

I fully endorse the notion that the board and the CEO should develop and agree on selection criteria for the new CEO, for three reasons. First, I have participated in far too many boardroom debates over the relative merits of various CEO candidates in which it is clear that at a surprisingly late stage in the selection process there is an incredible lack of consensus among board members about the most important professional attributes and personal qualities they are looking for in the next CEO. When that happens, it is hardly surprising that the board ties itself in knots trying to settle on a single candidate; how do you decide who is "best" when you can't agree on a definition of "best"? It seems painfully obvious, but the fact is that boards frequently get much too far down the succession road without taking the time to agree on what they're looking for.

The second issue is that assessment is essential for both development and selection, and there is no rational way to do assessment in the absence of explicit criteria. Establishing those criteria is the critical first step in measuring the distance between where candidates are today versus where they need to be, and then having a reasonably objective way to assess individual and comparative progress against the goals.

Third, explicit criteria are central to succession "story lines." One of the most useful tools in any succession situation is a well-developed, concise explanation of why the transition is happening, why it is happening now, and why the new CEO was the best possible choice—in other words, a "story line." And the easiest way to answer the question, "Why is this the best candidate?" is to be able to match the individual with the requirements, framed as a clear, concise set of criteria that squarely address the organization's biggest priorities and the one or two attributes that were the key differentiators among the top candidates; for example, "Our next CEO has to be someone with the deep knowledge of our company and our industry to lead a period of intense organic growth," or "To meet our growth projects, we need a CEO with global experience in world-class manufacturing operations."

In my experience, once you agree on the criteria, it's a simple matter to extrapolate from that all the essential communications, ranging from public announcements to very private conversations with the unsuccessful job candidates. The result is a message that is candid and consistent—one that will carry you through the entire succession event.

However, there is one caveat. The statement that the criteria "should be developed with the company's future strategic needs in mind" is absolutely true—but it would be a mistake to stop there. Here's why.

A few years ago, we were asked to help with the transition from one CEO to another at a major financial services company. The company's strategy was clear: the time was fast approaching when the company would need to become a publicly traded corporation. As a result, the retiring CEO/chairman made the personally difficult decision to look beyond his trusted circle of top executives, some of whom he had worked with for more than a quarter of a century, to find a CEO with senior-level experience at a public company within the same industry. He ultimately recruited a top executive away from a major competitor—a gentleman with precisely the credentials he was looking for, and a resume much more compatible with the skills and experience the new CEO would need.

Yet almost as soon as the appointment was announced, the outgoing CEO began feeling uncomfortable about his decision. He was disturbed by what struck him as his successor's arrogance, aloofness, and barely hidden disdain for the top managers he had inherited. And before long, the new CEO was embroiled in a highly publicized scandal involving his relationship with an employee and his use of corporate funds. In hindsight, there is little doubt the new CEO was technically qualified to address the company's immediate strategic challenges. What hadn't been examined as closely was whether he had the character to lead the company and build value over the long haul.

The point is that when it comes to developing succession criteria, focusing on the company's strategic challenges is a good place to start—but a terrible place to finish. Consider Gap; Mickey Drexler, with a great sense of fashion, made the clothing chain so successful that it eventually grew out of control. The owners ousted Drexler and replaced him with Paul Pressler, a Disney executive known for his financial prowess, and sure enough, he quickly brought financial discipline to the company, to the great delight of shareholders. But Pressler was a finance guy, not a fashion guy; he knew how to bring growth under control through financial discipline, but not how to generate growth through creative merchandising.

That's the phenomenon we refer to as the CEO's Act II.[5] A CEO is recruited to solve a particular problem—think of that as Act I. Assuming he or she is successful, the organization then moves on to a new set of challenges, often requiring entirely different management skills or leadership styles—we'll call that Act II. As it turns out, the very attributes that made the CEO the best possible candidate to attack the challenges in Act I will often be ill-suited to the problems in Act II and, in some cases, might even exacerbate them.

The implication for succession is that there is a huge risk in basing CEO selection criteria too narrowly on the specific attributes required to meet an immediate challenge. I am reminded of a recent board meeting of a small manufacturing company in desperate need of an immediate turnaround. The incumbent CEO had quit before the board had a chance to fire him, and now the board was reviewing a serious candidate to replace him. Initially, board members focused on his industry knowledge and turnaround experience. Gradually, questions turned to his operating experience, his ability to deal with customers, and his marketing savvy. After two hours, the board concluded that assuming he met the basic requirements in all the other areas, the three attributes they most cared about were his ability to recruit and effectively lead a great senior team, his decisiveness, and his personal integrity. My hunch is that they landed on a set of attributes that enabled them to hire a CEO who not only will do well in Act I, but will also be well suited to succeed in Act II.

Again, starting the selection criteria with the company's strategic requirements makes absolute sense. But as a best practice, the criteria should address the full range of requirements in the areas of strategy, operations, interpersonal relationships, and personal qualities.

5. Use Formal Assessment Processes

Formal assessment processes provide information that helps boards objectively assess candidates and identify development needs.

The standard performance appraisal tools most companies routinely employ rarely generate the kind of sophisticated data you'd like to have in front of you when it comes to planning who will lead your company into the future. That should come as no surprise. Despite enormous effort and great intentions, performance appraisals tend to become more perfunctory and less helpful the higher you go in the organization. Too often, they focus disproportionately on past performance rather than future development. They rarely indicate how the individual might do in a job with different requirements.

As a best practice, directors believe that potential CEO candidates should be subjected to periodic, formal assessments based on data gathered from a variety of sources who are asked to rate candidates against specific criteria. In particular, directors pay close attention to 360-degree feedback appraisals in which supervisors, peers, and direct reports rate each individual on such dimensions as management ability, leadership skill, strategic thinking, and operational knowledge.

Although there are any number of ways to design the assessments, I would argue strenuously in favor of customized sets of assessment tools carefully designed to meet the particular needs of each situation. Consider the following two very different examples.

At the media company referred to earlier, where we were asked to assess the viability of every senior team member as a potential CEO candidate, the assessment package we put together included

- A rating (arrived at together by the CEO and the executive chair) of each candidate on fifteen different selection criteria, including breadth of management experience, relevant business knowledge, customer focus, and emotional strength and maturity.
- An in-depth interview lasting two hours or more, conducted by one of our consultants and touching upon a host of personal and professional issues.
- An analysis of the widely respected Hogan Leadership Forecast, a psychometric instrument each candidate completed.
- Reports by each candidate describing their academic and professional backgrounds and explaining what they saw as the company's greatest strategic challenges and their ideas on how these should be addressed.

The result was a rich set of data on each candidate and a straightforward way to compare how closely each measured up to the selection criteria. But there's something missing: a 360-degree assessment. After much discussion, it was agreed to forego the 360 in this initial round of assessments because nearly the entire senior team had either been with the company, or in their current jobs, for such a short period of time that ratings by their peers and subordinates would have been next to meaningless. However, at the end of the project we strongly urged that 360s be introduced into the regular assessment process in the not-too-distant future.

In contrast, consider the assessment package we developed with a global financial services firm, an infinitely more stable organization in which senior executives had extensive experience with the company. The clear emphasis was on the 360-degree feedback, which was structured around a set of four key dimensions: strategic thinking, business results, people leadership, and personal effectiveness. The assessment included online feedback surveys involving numerical ratings from supervisors, peers, and employees, as well as confidential interviews (conducted by our consultants) with each executive's direct reports and a conversation with the CEO in which he provided numerical ratings, with color commentary, for each executive. The process concluded with a personal meeting between each executive and the CEO to go over the data and agree on developmental goals. The 360 was then repeated regularly, providing explicit data about each executive's progress—or lack thereof—in each critical area.

The two assessment approaches just described were dramatically different, and intentionally so; when it comes to assessment tools, CEO selection is not the place for a one-size-fits-all approach. These examples also illustrate some related best practices suggested by the directors in our NACD survey:

Conduct formal assessments early on, and use them regularly. Repeating the assessments at critical junctures in the succession process can benchmark executives' progress and highlight emerging issues that deserve special attention.

Use an independent third party. As self-serving as this sounds, directors said they found it helpful to have appraisals conducted by outsiders, who are viewed as more impartial and less threatening than internal people.

Assess all of the CEO's direct reports. The reality is that in any given situation, only a small number of top executives are viable CEO candidates. Nevertheless, periodic assessments of the entire senior team provide the board with valuable information about all the top executives, which can help them consider the entire pool of possible candidates before settling prematurely on just one or two of the most obvious contestants.

6. Develop Internal Candidates Rather Than Hiring Externally

Boards typically prefer developing internal candidates to recruiting externally for a new CEO.

Most directors in the NACD study said they strongly preferred developing home-grown talent rather than recruiting a CEO from the outside, and with good reason. Various studies suggest that hiring CEOs from the outside can result in everything from a mass exodus of top talent to an immediate drop in stock price to a long-term decline in company performance. Boards have concluded that it's just too hard to know what you're actually buying when you recruit a supposed superstar from the outside. For that reason, the hiring of outside CEOs at U.S. companies appears to have peaked in the mid-to-late 1990s; today, about two-thirds of CEOs are promoted from within.

The good news is that boards have learned from experience. The era of charismatic, celebrity CEOs led to a phenomenon in recent decades that Rakesh Khurana artfully captured in the title of his excellent book, *Searching for a Corporate Savior*.[6] These days, most boards seem to have tempered their expectations and adopted a more realistic approach.

I experienced that firsthand a few years ago at a digital media company where the CEO had departed unexpectedly. The board, though less than excited about the COO—let's call him John—decided that to maintain stability, it would have him act as CEO on an interim basis while they had a leading search firm line up some top-notch outside candidates. But a funny thing happened: John's performance was far better than any of the directors had expected. He didn't become any more charming or charismatic, but he quickly brought stability, focus, and, ultimately, forward momentum to a chaotic company at which key players had been streaming out the door. After six weeks, the director overseeing the search confided to me, "You know, I wouldn't go so far as to say I've fallen in love with John, but unless the headhunters come up with somebody who's so clearly head and shoulders above him that they knock my socks off, John's got the job."

That's the way the equation seems to be working out these days; the burden of proof is on the outside candidates to demonstrate that their potential performance far exceeds the internal candidates' established track record. In the battle of dueling succession clichés, "familiarity breeds contempt" gets trumped by "better the devil you know than the one you don't."

In this chapter we have already addressed some of the best practices specifically related to the development of internal candidates. In our NACD study, the directors described several specific approaches (see Figure 10.3). The most common is to provide top executives with a succession of progressively more responsible and challenging jobs, with the goal of guaranteeing that they experience a rigorous array of challenges that will test and tone them as they prepare for the top position.

7. Interact with Internal Candidates

Board members should be given ongoing opportunities to interact with internal candidates in various settings.

Notebooks filled with assessment data have their place, but at the end of the day, there is no substitute for personal observation. Most of us prefer to form our own judgments as to how a candidate answers questions, handles stress, and interacts with others. No headhunter "candidate summary" can fully describe someone's personal presence, communication skills, absence or abundance of charm and humor, or ability to think on his or her feet.

For outside candidates, that places disproportionate importance on the job interview, easily one of the most artificial and unrepresentative forms of human interaction ever devised. In theory, hiring from the inside should afford directors virtually infinite opportunities to size up each candidate over a significant period of time and in a wide variety of relatively meaningful situations. The question is whether that's what actually happens.

Question: How do boards develop internal candidates for the CEO position?	Board Member Has Experience With (%)	Board Member Rank Order of Effectiveness
Giving a candidate company assignments designed to broaden his or her experience	83	1
Having him or her work closely with the current CEO	83	2
Involving a candidate in multisource feedback or executive assessment process	83	3
Having board members interview a candidate and give him or her feedback	56	4
Having a candidate serve on another company's board	50	5
Providing him or her with coaching from a professional executive coach	61	6
Providing external education (such as executive M.B.A., leadership centers, and so on)	61	7
Other	6	NA

Figure 10.3. Development of Internal Candidates.

Once again, reality falls far short of the ideal. At many companies, the most common form of interaction between directors and potential CEO candidates continues to be the time-honored "dog and pony show," in which managers are ushered into the boardroom to deliver tightly scripted, well-rehearsed formal presentations on specific topics. Fortunately, many boards seem to be losing patience with this practice; they're spending less time on presentations, and more time on questions and discussion. That provides the board with better information about the topic at hand and better insights into what each manager has to offer beyond presentation skills.

Nevertheless, these infrequent appearances in the boardroom can have less than ideal outcomes. Not long ago, we helped the board of a publishing company identify a set of potential internal CEO candidates. We met with the board governance committee to discuss our findings, and one of the candidates—in fact, the one we rated number one—drew surprised reactions from board members. "Are you kidding?" one director asked. "You're seriously recommending that arrogant little s—t?"

We were somewhat taken aback. Certainly, the candidate—the head of one of the company's two most important divisions—came across as fairly self-assured, but we had also found him to be personable, funny, even charming. We took a closer look, and found that over the course of two years, the candidate had met with the board four times to provide updates on his division's performance. For this very ambitious young man, these board appearances induced massive anxiety and he overcompensated; rather than conveying confidence, he exuded arrogance. Nobody bothered to tell him how the board was reacting, so he kept doing the same thing each time he met with them. As a result, the board's view of him was dramatically different from the way he was seen in normal situations by his colleagues and employees.

From that standpoint, there is some cause for concern that directors in the NACD study put board presentations at the top of the list of practices that they find most helpful in developing insights about CEO candidates. The good news, as illustrated by the results shown in Figure 10.4, is that most directors in the study also found it helpful to engage with candidates outside the boardroom. Spending time with executives at company offsites seems to be a favorite, and it is easy to see why. Offsites generally provide a mix of both formal and informal sessions in a more relaxed

Question: How do board members meet and develop personal insights about the company's internal candidates?	Board Member Has Experience With (%)	Board Member Rank Order of Helpfulness
Executives make presentations at board meetings	67	1
Executives attend board offsite meetings or retreats	67	2
Executives meet individually with a board member or groups of board members	56	3
Executives attend board dinners or other social events	67	4
Other (please specify)	22	NA

Figure 10.4. Approaches to Meeting Internal Talent.

atmosphere than the office or the boardroom. They also allow directors to see how potential candidates interact not only with the board, but with their peers, as well.

The directors described other settings that can help round out the picture of candidates' personal and professional capabilities. Many boards invite key managers to join them at social events that coincide with board meetings, providing opportunities for relatively relaxed conversation. Some board members accompany top management on trips abroad or site visits. One director said that at his company, board members attend three meetings each year of divisional management committees, which allows them to see how candidates interact with their own people, and in the CEO's absence.

That last point raises a sticky issue: How deep into the organization should directors go in their search for complete information about CEO candidates? There is a delicate balancing act involved here, one that is increasingly common as directors feel more and more responsible for obtaining independent information—on a wide range of topics—unfiltered by top management. It makes perfect sense for directors to be curious about how potential CEOs behave in their natural environment, not just in the boardroom or at offsites under the CEO's watchful gaze. Realistically, however, there is endless potential for mischief, politicking, mixed messages, and unintended confusion whenever directors wander unattended into the dark reaches of the organization. That's not to say they should never go there—but clear ground rules can establish who goes where and says what.

8. Stage the Succession but Avoid Horse Races

The succession should be structured and supervised, but obvious horse races should be avoided.

Despite the now legendary three-way contest to select a successor to Jack Welch at GE, directors were emphatic in their belief that highly publicized horse races are rarely conducive to successful transitions. They might provide great entertainment to business journalists and office politics junkies, but their potential damage to the organization is immense.

Of course, even in the absence of any public announcement that the race is on, it is practically impossible to disguise the fact that a number of people are being prepped for Big Things in the future. That's only natural; you can't hide the fact that certain people keep taking on increasingly important roles, and after a while it becomes fairly obvious which emerging stars constitute the next generation of leaders. Given the inherently political nature of most organizations, it is not at all surprising that people try to handicap the competition and figure out where to place their personal bets. There is no practical way to stop any of that from happening, and little point in trying.

At the same time, there is almost nothing to be gained by publicly hoisting a starting pistol, announcing the candidates, and then orchestrating a head-to-head, winner-takes-all competition for the top job. As soon as that happens, people start to take sides, forming coalitions and alliances. Political considerations start to permeate business deliberations. Competition between individuals and factions can divert attention and sap morale. If things get out of control, outsiders get involved; as journalists and analysts speculate on who is ahead and what the implications might be, investors, suppliers, and customers can all get nervous. And once a choice is made, the one-time stars who have now been labeled "losers" usually feel they have no future at the company—as was the case after widely followed horse races at GE and Pfizer—and as a consequence, the company inevitably loses some of its top talent.

The reality of a horse race may be impossible to avoid, particularly in long-term succession processes that last three to five years. Most directors recommend that designating a clear front-runner—perhaps two years in advance—is the best way to defuse the competition, and that makes sense—just as long as you don't short-circuit the process prematurely, as suggested earlier, and find yourself with no backup plan should the front-runner suddenly drop out of the race.

9. Have the Outgoing CEO Leave or Stay On as Chair for a Limited Time

The outgoing CEO should either leave the board immediately or stay on as chair for a transitional period of six to eighteen months, maximum.

At many companies, the appointment of a new CEO often means that the retiring CEO will stay on for a while in some suitably altered role, often as board chair. But more than half the directors in the best practices survey recommended that the departing CEO should make a clean break—giving up both the CEO and chair roles—as soon as the new CEO takes over. What's more, the directors recommended that if there must be some period of transition during which the previous CEO remains as chair, then it should be for a very limited time, preferably six months and certainly no more than eighteen.

Needless to say, this is one of those decisions that is directly related to the specific circumstances of any given transition. For starters, what is the business situation surrounding the CEO's departure? Is the company doing poorly or well? Are major stakeholders demanding or expecting a major change, or are they looking for continuity? Is the new CEO an outside hire or a homegrown successor? Is the retiring CEO the founder, a major shareholder, or a member of the family that controls the company? And most important, does the board view the new CEO as a fully seasoned top executive, ready to take over from Day One, or did the board merely settle on the best available candidate without finding anyone they thought was fully prepared for the job?

The fact is that in various situations, and for a variety of reasons, some boards are extremely nervous about installing a CEO without retaining what is sometimes described, only partly in jest, as "adult supervision." The assumption is that the old CEO can provide oversight or an institutional memory to help avoid repeating past mistakes, and act as a sounding board or perhaps even a mentor and coach. That desire for an orderly and gradual transition is easy to understand—but it also involves some serious risks:

- It is extremely difficult for the new CEO to develop her own agenda and set a new course for the company without appearing to repudiate a predecessor who is sitting at the head of table.
- A new CEO will find it hard to exert leadership in the boardroom if directors continue to look to the old

CEO—in the most literal sense—for clues about how they should react.

- The most extreme risk is one we have seen play out time and time again in recent years at companies such as Dell, Nike, and Starbucks: the continued presence of the former CEO—particularly, though not exclusively, when the former CEO also happens to be the company founder—seriously increases the board's readiness to replace the new boss with the old boss. When a CEO hits a rough patch, it's all too easy for the board to hit the eject button if the former CEO is sitting right there and lobbying to get his old job back so he can return the company to its glory days. Even when things don't go that far, the new CEO becomes acutely aware that what the board and former CEO hath given, they can easily take away.

If, in spite of all that, the board decides that there should be some transition period in which the incoming and outgoing CEOs overlap (with the departing CEO as chair), there are some ways to manage and, it is hoped, limit the risks:

- The roles of the CEO and board chair should be defined with total clarity, removing any question about who is responsible for what.
- Everyone should pay attention to managing the symbols of power. For example, the old CEO simply has to give up his old office; better yet, he should move to a different floor, or a different building.
- The lead director should be prepared to act as mediator, as needed.
- Directors should be sensitive to their own behavior and the dynamics of the boardroom. Even simple things

such as automatically looking to the chair for his or her response when the new CEO says something controversial can take on enormous significance.

There is no overstating what an emotional minefield the transition period can be for both the new and departing CEOs, creating awkwardness or even friction between two leaders who might have previously enjoyed a terrific relationship. The principals generally brace themselves for a gradual change in their relationship; it always seems to come as a surprise that everything changes the very moment the transition is announced. "It's like someone switching on a light," one CEO told me. "It happens that fast." Suddenly, the balance of power in their long-term relationship gets stood on its head. In an instant, the retiring CEO becomes history and the new CEO becomes the center of attention.

The interplay of emotions is deep, intense, and somewhat unpredictable. In our experience, most of the key players involved—both the new and old CEOs—have told us that if they had it all to do over again, they would have shortened, if not totally eliminated, the transition period from one CEO to the next.

10. Prepare a Comprehensive Emergency Succession Plan

Emergency succession planning should be dealt with as soon as a new CEO takes the helm. The board should review the plan every year thereafter.

The lowest common denominator of succession planning is the question I heard a chairman put to his CEO: "Who takes over if you get hit by a truck?" It doesn't get much more basic than that. And yet, the directors interviewed for the best practices study estimated that one in ten companies have no emergency succession plan at all, and that at another 17 percent, the CEO prepares a letter with instructions to be opened only if there's a crisis, and nobody sees it, discusses the plan, or suggests that perhaps there might be other alternatives (see Figure 10.5).

In this day and age, given the variety of risks companies face and the speed with which news of the crisis can start eroding value and undermining the organization, it defies all logic for any company to go without an emergency succession plan. The stakes are simply too high.

In fact, the "what if the CEO gets hit by a truck" approach to emergency planning doesn't go nearly far enough. As one director suggested, boards ought to be thinking in terms of "an Eliot Spitzer scenario" in which some regulatory action, natural disaster, or wholly unanticipated chain of events somehow necessitates the immediate and wholesale replacement of not just the CEO, but the entire management team. A crisis of that scale is realistic in today's world, and it is inherently irresponsible for any board to ignore such a possibility and fail to plan for it.

Perhaps the ultimate "best practice," in terms of a board effectively handling a multiple-succession crisis, was the situation McDonald's experienced in 2004. When CEO Jim Cantalupo

On the basis of your experience as a board member, how do you believe that *most* boards treat emergency succession planning (used in the event of an unforeseen loss of corporate leadership)?

56%	There is an emergency succession plan in place that is reviewed at least annually.
17%	There is an emergency succession plan in place, but it is rarely reviewed.
17%	The CEO prepares a letter of instruction for emergency succession, to be opened if needed, but it is not discussed ahead of time.
11%	There is no emergency succession plan.

Figure 10.5. Emergency Succession Plans.

suffered a fatal heart attack, the board acted within hours to promote COO Charlie Bell to the top position and named one of its outside directors as non-executive chair. Then, just seven months later, Bell was diagnosed with terminal cancer, and the board acted quickly again to promote Jim Skinner, another well-prepared executive. The board handled two wholly unanticipated succession events within seven months of each other, reaping the benefits of solid emergency planning and an outstanding talent development process. As a result, the immensely successful turnaround that McDonald's launched in 2002 continued without interruption, despite the abrupt and tragic changes in the corporate suite.

The McDonald's situation was a wake-up call for many boards. Today, most leading companies have emergency succession plans, although it isn't clear whether all of them are dusted off and reviewed on a regular basis. For companies that have no plan, there is simply no excuse. As soon as a new CEO enters office, it is the duty of the board to instruct him or her immediately to develop an emergency succession plan, to discuss it with them, and then to review and update the plan with them on a regular basis.

Summary

We began this chapter by stipulating that the CEO succession process is hard work—much harder than it is often portrayed by governance experts or business journalists, who are quick to excoriate any board that suddenly finds itself with an empty CEO office and no obvious candidate in sight. Granted, in a perfect world, that would never happen, and every board should strive to make sure that it doesn't. But any endeavor that, at the end of the day, is all about a group of people trying to find the perfect person for an incredibly difficult job is bound to fall short of perfection.

There are any number of very specific and quite practical best practices that boards can employ in order to do a better job of developing top talent and selecting new leaders. The ten best practices discussed in this chapter combine the seasoned insights and experience in the trenches of directors at companies that have actually done succession well.

We have attempted to take those best practices one step further, adding additional texture to the succession picture by overlaying what we've experienced as the three ever-present dimensions of the process—analytics, emotions, and politics. The best succession processes acknowledge and integrate all three elements.

Clearly, the old approach to succession wasn't providing companies with the caliber of talent they needed to meet a host of new demands. In the past, the CEO would simply persuade the board that he had found a successor who had "the right stuff"—without a specific understanding of what constituted "the right stuff" or how it might actually equip someone to deal with the challenges awaiting the next CEO. More and more boards are moving way beyond that anachronistic model. At the same time, it would be equally foolhardy to think that succession can be reduced to an elaborate, objective process that somehow eliminates the human factor. Again, that's totally unreasonable. Instead, the true best practices combine the benefits of individual insight and observation with the analytical rigor of deliberate processes, with the goal of identifying and developing the optimal talent at the top.

11

Ending the CEO Succession Crisis

Ram Charan

We talk about leadership as though leaders—like Tolstoy's happy families—are all alike. But CEO leadership should be a subject apart because it is unique in scope and substance and of incomparable importance. CEOs' performance determines the fates of corporations, which collectively influence whole economies. Our standard of living depends upon excellence at the very top.

Who, then, would dispute that CEO selection deserves perpetual front-burner attention from the custodians of a company's welfare? Surely, when time or trauma ushers in change, organizations should be ready with a clear view of current and future needs and with carefully tended pools of candidates.

But they're not. The CEO succession process is broken in North America and is no better in many other parts of the world. Almost half of the companies with revenue greater than $500 million have no meaningful CEO succession plan, according to the National Association of Corporate Directors. Even those that have plans aren't happy with them. The Corporate Leadership Council (CLC), a human-resource research organization, surveyed 276 large companies last year and found that only 20 percent of responding HR executives were satisfied with their top-management succession processes.

That deficiency is simply inexcusable. A CEO or board that has been in place for six or seven years and has not yet provided a pool of qualified candidates, and a robust process for selecting the next leader, is a failure. Everyone talks about emulating such best practitioners as General Electric, but few work very hard at it.

The result of poor succession planning is often poor performance, which translates into higher turnover and corporate instability. As increased transparency, more vocal institutional investors, and more active boards make greater demands, CEO tenures continue to shrink. Booz Allen Hamilton reports that the global average is now just 7.6 years, down from 9.5 years in 1995. And two out of every five new CEOs fail in the first eighteen months, as Dan Ciampa cites in his article "Almost Ready" in *Harvard Business Review*.

The problem isn't just that more CEOs are being replaced. The problem is that, in many cases, CEOs are being replaced *badly*. Too often, new leaders are plucked from the well-worn Rolodexes of a small recruiting oligarchy and appointed by directors who have little experience hiring anyone for a position higher than COO, vice chair, CFO, or president of a large business unit. Hiring a CEO is simply different.

Coaxing former leaders out of retirement is another popular way to fill the void. Celebrated examples include Harry Stonecipher at Boeing, Bill Stavropoulos of Dow Chemical, and Jamie Houghton at Corning. But most "boomerang CEOs" return for just a couple of years, long enough to restore credibility and put a real succession candidate in place. They are not the long-term solution.

To increase their chances of finding a leader who will serve long and well, companies must do three things. First, they should have available a deep pool of internal candidates kept well stocked by a leadership development process that reaches from the bottom to the top. Second, boards should create, then continually update and refine, a succession plan and have in place a thoughtful process for making decisions about candidates. Finally, directors considering outside candidates should be exacting, informed drivers of the executive search process, leading recruiters rather than being led by them.

In my thirty-five years advising corporations, I have participated in dozens of CEO selections and have closely monitored numerous executive pipelines. Drawing on that experience, I will in these pages first explain why companies make poor appointments and then suggest what they can instead do to make good ones. Using these guidelines, organizations can ensure that all participants—directors, executive recruiters, and sitting CEOs—perform wisely and appropriately when it comes time to choose their next leader.

The Trouble with Outsiders

When companies lack the culture or the processes to grow their own heirs apparent, they have no choice but to look outside. More than a third (37 percent) of the *Fortune* 1000 companies are run by external recruits, according to the public affairs firm Burson-Marsteller. Although global data are harder to come by, the worldwide trend appears to be similar. But external candidates are in most cases a greater risk because directors and top management cannot know them as well as they know their own people.

Outsiders are generally chosen because they can do *a* job—turn around the company or restructure the portfolio. But *the* job is to lead a hugely complex organization over many years through an unpredictable progression of shifting markets and competitive terrains. Unfortunately, the requirements for that larger job are often not well defined by the board, which may be focused on finding a savior.

The results are not surprising. In North America, 55 percent of outside CEOs who departed in 2003 were forced to resign by their boards, compared with 34 percent of insiders, Booz Allen

Hamilton reports. In Europe, 70 percent of departing outsiders got the boot, compared with 55 percent of insiders. Some outside CEOs are barely around long enough to see their photographs hung in the headquarters lobby. Gil Amelio left Apple seventeen months after he arrived from National Semiconductor. Ex-IBMer Richard Thoman was out of the top spot at Xerox after thirteen months. David Siegel gave up the wheel at Avis Rent A Car for US Airways but departed two years later.

Even under the best circumstances, CEO selection is something of a batting average: companies will not hit successfully every time. But two or more consecutive outsider outs can have a devastating effect on employees, partners, and strategic position. New leaders import new teams and management styles. Continuity and momentum collapse, the energy to execute dwindles, and morale plummets as employees obsess about who will get the next pink slip. Rather than focus on the competition, companies start to look inward. Bad external appointments are also expensive, since even poor performance is rewarded with rich severance packages.

The Trouble with Insiders

Sometimes an external candidate exists, however, who is, very simply, the best available choice. A skillful, diligent board may discover an outstanding fit between an outsider and the job at hand. Lou Gerstner and IBM spring to mind. And boards must remember that just as outsiders are not uniformly bad choices, insiders are not uniformly good ones. In certain situations, internal candidates actually present the greater risk.

Some concerns about insiders, ironically, emerge from their very closeness to the company. For example, as "known quantities," they may sail through a lax due-diligence process. Or their social networks and psychological ties may complicate efforts to change the culture. Some will not have had the right experience or been tested in the right ways. Individuals from functional areas may not be up to the task of leading the entire business. Or a shift in the industry or market landscape may render carefully nurtured skills irrelevant. In some cases, the credibility of the outgoing CEO or management team may be so sullied that only a new broom can sweep the company clean.

What's more, companies that have no ongoing senior management development program (currently more the rule than the exception) will in all probability need to look outside, maybe for as long as the next ten to twenty years. Outside candidates, in other words, should always be an option. But so long as they remain the only option, and boards lack rigor in identifying and assessing them, succession is imperiled.

The Trouble with CEO Development

Many organizations do a decent job nurturing middle managers, but meaningful leadership development stops well below the apex. The problem manifests itself as a dearth of senior managers, for which companies must increasingly shop in other neighborhoods. Almost half of respondents to the CLC survey had hired a third or more of their senior executive teams from outside, but only 22 percent of those did so because they considered external candidates irresistibly appealing. Rather, 45 percent of all respondents judged that it would take too long or be too expensive to develop successors internally.

It's easy to understand why they feel that way. Even where strong development programs exist, very few leaders will ever be qualified to run the company. *Very few.* A $25 billion corporation with 70,000 employees, for instance, may have three thousand leaders, perhaps fifty to one hundred of whom would qualify for one of the ten jobs just below the top. That same company would be fortunate to field five strong internal candidates for CEO—and two or three is a more realistic number. General Electric had

The Secret of Session C

Lots of people know about Session C, General Electric's annual, dialogue-intensive review of how its leadership resources match up with its business direction. But inside Session C is a process that almost no one knows about. It's called "tandem assessment," and it is among GE's most potent tools for evaluating CEO candidates—and for helping those rising stars evaluate themselves.

Every year, GE selects a different set of twenty to twenty-five leaders who might grow into CEOs or top functional leaders and sits each one down for a three- to four-hour session with two human resource heads from outside the person's own business unit. The HR executives trace the budding leader's progression from early childhood (where the prospect grew up, how this person's parents influenced his or her style of thinking, what the prospect's early values were) through recent accomplishments. They then conduct an exhaustive fact-finding mission both inside and outside the organization, including 360-degree reviews, massive reference checks, and interviews with bosses, direct reports, customers, and peers. Largely eschewing psychology, tandem assessment concentrates instead on observed, measurable performance within the business.

The product of all this effort is a fifteen- to twenty-page document that charts the high potential's work and development over decades. The report—brimming with accolades but also detailing areas for improvement—goes to the nascent leader, who uses it to improve his or her game. It also goes to the individual's business head, the senior human-resource executive in the person's unit, and to corporate headquarters, where it is avidly perused by GE's chair, the three vice chairs, and Bill Conaty, senior vice president for corporate human resources. "I usually wait until the end of the workday to read one of these because it takes an hour or so," says Conaty. "You find out incredibly interesting things about people in this process."

Tandem assessment is so intensive that only those swimming closest to the C-suite headwaters undergo it. But GE also encourages business units to conduct their own miniversions of the exercise.

The process not only hands rising leaders a mirror but also broadens their support network. Using HR executives from outside the subject's business unit ensures objectivity and gives the promising star two new mentors and two new reality checks. "If something pops up during your career that doesn't feel quite right and you want outside calibration," Conaty explains, "you might call one of these individuals and say, 'Hey, look, everybody is telling me great things here, but this just happened. Would you read anything into it?'"

around 225,000 workers in 1993 when Jack Welch identified twenty potential successors; over seven years, he winnowed the number to three. In CEO succession, it takes a ton of ore to produce an ounce of gold.

Furthermore, the window in which to spot CEO talent is narrow. Companies require sufficiently seasoned candidates who can be counted on to hold the top job for ten years or more. That puts the age of accession at between forty-six and fifty-two. In my experience, for a candidate to be ready by forty-six, serious development should start by age thirty. Recognizing which five saplings in a three-thousand-tree forest are the ones to nurture requires a degree of discernment that most line managers and HR departments lack and few are developing.

Some companies do identify candidates early but then fail to evaluate them properly. Such organizations often turn evaluation over to HR, which may rely excessively on packaged databases of leadership traits developed by researchers in the human behavior field. Those programs compare internal high potentials with generic benchmarks along many dimensions, a process that creates fragmented profiles of some cookie-cutter ideal rather than nuanced, individualized portraits. What's more, most of those dimensions reflect only the personality traits and not the skills required of a CEO.

Nor do many companies properly nurture the candidates they identify. Some misjudge the business's needs and consequently emphasize the wrong talents. Only 24 percent of organizations the CLC surveyed believe their leadership development efforts are aligned with their strategic goals. And those goals can be a moving target, changing in response to sometimes tectonic shifts in the external environment. The marketplace changes. Technology changes. Employees' skills become obsolete even as they develop. What's more, very few in-house executive education programs are designed to impart the skills and know-how that a CEO needs.

But the larger issue is that true development happens on the job, not in a classroom. Few companies know how to get their best people the experiences that would prepare them for the CEO role or to rigorously evaluate them in the jobs they do perform. Many companies, for example, still equate leadership development with circulating candidates through multiple functions. In the 1970s, that was the rule at AT&T, IBM, and Xerox, companies that produced leaders who went on to become CEOs elsewhere—and in some cases failed.

The problem with that approach is that potential candidates don't stay long enough in one position to live with the consequences of their decisions. In addition, functional leaders learn to lead functions, not whole companies. Faced with external competition, they fall back on their functional expertise. You can mine all possible lessons from a turn as VP of marketing and still be blindsided by a P&L.

The Trouble with Boards

Bob Stemple's short stint as the head of General Motors ended ingloriously in 1992—and so did the accepted wisdom that boards should automatically bless the departing CEO's handpicked successor.

Yet while directors describe CEO succession as one of their most consuming issues, they don't appear consumed by it. In a survey by Mercer Delta and the University of Southern California, 40 percent of corporate directors called their involvement in CEO succession planning less than optimal. (I would hazard to add that far fewer are satisfied with the *outcome* of their involvement.) Only 21 percent responded that they were satisfied with their level of participation in developing internal candidates for senior management.

A packed agenda is the chief culprit: governance and fiduciary duties, in particular, command an outsize share of boards' attention. Mercer Delta asked directors to compare the amount of time they spend now with the amount they spent a year earlier on nine key activities. Large majorities reported devoting more or many more hours to monitoring accounting, Sarbanes-Oxley issues, risk, and financial performance. They also reported spending less time interacting with and preparing potential CEO successors than on any other activity. Yet boards' work on succession represents probably 80 percent of the value they deliver. If the choice of CEO successor is superb, all subsequent decisions become easier.

Another huge problem is that the vast majority of search committee members have had no experience working together on a CEO succession. As a result, they seldom coalesce into deep-delving bodies that get to the pith of their companies' fundamental needs. So they end up approaching their search with only the demands of the moment or—worse—the broadest of requirements.

As they audition candidates, directors may be seduced by reputation, particularly if they're considering a Wall Street or media darling. A few aspiring CEOs employ publicists who flog rosy stories to journalists; when those leaders are up for other jobs, their press-bestowed halos follow them. Board members can also be blinded by charisma, by the sheer leaderishness of a candidate. There is nothing intrinsically wrong with charisma, though some criticize it as the sheep's clothing in which hubris lurks. But too often directors become so focused on what candidates are *like* that they don't press hard enough to discover what candidates can and cannot *do*.

For example, one board looking for a new CEO after firing the old one asked for someone who could build a great team and get things done. The recruiter presented such a person—an energetic, focused candidate whose personal qualities quickly won over directors. What the organization really needed was someone who could create a stream of new products and win shelf space from powerful retailers in a volatile marketplace. Unfortunately, the directors never specified those requirements or raised them either during interviews or the background check.

The candidate's upstream-marketing skills were poor to nonexistent. The company's market share declined precipitously, and three years later the CEO was out on his ear. On its second try, the board concentrated so hard on marketing that it ignored execution. The next CEO was a visionary and a marketing genius but was unable to get things done. The company, once first in its market, will probably be sold or stumble into Chapter 11.

Finally, directors too often shunt due diligence onto recruiters. As a result, that process can be quite superficial. One company that left vetting to its recruiter and its investment banker found itself saddled with a leader who botched critical people issues. At a postmortem three years later, directors discovered that at his former company the CEO had routinely punted people problems to the board chair, who had been CEO before him and occupied the office next to his. That would have been nice to know before the pen touched the contract.

The Trouble with Recruiters

Executive recruiters are honest and highly professional. Still, they can wield disproportionate influence in CEO succession decisions. One reason is concentration. Just three recruiters control some 80 percent of the *Fortune* 100 CEO search market (a single firm claims fully 60 percent of it), and one or two people within those companies direct the most important searches. These firms' social networks are vast and powerful. Anyone with a smidgen of ambition in the corporate world knows whom they have to know to get ahead.

At the same time, board members' inexperience and consequent inability to precisely define their needs makes recruiters' task difficult. Recruiters must satisfy their clients yet also manage them, helping the search committee to gel so they can extract the criteria they need while keeping requirements broad enough to cast the widest talent net possible.

When committees don't gel, recruiters may step into the vacuum with their own criteria, and directors too often let them. Unfortunately, no executive recruiter can grasp the subtleties of a client's business as well as the client can. In the absence of effective direction, recruiters generally approach each search with a boilerplate of the twenty or so attributes they consider most desirable for any CEO. That formula tends to overemphasize generic qualities such as character and vision, as well as team building, change-management, and relationship skills. Psychology and chemistry are also very important to executive recruiters: like directors, they may let a personality surplus overshadow a skills deficit.

In one—granted, extreme—case, the longtime CEO of a company with four highly successful businesses and a huge debt level was retiring. The recruiter produced a list of six candidates, pressing one—the head of a very large division at a multinational company—hard on the board. Yet all the recruiter gave the directors was a page-and-a-half description of this candidate's leadership skills; a list of his extensive connections with unions, customers, and government bodies; and an outline of his swift rise through the organization.

A financial performance history for the candidate's division was not included and not publicly available, so a member of the search committee began to dig. He discovered that return on assets under the candidate's supervision was miniscule over the previous five years, even though his division was four times larger than the entire company considering him for CEO. Furthermore, this man had never earned cost of capital in his life. Even so, the recruiter wanted to put him in charge of a business that had certainly done so—and that hoped to rise to the next level.

Fortunately, after much debate, the committee vetoed the recommendation, opting instead for number three on the recruiter's list—the president of another company, who had consistently improved performance and delivered a 20 percent return on equity. In his first three years, this new CEO took the stock from 24 to 108 in a slow-moving industry. The board was happy. Management was happy. The recruiter's preferred candidate was happy when he was placed at another, larger company—but then he was fired in six months.

Executive recruiters also succumb to the usual-suspects bias, primarily looking for new heads above other companies' necks. It is just plain easier to compile a list of sitting CEOs than to make a case for—or take a risk on—a COO or an executive VP. Some recruiters go so far as to approach sitting CEOs, even with no specific jobs to dangle, and urge them to consider looking elsewhere. The recruiters' goal is to loosen a prized gem from its setting and thereby beat a fellow recruiter to the punch.

Sometimes, the board's selection of recruiter is flawed from the start. A director may jump the gun, recommending a recruiter he has worked well with even before the search committee is formed. Nor do most boards examine search firms' track records—that is, how many of the CEOs the firm has placed have succeeded and how many have failed. Even if directors did ask that question, they're not likely to get the answer because it appears no one is monitoring recruiters' performance. The stock-buying public, by contrast, knows exactly how well directors score on their CEO choices.

How to Succeed at Succession

Charlie Bell's ascension to the top spot at McDonald's within hours of Jim Cantalupo's death reflected well on a company that had its house in order, particularly when compared—as it inevitably was—with Coca-Cola's simultaneous travails. Similarly, NBC's early, orderly announcement that Brian Williams would replace network news anchor Tom Brokaw stands in stark relief to CBS's public uncertainty over Dan Rather's successor. (Anchors are not CEOs, of course, but they are even more visible and arguably as consequential to their organizations' fortunes.)

By now it should be clear that the most important thing companies can do to improve succession is to bolster their leadership development and focus on those very rare people in their ranks who might one day be CEO. Organizations must identify high-potential candidates early in their careers, and global companies must look in all the countries where they operate. As candidates enter the development pipeline, managers must constantly align their charges' education and on-the-job experience with the emerging landscape. And they must rigorously assess the candidates' performance at each developmental stage.

The very best preparation for CEOs is progression through positions with responsibility for steadily larger and more complex P&L centers. A candidate might start by managing a single product, then a customer segment, then a country, then several product lines, then a business unit, and then a division. Whatever the progression, P&L responsibility at every level is key. The Thomson Corporation, a global provider of information solutions, comprises more than one hundred P&Ls, so its top people have abundant opportunity to run a $50 million to $100 million business. "That's the best crucible for formulating leaders that I know of," says Jim Smith, executive vice president of human resources and administration.

Companies not set up to provide such opportunities should create jobs—large projects or small internal organizations—that exercise the P&L muscle. Otherwise, they risk elevating an internal candidate who is not prepared. For example, one $10 billion company in a highly capital-intensive and unionized industry has targeted as CEO successor the head of its smallest division. The candidate is a brilliant, articulate young man but has no experience running a big business in general or this type of business in particular (his own division is knowledge intensive, and unionized labor has no presence). The board is considering creating a deputy position within its largest division for this person and making the fifty-nine-year-old current division head (who will retire in three years) his coach, granting that coach a bonus if he ensures his successor's success.

Companies with inflexible functional structures will probably be forced to import P&L-tested leaders from outside and place them in very high positions. To reduce the risk, they should bring in such executives three or four years before the expected succession. That can be challenging, however, because many will demand appointment to the top spot in less than a year.

But leadership development is just part of the solution. Boards, too, can greatly improve the chances of finding a strong successor by acting vigilantly before and during the search. Senior executive development should be overseen by the board's compensation and organization committee, which needs to receive periodic reports on the entire pool of potential CEOs and regular updates on those bobbing near the top of it. The committee should spend a third of its time examining lists of the top twenty candidates in the leadership pipeline. In addition, at least 15 percent of the sixty or so hours that members meet as a full board should be devoted to succession. At minimum, the board ought to dedicate two sessions a year to hashing over at least five CEO candidates, both internal and external.

In addition, directors should personally get to know the company's rising stars. Promising leaders should be invited to board meetings and to the dinners that precede board meetings, and members should talk with them informally whenever possible. Directors should also meet with and observe candidates within the natural habitats of their business operations. In this way, when it comes time to single out CEO candidates, directors will be considering a set of very well-known quantities.

The "Fit" Imperative

The goal of all these interactions and deliberations is for board members to reach a highly refined but dynamic understanding of the CEO position and their options for it long before appointing a successor. Company leaders should be as well defined as puzzle pieces; their strengths and experiences must match the shape of their organizations' needs. That is, they simply must *fit*. Boards achieve fit by specifying, in terms as precise as possible, three or four aspects of talent, know-how, and experience that are nonnegotiable.

Ideally, these attributes pertain to the organization's dominant needs for the next several years, but they should also relate to future growth. In one recent CEO succession, the company, in conjunction with a boutique recruiting firm, began with impossibly broad criteria that included everything from industry leader to change agent. The process floundered until the search committee narrowed its focus to three qualities: experience in segmenting markets according to customer needs; the talent to grow the

The Living Succession Tree

Four years ago, top management at the Thomson Corporation realized that its CEO succession process had passed out of life and into a stagnant existence on paper. Leadership development chugged along separately from business planning. Human resource groups produced reams of documents and charts dense with the branches of succession trees. "We never used them," says Jim Smith, executive vice president of human resources and administration at the $7 billion global company. "I never saw anybody go to a chart and say, 'Let's look at this.'"

So the company decided to rethink talent management in order to field leaders who could run Thomson under whatever conditions might exist. The new process is built on two principles: succession planning should happen in lockstep with strategy making, and the current CEO should be intimately and visibly involved.

Each February, Thomson's two hundred top managers gather to review corporate initiatives.

Then in April, CEO Richard Harrington, CFO Robert Daleo, and Smith conduct strategy reviews with emerging leaders in every business unit. Goals coming out of those talks—related to markets, customers, products, and growth areas—accompany the trio into the next round of discussions, which takes place in June and focuses on management development.

At that point, Harrington, Daleo, and Smith devote eight full days to listening to senior executives (including CEO candidates) report on *their* highest potentials. The trio insists on concrete examples throughout. "It's so easy to generalize on how somebody's doing: 'He's a good guy' and 'She's terrific with people,'" says Smith. "We want to pin down the facts beneath that. 'You say she's good with people. Give me some examples of who she's developed. How many have been promoted?'"

The same people who attended the strategy meetings attend the leadership development meetings, so everyone in the room understands what talent the business requires. And when those same people reconvene again a few months later to discuss budgets, conclusions from the strategy and leadership development rounds inform their decisions. By year's end, Thomson has tightly integrated strategy, leadership, and budget plans. And Harrington and his senior team have spent many, many hours getting to know the company's most promising CEO candidates.

Smith has three recommendations for companies interested in crafting a similar system, which has proved constructive to managers and the board alike. First, make sure the CEO devotes considerable personal time to identifying, getting to know, and developing leaders. Second, treat leadership development as part of the process used to run the business. And finally, make the process informal enough to encourage conversation. "We used to produce books," says Smith. "Now we have conversations."

business organically; and a track record of building strong executive teams. Those three skills, in addition to general leadership traits, delineated the pond in which this company fished.

The job of defining such qualities belongs to the search committee, which should form well before succession is scheduled to take place. As they wrestle with requirements, committee members must constantly keep in mind the company's changing circumstances, so that an understanding of what currently works doesn't congeal into what works, period.

For example, Bank of America flourished under dealmaker par excellence Hugh McColl Jr. for years. But by the time he stepped down in 2001, integration, rather than acquisition, had become the dominant challenge. Having recognized the altered environment several years before, BOA's board chose not a leader in McColl's image but instead Ken Lewis, a company veteran proficient at integration of acquisitions and organic growth. (For an example of how a company integrates its leadership development with its strategy, see the sidebar "The Living Succession Tree.")

Specific, nonnegotiable criteria also let directors keep control when they work with executive recruiters. With good direction, search firms can be a valuable source of objectivity—benchmarking internal candidates against outsiders and making sure that board members consider all possibilities, even if they prefer an insider. Some companies even bring in recruiters to do independent assessments of insider candidates. Their concurrence with a board's judgment carries weight with shareholders and potential critics.

Search firms ask boards to recommend candidates, and they take those recommendations seriously. But, ultimately, it is the recruiter who compiles the list, and the compiler of the list wields considerable influence. Directors must require from recruiters detailed explanations of how the candidates fulfill their criteria. A ten-page report on each is reasonable.

When the time comes to select the new CEO, directors—ordinarily a polite breed, unaccustomed to challenging one another or asking discomforting questions—must engage in a vigorous discussion of the candidates' comparative merits. One search committee that did an outstanding job making the final decision invited five candidates (two internal and three external) to a hotel for a couple of days. The two internal candidates were favorites of two different directors. On the first day, the committee interviewed three candidates, two external and one internal. The directors split into two groups of three, and each group spoke with one candidate for ninety minutes. After these interviews, the directors broke for forty-five minutes to share impressions, then switched candidates. Then the two groups of directors took turns interviewing the third candidate, similarly sharing impressions informally. At the end of the first day, the committee members debated over dinner, and the director who had originally advocated for the internal candidate volunteered that he was indeed not the strongest choice. The next day, they repeated the process with the two other candidates, and the results were remarkably the same, with the director who had originally advocated for the internal candidate changing his mind. In the course of these discussions, all hidden agendas fell away, requirements were honed, and directors were able to reach consensus.

Finally, board members must do due diligence on outside candidates—and do it well. Directors must seek reliable external sources and demand candor from them. Board members should ask first about the candidate's natural talents. If those gifts—admirable as they may be—do not match the position's specific profile, that candidate is not worth pursuing. Needless to say, due diligence is also the time to root out any fatal character flaws.

At this point, the role of the outgoing CEO is chiefly consultative. He or she must be active in spotting and grooming talent, help define the job's requirements, provide accurate information about both internal and external candidates, and facilitate discussions between candidates and directors. But when the choice of successor is imminent, make no mistake: that decision belongs to the board.

Inside a Development Engine

Despite the current crisis, we know it is possible to build organizations that reliably produce great CEOs. Starting after World War II, a few corporations emerged as veritable leadership factories. Companies such as General Electric, Emerson Electric, Sherwin-Williams, Procter & Gamble, and Johnson & Johnson managed to stock not only their own corner offices but also many others. (Of course even great companies sometimes stumble: Procter &

Gamble had a failure from within when it promoted Durk Jager to the top spot. But it is going great guns under the stewardship of company veteran A. G. Lafley.)

Reuben Mark has sat atop Colgate-Palmolive for twenty years, so the company's CEO succession chops have not been recently proven. But I believe the consumer products giant has a first-rate process for identifying and developing CEO talent. At the very least it produced three internal candidates who are excellent prospects for the job.

Colgate-Palmolive does business in more than two hundred countries, and its emerging leaders are correspondingly international and diverse. Leadership evaluation begins during the first year of employment. "It may seem strange to talk about someone who's been here just a year when discussing the pipeline to the CEO," says Bob Joy, senior vice president of global human resources. "But the earlier you start to identify talent, the earlier you can provide the job assignments and develop the broad business experience needed by a CEO candidate."

Each subsidiary identifies its own high potentials and submits that list to local general managers, who add and subtract names and then hand the list off to the division heads. These lists wend their way up the chain until they reach the Colgate-Palmolive Human Resource (CPHR) committee, composed of Colgate's CEO, president, and COO, the senior VP of HR, and the senior candidates up for the top job. CPHR modifies and consolidates the lists into a single master list, dispatching it back down the ranks where managers can contest decisions made by those above them. The process takes place once a year.

Those who make the cut are deployed in one of three tracks. The first track, local talent, is for relatively junior staff who might become the direct reports of a general manager. Someone more advanced would be designated regional talent, and given, for example, a significant position in Asia. The most elevated track—global talent—is the reservoir from which the most senior jobs are filled.

Throughout their careers, all these high potentials receive assignments that stretch their abilities and expand their knowledge, exposing them to a variety of markets, cultures, consumers, and business circumstances. CPHR itself designs career paths for general managers and higher positions because the committee is at the same time dynamically developing the profile of Colgate's future leadership team. (Also, says Joy, "you can imagine the kind of resistance you'd get from a division president who would like to keep his high-potential people in his own area.") The thousand or so highest high potentials (out of a total pool of about two thousand) receive outside executive coaching, which includes 360-degree feedback on current and past assignments.

Having identified its high potentials, Colgate strives to bolster their connection to the company. One tactic is recognition: "If you're talking about the future leaders of your company, you want them to feel special," says Joy. "You want them to have Colgate in their veins." Toward that end, the company sponsors a series of "visibility programs." One, for example, gathers high potentials from all over the world at Colgate's New York headquarters for week-long sessions during which they meet with every senior leader in the company. In addition, each high potential receives a special stock grant, which arrives with a personal letter from the CEO.

Colgate's global growth program mandates that all senior managers retain 90 percent of their high potentials or lose some compensation. If a high potential at any level, anywhere in the world, does resign, the CEO, the COO, the president, and Joy are alerted within twenty-four hours and move immediately to retain that person.

Perhaps most important, Joy collaborates with the office of the board chair to connect directors early and often with high potentials in all areas. At the most senior level, functional leaders introduce the board to the top two or three most promising heirs for their own positions, adding detailed analyses of those candidates' strengths and weaknesses. Emerging leaders routinely take part in presentations to the board and meet informally with directors over lunch. Board members closely track the progress not of one or two people but of the top two hundred, frequently discussing how each piece fits into the puzzle and what experiences or skills might improve that fit.

As a result, when CEO succession looms, the board and top management will be able to select from candidates they have spent many, many years observing and evaluating. "If you start five years or even ten years before the CEO is going to retire," says Joy, "it may be too late."

Of course Colgate-Palmolive—like General Electric—tackles succession from a position of strength. Its CEO has been two decades in the saddle, and he is passionate on the subject of an heir. Companies with less-veteran chiefs—and whose boards have been negligent in this area—will probably need to line up candidates quickly, while laying a deeper pipeline. They will in all likelihood have to bring in outsiders and position them to gain the requisite business and industry experience. That may mean shaking up the leadership team and reporting structures to free up slots in which outsiders can be tested. This restructuring will probably be resented, but it is necessary pain.

A quick infusion of talent may be a company's only course, but it is no way to run a railroad. Organizations without meaningful pipelines must start now to put them in place. Young companies should create the processes that will come to fruition in five or ten years' time. Choosing the CEO's successor is not one decision but the amalgam of thousands of decisions made by many people every day over years and years. Such meticulous, steady attention to defining needs and evaluating candidates produces strong leaders and inspires succession planners at lower levels to exercise the same discipline.

The trend of CEO failures must be reversed. CEO succession is all boards' paramount responsibility; nothing else so profoundly affects their companies' futures. Directors must start investing their time and energy today. The call for a new leader could come tomorrow.

Part IV

Improving Your Board's Performance and Impact

12

How Your Board Can Leverage Team Practices for Better Performance

Elise Walton

It sounds like an ideal situation: gather a diverse group of accomplished, energetic, dedicated leaders from all walks of the public and private sectors; give them stewardship of an important enterprise; and let them prioritize the relevant issues and make good decisions for present and future shareholder value. A dream story, but it doesn't always work like magic. Achieving high performance from a group of high-performance individuals blends practice, protocol, and art. To lead as a board, directors should leverage the practices of good teams.

Expectations for board oversight of corporate performance are high and are getting higher. Delivering shareholder returns, quality products, operational efficiency, and regulatory compliance are the basics expected of today's publicly listed corporation. Business continuity, sustainability, stakeholder and shareholder accountability, and good citizenship are emerging as new performance demands. The pressures this creates for boards are captured in studies and surveys by renowned professional organizations such as Risk Metrics, Heidrick & Struggles, McKinsey, the National Association of Corporate Directors (NACD), the Center for Organization Effectiveness, Spencer Stuart, and the Corporate Library—to name a few.

To provide proper oversight and leadership, the directors must work interdependently with each other, as a board, to achieve goals that no director could accomplish on his or her own. The duty of care, of overseeing management activity and corporate performance, surpasses the capability of any individual director, and is more than the simple sum of individual director activities. Directors must build common knowledge, align behind common goals, and live with the collective result. In effect, they must act as a team.

One needs look no further than recent press to see the consequences of a board that lacks the coordination of a team. Most notoriously, the Hewlett-Packard (HP) board has had one public dispute after another. In 2002, Walter Hewlett registered an eleventh-hour opposition to the board-approved purchase of Compaq that ended up in court. In 2005, the board orchestrated a last-minute termination of CEO Carly Fiorina, with no clear replacement strategy in place. In 2006, an investigation by the non-executive chair into board leaks drew accusations of illegal spying that led to an investigation by the attorney general as well as the termination of several directors and executives. The conflicts within this board undermined the corporation's ability to get on with business, hurt the firm's corporate reputation and investor relations, and demoralized staff and executives. Aligned goals and good team processes were not first principles for this board.

In contrast, Tyco CEO Ed Breen and lead director Jack Krol (also former CEO of DuPont) worked closely together to build an effective board after the Tyco meltdown in 2002. The departing CEO Dennis Kozlowski left Tyco with regulatory investigations on tax, fraud, and corruption, and a precipitous stock decline. Breen and Krol quickly replaced the entire board. The new directors were selected for their strong ethics and integrity. Krol and Breen worked together to ensure effective engagement and oversight on the part of the board. Subsequently, as the corporation began to examine its ability to create shareholder value as a multi-industry conglomerate, the board had to work through a major decision regarding a corporate separation. Work was done with clear, meaningful participation among the directors—different views were aired and debated. The decision was ultimately made and executed effectively, with no public acrimony or spillover. The goal alignment and teamwork on the board paid off for the company.[1]

The contrast between these two corporate boards demonstrates the value of a board that works well together as a team. Working well together requires dealing with complex, material decisions in a way that satisfies the duty of care entrusted to the board. This chapter examines the context of the board's work—what are the unique and challenging circumstances board directors face in order to work effectively together? In the context of these challenges, we identify practices that foster effective and appropriate teamwork and alignment. In conclusion, this chapter examines how current concepts of good governance support or undermine effective teamwork. If the board is a strategic asset to the firm, there can be nothing more important than boardroom practices that increase the board's ability to perform its duties well.

The Teamwork Context

Like any other team, board directors have a shared destiny. It is ultimately the *group's* performance that counts, regardless of individual performance or who calls the plays. The courts have indicated that no one director may be held uniquely liable for any one decision or any material oversight—that there are only board decisions, not individual director decisions. Directors enjoy or suffer the personal, reputation, and financial consequences of corporate results gone right or wrong, regardless of the individual role they may have played.

In the context of team design, the task shapes the work of the board and how it can provide leadership. Teams work well when they have a clear, compelling, common goal; good processes; the right mix and number of members; and a means by which they can evaluate effectiveness. For instance, sports teams have a clear goal—to score more than the opposing team. They have clear mechanisms for doing this—players, goals, courts, balls, rules, and so forth. Where a sports team has specificity and clarity, directors in contrast have ambiguity, diversity, and multiple goals. The board's context creates challenges for performing effectively as a team. Consider the following circumstances confronting boardrooms.

Complex goals. Boards have to manage a complex set of interdependent goals, which may be strict trade-offs (cash returned to shareholders or cash invested in internal projects) or synergistic (investments in supply chain increase cost effectiveness and customer satisfaction). The original impetus for boards—to represent the interests of the investors and shareowners—created a simple decision principle: directors have responsibility to achieve the highest share price possible. If the shares are trading at $10, a $15 a share offer should be taken. But the diversity of shareholder groups and shareholder objectives makes even a straightforward decision principle more complex. Value for which shareholders? Over what time frame? With what risk? The 2008 sale of Bear Sterns to JPMorgan for less than a tenth of its 2007 market value demonstrates the conflicts between long-term holders, short-term holders, traders, employees (who had incentives both to sell and not to sell), the buyer, and the government as to what constitutes an acceptable price.

However, even the overarching goal of shareholder value is coming under question from regulators, lawyers, unions, and even investors. Many corporations are moving beyond the singular ideal of shareholder value and expressly publish governance principles that indicate the board should consider a broader group of stakeholders—employees, customers, and even society at large. The multiplicity of goals and desired outcomes makes one parameter of teamwork—a definitive or singular goal—challenging.

Ambiguous and inconclusive material. The board adds value by how the directors, as a team, sort through complex information and use it to guide attention and action. The information is abstract, complex, and interdependent. When one business case seems solid, new information comes to light that may raise doubts. There are multiple measures for even the simple concepts of revenue and return. Different time horizons add to the ambiguity of the data—and how boards distribute value over time. Certain sure-thing decisions have failed the test of time, while some seemingly big risks have proven brilliant. The 2002 HP decision to acquire Compaq, described earlier, caused significant debate about the wisdom of that course of action, but years later, that decision was heralded as a great success. The issues and their solutions are indeterminate—there is no formulaic path, no defining variable or guaranteed process even when a goal is clear.

Big bets. The task of boards means that primarily the biggest investments and issues come to the directors, and the magnitude of the decisions makes the board's decisions weightier. Board-level decisions such as a sale, or a large capital investment, or a CEO selection require greater debate because once done, they are hard to undo. For example, the Yahoo! board has resisted the 2008 takeover offer extended by Microsoft, despite the apparent premium over Yahoo!'s trading stock price. The benefits and costs of the proposed merger aside, this merger is a highly consequential, bet-the-company, one-shot decision. America Online purchased Time Warner to combine the power of the Internet with traditional media strength. AOL Time Warner, the product of the merger, combined several lines of business and faced significant business challenges, including large losses. There is no going back to the old AOL. With consequential or irrevocable decisions, deliberations become more arduous.

Increasing accountability. Governance and shareholder activists are holding directors to ever-greater accountability on performance and key decisions. For instance, the Children's Investment Fund Management group has called on four Merrill Lynch directors to describe what they did to protect shareholders from excessive mortgage-related risk over the past two years and the estimated loss of $35 billion to shareholders in 2007.[2] In 2007, Breeden Capital Management wrote to the SEC, "H&R Block's stock has significantly underperformed the S&P 500 index for the five years ended June 15, 2007. As shareholders, we believe that five years is long enough to wait for H&R Block to achieve attractive returns for shareholders. This board needs fresh perspectives and new energy, which we intend to supply, to tackle the company's problems." Breeden Capital Management prevailed in its proxy fight at H&R Block, winning all three board seats up for election at the tax-return-preparation firm. Whether activism leads to new directors or new conversations with shareholders, the board members will find great scrutiny of their actions, and boards will be expected to have greater transparency in the future. Furthermore, directors now have, on average, longer service to a company in their role than the CEOs they oversee, placing them squarely responsible for key corporate decisions.

Intermittent interactions. Although boards are increasing the frequency of their interactions—via monthly phone calls, more frequent meetings, and meetings held in venues other than the boardroom—these interactions are still not as regular as those of management teams, research teams, or other knowledge-based teams. Their relative infrequency makes it harder to develop and use social norms in discovering, understanding, and utilizing complex, ambiguous information.

Fluctuating demands. Boards may quickly change their involvement under conditions of shareholder activism, lawsuits, product recalls, regulatory activity, or unexpected succession events such as a CEO death, to name a few. Major industry events—the dot-com bust or the mortgage and liquidity crises—drive immediate and significant demands on the directors serving firms in affected industries. The NACD 2007 survey estimates directors work two hundred hours a year for the boards they serve, but no doubt hours vary widely depending on the work demands facing the board.

The context just described—growing scope and volatility, increased accountability, fluctuating demands—create a formidable challenge for the board's leadership and work as a team. What can board directors do to ensure that they are ready—as a team—to step in and protect the long-term value of the firm? What practices can the board directors use to function effectively and get the most out of their time and knowledge?

Emerging board practices, coupled with knowledge of effective group process, can provide guidance to how directors are working together effectively. These practices help the board turn data into information, and information into insight, and insight into action. Though no practice can guarantee success, these nine team-based practices summarized in Figure 12.1 can enhance a board's ability to provide the leadership the corporation requires.

The Teamwork Practices: From Information to Insight to Informed Action

Practice 1: Build a Shared View of the Corporate Context

Boards and directors need a holistic, common understanding of the enterprise that provides the foundation for informed debate and decision. The corporate context includes the vision, the goals, the values, and the performance expectations of the enterprise. It provides a comprehensive view that goes well beyond financial pro formas. Understanding the context encompasses business fundamentals as well as the venues and stakeholders of the firm—including markets, customers, employees, investors, regulators, and so forth.

The challenge in understanding the corporate context is identifying the most relevant information. Basic knowledge is important, and understanding nuances and alternative views can make the difference in a board's ability to add value. Obviously the board agenda—the topics covered during the directors' time together—is a primary venue for building common understanding

Practice 1: Build a shared view of the corporate context. What is important to board effectiveness is that there is a baseline of common knowledge to work with, and a shared view of the values.
Practice 2: Diversify your data sources. Directors are looking to additional sources of information about the company—and may extend their reach to seek second opinions from advisers, to gain insight from executive management, and even to solicit ideas from investors or customers.
Practice 3: Use tools to synthesize and prioritize information. From committees to scorecards, boards need ways of digesting the massive scope of information in their purview.
Practice 4: Set the tone for active learning. Directors need to be engaged in a learning effort. Being active learners means directors shape the agenda and content of what the board needs to understand.
Practice 5: Practice productive debate. Regardless of the regulation, effective independence can only be created in a group that values dissent and handles conflict productively. Debate enables directors to assimilate individual knowledge into collective understanding.
Practice 6: Go beyond the expected. Teams that prepare for the unexpected handle surprise events better when they arise. Whether it is a planned and orderly CEO succession or a surprise hostile bid, preparation facilitates the capacity to act.
Practice 7: Actively manage director composition. Boards regularly examine the mix of directors over time—looking for skills, orientation, and experience that will help the group gain insight into the corporation, its opportunities, and its value.
Practice 8: Stay relevant, individually and collectively. Whether sponsored by the company or not, good directors and boards actively examine their contribution and their perspective. Directors must stay attuned to how their views and self-interests support or undermine their effective contribution.
Practice 9: Be versatile. To create the kind of leadership required by boards today, directors need to stay open to new information and know when to change.

Figure 12.1. Leading as a Team: Nine Best Practices of Effective Boards.

of the corporate context. Fundamental firm performance and financial data is necessary but not sufficient. What else should be on the board agenda?

To expand their view of the corporate context, boards are looking to nonfinancial indicators that predict future competitiveness and market conditions (production rates, inventories and shipment forecasts, customer satisfaction) in order to fully understand the context of their decision making. A 2007 PricewaterhouseCoopers survey found that over half the boards surveyed receive data on customer satisfaction.[3] Though directors feel the greatest responsibility toward long-term shareholders and investors, customers and employees are meaningful constituencies. The survey noted that earnings restatement is still the most important signal that the board should take a more active role. The second most important prompt is data showing a poor customer satisfaction track record. Boards need to see formal customer data—satisfaction measures, repeat purchase rates, or whatever metrics are most meaningful—to accurately assess the customer aspect of their corporate context. In fact, one board decided that directors should periodically review actual customer comments to get a visceral feel for what customers are saying.

Boards are also looking more carefully at key stakeholders as part of the corporate context. Now, for instance, one board does a biannual review of the shareholders—who holds their shares and why, who is buying, and who is selling. Another board is formalizing a shareholder relations policy, advocating regular meetings between two designated directors and major shareholders.

Having the right information and a shared view of the corporate context is foundational for the critical conversations the board—as a team—must have, and for the leadership decisions the board must make. The context tells the board *what* to pay attention to. The next practice looks not only at what information but at the sources of information.

Practice 2: Diversify Your Data Sources

Using the data in the 2007 NACD Public Company Survey, an analysis identified correlates of the board effectiveness ratings. *Information sharing* dominated other variables in terms of correlation with overall board effectiveness (particularly in the areas of strategic planning and corporate valuation). Information-sharing variables had higher correlations with effectiveness ratings than did items related to directors' skills. Notably, information provided by the CEO *and* information provided by outside advisers were both important correlates of effectiveness.[4] A related finding comes from the Center for Effective Organizations' and Heidrick & Struggles' 2007 board survey, in which less than a third of the respondents reported that they had good access to independent information, suggesting that a sizable majority might like better information from other sources.[5] If boards see benefits from nontraditional sources of information, where should they look to get other data and points of view?

One concrete example of getting information from diverse sources is a structured board trip. With increasing frequency over the past few years, U.S. CEOs have begun to take their boards to China and India to better understand how those economies affect the company and its options. Through this kind of direct experience in different countries and economies, the directors develop a broader, deeper understanding of the global realities within which the company operates.

Site visits, to stores, plants, or business units, can similarly provide diverse views on corporate performance. Several companies—Home Depot and GE, among others—require these. These visits provide a direct, personal experience of what's going on in the business. Hearing from suppliers, employees, and customers provides important insight into the work of the company, the state of the workforce, and customer-related activities. Shareholder meetings, partner meetings, or other large-group events in which other stakeholders have a voice provide additional perspective.

Diversifying data sources can be reflected in board calendars and agendas. For instance, one board makes sure it has a presentation from a major advertising service provider at least once a year. Another board sponsors educational events for the board, inviting academics, news commentators, and public activists, among others, to speak with directors. Others have set up one-on-one mentoring relationships between specific directors and key executives. Some boards institutionalize practices that allow directors to draw on diverse data sources, such as requiring second opinions on major advisory recommendations in business decisions. All of these, while demanding time, expand the directors' ability to comprehend the complexity of the company and the context they oversee.

This practice helps boards avoid developing a unitary or parochial perspective. By continually exposing themselves to different views, directors are less likely to be surprised by events that fall outside the corporate frame or prevailing internal viewpoints. By diversifying data sources, directors are more likely to hear perspectives that enable independent thinking. As James Surowiecki asserts in *The Wisdom of Crowds*, it's hard to have a collectively intelligent group without diversity.[6]

Practice 3: Use Tools to Synthesize and Prioritize Information

Directors often ask for more information but are inarticulate about what specifically they need. CEOs and general counsels complain, "I don't know what else to give them!" This phenomenon repeats itself from board to board and reflects the information processing challenge that the boards and directors confront. The challenge is not insufficient information; in fact, information is "oversufficient."

A monumental amount of information accumulates at the top of the corporation. Information complexity is an issue faced by boards, CEOs, and those that hold them accountable. Even the SEC has begun to address the issue of information complexity, requiring that compensation disclosures be in "plain English." The request for more information is usually, in fact, a request for useful information.

Good practice focuses information and data in a way that helps the directors build common board insight and knowledge. Focusing tools help directors get information out of data more quickly, so they can spend less time reviewing the data and more time on discussion. Boards' routines, such as a discussion protocol for particular topics, can help directors move through a specific information chain more rapidly. As the board repeats structured experiences with information, its ability to assimilate information improves.

Some boards use a risk map to cover the range of strategic, financial, and operational risks (from brand risk, human capital risk, share erosion, and so on). These provide at-a-glance insight into issues the board should pay attention to. Many boards use a company or CEO scorecard—complete with red, yellow, and green scoring—to consistently review performance in key areas (financial, customer, employee, and growth). These structuring tools provide a comprehensive, executive view of what the board should consider. With repeated use, directors learn "what to look for" in the data they can see.

Committees are a synthesizing tool, and the core committees—governance and nominating, compensation, and audit—do just that for many boards. Committees are where most of the work gets done. Boards also create issue-specific committees or special purpose or time-bounded committees to deal with specific information challenges. Strategy, finance, sustainability, or merger and acquisition (M&A) committees have been adopted by some companies when there is substantial information to be reviewed and the board's objective is collaborative engagement. In some boards, the lead director has an executive committee comprising committee heads so that a small subgroup can synthesize the information and knowledge developed at the committee level.

When a board needs to process a unique set of information consistently, a tool may be preferable to an undesignated group doing work informally out in front of the board. One board, working with a company that had an acquisitive growth strategy, found itself reviewing acquisition proposals frequently. A subset of the directors—those with more M&A experience—had informal, individual conversations around the "fit" of certain proposed acquisitions and occasionally spearheaded challenges to specific proposals. In fact, the informal director group proposed the board operationalize itself as an M&A committee. The CEO felt the informal group, and the proposed committee, were disempowering and were second-guessing the company's M&A team and its work. This board evaluated choices for synthesizing the flow of M&A proposals, including an improved M&A management process, a liaison director to the M&A team, and M&A subcommittee (permanent or temporary), among others. Eventually, having reaffirmed the corporate strategy and context, the board and the CEO agreed on criteria for which deals fit and which did not fit the strategy. This tool made board consideration and action on M&A proposals much more effective and less polarizing.

Of course, agenda planning and time management are important tools for helping directors absorb and synthesize information. Frequent conversations help, and some boards have instituted sixty- or ninety-minute monthly phone calls with the CEO for a business update. This frequency allows directors to stay current and digest information over time, rather than loading all information into full board meetings—which often overload directors with too many topics and too much information. Too often, the failure to structure the discussion correctly not only undermines learning but frustrates directors and the board. As one director said, "All new lead directors should have a review of good meeting practice—a kind of Robert's Rules of Order, but not so parliamentarian." Basic actions that lead to successful meetings include the following: (1) planning an achievable agenda that focuses on the right topics, (2) managing time effectively, (3) having a clear sense of discussion intent (information sharing, debate, decision), (4) using good listening and conversation skills, (5) ensuring that all directors get a chance to participate in the discussion, (6) formally checking with all members before reaching a major decision, and (7) checking in on performance informally at the conclusion of the meeting. And finally, the boardroom conversation needs sufficient time to make sense of issues, but it cannot take so much time that it tests patience and attention, or digresses into areas outside the board's realm.

Practice 4: Set the Tone for Active Learning

The concept of active learning puts responsibility for learning with learners and asserts that engagement is critical for effective learning. In this line of thinking, directors are not just receivers of information but also proactive in seeking and shaping relevant board content.

Time is an important enabler for active learning. Boards and companies are rightly concerned that directors who are spread thin will not devote sufficient attention, or *share of mind*, to their duties on the company's board. The Center for Effective Organizations and Heidrick & Struggles' report finds that 40 percent of the firms in their survey limit the number of boards on which outside directors can serve, a major increase from just 3 percent in 2001.[7] The "over-boarded" director may have too many commitments to be valuable to any one company and certainly won't be working with his or her team to develop the learning agenda.

One practice that supports active learning is corporate-funded directors' education, including director education programs, general business programs, and forums and conferences on board-relevant topics. When directors have opportunities to understand broad trends and issues, to hear about other boards, and to educate themselves on regulatory changes, they are better able to learn and contribute to their own board. In-boardroom programs are particularly powerful experiences because the team can hear the information and learn *together*. Going through the experience *together* enables the directors to improve their common knowledge base and collective wisdom. It also provides a venue for building skills in productive conversation, relevance, and vigilance.

Another practice to build active learning is to formally outline protocols of inquiry. For instance, one board developed five standard and straightforward questions for every big strategic decision (Does this fit with the strategy? What is the cost of not doing this? What are the alternatives? What are the unseen risks?

Who would oppose this?). This tool helped synthesize information, but also created etiquette for the boardroom that gave directors polite permission to challenge. When a director asked one of these five questions, it was commonly acknowledged that the speaker's intent was not rude or hostile, but the speaker was following an agreed practice to ensure diligent discovery and decision making. Further, the question list put the onus on directors to explore proposals and codified a board culture in which the directors proactively shaped learning and board discussion.

Active learning for boards must be a team phenomenon, because the consequent knowledge gained from active learning must be useful to the full group. As such, learning requires not only inquiry and logic but also social norms and expected behavior. For example, is it okay to ask questions? Is it okay to challenge assumptions? Is enough time allocated to having the board develop a point of view, including contrarian points of view? Is a learning orientation valued? By accepting different views and welcoming the uninformed question, the board ensures that it is getting the best thinking from its resources. In fact, Jim Surowiecki argues that having an uninformed view or the "naïve" question may be essential to group effectiveness.[8]

Practice 5: Practice Productive Debate

Boardroom conversation has to be well managed so that different points of view are heard, contemplated, debated, and synthesized. Conversation should incorporate specialized knowledge but not allow specialists or experts to dominate the decisions. It should unearth disagreement but not make divisiveness its only result. Productive debate knits together individual perspectives into a fabric for common knowledge and collective action.

Productive debate requires fundamental skills in dialogue and debate. Simple techniques for achieving conversational clarity have been developed over the past few decades—for example, being clear on separating observations and inferences made from those observations, making direct proposals versus disguised proposals, summarizing discussion points, and calling for a decision when needed. Productive debate and constructive conversation go beyond the norm of "no such thing as a stupid question" to norms about how to ask good questions, how to build on a line of questioning, and how to deal with unsatisfactory answers. Chapter Four, by Katharina Pick, illustrates how a board chair can foster productive dialogue and debate.

Focused and thorough inquiry is essential, not merely the ability to ask any question. Legal experts argue that the greatest liability when confronted with a shareholders' lawsuit or other legal action is finding that questions were raised but no resolution was sought. That is, once an issue is raised, the directors must discharge their duty by tracking down an acceptable answer. A board skilled at productive debate will be able to use the collective experience and knowledge of directors to pursue the understanding and resolution of critical issues.

An essential venue for building active debate is the board retreat. Retreats allow for immersion and dialogue, customer stories, outsider perspectives, and informal time with a broader set of company leaders. A two-day retreat is common, but some boards now have full-week strategy retreats. The extended time together provides the opportunity to get deeper into discussion than does the tightly scheduled board meeting. Board trips and in-boardroom education can provide similar opportunities to build debate and immersion.

Of course, debate must be complemented with decision and closure. Directors and executives often have a bias for action and decry time spent on information and debate. Yet debate is the underpinning of agreement and alignment. Without sufficient debate and the consequent understanding, decisions are delayed, opportunities are missed, and, worst of all, decisions made are second-guessed in public.

Practice 6: Go Beyond the Expected

As the corporate context becomes increasingly volatile, being prepared for major change is a strategic advantage. The practices thus far focus on fundamentals such as getting relevant information and having productive discussions. This practice takes board discussions beyond the fundamentals, from the likely into the unlikely. By anticipating change and constructing different scenarios, boards come to a reasoned understanding of their options, which allows them to act quickly when opportunities or threats arise.

One bank director makes the point: "A big strategy conversation should never be a surprise. We regularly cover alternative scenarios, and so when a big acquisition opportunity came along, the board was well prepared to make a decision quickly—because we'd discussed it several times in the past. When you look at ABN Amro, you get the sense from a distance that they hadn't given their options much thought before the bids started coming in." Another director echoed the same, saying, "You never want to be forced to make a snap decision with poor information. Boards don't work well that way. You can see that in some of the bidding fiascos, where buyers seemed to be unaware of the pitfalls in their approach to the acquisition target."[9]

Going beyond the expected places a value on scenarios—possible events that are not contemplated by the stated plans and goals of the organization. For instance, one board walked through scenarios including a major supply disruption from Asia, a major pandemic, and a dramatic change in the major competitor's behavior. While none of these were presumed likely, the discussion allowed the board to debate alternative responses in a hypothetical context. This exercise built the board's ability to envision future events, and enhanced its capacity to act should one of the unlikely events unfold.

Going beyond the expected requires time for "what if" discussions and long-range thinking. Envisioning future scenarios helps a board build leadership thinking by being out ahead of events. Going beyond the expected helps boards consider what relationships the board might need, and can encourage directors to ensure those relationships exist before an emergency when they might be needed.

Practice 7: Actively Manage Director Composition

Greater director capability, knowledge, and skill are the products of greater board accountability. Boards must regularly take stock of their membership, size, and committees to be sure they have the right skills for their situation. Actively managing composition means finding the right mix of skills, as well as knowing how to leverage current directors' skills, experience, and orientation to address topics of concern to the corporation and its shareholders. This is an ongoing effort and involves change in directors as well as changing directors—that is, development, recruitment, and replacement. Chapter Six, by Richard Leblanc, explores this critical topic as well.

CEOs and directors are using several strategies to manage composition. Boards are developing director-profile strategies for the right mix of directors. In recent years, boards have added a substantially greater mix of skills—more finance experts, more globally experienced directors (specifically in emerging markets, Asia-Pacific, and China), and more operational executives, as well as technology and marketing directors. Diversity also remains an objective, with mixed success: women are increasing in the population of directors, while minorities have made smaller gains. As firms extend their search for new and different skills, directors and CEOs are extending beyond traditional networks to more frequent use of search firms, extending their personal networks, alumni networks, and independently listed directors in venues such as the NACD database, among others.

Annual elections are an opportunity to manage composition—specifically, to manage the mix. In one case, a board's governance and nominating committee assessed the portfolio of director skills and felt that there were not enough directors with operational experience and too many directors with investing backgrounds. After some debate, the lead director asked an "investor" director to step down from election, explaining that the board needed the spot for a specific expertise.

Director assessment is also a tool that companies can employ to manage the "soft side" of composition—that is, helping existing directors contribute. Properly handled, director assessments can give directors insight into how their personal contributions are seen by other directors and what they can do to increase the value they bring to the board. Director assessments sometimes provoke composition changes as well. Said one CEO, "It was some time after our merger, and it was clear that one of the inherited directors wasn't engaged or productive. We hired a third party to conduct director assessments. Through this process, it became clear that the full board felt this director wasn't contributing. Once that became known, I think he had little choice but to step down."

Right-sizing the board is another practice for matching director composition to need, with a growing preference among public companies for smaller-sized boards. One director described the problem with his thirteen-person board meeting: "After the meeting, we had dinner and a few of us were complaining about how board size made it hard to have a good conversation. One of the management team who presented to us was at the table and, overhearing our conversation, commented on his presentations to us: 'I got twenty-six questions in rapid fire, none of which had anything to do with any other question. We went overtime, and no one really learned much about what I had to share.'"

Richard Hackman's research on teams suggests that a team should be slightly smaller than the task requires, and some empirical studies have correlated board effectiveness with smaller board size.[10] The most recent NACD study indicated that although directors tend to endorse the size of the board they serve on, the preferred board size is between seven and nine directors.[11] Spencer Stuart's 2007 report notes a trend toward smaller boards, with the greatest decrease occurring in boards of twelve or more members.[12]

Smaller boards confer benefits for directors and for board performance. Directors can get to know each other better, which can foster greater collaboration and deeper conversation. Larger boards may focus on ratifying, as they have limited ability for debate and full participation by all.[13] Smaller boards are often more attractive candidates, and an undersized board can add a director more easily if a good candidate becomes available. However, boards can be too small, and must be able to staff key committees. Fewer than seven directors creates a risk of not being able to fill committees appropriately, and, in general, boards need a "cushion" to deal with an unanticipated event.[14]

Practice 8: Stay Relevant, Individually and Collectively

Directors belong to boards because they have something to offer, but their experience, skills, and objectives need to be put into context and kept "fresh" to be of value. Directors need to make sure their knowledge and insight are relevant and translate effectively to the board requirements and corporate context. Independent directors inevitably bring their unique lens to a problem, but they need to be aware of the limits of that lens. For instance, one director described the challenge associated with a peer director whose background was too close to the business. With a strong consulting background on the company's product and technology, this director frequently "turned consultant" in the boardroom. Unfortunately, he went into too much detail, as if to demonstrate his breadth, rather than contribute to a discussion of equals.

In a more positive example, a lead director brought a focus on risk management—an important area for a growing diversified services company he served. However, this director came from a materials and manufacturing company, for which hazard risk—the potential for harm to people, property, or the environment—is significant. One executive noted, "Risk assessments are good, but some directors' questions obviously come from a different background. Chemical hazards aren't very relevant in a services company." After some calibration, this director translated his extensive experience and knowledge into questions more relevant to the corporate context of the services firm.

A full board assessment process can help directors, individually and collectively, stay relevant. The full board assessment process goes beyond the required surveys. Board surveys, though efficient, are often not textured enough to provide useful, actionable data. Typically, with a survey scale of 1 to 5, results range from 3.9 to 4.5, providing little differentiation in terms of highs and lows. Year-over-year changes can be informative but are rarely dramatic. This common pattern leaves directors looking at marginal changes and underwhelming data.

For this reason, boards conduct a full board assessment, complementing surveys with in-depth director and management interviews. Interviews supplement the consistent, quantifiable survey data with interpretive, qualitative information that directly addresses the issues on the minds of directors and executives. These interviews more effectively surface specific actions that may need to be taken. Finally, the full assessment process provides better insight into perceptions about board and director contribution and relevance. Boards typically conduct this type of in-depth assessment on a three-year cycle, or at such time when company events suggest better insight into directors' thinking would be important. Chapters Five and Six both explore assessments in greater detail.

A few boards are experimenting with a related practice—the board coach. Like coaches who help executives and executive teams work together more effectively, board coaches provide support, usually via the lead director or the CEO, to the group, to the general counsel, and to key board-support resources. In some cases, boards have informally anointed member-coaches—that is, one or two directors take unique responsibility for improving conversations and individual effectiveness. Board education outside the boardroom can also help directors stay relevant. By learning what other boards and directors are doing, a director can compare and contrast the skills and practices of his or her own board with others, and also calibrate his or her skills in a broader population of directors.

Keeping one's contribution relevant is ultimately the individual director's responsibility and depends greatly on individual self-awareness. Feedback can be helpful, but the individual director needs to be open to insight and to continual and ruthless examination of the value and objectivity of his or her directorship. In some cases, directors may need to examine and adjust their engagement. In a positive example, one director's self-examination led him to a difficult decision—leaving the board. He commented, "It was hard to leave the board—I care a lot about the company, there are a lot of good things they are doing. But I was uncomfortable with what management was doing. It was almost an integrity issue, so I decided I shouldn't continue." Though this director had plenty of reasons to stay with the status quo, his self-examination led him to a tough decision. In a less positive example on another board, a director continually pressed his board to consider replacing the CEO. However, it was clear to many whom this director had in mind as the CEO's replacement—himself. His colleagues on the board noted his apparent objective. One peer commented, "We saw some conflict of interest in that approach." This director failed to stay objective in making his contribution.

Staying relevant is an essential to director independence. To be independent and objective, directors must understand their own agendas and vulnerabilities. Board leadership requires that directors continually assess their individual perspectives, biases, and viewpoints to ascertain whether they are able to provide oversight that is valuable and independent. When skills are no longer relevant, or independence is jeopardized, directors must be willing to make tough decisions.

Practice 9: Be Versatile

Versatility, as used here, takes the definition of "turning with ease from one thing to another." One constant for boards is change, and dealing with change requires versatility on the part of the board and its directors. Some versatility is implied in formalized requirements, such as term limits and rotation among committee assignments. But versatility is part of behavior and norms. Directors must be flexible in adapting the contributions they offer or they risk being pigeonholed as the predictable advocate of one point of view, or as narrowly skilled in only one area.

Versatility suggests that all directors can contribute across the spectrum of board work. Diverse information and skills will not make a difference unless the board, as a team, values the diversity. Enron's board, for example, had competent, experienced directors and was a top-rated board though, apparently, the experienced directors were not the ones who were challenging some of the unusual practices.[15] In fact, it is often the less-business-based directors—those with government or public-sector backgrounds—who raise some of the most important and fundamental questions. Therefore, being able to debate and synthesize information *with an open mind* is an important skill, and this requires versatility of director input and roles.

How does the board, as a team, stay versatile? Circumstances dictate: an oversight board may need to become more operational, or a highly engaged board may need to ratchet back. Individual directors may need to shift roles and activities. Equally difficult, even unnatural, is for directors to oversee and advocate for a change in course that they may have sponsored and invested time, money, and reputation in. When AT&T finally spun out its cable unit to ATT Comcast, the board had long known that AT&T's cable investment, which they had supported, had not worked.[16]

The ability to recognize and act on a failed course of action is a critical aspect of versatility for the board that provides leadership.

No group—managers, regulators, academics, directors—has a perfect record of identifying dramatic changes in advance. Over the past two decades, one can easily find the CEO, board, or company heralded as a role model in one year, only to fail and be pilloried the following year. In the moment, it can be impossible to differentiate between a few tough quarters, naturally occurring variance, and an emerging disaster. Versatility requires attentiveness to the context and its demands—anticipating when change is required. Acting on slow-moving change—the erosion of share, glacial industry shifts that leave a company on the outside, the failure to maintain assets such that a worn infrastructure is incapable of meeting customer expectations or safety requirement—is a venue for boards to provide leadership. A strong board should address these trends before they develop into problems.

Reflections and Conclusion

As the role of board evolves, directors and the boards they serve will seek new ways of leading as a team. Equally important, the effective board can be construed as a strategic asset, one that can positively improve the value of a firm.[17] Directors in this century will have further responsibility to work as a team to provide leadership that differentiates between corporate success and corporate failure—in the context determined.

The practices described in this chapter are designed to improve the board's ability to lead as a team. As such, they are *not* about creating director independence, but about creating *appropriate interdependence*. Independence is an important goal for boards, and independent directors become required for most public company boards.[18] Independence criteria are spelled out specifically by the SEC and the NYSE and in many corporations' governance principles. However, these definitions, which focus on economic or employment ties, are somewhat limited, and it is unclear how best to define director independence or even whether an all-independent director board does a better job on corporate governance or overall firm performance.

Returning to the context of team design, some principles suggest limits to the ideal of independence. For instance, psychological research has shown that even the most subtle contextual elements—say, finding a dime in a phone booth—can affect altruistic behavior.[19] To argue an extreme, serving lunch to directors could create feelings of altruism, thereby making the board more likely to approve a management-recommended acquisition, and less independent.

Furthermore, effective teams are characterized by a supportive environment. Positive expectations facilitate individual contribution, while familiarity and shared mental models contribute to the capability of individuals to work together to achieve common goals. Thus boards in which directors have positive regard for peers might be more effective. Finally, shared direction is an important element of an effective team—it guides and shapes behavior in ways that allow the team members to coordinate activity for higher performance. This focus on interdependence reflects what directors and CEOs already know—"fit" is important. Said one director, "When you decide to go on a board, make sure you can support the CEO's direction." One CEO agrees, "I don't think the directors who believe their role is to distrust management are actually good directors."

The calculus of working relationships is complex, to say the least. The elements that help the board to lead as a team—common goals, positive expectations, and interdependence—can also, paradoxically, undermine the board performance. Positive regard may be a threat to independence if directors avoid conflict with esteemed colleagues. An aligned team can reinforce homogeneity and, at an extreme, succumb to "groupthink"—the phenomenon found in highly cohesive groups whose desire for unanimity overrides a realistic appraisal of a situation or course of action. But "groupthink" occurs in a variety of ways, not only as blind support of management proposals. The financial industry in 2007 arguably suffered from "industry sector think," with CEOs and boards failing to address the mix-and-match investment confusions created by the securitization of mortgages and inadequate risk management practices. Boards only addressed the crises after the markets had outed the problems. A board can also fall under the spell of a charismatic and ambitious director, who might lead the board down a self-serving or ill-advised path. The focus on independence must be modified to something more textured, something that reflects the various nuances of independence, and even perhaps acknowledges the existence of interdependence.

The team practices that we have been describing aim to maintain *independent thinking*, enabling the board to provide strategic leadership in validating and promoting the appropriate path for the firm. They include the practices of developing a shared context, using tools to synthesize information, diversifying data sources, and anticipating the unexpected to ensure that the board is acting on an informed basis. Practices such as active learning, productive conflict, staying relevant, and maintaining versatility create a context in which a board, as a team, can approach issues objectively and with open minds. Together, these practices vaccinate against unexamined CEO (or other) dependence, uninformed action, and groupthink by encouraging a thoughtful context for learning, insight, and action. Furthermore, by making use of the full capability and wisdom of the team, these practices promote team insight and action that allow the board to fulfill its duties appropriately and lead effectively.

Bibliography

Ancona, D. G., and Bresman, H. *X-Teams: How to Build Teams That Lead, Innovate, and Succeed.* Boston: Harvard Business School Press, 2007.

Beecher-Monas, E. "Marrying Diversity and Independence in the Boardroom: Just How Far Have You Come, Baby?" Wayne State University Law School research paper no. 07–17. [http://ssrn.con/abstract=985339].

Bogle, J. *Saving the Soul of Capitalism*. New Haven, Conn.: Yale University Press, 2005.

"CSX Directors May Get De-Railed (CSX)," December 20, 2007. [http://www.takingthestreet.com/csx-directors-may-get-de-railed-csx].

"Investment Fund Seeks Changes at CSX," Oct. 16, 2007. [http://www.usatoday.com/money/economy/2007–10–16–1398990619_x.htm].

Jensen, M. A. *A Theory of the Firm: Governance, Residual Claims, and Organizational Forms*. Cambridge, Mass.: Harvard University Press, 2003.

Merced, M. "Activist Hedge Fund Presses CSX for Change," Oct. 17, 2007. [http://www.nytimes.com/2007/10/17/business/17hedge.html?_r=1&dlbk&oref=slogin].

Moscow, C., and Gudmundsson, H. "Independent Directors: Towards a Universal Definition of Director Independence in Corporate Law." *Advanced Corporate Law*, November 29, 2005.

Nadler, D. "Building Better Boards," *Harvard Business Review*, DOI: 10.1225/R0405G, May 1, 2004.

Nadler, D. A., Behan, B. A., and Nadler, M. B. *Building Better Boards*. San Francisco: Jossey-Bass, 2006.

Postseason Report: A Closer Look at Accountability and Engagement. New York: RiskMetrics Group, October 2007.

Senge, P. *The Fifth Discipline: The Art and Science of the Learning Organization*. New York: Doubleday, 2000.

Spears, L.C. (ed.). *Insights on Leadership: Service, Stewardship, Spirit, and Servant-Leadership*. Hoboken, N.J.: John Wiley and Sons, 1998.

13

What Your Board Needs to Know: Early Warning Signs That Provide Insight to What Is Really Going On in Companies

Sydney Finkelstein

Boards of directors have a tough job. They are responsible for the hiring and firing of senior executives, especially the CEO, and they are expected to provide advice and counsel to management. All important, but there is one overarching challenge boards face that can make or break companies, and board member reputations—avoiding failure, by ensuring that the company and its leaders are behaving in an ethical manner, are engaging in well thought-out strategic initiatives, and are attuned to the changing landscape of business. There are many things that might go wrong in a company, but "blow-up-the-company" mistakes simply cannot happen. There is virtually no level of acceptable risk that board members are willing to take on when it comes to the risk of business breakdowns. In the post-Sarbanes-Oxley world in which boards live, there is no question that individual directors are ultimately responsible for major mistakes that occur on their watch.

The same challenge confronts individual directors contemplating invitations to join boards. What are the warning signs to look out for that might lead potential directors to say "no thanks" when offered a board seat? There are some boards on which the potential for trouble will outweigh the opportunities associated with serving. These boards need to be avoided.

Of course there is no vaccine to preempt failure. And there is no smoke alarm that is sure to go off in time to save a failing business. But there are many clues. In this chapter we identify some of the most important ones. On the basis of a six-year study of business breakdowns and failures, it is now possible to point to specific areas of concern that board members must be on the alert for. Are these warning signs a guarantee that a business breakdown will occur? Of course not! But they are warning signs—indications that something is at work that has caused severe problems in other companies and that requires special attention. We can never be fully predictive, of course; life is much too complex for that. But think about how valuable it would be to be able to recognize the critical signals that foreshadow a business failure. These are the early warning signs that let us take a peek into the future, imperfectly to be sure, but they provide a window nonetheless into what might happen.

There are two things to keep in mind as we begin. First, whenever possible, we will look to identify those warning signs that would or should be visible to board members. There will be no neon signs blazing with the words *DANGER—DO NOT ENTER*, but there are a surprising number of insights available when we are on alert and know what to look for. And second, if we see a warning sign, it is nothing more, or less, than that—a warning. One way to put this in perspective is to consider how the government or military evaluates threats. As the severity of the threat increases—presumably because of an accumulation of warning signs—they shift to a higher level of alert. So as we see the warning signs of potential failure in companies, we need to pay even more attention and be ready to act, if necessary. The following sections describe the key warning signs we identified in our research. There are five categories of problems, as illustrated in Figure 13.1. We begin with "Unnecessary Complexity."

I. Unnecessary Complexity

1. Is the organizational structure convoluted or complex?
2. Is the strategy unnecessarily complex for an otherwise simple problem?
3. Is the accounting overly complicated, nontransparent, or nonstandard?
4. Is the company employing complicated or nonstandard terminology?

II. Speeding Out of Control

5. Is there sufficient experience on the management team to handle the growth?
6. Are there small, yet nontrivial, details or problems that seem to be getting overlooked by management?
7. Is management ignoring warnings now that could lead to problems later?
8. Is the company so successful or so dominant that it is no longer in touch with what it needs to do to remain on top?
9. Does the unplanned departure of senior executives signify deeper problems at the company?

III. The Distracted CEO

10. Is the company pursuing an overly ambitious and potentially self-destructive strategy?
11. Are there unanswered questions about the CEO's background and talent?
12. Is the CEO authorizing significant expenditures to fulfill personal preferences that have questionable benefits to the company at best?
13. Is the company so consumed by money and greed that it is taking questionable or inappropriate actions?

IV. Excessive Hype

14. Is the excitement around the company's new product really just unfulfilled hype?
15. Is the excitement around the company's merger or acquisition just unfulfilled hype?
16. Is the excitement around the company's prospects just unfulfilled hype?
17. Is the latest missed milestone part of a pattern that could signify deeper problems?

V. A Question of Character

18. Is the character of the CEO and other senior executives so aggressive or overconfident that you do not really trust them?

Figure 13.1. Key Questions to Ask About Early Warning Signs.

Unnecessary Complexity

Some things are by their very nature quite complex, like the theory of relativity or derivative-based hedging strategies, whereas others are made complex. This latter complexity can manifest itself in structures, strategies, accounting practices, and even the terminology employed to talk about the business. Whatever form it takes, what they all share in common is that they are unnecessary, complications that create bigger problem than they solve. Hence, when we see unnecessary complexity, whether in the form of indecipherable organizational charts or financial transactions that few can understand, we are really seeing a warning sign, because a company has chosen to create complexity where none was needed.

But why make something more complex in the first place? Occasionally, complexity is a practiced approach, providing legitimacy to a course of action preferred by decision makers. In other words, it provides cover. For example, when Motorola missed the digital mobile phone revolution, they relied on a sophisticated, complex forecasting model to assess the potential of digital cell phones rather than direct customer feedback—of which there was plenty. Why? It may well be because they didn't really want to go to digital, and no one on the board was willing to challenge that misguided decision.

More often, complexity arises to address a problem that could more easily be handled with a simpler solution. For example, companies sometimes end up dealing with the complexity of an acquisition when some type of strategic alliance would have been much less costly and easier to implement. Unnecessary complexity most often occurs without anyone realizing what is happening until it is too late. In some cases, over a period of time it can creep into a process or into how an organization chooses to be structured, as decisions are layered one on top of the other, leaving a complicated mess. Often the mess itself is what leads to problems, as it may hide issues from executives who then make poor decisions.

So how do you spot unnecessary complexity when those closest to the situation often can't see it themselves? It starts with knowing where to look, and what to look for.

Convoluted or Complex Organizational Structures and Processes

All systems of organization are subject to breakdown. For example, one of the reasons U.S. fighter jets accidentally shot down two U.S. Black Hawk helicopters over the no-fly zone in Iraq in 1994 was because personnel in the AWACs radar plane assumed someone else was watching the flight zone at the time of the accident. Why would they make this assumption? Because of the principle of "diffuse responsibility," which translates into having more than one person responsible for the same coordinates in a hostile region. With two people paying attention, there's much less likelihood that something will get overlooked. Unfortunately, it was precisely because personnel knew there was someone else with overlapping responsibility that they felt empowered *to pay less attention.*[1] This is exactly the same phenomenon that accounted for the Kitty Genovese incident in Queens, New York, in 1964. On a hot summer night, Kitty was attacked in full view of dozens of people, but no one called the police because they assumed, with so many other people viewing the same scene, that someone else had probably already done so.[2]

The pressure to make mergers and acquisitions work sometimes leads to convoluted management structures. One of the worst scenarios is when two giants merge. For example, when Pharmacia and Upjohn combined in 1995, fears that one side would dominate if corporate head offices were consolidated in one country prompted the merged business to set up a new head office in London. Unfortunately, because Pharmacia and Upjohn did not close down corporate offices in Sweden or the United States, this only served to create a new layer of management that duplicated existing structures. The net result of missteps went like this: several senior executives (including the new CEO) and top R&D people departed, and merger and acquisition (M&A) restructuring costs mushroomed to $800 million, one-third more than originally anticipated. By 1998 the company had finally settled on a single corporate headquarters in New Jersey.

The best (or worst, actually) example of creating unnecessary complexity in M&As is the classic story of co-CEOs. Why is this a good idea? Is there anyone who really believes that two people who have made it to the top of their businesses through enormous dedication, sacrifice, and ambition will do better when they share responsibilities at the top? How long did Bob Eaton of Chrysler last with Jürgen Schrempp of Daimler? John Reed (Citicorp) and Sandy Weill (Travelers) barely shared the executive suite at Citigroup before Reed moved on. The creation of co-CEO positions following a merger should be seen for what it is—a temporary face-saving way to get both eight-hundred-pound gorillas to say yes.[3]

Unnecessarily Complex Strategies or Solutions to Otherwise Simple Problems

So you're traveling in Southeast Asia in 1990 and you need to make a call, but you can't because there is no cell phone service. The first thing that jumps into your mind is, obviously, a constellation of low-Earth-orbiting satellites. You think briefly about just building some more cell towers and expanding service. That might seem easier, you admit, but not nearly as sexy as the satellites. And just think about the contracts to build those things. Besides, nobody is going to expand cell service to these places, are they? Result: Iridium, the failed telecommunications company.

Now let's say you are back at home in the United States in 1996 and you don't have time to drive to the grocery store, but you need to stock up on a few basics. You come up with the perfect solution. You will build twenty-six high-tech distribution centers, each costing $50 million, and offer home delivery over the Internet without a delivery fee. OK, I guess that works, but what about just hiring young, low-wage delivery people for $6.50 an hour to do it? Too expensive you say? You're right, let's spend the $1 billion plus instead. Result: Webvan, the failed Internet startup.

Complex solutions can be appropriate, and powerful, when they are employed to solve very complex problems. For example, Intel's microchip fabrication plants are marvels to behold, but they enable Intel to compete not just on technical specs but on low costs as well. In that industry, dual capabilities are important, and there aren't a heck of a lot of reasonable alternatives if you want to be a big-time player. It is when a company adopts a solution way out of proportion to the problem they are trying to solve that trouble occurs.

Unnecessarily complex strategies or solutions are good warning signs because they often hide flaws or overshadow simpler options. Management or investors can get so caught up in the grandness of the plan or the details of the execution or the gee-whiz factor of the technology that they forget to ask whether it is a good idea in the first place. For example, Marc Porat, the former CEO of General Magic, told us that the company took on too many related strategic initiatives at once, and were unable to succeed at any: "We tried to create an operating system, a handheld device, and the communication network software—and thereby tried to create two markets. That was problem number one."[4] The best defense against such seductive strategies is to keep an open mind and ask, is this the best way? Is there a simpler, perhaps even more effective, solution? Other times, boards will hear senior executives describe multistage investments to reach some ultimate goal that may or may not be worth all those investments. This is one time when intuition that it is a bad idea makes sense—if board members can't see the logic, then it might not actually be there!

Overly Complicated, Nontransparent, or Nonstandard Accounting

Despite many who believe otherwise, accounting rules are not intentionally designed to be complicated. The goal of accounting is to illuminate the true financial performance of an organization for all to see, not to confuse or hide it. If it is confusing or unusual or inconsistent, it's time to take a closer look. Don't be fooled by those who call it innovative; Enron's use of off-balance-sheet partnerships was very innovative, after all. A good rule of thumb is this: nonstandard or unusual accounting can make a company look better than it is, but it will rarely make the company better than it is, and it often is a warning sign that the company is actually worse than it appears.

Three of the biggest U.S. bankruptcies ever—Enron, WorldCom, and Conseco—followed a pattern of aggressive and creative accounting arrangements ranging from off-balance-sheet manipulations (Enron) to systematic capitalization of expenses (WorldCom) to shifting acquisition accounting to and from the income statement (Conseco). Internet companies were notorious for pushing the accounting envelope. One common practice was to trade ad space with other dot-coms, booking the barter as revenue. Other times, companies recorded non-cash revenues by swapping services for stock. Because the valuation of most dot-coms was based on revenues and not cash flow, let alone earnings, this practice could give a quick boost to a company's stock price. The SEC eventually started cracking down on some of these games, but by then it was far too late for many investors.[5]

Nonstandard accounting is not always easy to see; however, if you understand when a company is most likely to benefit from it, you will have a better chance of spotting it. For Internet companies, the emphasis was on revenues more than profits, so revenue recognition games became a hot button. For other companies, such as Enron, the strength of the balance sheet was a particular concern, thus the off-balance-sheet partnerships. Pay attention to the prominent metrics in an industry, because if nonstandard accounting is going to appear anywhere, it will be there.

Complicated or Nonstandard Terminology

Internet entrepreneurs and managers created a whole new vocabulary of business terminology, separate from that used in the "old economy." Rather than speak of "strategy," Internet startups boasted "business models." Online companies and venture capitalists emphasized the importance of "reach" and "stickiness," when what they really meant was that Internet startups must have "customers," and that these customers must make "repeat purchases." Internet companies did not compete in a "market"; they competed in a "space." In some ways, you could see how this would come about. After all, what would you rather tell your shareholders—that your "burn rate" was $500,000 per month or that you were going to lose $6 million next year?

To go along with their new terminology, many of the dot-coms of the late 1990s asked Wall Street and their investors to use a new set of accounting standards to evaluate their businesses. They talked about how the new economy needed new rules to accommodate a changed world, especially because the old accounting standbys such as EPS and P/E ratios were not very effective when you had no "E." In the end, of course, the standard accounting principles did their job just fine, as they accurately captured the fact that these companies were not creating value for shareholders.

Even several large technology companies tried to play the terminology game. For example, Nortel Networks Corp asked investors to focus on a measure it called "net earnings from operations," which excluded amortization of goodwill and development costs, and gains and charges. In 2000, Nortel reported "net earnings from operations" of $2.31 billion, or 71 cents a share, while according to generally accepted accounting principles the company actually lost $3.47 billion, or $1.17 a share.[6]

Speeding Out of Control

How many times have you read about a company whose insiders in looking back describe the organization with phrases like "speeding out of control" or "we couldn't get out of our own way" or "complete chaos"? Now think about how often executives describe their current situation that way? Not nearly as often, right! So why is it that no one seems to notice that their company is out of control until it is too late?

Companies that are speeding out of control make costly mistakes because executives are overwhelmed. This most commonly occurs in companies that are experiencing rapid growth, but it can also take place in companies that are adjusting to technological change or are dealing with management turnover or are in any situation that can create frantic behavior.

The costs of poor decisions made while speeding out of control can be severe. In the rush for first mover advantage, bet-the-company decisions are sometimes made that ultimately lead to the downfall of a company, like Webvan. This Internet startup became fixated with becoming the number one firm in its market—online ordering and delivery of groceries. To accomplish that goal, speed was among the most powerful weapons, leading to decisions to extend its business model before getting the core business to work, and expanding its distribution and warehouse facilities around the country before perfecting the model in any one location. The net result was that billions of dollars were invested in infrastructure that never paid off, as the company could not even establish its initial position in the industry. In the end, Webvan declared bankruptcy after running through investors' cash in record time.

While riding the crest of success, a company might allow itself to become unprepared for the next technological jump and find itself on the outside, like J&J in the stent business. Even if a company can avoid the big strategic mistakes, that doesn't mean it is out of the woods yet, for the abundance of little details that can get messed up when a company is speeding out of control can be just as devastating.

So back to why no one can ever seem to tell when their company is out of control. Part of it is no doubt because everything is moving too fast, but more important, it's because they usually don't know the warning signs. Board members and would-be board members need to know what to look for.

Who Knows How to Drive This Thing? Insufficient Experience to Manage Growth

Picture a company that is growing at breakneck speed. Now add in a management team with a little too much "milk on their lips." Finally, give the inexperienced executives lots of money and little adult supervision. That, in a nutshell, was the classic formula for Internet startups during the boom years. Each one of these elements—rapid growth, inexperienced management, free cash flow, and weak board governance—can bring a company to grief, but when all four are present at the same time, watch out!

In 1994 Dale Sundby founded PowerAgent, an online startup poised to revolutionize advertising by matching companies with customers in a classic one-to-one marketing scheme. Sundby, a law firm CEO and former IBM executive, had never worked in advertising, yet he managed to raise $16 million by 1996. In search of the elusive first mover advantage, PowerAgent went haywire employing multiple software developers doing redundant work in an effort to get its customer interface in place, and hiring experienced sales executives before the product was even available. Actually, despite a burn rate that reached more than $2 million a month (slick promotional video for $500,000; high-profile parties; well-furnished offices in several cities), the product never did become available. As one industry veteran brought in to make sense of the mess put it, "I took one look at the product right after getting there and said, 'you've got to be kidding. We can't launch anything that looks like this. This is awful. Awful.'"[7] And the board of directors in this story? Mostly absentee investors hoping to cash in on the Internet gravy train.[8] From there, it was only a matter of months before the company folded.

Although some early warning signs are more shrouded than others, board members must read the S-1 statement the SEC requires in advance of IPOs, and the 10-K for companies that are already public, both of which contain information on management experience, capitalization and funding, and management plans moving forward. The business press—though far from accurate in their subjective assessments of a company's prospects—occasionally do publish actual facts. Both sources of information would have told an interesting story about Webvan, which raised hundreds of millions of dollars and adopted an extraordinarily aggressive growth strategy. The fast-paced rise of Mossimo was well chronicled by the press as well. Founder Mossimo Giannulli was a twenty-something entrepreneur who hit it big with his line of surfer clothes in southern California. While he had a knack for design, as the company's sales took off he began to believe he also had a knack for all the other things that companies do—generating consistent and reliable sales, managing inventory, building management talent, and so on. Unfortunately, he didn't, and his company collapsed.

Most of all, there was a whole community of big spenders at loose running Internet startups, leaving a trail of high-octane expenditures. For example, Boo.com, the high-profile European Internet startup that raised $135 million, boasted six luxurious offices set up in different cities and insisted that management—traveling with an entourage—stay at the best hotels. One prospective investor said in describing the elaborate efforts the company went through to build their Website, "It was like they were trying to build a Mercedes-Benz by hand." In the end the startup declared bankruptcy, selling its back-end shipping technology for $375,000.[9]

Broken Windows: Tolerance of the Little Mistake May Foreshadow the Big Ones

You don't have to tour a company's facilities to see broken windows. As with any warning sign, it's all about knowing what to look for. For manufacturing companies, it might be a minor quality problem now that leads to a bigger one later. For service companies, it might be the loss of a smaller client that foreshadows bigger client failures. Execution errors may not be the root cause of failure, but they can be symptomatic of something more serious.

You might not know that WorldCom was systematically overcharging customers by switching millions to more expensive plans without their knowledge, or refusing to adjust billing errors[10]—practices that cost the company hundreds of millions in class action suits and proceedings brought by several state attorney generals[11]—but you could have paid attention to such things as (1) WorldCom's number one ranking in long-distance slamming complaints to the FCC, or (2) PlanetFeedBack's[12] rating of several of WorldCom's business units in the top ten worst companies for customer service and billing errors.[13]

There is an even more basic way to get a handle on not just the cost of a broken window but also a strategy of excess that is characteristic of wild companies speeding out of control. Follow the cash and don't get deceived by relying on a company's net income as the only measure of financial health. The cable industry in the 1990s was a classic example of an industry in which firms boasted strong operating income but had insatiable appetites for cash, as competition forced companies to spend heavily on upgrading their networks. When debt balloons up in response, it's important to look at a company's ability to cover the payments. In much the same way that banks assess personal income and expenses when writing home mortgages, corporate lenders issue covenants to ensure that a company has adequate resources to cover the cost of the debt. When companies go bankrupt, it is often the case that lenders have decided to cut their losses because loan covenants have been violated.

Finally, don't be afraid to look at an even simpler measure—whether there is cash in the bank. It may well be the single most important indicator of health for a company, especially in technology and biotech.

Where There's Smoke . . . Ignoring Warnings

Companies do not have to be small, fast-growing dynamos to succumb to the pitfalls of speeding out of control. Large companies with experienced management teams have speeded past a lot more than just broken windows. At J&J's stent business, management failed to notice that the building was on fire before it was too late. The smoke was there for anyone to see—the erosion of European market share and the lack of ongoing innovation in a business that requires it. As a manager, these are your warning signs. But as a board member, the real warning sign is when conditions like these are present, and no one seems to be doing anything about it. As John Keogh, president of an insurance company that writes policies to cover corporate directors and officers (D&O insurance) told us, "My experience anecdotally is that where there is smoke there is fire so if you find a problem in one piece of the business it's probably an early indicator of a bigger problem. When management finds there is a bigger problem, the sooner they deal with and manage it obviously the better. It's the ones that take longer to come to the surface that tend to be the ones that destroy companies."[14]

We saw plenty of examples of what Keogh was referring to: RJ Reynold's Project Spa was a smoker's fantasy that never should have moved as far as it did. Customers hated the taste and told the development team exactly that in no uncertain terms. Customers sent overt warnings to Motorola as it stonewalled against digital mobile phones and to Rubbermaid as it tried to pass along ever-higher costs to retailers. The warnings need not come from customers—people inside a company sometimes summon the courage to speak out, but executives at the top don't always listen, as was the case at Enron.[15]

Unheeded warnings are common in M&A transactions. Companies become so focused on the end result or on getting to the next deal that they gloss over potential differences. Unfortunately, the one certainty in acquisitions is that what you don't resolve before the deal is completed, you end up addressing one way or the other afterwards. Often, the unheeded warnings you see may not lead to the downfall of the company or the deal, but they may be indicative of a pattern that will.

In the case of Snow Brands—at one point Japan's leading producer of milk and dairy products that failed to address a product contamination outbreak—by the time anyone noticed that warnings were going unheeded in the milk business, it was too late. But it was not too late to notice the culture of unheeded warnings and the impact that this might have on the rest of the business. In the D&O insurance industry, insurers typically look at lawsuits that have been settled in a very different way than in the market. Investors often think of a suit settlement as a sign that the company has put these problems behind them. Insurers look at it as a warning sign of a culture that may well have committed another offense that will eventually lead to more lawsuits.[16]

Humpty Dumpty Sat on the Wall: The Dangers of Being Too Successful

Here's a surprise. Want to know one of the best generic warning signs you can look for? How about success, lots of it! Leaving aside the unfortunate reality that many of the companies we studied were quite successful before the really bad stuff happened—Rubbermaid, Motorola, Wang Labs, Sony, Conseco, Johnson & Johnson, Snow Brand Milk, LTCM, Barneys, the list goes on—there are several reasons why directors should be on the alert. First, virtually every company we studied was successful at one time, but they fell into a wide swath of bad attitudes that were an outgrowth of that success. Second, companies that are successful in their marketplace act as an advertisement for others to enter the same arena. Lacking powerful barriers to entry, new companies will take some share away from incumbents. Third, success breeds arrogance. Even a company as powerful as Microsoft was not immune to the perils of success, and probably should count itself lucky that the antitrust suit ended up where it did. Fourth, it's easy to let our guard down when we are awash in profits. It's only natural; "there is a common failing of mankind, never to anticipate a storm when the sea is calm."[17] Finally, success creates its own momentum that in the scheme of things is remarkably difficult to maintain. One of the reasons WorldCom turned to fraudulent accounting was because that was the only way they could keep the great numbers up; the regular course of business was no longer doing it.

When a company is doing really well, it's easy to bask in the glow of success. Few companies evaluate why business is working, often defaulting to a "CEO is genius" attribution. But without really understanding why success is happening, it becomes difficult to identify and act when mid-term adjustments are needed. Then, you wake up one morning, and it looks like everything went bad overnight. But it didn't—it is a slow process that can often be seen if energy is directed to the task. For example, as retailer Gap began its downfall, there was more bafflement than analysis. CEO Mickey Drexler had made the right calls before, and it was assumed that he would continue to make the right calls to turn things around. Unfortunately, the triggers for turnaround—critical dissent, talent bench strength, and open-mindedness—were all missing. Drexler's personal style coupled with his successful track record made it difficult to challenge him, and the company's "We set fashion, we don't respond to it" ethic shut down debate.[18] Directors need to be on the alert for the warning signs of arrogance—executives who don't have thoughtful answers to questions about competitors and potential competitors, CEOs who shut down real debate and seem only to share the minimum amount of information with the board, and CEOs who are unable to identify areas where improvements are needed.

The extreme case of a successful company that lost all semblance of constraint and responsibility to standard norms of business conduct may well be Adelphia. When we think of Adelphia, we think of the classic Mel Brooks movie, *Blazing Saddles*. There's a scene in the film when everyone converges on this one town where the saloon, the stores, the bank, and even the sheriff share the same name—Johnson. The town is totally dominated by this one man and his family, and while Mel Brooks used the name Johnson, in reality at Adelphia the name was Rigas. John Rigas and his family were the kings of the town of Coudersport, Pennsylvania. Most of the people in town worked for Adelphia, and Adelphia and the Rigas family owned most of the town. The real estate, the restaurant, the movie theater, the golf course—all were part of the family. And perhaps the defining principle of the company, and the family, was that "you took care of your own." So John's wife Doris decorated the Adelphia buildings with $12.4 million in furniture from a Rigas family business;[19] son-in-law Peter Venetis ran a venture capital fund with company money; when the company needed a vehicle, they bought it from the family car dealership; snow removal, lawn mowing, maintenance—that's right—all from family-run businesses.[20] The Rigas family created Adelphia—the word itself means "brothers" in Greek—as an island onto itself, but when they ventured to the outside world in search of capital, and proceeded to abuse that capital, the game was up.[21]

The Adelphia story provides a window to that world. When a company shuts itself off from common norms of behavior; when a company takes the positive of a "family business" and turns it into a kingdom with little access to the outside world; when a company owns too much, and controls too much, and dominates too much; when all of these things are happening it is time to take a closer look. Fantastic success or overwhelming dominance does not mean that bad things are happening or will happen. However, there are an extraordinary number of times when precisely these attributes are in place in companies that run up against failure. Attention must be paid to such a company, and the board of directors is the primary line of defense.

Boards of directors need to come prepared to board meetings, ready for real debate and discussion. It is not inappropriate to ask executives why they believe their assumptions about the business are correct. Just a simple examination of the history of business indicates that there are not any companies that stay at the top forever, and this simple awareness should empower directors to do whatever they can to ensure that their firms don't falter on their watch.

Will the Last Person Turn Off the Light . . . Unplanned Executive Departures

Between 1999 and 2001, four of the five senior executives at Gap left the company, culminating in the resignation of CEO Mickey Drexler as the company's year-over-year same-store sales continued to decrease. Over a two-year period in 1999 and 2000, six direct reports to Mattel CEO Jill Barad resigned for "personal reasons." Not long afterward, CEO Barad stepped down. CEO Jeff Skilling left Enron in August 2001, just three months before Enron's problems made front-page news. Kmart averaged 38 percent annual turnover in the top executive ranks throughout the decade of the 1990s. Silicon Graphics lost 40 percent of its top management team in the two years preceding its 1996 stock meltdown. Almost all of the top sixty-four executives at Cordis left following the 1995 acquisition of that company by Johnson & Johnson.

How clear can a pattern be? A revolving door at the top is very often a strong signal that there is real trouble in a company. It may be an indication that the CEO is pushing out other top executives who have different views on the company's direction, or it may reflect inside information senior executives are acting on. It is standard practice for analysts and many investors to track insider sales of stock, but what stronger statement can an executive make than to leave his job and the company entirely? Boards can certainly track this data very closely.

Even when a company appears to be strong, or at least a stalwart in an industry sector, there can be important information contained in executive departures. Consider Sun Microsystems. On May 1, 2002, Sun Microsystems announced that President Edward Zander was resigning from the company, making him the fourth senior executive to leave Sun in a two-week period. Sun CEO Scott McNealy characterized these moves as "positive and planned out," yet just five months later Sun announced an unexpected revenue decline for the first quarter of fiscal 2003 along with layoffs of 11 percent of its workforce, or 4,400 people. Interestingly, McNealy continued to defend the company's position ("Sun is in great shape. I am having a blast"); in the five months between Zander's resignation and the layoff announcement Sun's stock price went from $8.18 to $2.99, a decline of 63 percent.[22]

The Distracted CEO

CEOs play a big role in deciding the agenda of the board. Of course, it's true that independent chairs, or lead directors, have formal authority to manage board time, but it has been our experience that this important task is usually delegated to the CEO. After all, it is the CEO who has the information and insight on the direction of the company. In one extreme case, when we investigated how the board spent its time, we found that the compensation committee was actually meeting more often than the audit committee. In our post-Sarbanes-Oxley world, we wouldn't expect to see this very much, yet when asked why directors were so engrossed in compensation issues we heard that executive compensation is very complex and merits in-depth consideration. But does that imply that the company's financials are not complex and, hence, merit *less* attention?

In our experience, the easiest way to spot a company that is out of focus is to look at the CEO. Organizations take their lead from the top, and distraction or misdirection at the CEO level can have serious consequences. Studying a CEO for signs that he or she has become sidetracked will never yield a black or white answer, but there are some patterns that emerged in the failures we studied that provide some clues.

The Napoleon Complex—Strategies Designed to Conquer the World

Remember the Saatchi brothers' chase to be number one? First they acquired as many advertising agencies as they could, and then professional services, and later still it was on to banking. Maurice Saatchi actually described himself as "afflicted by . . . insecurity and paranoia" and admitted that hubris was a driving factor in the company's strategy.[23] All of which might explain how a company could pursue a strategy that almost matches Napoleon's in its grandness, and in its ultimate conclusion.

The saga of the Saatchi brothers is a good example of the difference between an aggressive growth plan and a destructive loss of focus in pursuit of the wrong thing. In the case of the Saatchis it was unattainable glory they chased. At Enron, Ken Lay stated that his ambition was to grow Enron into "one of the biggest, most successful companies in the world."[24] His successor, Jeffrey Skilling, was quoted as saying, "there is a very reasonable chance that [Enron] will become the biggest corporation in the world."[25] The CEO of now defunct Internet consulting firm Razorfish laid out his ambition this way: "There are sheep and there are shepherds, and I fancy myself to be the latter."[26]

By the time strategies like these are announced or implemented, a lot of damage has already been done. People are out of control, strategies are out of control, and it becomes very difficult to undo what has already been done without considerable disruption. There are three types of early warning signs—visible to board members who do the digging and know what to look for—that can flag CEO trouble ahead.

Did Anybody Check Their Background? Unanswered Questions About the CEO

Sam Waksal was the founder of ImClone and the man Bristol-Myers Squibb (BMS) decided to bet $2 billion on when they took a

20 percent stake in the biotech firm and its only product, the cancer drug Erbitux. When the FDA turned down ImClone's application for the drug, BMS was left to explain what happened. When it was subsequently revealed that ImClone had known about FDA concerns months beforehand, and the company had apparently provided inaccurate data to the FDA,[27] more explaining was necessary. When the related insider trading scandal broke (eventually leading to Waksal's indictment and drawing in such pivotal figures of the New York social scene as Martha Stewart), BMS was left to explain why they decided to partner with Waksal in the first place.

This was an unfortunate episode, but who could have predicted that things would go so wrong? Actually, while no one could have predicted exactly what did happen, there were big-time clues that Sam Waksal might not be the best business partner for a prestigious pharmaceutical company. There's no question Waksal had the brains and the charisma, but a look into his past might have revealed some disquieting concerns about just how these prodigious talents were used.

After earning a Ph.D., Sam Waksal went through a succession of prestigious jobs, but left under a cloud each time. First was a position at a lab at Stanford, which ended when Waksal was asked to leave after he misled the top scientist there about how he had procured a supply of difficult-to-produce antibodies. Afterward, he managed to land at the National Cancer Institute for a sojourn that lasted less than three years. This time his contract was not renewed because of a series of experiment-ending problems that mysteriously occurred just when Waksal was due to deliver his work to his collaborators.

His next stop was Tufts University, where once again the same pattern of charm coupled with questionable ethics spilled out. The last straw for Tufts was when Waksal's brother, Harlan, a medical resident at Tufts, was arrested for the possession of cocaine and Sam, not a medical doctor, covered for his brother by seeing his patients while Harlan was "indisposed." A few years later, while working at Mount Sinai School of Medicine in New York, he was accused of falsifying data in an experiment, ending his time at that institution. Finally, Sam Waksal was ready to go into business for himself! He founded ImClone in 1985, bringing his brother Harlan with him soon afterward.[28]

There is of course no certainty that a CEO with a checkered past will be untrustworthy in the future, but if we don't pay attention to the data we can collect on a CEO's background, the odds are we will be unhappily surprised. Just as careful underwriters of D&O insurance have found that past lawsuits are actually a predictor of lawsuits still to come, we've got to go with the pattern of data we discover. That is the essence of what an early warning sign is, after all. Directors need to know well the histories of their CEOs.

And when we consider the data that emerge from the companies we studied, one other fact that seems to stand out is the high number of family-run businesses that ended up in ruins. Schwinn, Barneys, and Rite Aid were run by follow-on generations from the founders, and all went bankrupt or close to it. Companies such as Samsung and Levi Strauss were controlled by their founding families when they ran into trouble as well. The truth is that it *is* possible for a CEO to own too much stock, because once past some level of ownership there is virtually no limit to a CEO's power. Whether this power is turned into positive or negative outcomes cannot be predetermined, though the fact remains that CEOs in a family line have not been vetted in the same way that executives working their way up a hierarchy have been. The one thing we should expect with some confidence, however, is that companies run by a founder's family are likely to produce more volatile results because their power gives them the freedom to choose higher risk strategies that can yield widely varying outcomes.[29]

Show Me the Behavior . . . Authorizing Expenditures for Personal Needs

The second type of early warning sign requires even less effort on the part of board members to pick up on. This is because the types of behavior that are exhibited by CEOs in the throes of Napoleonic fervor tend to be so blatant they can't be missed.

It all starts with making sure you as the CEO are the center of attention, ideally with a "very cool" crowd. So the Saatchi brothers are active with the Tory Party in the United Kingdom. Kun-Hee Lee, the chairman of Samsung who undertook a multibillion-dollar venture into automobiles that was a massive failure, says his entry to the auto business was "for the sake of the nation."[30] Sam Waksal buys a swank SoHo apartment, decorates it with expensive art, and joins the Manhattan smart set. Edward McCracken, the former CEO of Silicon Graphics, was a regular at White House events in the 1990s. Ken Lay was never more than a phone call away from close friend President George W. Bush.

What is remarkable about all these people is that while they chose to live the high life, hobnobbing with celebrities and politicians, and spending lavishly on pet projects or misdirected strategies, the companies for which they had fiduciary responsibility suffered huge losses. Being a CEO is more than a full-time job, and perhaps the same can be said for being a jetsetter Hollywood celebrity or a well-connected Washington lobbyist. There is a role for CEOs to play on issues of public interest, but when this segues from making a contribution to adopting a lifestyle, bad things tend to happen.

Unfortunately, in some companies there are even more extreme forms of this self-aggrandizing behavior, as CEOs who spend to their heart's content not only drain their companies of leadership, they also drain it of resources. Guber and Peters spent millions on studio renovations at Sony Pictures in the early 1990s while enroute to a \$3.2 billion write-down. William Farley, CEO of Fruit of the Loom, "worked in an unbelievably beautiful office with terrific artwork in Chicago, not in Bowling Green where the [Fruit of the Loom] plant was."[31] John Rigas used Adelphia money to buy the Buffalo Sabres hockey team and build a \$13 million golf course on property owned by Adelphia.[32]

What could be worse than this? How about when a company begins building a striking new headquarters, designed to serve as a corporate symbol? In addition to distracting the CEO from his or her most important tasks, this kind of project can absorb most of the attention of senior executives for months on end. Whose design ideas will be incorporated into the final plan? Whose department will get what space? Which executives will be assigned which offices? The possibilities for disputes and plotting are almost endless. Yet none of the efforts that the new building absorbs are likely to have anything but a negative effect on corporate performance. The executives at the Money Store provide a classic example. During the period before their 1998 acquisition by First Union, they were so preoccupied with building a new headquarters shaped like a Mayan pyramid that internal controls all but lapsed, and the business was running almost as though it had no senior management at all.[33]

Our personal favorite in the category of "Big Fat Warning Sign" is when a company decides to acquire the naming rights for a new sports arena or stadium. For example, when CMGI (an Internet holding company with a variety of businesses under different names), ponied up a cool $114 million for a fifteen-year deal to plaster their name on the New England Patriots' new stadium in 2000, there wasn't much of a business case to support it. After all, as a holding company there was no consumer brand to market, and there was no product or service called CMGI that anyone could purchase. Add to this the little fact that CMGI lost more than $5.4 *billion* in 2001, and continues to struggle in the post-Internet era, and the folly of buying stadium-naming rights is rather apparent.[34]

Remarkably, CMGI is not alone. A surprising number of companies that paid millions of dollars to have their corporate logo and name adorn sports stadiums and arenas in the last five years ended up with severe financial difficulties. Besides the no less than eight airlines making such investments, some of the other "winners" and what they spent were:[35]

Fruit of the Loom	Pro Player Stadium, Miami	Florida Marlins, Miami Dolphins	$20 million
Enron	Enron Field	Houston Astros	$100 million
Conseco	Conseco Fieldhouse	Indiana Pacers	$40 million
PSINet	PSINet Stadium	Baltimore Ravens	$100 million

The pattern of elaborate spending on sports stadiums, headquarters buildings, offices, and golf courses goes beyond what we saw earlier in fast-growing, inexperienced, "born to be wild" startups. The entrepreneurial companies overspent because they lacked the financial discipline and experience needed to be careful stewards of company assets. Here there is a willful desire to spend to advance one's personal standing, for ego gratification reasons, and as a manifestation of an illusion of preeminence. Board members can see this if they are looking; the question is whether they are looking. The underlying dynamics of how leaders develop the belief they are above everyone else are subtle, self-reinforcing, and powerful, but the symptoms will always show up, and that is the point where action must be taken.

Show Me the Money . . . Consumed by Greed

When we asked Russell Lewis, the CEO of the *New York Times*, what warning signs he believes are potential markers for trouble, the first thing he mentioned was, "if the compensation is disproportionately high to the size of the business and the performance, I'd get the hell out of that investment in a hurry."[36] Good advice, echoed by some other experts we spoke to, but we'd go even further. When the company itself becomes consumed with money, and with greed, it's time to take a closer look, if not get out altogether as a board director. And the poster children for the "greed is good" fixation are none other than those kings of bankruptcy, WorldCom and Enron.

WorldCom under CEO Bernie Ebbers and CFO Scott Sullivan reminds us of nothing so much as the movie *Chocolat*, whose climax featured one of the main characters totally engorged with chocolate. Unable to stop eating, unable to control his obsession, he finally falls asleep in the window display of the chocolate shop. At WorldCom, money and profits took the place of chocolate, and there was no limit to their hunger. The board authorized loans to Ebbers of $400 million; sales representatives systematically double-billed customers, boosting their commissions; during analyst meetings, Ebbers would only discuss the company's stock price, showing a graph of an increasing share price and asking, "any questions?"; the company boosted earnings by taking down reserves whenever they wanted to goose the numbers; operating expenses were regularly capitalized (one employee was even told to capitalize plane tickets when visiting company sites); when all else failed, CFO Sullivan allegedly invented financial numbers to boost earnings.[37]

The Enron story is even more well-known than that of WorldCom, and the story that has emerged is also of a company that lost control, had no limits, and cared for nothing but money—for individual executives and for the company as a whole. The off-balance-sheet partnerships are now well established as a remarkably brazen tool to enrich CFO Andrew Fastow and a select few at the company. Actually, the idea that money comes first dates back to as early as 1987, when auditors uncovered a huge oil trading scandal at Enron. Traders who were found guilty of generating false transactions to increase volume, and not incidentally their bonuses, were not fired by then CEO Ken Lay until the scam became public.[38] Within Enron, this was considered business as usual.

These types of incredibly egregious actions by key executives are not always as visible to outsiders as excessive compensation, but when it takes over the culture of a company—as it did at both WorldCom and Enron—then virtually everyone on the inside should have some inkling. This includes board members, of course. But it also includes managers up and down the hierarchy, who have special insight to warning signs such as these. Boards need to spend at least some time with middle managers, and speak to them directly and without the CEO present. Boards also need to ensure that there are multiple, and safe, avenues open to managers who wish to report on potential problems. For boards, the lesson is that as easy as it is to get caught up in the excitement of a company like Enron that is breaking all the rules, or like WorldCom that is building the new AT&T via astute acquisitions, the reality is never as straightforward. In this regard, it's also a story of hype, which brings us to the next type of common warning sign.

Excessive Hype

The world of hype peaked with the Internet bubble, yet this practice is far from gone. Why would hype be a good warning sign? Let's start by looking at the definition of the word. *Hype: noun (1) Excessive publicity and the ensuing commotion; (2) Exaggerated or extravagant claims made especially in advertising or promotional material; (3) Something deliberately misleading; a deception.*[39] It doesn't sound so harmless when you look at it this way, and it wasn't so harmless to the countless investors who got caught up in the hype of the Internet boom.

Hyping Products Before They Exist

Marketing a product before it comes out and creating a little hype for its release is common practice in business. Think no further than the film business, where the promotion machine goes into high gear even before a movie opens. However, the last time we looked, there weren't too many films being hyped even before shooting begins! But that's what happened with General Magic and Iridium. To some extent the engineers in charge couldn't help it; remember, these were both classic stories of "techtosterone." But when something sounds too good to be true—it usually is.

One of the businesses that is most vulnerable to hype gone wild is the pharmaceutical industry. When your health and the health of loved ones is at stake, there's little you won't do, and even less you won't believe in. In other words, this is the perfect setting for making outlandish claims that generate free publicity. The remedy within the industry is the FDA, which is charged with overseeing and approving drugs.

Enter Sam Waksal, scientist, CEO, and Manhattan socialite. As his company, ImClone, was developing the cancer drug Erbitux, the hype machine went into overdrive. Waksal declared that Erbitux "is going to be the most important new oncology launch ever."[40] He made the cover of *BusinessWeek*, ImClone's stock took off, and Bristol-Myers Squibb announced its $2 billion investment in the high-flying biotech. The only problem was that the FDA rejected ImClone's application for Erbitux on December 28, 2001, sending the stock of both ImClone and Bristol into a tailspin. One of the most amazing things about the story is that in its seventeen years in existence, ImClone had not produced a single drug or had even one profitable year, yet this never seemed to concern anyone as its stock price skyrocketed. For an investor, the lessons of the post-Internet boom are clear. Holding onto a stock whose value is predicated on the hype of its "product to be" can be disastrous. In many cases, most of the upside is already factored in due to the hype, leaving only significant downside exposure. As one shortseller put it, "When I hear management make overstatements, I get interested."[41]

As a director, here is what you should be on the lookout for. Are pro forma financial statements based on reasonable assumptions, assumptions that have been tested and kicked around? Are these assumptions being updated with current data? What made sense nine months ago does not necessarily make sense today. How accurate are competitor data? If the board is told that competitors are far behind in a product or service offering, it is essential to probe. How do we know? What would happen if this forecast was wrong? More generally, to what extent is there scenario planning and "war gaming" going on? We found several instances in which management teams didn't really have a solid grasp on the strategies of their key competitors. All of these examples can lead to excessive hype, and it is the board's responsibility to not let that happen.

Hyping Mergers and Acquisitions

The one place where dishing out hype has been elevated to an art form is in the merger and acquisition game. With a losing track record, a pattern of underestimating costs and overestimating benefits, big acquisition premiums, and hero CEOs pushing for deals, the pressure to make the big picture look good is enormous. To see an uptick in the stock price in the first couple of days after the deal is announced is an immediate affirmation that this acquisition is different.

Often involving coordinated attack by the acquiring company CEO, investment bankers, and professional public relations firms hired solely for this purpose, the goal is to get a favorable spin in the first press articles that appear after the deal is announced. For example, when Novell announced the acquisition of WordPerfect for stock valued at $1.4 billion on March 21, 1994, the CEO said, "The combination positions WordPerfect to be central to the next generation of applications. We are helping Novell create a software powerhouse." After struggling against Microsoft, internal dissension, and the market for two years, the same Novell CEO announced the sale of WordPerfect to Corel for $124 million in stock and cash and a licensing arrangement by noting that the sale "allows Novell to focus on what we do best, and that's networking" software. In the Daimler-Benz merger with Chrysler, the talk was of $3 billion in cost savings, a target so outlandish that even Daimler executives quickly stopped trying to calculate the magnitude of savings they could actually generate.

In a fascinating article in the *Wall Street Journal,* journalists Nikhil Deogun and Steven Lipin compared statements the acquiring company CEO made when a deal was proclaimed, and then

Table 13.1. CEO Statements at Acquisition and at Divestiture.

Deal	Dates Bought and Sold	CEO Before	CEO After
AT&T buys NCR	1991–1995	"Ours will be a future of promises fulfilled."	"The world has changed."
SmithKline Beecham buys Diversified Pharmaceutical Benefits	1994–1999	"Unique alliance . . . positions us to win."	"We [need] a sharper focus."
Eli Lilly buys PCS Health Systems	1994–1998	"Jewel at a very attractive price."	"Business can benefit from new ownership arrangements."
Quaker Oats buys Snapple	1994–1997	"Tremendous growth potential."	"Remove financial burdens and risks Snapple brought."

later, when the subsequent sale of the acquired company was announced (see Table 13.1).[42] As these examples attest, hype is alive and well in the M&A business. The good news is that we can be on the alert for this type of hype, and recognize it for what it is—a transparent attempt to manipulate investors.

Hyping the Company's Prospects

The hype that some companies exude must be taken with a grain of salt by board members. Consider these examples:

> "We're in a horse race to be the biggest television network. Our competitors are CBS, NBC and ABC."
>
> **Josh Harris, founder of Pseudo Programs in 1998.**[43]

> "I'm creating the next Time Warner, the next Conde Nast. I'll become the next Michael Eisner or Barry Diller or Steve Case."

Jason McCabe Calacanis, editor, Silicon Alley Reporter.[44]

> "We like to think of ourselves as the IBM of the garment industry."

Jay Margolis, senior executive of Liz Claiborne in 1989.[45]

Pseudo Programs shut down in 2001 after burning through tens of millions of dollars of venture capital, as did the Silicon Alley Reporter the same year; Liz Claiborne went into a serious tailspin for several years following the time of this quote. These examples all suggest that such overwrought declarations are a wonderful signal, not so much to get excited about a company, but rather to pay a little more, not less, attention to what is going on.

The same recommendation holds when the hype comes from sources outside of the company. While it is certainly not always the case, we can't help but be struck at the number of times business and trade publications anoint sainthood on a company or individual that stumbles shortly thereafter. We've already seen Rubbermaid fall from America's Most Admired Company in *Fortune* magazine (former CEO Stanley Gault made a point of telling us that he believed his predecessor, Wolfgang Schmitt, "believed his original press clippings"[46]), but did you know that former Enron CFO Andrew Fastow, who was at the center of the off-balance-sheet partnerships that contributed to the company's downfall, earned the CFO Excellence Award for Capital Structure Management from *CFO Magazine* in October 1999, a little more than two years before Enron's bankruptcy declaration? Not to be outmatched, *Chief Executive* magazine named Enron one of their top five corporate boards around the same time. And the Newspaper Association of America honored Kmart as the "Retailer of the Year" on January 21, 2002, unfortunate timing to be sure as the following day Kmart filed for Chapter 11. Mattel's Jill Barad was feted on the cover by *BusinessWeek* in 1998 (almost exactly one year before Mattel acquired The Learning Company, a decision that was the beginning of the end for her tenure), while other cover stories on Dennis Kozlowski of Tyco (*BusinessWeek* in 2001) and Mickey Drexler of Gap (*Fortune* in 1998, just before Gap began its losing streak) have also appeared.

The "glowing press reports" indicator may not be limited to the United States alone. In January 1994, Metallgesellschaft (MG), the German metals and services conglomerate, was rescued from bankruptcy by a DM3.4 billion bailout by a consortium of German banks after an ill-conceived venture into the financial derivatives market by their U.S. subsidiary. Just over two years earlier MG's CEO, Heinz Schimmelbusch, was named Germany's Manager of the Year.

The End of Hype: Missing Milestones

One of the best warning signs that a company may be relying on hype is the missed milestone. Whenever a company announces that its quarterly earnings are below forecast, the market reacts negatively to the news. The magnitude of the reaction will depend on the track record of the company or CEO. As with our criminal justice system, first-time offenders are treated much more leniently than repeat offenders.

Jill Barad, the former CEO at Mattel, went through a streak of missing earnings targets four quarters in a row, yet each time she would pronounce that better times lay ahead ("we continue to be confident in the future of this company"[47]). Her penchant for promotion and publicity (she did, after all, rise to the CEO position on her amazing success building Barbie dolls into an almost $2 billion business) didn't play out so well on Wall Street, however. Her assurances to investors were taken at face value, and when she couldn't deliver, her credibility was gone and so was she.

By the time a company reports a missed earnings target, it is often too late to save yourself money as an investor. However, there are other types of missed milestones that often precede the disastrous earnings report. Advance Micro Devices, for example, has a long history of product development and production delays that have led to poor earnings. The launch of its K5 chip in 1996 was a full year behind plan, leaving its new production facility greatly underutilized and unprofitable. Although designed for speeds 30 percent greater than Intel's Pentium processor, the K5 performance levels at volume production were no better than Pentium speeds. Mike Johnson, AMD's chief designer, admits the young K5 team failed to devise adequate software tests, so they were unaware the chip ran real software programs more slowly than expected.[48] Given AMD's track record and the early warning signs for this chip, the problems AMD has encountered in competing against Intel should not be surprising.

A Question of Character

Perhaps the single most important indicator of potential trouble is the one that is hardest to precisely define—the question of character: a person with high ethical standards and deep competence, who has a desire to succeed by helping others to be better than they would otherwise be on their own, who can face reality even when it is not so pleasant and acknowledge when something is wrong, and who engenders trust and promotes honesty in the organizations he or she creates and leads. That may sound like a tall order, but the real problem is that for some of the executives at the helm of companies we studied, they weren't even close. Tony Galban, a D&O underwriter at Chubb, zeroed right in on this issue: "The three things behind every bad directors and officers liability situation are greed, cronyism, and denial. And if you were to watch people on the stands over the last six or eight months you would see an extraordinary amount of denial, some of which is almost not credible."[49]

Even many of the scrupulously honest executives we studied—and there were many—stumbled when they couldn't accept the reality of a changed world. For these executives, the problem wasn't one of ethics, but of defensiveness. How can we spot this warning sign? Here's one suggestion from Tony:

"Always listen to the analysts' calls because that gives you a sense of how an individual thinks on their seat. They give you a sense of whether they're in denial or whether they're being professional. I've seen even the most polished people make very revealing comments in the heat of press questioning . . . you know, where you want to concentrate on subject A and you touch upon subject B but they keep grilling you on subject B . . . by the time the third question comes on subject B watch how testy the CEO gets. 'I thought we covered that,' or 'It's just what I said earlier' . . . just very unresponsive, testy remarks which means, 'I'm here to talk about subject A. I've been rehearsing subject A all night and now you're going to sit here and poke me on this marginal subject B and I don't want to talk about it.'"[50]

Board members are in a terrific position to see how the CEO deals with adverse circumstances. John Keogh, another big-time underwriter of D&O insurance, pointed out what he looks for when CEOs are in the hot seat: "How well [do] they understand their business . . . [was] the management team incredibly arrogant . . . [did the CEO or CFO] have all the answers and is pretty [much] on top of his or her game."[51] As these quotes indicate, boards need to watch out for certain behaviors or characteristics of CEOs that can lead to trouble. In our own work with boards, we have identified several key warning signs when it comes to character:

- Does the CEO believe that he or she is considerably smarter, or better, than other people?
- Does the CEO believe that change is simply a matter of exerting his or her will on other stakeholders, whether they are customers, employees, or regulators?

- Does the CEO always seem to have the "answer" to problems, showing no sign of drawing on the strengths of his or her management team? (In this regard, when the CEO is the only senior executive directors meet at board meetings, you know you have a problem.)
- Does the CEO spend an inordinate amount of time talking about public relations and image relative to strategy and execution?
- Does the CEO rely on solutions to new problems that are no different from what he or she has done in the past?

All of these questions need to be in the backs of the heads of vigilant board members. Any one such attribute may be excused, but when a pattern starts to form the question of character comes to the fore.

Consider the letter to shareholders. Implicit in some of the warning signs we've discussed is a degree of aggressiveness, or overconfidence, and the letter can sometimes provide clues. Tony Galban teaches the D&O underwriters that work for him to "go through the letter and circle all the adjectives because, remember, that's been distilled . . . that letter has been distilled through General Counsel, that letter has been distilled through all the other people who looked at it to make sure they're being careful. What you are wary of are people that have an excessively aggressive sense of control, and people that are cowboys. They tend to be the worst personality fits for what I call a sanguine CEO. You're looking for people that speak in overly aggressive terms about what they will accomplish, people that have a self-righteous indignation about failures, people that are defensive about having bad years, people that are in simple denial. I mean, you'll see these 'Well, sales are off 60 percent this year but so are everybody's,' or 'Sales were off 60 percent this year but that was an aberration,' or 'Sales are off 60 percent this year but believe it or not we're in better shape than ever.' These are the kinds of sort of mass denials that you want to get to, so the letter to the shareholders is a good place to find it."[52]

So the experts who are actually on the line for corporate malfeasance pay a lot of attention to character. In some ways, if we don't trust the CEO and other senior executives, it is the ultimate warning sign. In all, it seems clear that there are clues to what might happen in a company, and although there is a great deal of uncertainty around these clues, they offer board members important insights to the future. The question of character may well be the most important of them all.

In sum, board members have a huge responsibility. Paying attention to the warning signs that are around them is essential to fulfilling their duty of vigilance. Many of the failing boards in recent years had ample opportunities to see what was going on during their watch, but simply didn't know where to look, or did an ineffective job looking or rationalized the issue away. The same discipline also applies to those considering taking on new board seats—it is critical to know what to look for before finding yourself enmeshed in something much more than you bargained for. In this chapter, we have put together a set of specific questions that boards, and potential board members, should be asking on a regular basis about the companies for which they have critical oversight responsibility today, or potentially tomorrow. The bottom line is that board members need to track these warning signs as if their companies' futures depended on it, because they do.

14

Globalizing the Company Board: Lessons from China's Lenovo

Michael Useem and Neng Liang

The rise of the Indian and Chinese economies during the past decade is transforming how executives and directors think about company governance. In both countries, corporate boards had traditionally played a modest role in company decisions. And even when more actively involved, they had often pulled decisions toward objectives not entirely in keeping with governance ideals. If directors are in theory the eyes and ears of all company owners, in practice they sometimes favored family owners over others in India, and state holders over others in China.

The sustained growth of the Indian and Chinese economies, however, has forced regulators, shareholders, and companies in both countries to reexamine their governance practices for two reasons. First, international investors increasingly moved cash across country lines, and as they took greater ownership in publicly traded companies outside their home countries, they also brought home-country biases for independent, informed, and even-handed directors. Second, Indian and Chinese executives increasingly moved their operations across national boundaries, and as they entered demanding international markets, they also learned that independent, informed, and even-handed directors can constitute a source of company advantage.

The broader outlines of these trends are reasonably well known, but what is less understood is how companies remake their boards to reflect the emerging reality of global equity and operating markets. This chapter seeks to identify the process by which company leaders are restructuring their governance through investigation of how one of China's more prominent companies, Lenovo, transformed its board following acquisition of IBM's personal computer operation in 2005.

Founded in 1984, Lenovo had emerged two decades later as China's largest computer maker. It had captured 27 percent of China's rapidly expanding computer market, with annual revenue exceeding $3 billion. The company concluded, however, that its long-term growth depended on its becoming an international player, just as many American and European companies had concluded in years past. "In our world," explained executive chairman Yang Yuanqing, "a high growth rate is hard to sustain if you only try to maintain your position in the China market."[1]

After thirteen months of negotiations, Lenovo and IBM announced that Lenovo would acquire IBM's Personal Computing Division for $1.75 billion. Founder Liu Chuanzhi declared that globalization had become a necessity, the company's only option for growth and survival. In the months that followed, Lenovo restructured its governing board as well, and we focus here on the governance decisions that drove that change.

Governance Decisions

We define governance decisions to be those moments when governing-board directors face a discrete and realistic opportunity to commit company resources to one course or another on behalf of the enterprise's objectives. This is akin to Barnard's characterization of top company decisions as a "choice of means to accomplish ends which are not personal."[2] Few top decisions are taken without the input of others, and researchers report that decisions often evolve out of numerous discussions, competing agendas, and unanticipated events.[3] In focusing on governance decisions, we do not mean to imply that directors are solely responsible for their decisions, nor that all of their decisions can be identified. Yet boards of directors do take the principal role in governance decisions, and many of the directors' major decisions can be pinpointed and evaluated.[4]

We know a great deal about the visible features of corporate governance that make a difference in company behavior, ranging from firm profitability and fraudulent activity to protecting the environment and picking a chief executive.[5] Although the outward features of the board are useful predictors of company behavior, the board's inside decisions drive much of that behavior. The "front-stage performance" of governing boards, concluded one researcher, is a product of their "back-stage activity," and peering into that backstage can be essential for appreciating what reaches the frontstage.[6] By way of example, consider Enron's board just prior to the company's bankruptcy in December 2001. It was a relatively well-composed board, with many prominent independent directors and only two Enron executives serving on the board. An accounting professor had served as its audit committee chair since 1985. The board itself was led by a chair who was not also the chief executive officer, one more outward sign of good governance. Whatever the outside appearance, however, when directors reached their decisions inside the boardroom, their actual decisions were suboptimal, including approval of the special-purpose entities that hid Enron debt from the market and suspension of the company's code of ethics. The board's favorable outward features notwithstanding, the directors' inside decisions directly contributed to the company's downfall.[7]

The challenge is to find a method for witnessing the backstage decisions, and for that we have chosen to focus on Lenovo's experience in restructuring its governance. With direct access to the company's leaders, we have sought to identify the decisions that its directors had taken behind closed doors, decisions that played a critical role, we believe, in driving the restructuring. Lenovo's experience is illustrative of what other companies are likely to undergo as they face increasingly international markets. Our analysis points to the central role of governance decisions in driving that change.

Five Conceptions of Decision Making in Corporate Governance

Before we enter the boardroom backstage to examine director decisions, it is useful to identify the major potential areas in which directors may make decisions. We are primarily concerned with directors' explicit involvement in company decisions and the criteria that they apply in reaching those decisions under varying market conditions. From prior research and theory we anticipate that directors may engage in four areas of decision making, each with its own set of distinct criteria.

Monitoring Management

One well-established conception of the firm views directors as largely serving as the eyes and ears of the shareholders, ensuring that company executives conduct themselves properly on behalf of the owners. The decisions that directors take are therefore inferred or prescribed to be directed at monitoring the decisions that executives make.[8] This is the formal view that big business sometimes even takes of its own boardrooms. "The board of directors has the important role of overseeing management performance on behalf of shareholders," declared the Business Roundtable, and "directors are diligent monitors, but not managers, of business operations."[9] By way of illustration, directors often take decisions to ensure that their executives do not enrich themselves at the expenses of shareholders, nor that they enter into sweetheart deals with other companies controlled by the executives' families.

Partnering with Management

A long-standing alternative conception of corporate governance suggests that directors are decision partners with the top executives, joining with them in making the company's most important choices. Directors are seen as coproducers of the firm's strategic decisions.[10] This is the informal view that business executives often take of themselves. The chief executive of a large financial-services firm, for instance, spoke for many in describing the decisions that directors reach in his boardroom. They are, he said, those that are "strategically impactful" and those that will "change the future."[11] If a company's executives are seeking to integrate newly acquired international operations, for example, directors may collaborate with the executives in reaching key decisions on how to optimize the process.

Legitimating Management

A third conception of corporate governance sees the directors as legitimating management to outside constituencies, especially owners but also regulators and even customers. From the standpoint of this framework, the company selects directors whose stature and visibility reassure shareholders and others that backstage board decisions will be well taken. This view is less frequently articulated by business executives and academic researchers alike, but it does emerge from time to time as an explanatory factor in studies ranging from company reputation to corporate codes.[12] For instance, if a company is seeking to reassure its corporate customers, institutional investors, and equity analysts, company executives may reference their prominent directors to suggest that that confidence is well placed because the directors can be expected to make good decisions inside the boardroom.

Controlling Management

A fourth conception of corporate governance describes directors as controlling management on behalf of a dominant ownership group, whether family or government. This framing is commonplace in India, where families such as the Ambanis and Tatas remain powerfully involved in companies they founded, and in China, where public agencies and party officials remain powerfully involved in state-owned enterprises. In China, Company Law (Article 17) specifies that "the activities of the local branch units of the Chinese Communist Party (CCP) shall be carried out in accordance with the Constitution of the CCP," which grants the local party committee the rights "to supervise party cadres and any other personnel."[13] The deputy governor of the nation's central bank, People's Bank of China, thus affirmed that members of the Communist Party should serve on boards of state-owned banks to ensure that "they will carry out in a loyal way" their "responsibility" to "implement the Party's general and specific policies" and thus ensure the "Party's supervision over cadres." One consequence, for instance, could be for directors to direct company business to other firms with which the directors are associated (even though research has suggested suboptimal performance consequences).[14]

Controlled by Management

A fifth implicit conception of corporate governance takes the position that directors make few significant decisions of any kind. In this framing, boardrooms must be filled by regulatory requirement, but beyond meeting compliance obligations, directors contribute little to the firm's decisions. Among the better-known examples of this view is an appraisal of American governance practices by academician Jay Lorsch titled *Pawns or Potentates*. His answer to the implicit question came closer to the former than the latter.[15] By way of illustration, when Walt Disney chief executive Michael Eisner hired friend Michael Ovitz as chief operating office and heir apparent in 1995, he did not allow the directors to fully consider a decision that ordinarily would be deemed a board prerogative. Similarly, when executives at HealthSouth, Tyco International, and WorldCom decided to engage in fraudulent accounting in 1998–2001, they shielded those decisions from their boards.[16]

The first four conceptions of boardroom decision making are not mutually exclusive. In selecting a new chief executive, for instance, directors often appear to decide on a candidate both for the promise of enhancing shareholder value and for following a preferred strategy. What remains unclear is the relative extent to which these several conceptions characterize the directors' decisions, and how that mix is altered by changes in market conditions. The five conceptions are summarized in Table 14.1.

We also theorize that governance changes in response to market changes are a product of explicit director decisions. Transformations in the governing board come not only from the subtle impact of market changes but also from explicit understanding of those changes by directors and their subsequent decisions in response to the changes. While the invisible hand of the market sets the stage, the directors' visible hand makes the change, with new decision criteria coming to the fore in the boardroom as other criteria recede.

Ownership and Governance in China

The five conceptions of decision making in corporate governance have been largely developed from observation of boards in the United States, and they are thus partly rooted in the distinctive ownership patterns that have characterized large publicly traded American companies in recent years, especially the wide diffusion of ownership among large institutional holders.[17] The ownership of Chinese companies has been marked by far less diffusion, and as a result, two of the five conceptions—"controlling management" and "controlled by management"—appear more relatively prevalent among large publicly listed Chinese companies.

Most listed companies in China report three distinct groups of shareholders: the state, "legal persons," and individual investors. Legal persons are domestic legal entities and institutions, many

Table 14.1. Five Conceptions of Decision Making in Corporate Governance.

Governance Conception	Decision Criteria	Characterization	Illustration
Monitoring management	Optimize shareholder value	Directors take decisions that monitor executive actions	Directors decide to prevent executive self-enrichment
Partnering with management	Guide company strategy	Directors co-make strategic decisions with executives	Directors decide with executives how to integrate acquisitions
Legitimating management	Reassure investors, regulators, and customers	Director stature implies good director decisions	International directors are presumed to make globally savvy decisions
Controlling management	Protect dominant owners	Director decisions favor dominant owners	Directors direct business to owner-affiliated companies
Controlled by management	Endorse management decisions	Directors make no substantial decisions	Directors make no decisions to prevent executive fraud

controlled by the state. Drawing on 2003 data, for instance, the Shanghai Stock Exchange (China's premier exchange) estimated that the government held 49.9 percent of its listed shares, whereas individual investors accounted for 35.3 percent and legal persons 14.8 percent. Further analysis of the governance patterns of the exchange's listed companies led researchers to classify most of the firms as falling into one of two governance categories that they termed "majority owner control" or "insider control."[18]

The implication for governance decision making among publicly listed Chinese firms is that their directors have been able to exercise relatively little discretion in the boardroom. State agencies and state-controlled organizations tended to exercise control over the board and management—or management tended to exercise control over the board. Of the five conceptions of decision making in corporate governance largely derived from U.S. experience (displayed in Table 14.1), the most apt descriptors, drawing on the Shanghai Stock Exchange's appraisal, are either "controlling management" or "controlled by management." In both conditions, directors are viewed as under the thumb of either a dominant owner—the state, in the case of Chinese firms—or top management.[19] Consistent with this assessment, an investigator who studied the governance of a set of publicly listed firms in the late 1990s concluded that Chinese boards are "rubber-stamps" and independent directors little more than "window-dressing."[20]

Until recently, China's Security Regulatory Commission had reinforced the two governance conceptions of "controlling management" or "controlled by management" by prohibiting stock trading by both state and legal-person entities. Yet even with the commission's dropping of the trading prohibition in 2005, little active trading by those entities followed, thereby inhibiting emergence of an active market for corporate control, one of the forces that had emboldened boards in the United States during the past two decades. As a result, Chinese boards remained relatively weak compared with American boards, leaving them subject to control by either management or the state. Indeed, the boundary between the state and the firm has not always been as sharply drawn as in the West, allowing state agents to exercise direct influence over management at some firms.[21]

Because the governance structure of an economy is not exogenous, but rather the revealed preference of its various stakeholders, the recent entry of Chinese companies into world markets is likely to challenge these traditional conceptions of governance. Led by such firms as Haier (household appliances), TCL (electronics), China National Offshore Oil Corporation, and Lenovo, Chinese firms have in the past decade increasingly sought sales, supplies, and shareholders abroad.[22] As they now have to face investors, customers, suppliers, employees, and regulators in a global context, we anticipate that they will transform their governance, moving away from the traditional conceptions of controlling management or controlled by management toward the alternative conceptions of monitoring, partnering with, and legitimating management. We expect new decision criteria as a result to come to the fore in the boardroom, and we also expect that these changes will come through explicit decisions by company directors.

Research Method

To see the exercise of the directors' visible hand in the board's backstage, we have sought direct access to a Chinese company that faced a rapidly changing market and responded by expanding wellbeyond its national borders. Lenovo fit these criteria well, confronting and reacting to fast-growing but highly competitive and habitually unpredictable domestic and global markets for personal computers. Lenovo was also prepared to allow us to learn about its backstage decisions.

During the late 1990s and early 2000s, Lenovo had attempted to diversify beyond its manufacturing and sale of personal computers in China, but that effort largely failed. In the meantime, its PC dominance within the Chinese market was coming under increasingly successful attack by Hewlett-Packard, Dell, and other foreign and domestic makers. In 1994, Lenovo held 4 percent of the Chinese PC market, and by 2000 its fraction had risen to 29 percent, but its market share then dropped back to 27 percent in 2003 and 26 percent in 2004. Top management concluded that for continued growth, international expansion had become essential. It also concluded that it would have to change its original name—Legend—to Lenovo, because the name of Legend was already used by other companies in other countries.[23]

At the time, however, Lenovo had no foothold outside greater China. By coincidence, IBM approached Lenovo on the possibility of the Chinese company acquiring IBM's personal-computer division, and Lenovo's management swiftly embraced the offer, even though IBM's operation drew four times the revenue of Lenovo. But IBM was losing money on its personal-computer sales, and Lenovo's due diligence convinced management that it could turn the much larger IBM operation around. "We finally came to believe that in IBM's hands the PC division would continue to suffer annual losses," reported Liu Chuanzhi, then executive chairman of Lenovo, but he felt that in his own hands the IBM operation "could be profitable." That conclusion was partly based on analysis of overhead that the IBM parent allocated to its PC division. The division would have been profitable were it not for the high headquarters overhead imposed on it. And it could have been even more profitable had it adopted Lenovo's lean manufacturing methods. Assembling a PC in the United States at the time cost $24, compared with $4 in China.[24]

Lenovo announced the IBM acquisition on December 7, 2004, at a Beijing news conference attended by some five hundred Chinese and Western journalists, and it completed the acquisition in April 2005. From a dominant but faltering place in the Chinese computer market, Lenovo became a substantial and rising force in the global computer market. The IBM acquisition moved Lenovo from the eighth to third largest computer maker worldwide after Dell and Hewlett-Packard. In the year after the acquisition, Lenovo doubled its workforce to twenty thousand and quadrupled its revenue to $12 billion.

Lenovo's share of the world PC market rose from 2.3 percent in 2004 to 6.2 percent in 2005 and 7.9 percent in early 2007, as seen in Table 14.2. Years earlier, when Lenovo had fewer than a dozen employees, Liu Chuanzhi had vowed that it would one day become "the IBM of China." Now, owning IBM in China and well beyond, it had become far more global. Executive chairman Yang Yuanqing declared, "No matter where you are in the world, you must now be an enterprise that is internationally competitive. Internationalization has therefore become a key goal for us."[25]

To appreciate the impact on backstage governance decisions of this transformation of a largely domestic Chinese manufacturer into a significant international maker, we interviewed the key decision makers in 2007–2008. They included Liu Chuanzhi, Lenovo's founder and executive chairman just prior to the IBM acquisition; Yang Yuanqing, Lenovo's chief executive before the acquisition and executive chairman afterward; William Amelio, Lenovo's second chief executive officer; Shan Weijian, a non-executive director of Lenovo representing one of its major private investors; and two other top executives at Lenovo. We kept detailed notes on the interviews, and we recorded the interviews with Liu, Yang, and Amelio (and two interviews with Liu in August 2004, several months before the acquisition[26]). The analysis that follows emerges from our systematic immersion—in

Table 14.2. Worldwide Market Share of Personal Computers by Vendor, 2004–2007.

	Vendor Percentage Share			
	2004	2005	2006	2007
Hewlett-Packard	17.7	18.1	18.2	18.3
Dell	15.7	15.6	15.0	15.5
Lenovo	2.3	6.2	8.0	7.9
Acer	3.6	4.7	7.2	6.8

Source: Gartner Dataquest, International Data Corporation, and iSuppli Corporation via www.eMarketer.com (accessed December 19, 2007). The data for 2006 and 2007 are for the end of the second quarter.

keeping with the classic guidelines of Glaser and Strauss—in the interviews and in a host of documents provided by the company and other sources. Quotes not attributed to a written source are from the interviews.[27]

Globalization of Lenovo's Sales, Manufacturing, and Ownership

Prior to the IBM acquisition in 2004, Lenovo was a largely Chinese company, with headquarters in Beijing and most of its sales and all of its operations in greater China. After the acquisition, it moved its executive offices to Raleigh (North Carolina), Beijing, and Singapore. It divided its research operations among Raleigh, Yamato (Japan), Beijing, Shanghai, and three other Chinese cities. It transferred marketing operations to Bangalore, India. It spread manufacturing operations across Australia, Brazil, China, Hungary, India, Japan, Malaysia, Mexico, the United States, and the United Kingdom. In 2004, none of its PC sales came from outside greater China; three years later, it drew more than three-fifths from foreign shores, as seen in Table 14.3. Symbolizing the international commitment, the executive chairman Yang Yuanqing moved his family to the United States.

Table 14.3. Percentage of Lenovo Sales from Greater China and Elsewhere, 2004–2007.

	Region Percentage Share			
	2004	2005	2006	2007
Greater China	100	100	36	38
Americas	0	0	30	28
Europe, Middle East, and Africa	0	0	21	21
Asia Pacific	0	0	13	13

Source: Lenovo Annual Report, 2004–05, 2005–06, 2006–07.

Relinquishing direct operating control of Lenovo, founder Liu Chuanzhi remained as president of the parent company, Legend Holdings, and installed Yang Yuanqing, who had served at Lenovo since 1989, as executive chairman of Lenovo. Together they recruited the executive responsible for the IBM PC division, Stephen Ward, as Lenovo's first chief executive officer, and then several months later the chief of Dell's Asian operations, William Amelio, to serve as the second CEO. Amelio established his office in Singapore, Liu in Beijing, and Yang in Raleigh. "The distributed logic of worldsourcing," explained Amelio, "suggests a radically decentralized organizational model." A "meeting of my company's senior managers," he added, "looks like the United Nations General Assembly." Chinese has always been the language of Lenovo, but the company declared two weeks after the IBM acquisition that English would constitute its official language.

Lenovo in parallel diversified its ownership (Table 14.4). The government's Chinese Academy of Sciences had been the majority holder through Legend Holdings, but after the IBM acquisition, IBM held a significant stake in the company, as did three American-based private equity companies: Texas Pacific Group (TPG; $30 billion under management), General Atlantic (GA; $15 billion under management), and Newbridge Capital ($2 billion under management and affiliated with TPG).

Globalization of Lenovo's Board of Directors

Lenovo's market and organizational remake also brought a remake of the governing board. In 2003, nonindependent directors outnumbered the independent directors four to three. The post-acquisition board, by contrast, was divided between five executive and nonindependent directors, three private-equity directors, and three independent directors. Prior to the acquisition, all seven of the directors were Chinese or of greater China origin. After the acquisition, four of the eleven directors were Americans, as seen

Table 14.4. Lenovo Ownership by Holder, 2003, 2005, and 2007.

	Holder Percentage Ownership		
	2003	2005	2007
Legend Holdings Limited	57.8	57.0	41.9
Public shares	39.9	20.4	43.1
Private equity companies	0	9.5	6.5
IBM	0	12.3	7.9
Directors	0.3	0.8	0.6

Source: For 2003, *Report of the Directors*, Lenovo, for the year ending March 31, 2003, pp. 64–65; for 2005, *Report of the Directors*, Lenovo, for the year ending March 31, 2005, pp. 42–43; for 2007, company Website at http://www.pc.ibm.com/ww/lenovo/investor_factsheet.html (accessed on December 23, 2007). Lenovo's number of outstanding shares is from Osiris company report on Lenovo (www.bvdep.com/en/OSIRIS.html, accessed on December 21, 2007). Of the Legend Holdings Limited in 2007, the Chinese Academy of Sciences held 65 percent, and the Employees' Shareholding Society of Legend Holdings Ltd. held 35 percent. The share of public funds in 2007 included significant holdings by institutional investors Matthews International Capital Management (3.9%), Capital Group (1.5%), Legg Mason (1.44%), HSBC (0.9%), and Fidelity Investments (0.9%).

in Table 14.5. Before the acquisition, board meetings had always been conducted in Chinese; after the acquisition, because all but one director spoke English and several spoke no Chinese, English became the medium of expression. Going into the acquisition, the executive chairman and chief executive were both Chinese; coming out of the acquisition, the executive chairman was Chinese and the CEO American. Of the top management team in 2004, all were Chinese; of the eighteen members of the top management team in 2007, six were from greater China, one from Europe, and eleven from the United States. Ma Xuezheng [Mary Ma], the company's CFO at the acquisition moment, declared at the time, "This is going to be very much an international company operated in an international fashion."[28]

Compared with publicly traded companies worldwide, Lenovo's post-acquisition governance reached international

Table 14.5. Lenovo Directors, 2003, 2005, and 2007

2003			
Executive and Non-Independent Directors			
Liu Chuanzhi	China	Executive chairman	Founded Legend in 1984; Chairman, Legend Holdings
Yang Yuanqing	China	Chief executive officer	Joined Legend in 1989, CEO in 2001
Ma Xuezheng	China	Chief financial officer	Joined Legend in 1992; formerly Chinese Academy of Sciences (CAS)
Zeng Maochao	China	Non-executive director	Former director, Institute of Computing Technology, CAS
Independent Non-Executive Directors			
Chia-Wei Woo	Hong Kong	Non-executive director	Former president of Hong Kong University of Science & Technology
Lee Sen Ting	U.S.	Non-executive director	Managing director, WR Hambrecht & Co.; formerly Hewlett-Packard
Wai Ming Wong	U.K.	Non-executive director	Chartered accountant; CEO of Roly International Holdings (Singapore)
2005*			
Executive and Non-Independent Directors			
Yang Yuanqing	China	Executive chairman	Joined Legend in 1989, CEO in 2001
Steven M. Ward	U.S.	Chief executive officer	Formerly general manager, Personal Systems Group, IBM
Ma Xuezheng	China	Chief financial officer	Joined Legend in 1992; formerly Chinese Academy of Sciences (CAS)

Liu Chuanzhi	China	Non-executive director	Legend founder; Chairman, Legend Holdings; formerly of CAS
Zhu Linan	China	Non-executive director	Joined Legend in 1989; Managing director, Legend Capital
Private-Equity Directors			
James Coulter	U.S.	Non-executive director	Founding partner, private-equity investor Texas Pacific Group (TPG)
William Grabe	U.S.	Non-executive director	Managing director, private-equity investor General Atlantic (GA)
Shan Weijian	China	Non-executive director	Managing director, private-equity investor Newbridge Capital
Independent Non-Executive Directors			
Wai Ming Wong	U.K.	Non-executive director	Chartered accountant; CEO of Roly International Holdings (Singapore)
Lee Sen Ting	U.S.	Non-executive director	Managing director, WR Hambrecht & Co.; formerly Hewlett-Packard
Chia-Wei Woo	Hong Kong	Non-executive director	Former president of Hong Kong University of Science & Technology
2007**			
Executive and Non-Independent Directors			
Yang Yuanqing	China	Executive chairman	Joined Legend in 1989, CEO in 2001
William Amelio	U.S.	Chief executive officer	Formerly VP-Asia for Dell; NCR; Honeywell; IBM
Ma Xuezheng	China	Chief financial officer	Joined Legend in 1992; formerly Chinese Academy of Sciences (CAS)

(Continued)

Table 14.5. Lenovo Directors, 2003, 2005, and 2007 (Cont'd)

2007			
Executive and Non-Independent Directors			
Liu Chuanzhi	China	Non-executive director	Legend founder; Chairman, Legend Holdings; formerly of CAS
Zhu Linan	China	Non-executive director	Joined Legend in 1989; Managing Director, Legend Capital
Private-Equity Directors			
James Coulter	U.S.	Non-executive director	Founding partner, Texas Pacific Group (TPG)
William Grabe	U.S.	Non-executive director	Managing director, private-equity investor General Atlantic (GA)
Shan Weijian	China	Non-executive director	Managing director, private-equity investor Newbridge Capital
Independent Non-Executive Directors			
John W. Barter	U.S.	Non-executive director	Director of BMC Software; formerly CFO, Allied Signal
Chia-Wei Woo	Hong Kong	Non-executive director	Former president of Hong Kong University of Science & Technology
Lee Sen Ting	U.S.	Non-executive director	Managing director, WR Hambrecht & Co.; formerly Hewlett-Packard
Wai Ming Wong	U.K.	Non-executive director	Chartered accountant; CEO of Roly International Holdings (Singapore)

Notes: *After May 17
**Before May 22

Source: Company records.

norms. To see this, we turn to Institutional Shareholder Services (ISS), which furnishes institutional investors with independent appraisals of company governance, drawing upon publicly available data sources. ISS gathered data on 236 governance features, ranging from board composition and executive compensation to takeover defenses and stock-option expensing. ISS provides an overall measure of a company's governance with its Corporate Governance Quotient (CGQ). The CGQ compares Lenovo's governance with that of publicly traded non-U.S. companies (those included in Morgan Stanley Capital International's EAFE index and the *Financial Times'* All Shares and World Developed indices). ISS also compares Lenovo with a subset of technology and hardware equipment makers outside the United States. ISS terms the first comparison a company's *Index* CGQ, and the second a company's *Industry* CGQ. The CGQ scores represent a company's percentile ranking, with a score of 50 implying that the company's governance ranks better than half the comparison firms and worse than half.[29]

Figure 14.1 reveals that Lenovo's governance ranked at about the 25th percentile on both measures during the year of the acquisition (the first year ISS appraised Lenovo's governance). During the two years that followed, however, Lenovo had elevated its governance ranking above the 40th percentile compared with all companies, and above the 50th percentile compared with other firms in the technology hardware and equipment industry. By these measures, Lenovo had moved its outward features of governance into the middle range of company governance worldwide.

Partnering with Management

Our interview evidence regarding the remaking of Lenovo's governing board points toward a transformation of the board from a limited version of monitoring management or even controlled by management to a partnership with management. Company

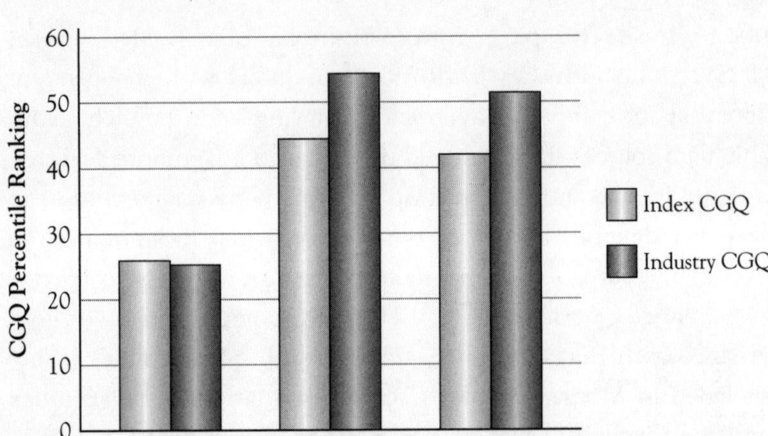

Figure 14.1. Lenovo's Index and Industry Corporate Governance Quotient (CGQ) by Institutional Shareholder Services, 2005–2007.

executives instigated the change in the immediate wake of the decision to expand rapidly outside of China through the acquisition of the personal computer division of IBM.

"The IBM PC acquisition is a watershed," observed Liu Chuanzhi. "Before that point," he said, "the board of directors did not play much [of a] role." The board had mainly been concerned with company audit and executive pay. The board played a modest monitoring function on behalf of nonstate investors, but was otherwise little involved in the firm's strategic decisions. During the late 1990s, for example, the chief technology officer Ni Guangnan of Lenovo (the company was then known as Legend) and its chief executive Liu Chuanzhi came to sharp disagreement on the company's fundamental strategy. Rather than taking the issue up to the board, Guangnan lodged charges against Liu's leadership with the Chinese government, provoking the Chinese premier, Zhu Rongji, to send an investigating team. The Chinese Academy of Sciences finally intervened to resolve the issue, and it did so without board involvement. Though a final decision was nominally taken in the name of the board on September 2, 1999, "one word from the Academy [had] settled the matter," Liu recalled, and the company forced out Ni. But "all this changed after the IBM PC acquisition," he affirmed in referencing the board's decision engagement.

Lenovo has been listed on the Hong Kong Stock Exchange (and through an American Depository Receipt on the New York Stock Exchange), and in keeping with Hong Kong tradition, independent non-executive directors prior to the IBM acquisition were viewed by the company as largely present to protect minority stockholders—in this case, investors other than the Chinese Academy of Sciences. Liu and Yang reconstituted the board to go well beyond that focus, adding the international directors, improving board capacity to render guidance to the executive team, and, more generally, creating a governing body that is more globally informed and independent, important prerequisites for partnering with management rather than just monitoring or bowing to management.

The decision to add international directors, for instance, was largely driven by the reported need for the board to bring global "vision" into the boardroom. "Now," said Yang, "internationalization is our key consideration as we are taking on international business." This in his view required directors who would bring fresh insight into how Lenovo could make inroads into the worldwide market share of its larger rivals—Dell Computer at 18 percent and Hewlett-Packard at 16 percent in 2005—and at the same time hold onto its market share against its smaller rivals, including Acer at 5 percent and Fujitsu at 4 percent in 2005.[30] Although Lenovo was still the biggest player in the Chinese market—the nearest rival, Founder Technology Group, held less than half its market share—domestic dominance provided no assurance of growth abroad. "If you have a highly successful business in one country," warned Amelio, "it does not mean that you will have a highly successful business in a global operation," and that is where the counsel of the non-executive directors would prove particularly valuable. And their counsel pointed toward equal footing for the Chinese and American operations. Non-executive director Shan Weijian explained, "We don't want people to have a feeling of takeover [by a] Chinese company of the American company. We want an integration process which doesn't involve which part takes which part. What we want is [to be] integrated into [a single] global operation." That consideration proved a major factor in the board's selection of an American chief executive. "If we choose a Chinese CEO," Shan reported, "no matter how well he speaks English, that would [make it] much more challenging to manage the American workforce," in contrast to the Chinese workforce, he observed, which would have been more open to an American CEO.

The restructuring of the Lenovo board following the IBM purchase also brought the directors into direct guidance of the integration of Lenovo's and IBM's distinct operating styles. IBM had built up strong, enduring relations with its select corporate customers; Lenovo had by contrast created a largely "transactional" exchange with its many retail customers. Although large enterprise relations had been the staple of IBM's PC sales, management anticipated greater growth among small consumers. But identifying the optimal areas for growth outside of China and identifying effective ways of reaching them were uncertain and risky judgment calls, and in making them management sought director guidance.

Facing many decisions of this kind in the wake of the acquisition, the company formed a strategy committee, charged with vetting the company's mid- and long-term decisions on behalf of the board. As a step toward internationalization, the company placed two Chinese directors—Yang Yuanqing and Liu Chuanzhi—on the strategy committee along with two Americans—James Coulter and William Grabe. The board met quarterly, but the strategy committee met monthly to focus on issues ranging from competitive strategy to cultural integration. Regarding the latter, for example, Yang viewed the non-executive directors as an "impartial third party" that would help prevent a "confrontation of two teams, two cultures, and two mentalities." With their own money invested in the company, the "third party" private-equity representatives would not be reluctant to resolve the differences, or for that matter to delve into other significant issues. "In order to build a world-class organization," said private-equity director representative Shan Weijian, "you really have to have world-class challenge." The directors were ready to provide it, and company executives sought it. In CEO William Amelio's words, the role of the directors on the strategy committee was to pick from an array of choices "the right idea that is going to maximize the core competence of the company."

Lenovo's board also became directly engaged in decisions on executive succession, an arena that had also not previously been its prerogative. Two non-executive directors from the private-equity groups in 2005, for instance, played a pivotal role in replacing the first CEO after the acquisition. At the time of the purchase, the IBM executive responsible for the PC division, Stephen Ward, had been the logical candidate for the role of chief executive, with Yang to serve as executive chairman. Their dual appointment was largely an executive decision, but within months it became evident to the board's strategy committee that the former IBM executive was not the right person to lead the combined enterprise given the specific challenges it faced, topped by the need for greater supply-chain efficiencies. Yang and Liu worried, however, that an unexpected exit of the top American executive so soon after the acquisition would cast a shadow over their effort to internationalize the firm. Neither knew the international computer industry well enough to identify a strong replacement, and it was American non-executive directors James Coulter and William Grabe who identified several candidates for succession, including William Amelio, then head of Dell Computer's Asian operations, who eventually became the successor. Nor were

Yang and Liu familiar with the process of replacing an American chief executive, but the private-equity directors on the Lenovo board represented firms that had often done so. Said one of the private-equity directors, "we have done this repeatedly, and we are familiar with the U.S. market and the practice over there, the environment, and how to do it."

Private-equity firms generally seek direct engagement in company decision making through service on the governing board. Texas Pacific Group and General Atlantic were no exception, and both were already well familiar with the IBM operation. TPG had hoped itself to buy out the IBM PC division, and had conducted its own due diligence. GA had been asked by Liu Chuanzhi to advise him on whether to buy the IBM division, and it too had gathered detailed data on the IBM operation. Though other bidders emerged, Lenovo and TPG became the two finalists, and IBM notified Lenovo that it had won and TPG that it had lost just thirty minutes apart. Consequently, James Coulter of TPG and William Grabe of GA were already well versed in the personal computer business when they joined the Lenovo board and its strategy committee. Executives as a result treated them like partners rather than minority investors, reported Coulter. Vince Feng, a GA partner who managed its investments in China and East Asia, affirmed the same, reporting that "our influence comes less from ownership than having been trusted advisors for Lenovo's key decision makers for a long time."[31]

Similarly, the criteria for bringing specific non-executive directors onto the board after the IBM acquisition reflected a preference for directors who would partner with management more than monitor or defer to management. The selection standards for the new board members, reported Yang, included their industry experience, "strategic vision," personal reputation, and functional expertise in such areas as finance, strategy, and marketing. For example, in the case of the appointment of John Barter, who had served as Allied Signal's chief financial officer and president of its thirty-five-thousand-employee automotive division, Yang and his colleagues had identified more than twenty candidates, narrowed the list to four finalists, and then selected Barter because of his "very solid background" in finance and management with publicly traded American companies. Equally important was his extensive experience on the boards of American companies—including NYSE-listed BMC Software—because he would bring an understanding of best practices in American corporate governance to the Lenovo board. "As we are going international," said Yang, "we'd like to learn from American companies. That's why we invited people like John Barter to join us." Added Amelio in reference to one of the private-equity investors, "TPG wanted to be part of us" because they believed that "they could bring value to the table to help to make this thing a real global powerhouse," and "the fact is" that they have been "very successful in helping us" do so.

Our interviews revealed that a host of other major issues—how long to retain the IBM logo, what acquisitions to make, which "adjacencies" such as servers to consider, and whether to build devices that bridge laptops and telephones—now came to the directors for vetting and decision making. Before the acquisition, the board's decision domain had been largely limited to audit and reporting issues. "The board of directors during that period," said Liu, was "mainly to ensure transparency" and played little "role in business or strategy decisions." But after the acquisition, the board frequently engaged in both business and strategy decisions. Lenovo subsequently considered acquiring personal-computer makers Packard Bell, for instance, and the directors took an active role in deciding on whether to proceed and what to pay. "Everybody was involved," reported non-executive director Shan Weijian, "because this is a large issue for the entire company." Lenovo decided to back off—another PC maker, Gateway, was later acquired by Taiwan PC maker Acer—and the board's deliberations proved critical in reaching that decision.

Top management saw it the same way. "I say it's good to have a sounding board," offered chief executive William Amelio, for "you can talk about what your plans are because you get more independent views than you would from your own team given the fact they are more biased inside the company." He explained why: "People who work for you" will "act differently than people that you report to," and thus you get "more independent views or opinions on strategy" from the latter than the former. Referencing what Lenovo learned from its three private-equity directors, Amelio offered, "They have under their watch literally eighty other CEOs [of companies in which they have invested]. We get that knowledge brought in best practices, what other companies are doing."[32]

By way of illustration of the value of independent director "opinions on strategy," consider Lenovo's focus on operational efficiency in the wake of the IBM purchase. Lenovo found that certain points in the chain inherited from IBM enhanced value while others reduced value, and Lenovo believed that the key to turning the IBM operations from money-losing to moneymaking was the effective "worldsourcing" of its supply chain. "We have been relentless in trying to squeeze every penny out of this process," observed non-executive director Shan Weijian, for "making sure the process is as efficient as possible."

Although the American Business Roundtable had warned that directors should be "monitors, not managers," Lenovo drew its directors directly into decisions on worldwide sourcing. "We need thinkers that are on the board that can help us make sure that we are in the process of maximizing this concept of Worldsourcing," affirmed Amelio. Whatever the optimal way to produce computers, you have to "gravitate to it rapidly in order for you to have the most competitive offerings for your customers," he added, and that pointed to engaging directors directly in decisions on manufacturing operations. When Lenovo looked at the recruitment of new directors, pragmatic operational experience proved an important criterion. The preferred expertise could range from knowing the pitfalls of SAP software implementation to identifying the best foreign suppliers of computer components and best foreign sources of computer engineers.

The strategy committee played a particularly important role on behalf of the board in partnering with management. The strategy committee, Amelio reported, "goes through all the options, and thoroughly" vets "the pros and cons on various courses of action." This has proven especially valuable as the company considered potential acquisitions. The directors representing the private-equity firms brought extensive acquisition experience to the boardroom, and "that's why the private-equity guys," said Amelio, "become totally invaluable, because the name of their game is lots of acquisitions and lots of mergers." The board's strategy committee became a venue for intense debate on these company decisions. "We are trying to maximize how to get the best from the East and the West," said Amelio, "to make sure we have the best ideas."

The strategy committee also conducted an annual performance review of the executive chairman and chief executive, signifying that monitoring coexisted along with partnering. The chairman and CEO submitted self-assessments to the board, and the directors then appraised the extent to which the executives had achieved their annual plan's financial, market-share, talent-acquisition, and related goals. In keeping with the partnership principle, the chairman and CEO also completed 360-degree reviews of themselves and reported the results to the directors.

The culture of the boardroom changed in the wake of the IBM purchase as well. Formality and conflict-aversion gave way to informality and active debate. Lee Ting served on the Lenovo board both before and after the acquisition, and as a veteran of both American and Chinese boardrooms, he brought comparative insight to the table. "Chinese boards are very formal in their structures," he observed. "It's 'Mr. This,' or 'Chairman That.' The meetings are primarily meant to approve financial results. There isn't as much open debate and questioning as you might find on a U.S. board, and there isn't as much discussion about strategy." Moreover, "you might make comments and suggestions [at the meetings], but you don't get a lot of feedback and don't know if management has heard you." A year and a half after the IBM acquisition, by contrast, he reported that the Lenovo board now "operates more as an international board."[33]

One of Lenovo's senior managers confirmed that point when he appeared at a meeting of the governing board. The directors, he found, displayed an engaged concern with the larger issues of the moment, ranging from the company's marketing strategy and protecting the company's "Thinkpad" brand to product development, sales revenue, operational efficiency, and core competencies. One of the directors, for instance, insisted that management "guarantee" the company's continued "leadership with the Thinkpad." Liu summed up what others had inferred or implied: "All major decisions were [now] made at the board level."[34]

By way of example, Liu Jun had been serving as senior vice president for the global supply chain of Lenovo after the IBM acquisition. His performance had been strong, and both executive chairman Yang Yuanqing and non-executive director Liu Chuanzhi backed his continued service. That would have been more than sufficient before the acquisition, but the post-acquisition board had taken such decisions into its own hands and it decided at its August 2006 meeting to replace Liu Jun with an executive from Dell Computer. Liu Chuanzhi voiced support for Liu Jun at the meeting. "But whether others [on the board] agreed with me was another matter," he recalled. "On the one hand, others respected my judgment; on the other hand, they also have their own opinion," and it was the latter that prevailed at the meeting.[35]

By peering into the Lenovo boardroom we see a sharp divide between the company's governance before and after its decision to build out globally through the IBM purchase. Prior to the acquisition, the board had operated without a strategy committee or performance review. Now it had both. Director decisions had been largely limited to proper audit for protecting small shareholders. Now their decisions ranged from branding to sourcing. Executive succession and director selection had been the prerogatives of management. Now they were shared decisions with directors. The boardroom norms had been high in formality and low in content. Now they were the opposite. A limited form of director monitoring and management control had been superseded by director partnering in reaching the company's major decisions (Table 14.6).

Table 14.6. Lenovo Directors Partnering with Management in Reaching Governance Decisions.

Partnering with Management	Before IBM Acquisition	After IBM Acquisition
Board organization	No strategy committee	Strategy committee with non-executive directors
Executive succession	Decided by executives	Decided by directors
Director selection	Able to protect minority holders	Bring strategic vision, knowledge of operations and the industry, impartiality, and credibility to key stakeholders
Decision domains	Limited (for example, audit)	Extensive (such as branding, acquisitions, products, sourcing)
Performance reviews	Informal	Conducted formally on executive chairman and CEO
Boardroom norms	Formal	Informal and engaged

Legitimating Management

Lenovo's governing board also reconstituted itself to help legitimate management with the major domestic owner, large international investors, a global workforce, and other key stakeholders. It achieved this by both reorganizing the board and introducing new directors onto the board.

Lenovo restructured the board's organization to bring it into compliance with U.S. governance standards. The Sarbanes-Oxley Act of 2002 and the revised New York Stock Exchange listing criteria of 2003 require that company boards constitute audit, compensation, and governance committees. Prior to the IBM acquisition, the Lenovo board had created an audit and compensation committee, but in the wake of the purchase it added a governance committee. The new governance committee not only vetted nominees for the board but also conducted an annual evaluation of the CEO, relatively unheard of among Chinese companies but increasingly common among American firms.

This remake was particularly important given the poor reputation of Chinese corporate governance. Lenovo would be implicitly saddled with the country's lagging reputation if it did not take explicit steps to overcome it. A study in 2007 of the ten largest Chinese companies whose American depository receipts were traded on the New York Stock Exchange reported, for instance, that they suffered from "inadequate governance standards." A study conducted in 2005–2006 by an executive-search firm and Fudan University found that many Chinese companies were characterized by a "weak board" with non-executive directors exercising only limited influence on board decisions. The Asian Corporate Governance Association conducted annual surveys of the governance climate in Asian markets, and drawing on eighty-seven criteria—such as whether a nation's reporting standards compared favorably with international standards and whether financial regulators enforced the standards—the 2006 survey ranked China ninth among eleven Asian markets. Still another survey of Asian fund managers and equity analysts in 2006 rated Chinese governance practices last among nine Asian economies. Such shortcomings mattered to both international and domestic investors. A 2006 study of investors worldwide, for instance, reported that Chinese investors placed greater emphasis on corporate governance than did investors in other major markets, with board organization, composition, and independence their chief concerns.[36]

Lenovo thus reconstituted the board's membership to project a more reputable image to its investors, customers, and global workforce. "Because the IBM PC acquisition is a case of a small firm from a developing country acquiring a part of a large firm from a developed country," Liu Chuanzhi explained, Lenovo suffered a certain "credibility liability." Without the internationalization of the board, he said, "if I told people that I or Yang understand [global] business, who will believe us?" The board's new membership would help "make the company more transparent" to the "society at large" and "solidify our reputation for being an ethical organization." As described by William Amelio, "global companies . . . must create trust" by "adhering to the highest standards of governance, transparency, compliance and quality."[37]

Lenovo also reconstituted the board's leadership. Prior to the IBM acquisition, Yang had served as chief executive and Liu Chuanzhi as executive chairman. After the acquisition, Yang and Liu elevated Yang to executive chairman and appointed an American as chief executive—first Ward and then Amelio—but this came at a cost. Yang and Liu had worked closely together for fifteen years, whereas Yang and Amelio had never worked together, and they brought contrasting styles to the boardroom and executive suite. "Chinese are more reserved while the Americans are more frank," Yang observed. As a result, "I express myself implicitly, but the American people don't understand me. They would rather have me say it directly." Disagreement on strategic and operational issues between the two executives was sometimes unavoidable, but the downsides of disagreement were more than compensated by the public projection of diverse citizenship at the top.

Lenovo wanted customers, competitors, and investors, said Yang, to see it as an "international company," and for this "a Chinese chairman with an American CEO is a perfect signal." It indicated national diversity at the top but also global competence. Liu Chuanzhi has viewed the installation of a non-Chinese chief executive at Lenovo as essential for this reason. "We must be aware that we are not sufficiently familiar with the global markets," he explained. "Under such conditions, we should fully respect and rely on international executives. No Chinese companies making acquisitions abroad should seek the CEO's position; even if you can get it, it is not good for you."[38]

As most Chinese listed firms are controlled by a non-listed state-owned entity, Lenovo's largest shareholder, Legend Holding, is majority-owned by the Chinese Academy of Sciences. Managing the relationship with the Academy was thus very important to Lenovo. To prove the business value of the IBM acquisition to Lenovo's most important holder, Yang and Liu concluded that they should bring international private-equity representatives onto the board and into its ownership. Yang observed that adding directors from international private equity was very important "for us to convince our large shareholder." That would help persuade the Academy of the value, in Yang's words, of the "snake-swallowing-an-elephant acquisition." If tough-minded international investors thought it worthwhile and were willing to put their money at risk, the Academy would be encouraged to conclude the same.

Still, the reconstitution of the board's membership in the wake of the IBM acquisition was almost entirely an executive-driven affair. The decisions on who to bring onto the Lenovo board after the IBM acquisition were largely taken by executive directors Yang, Liu, and, to a lesser degree, Ma Xuezheng [Mary Ma], Lenovo's chief financial officer who also served on the board. When asked who participated in the recomposition of the board, Yang responded, "The key participants are executive directors. Namely, Mr. Liu and I are the key decision makers." When asked if any other board members played a role in deciding on the board's reconstituted membership, he responded, "That would be Mary Ma, our CFO and board member." When asked if any of the independent non-executive directors played any role, Yang responded that they "did participate," but "in fact it was the management/executive directors who made the decisions." When asked if any directors pushed back against the executive decisions on the board's reconstitution, Yang reported, "I don't remember any difficulties."

Prior to the acquisition, Liu served as the principal liaison between the company and its primary owner, the Chinese Academy of Sciences. After the acquisition, he continued to play that role, but the non-executive directors played an investor-liaison role as well—in their case with international capital. "The private-equity guys," observed Amelio, spoke with "enthusiasm" about Lenovo when they met prospective investors.

Upon opening the Lenovo boardroom, we have found a marked emphasis on the credibility that directors could add to the company following the IBM acquisition. Prior to the purchase, the company worried little about investor credibility. Much of the relationship between the company and the Chinese Academy of Sciences had been privately managed by Liu Chuanzhi. After the purchase, by contrast, the company added a governance committee as expected by U.S. regulators.

In the aftermath of its decision to globalize with the IBM acquisition, Lenovo sought to bolster its credibility with customers, suppliers, employees, and regulators outside of China. It recruited an American chief executive to work with a Chinese executive chairman, projecting an international image at the top.

Table 14.7. Lenovo Directors Legitimating Management.

Legitimating Management	Before IBM Acquisition	After IBM Acquisition
Board organization	No governance committee	Governance committee
Executive leadership	Chinese executive chairman and Chinese CEO	Chinese executive chairman and American CEO
Director nationality	All Chinese	Chinese and Americans
Investor ownership	All Chinese	IBM and American private-equity
Investor relations	Executive chairman met with dominant Chinese owner	Executives and non-executive directors meet with international investors

And it solicited international private-equity holdings, bolstering an image of investor responsiveness. A limited form of director monitoring and management control had been superseded by not only a director partnership with management but also a director legitimization of management (Table 14.7).

Impersonal Market Versus the Visible Hand

Lenovo's restructuring of its governing board was shaped by changes in its market, but its specific changes in the board were not predetermined by the market. The invisible hand of the market set the stage, but on that stage the directors' hand charted the particular features of the remake. Within wide boundaries set by the market, their leadership decisions set the course.

The discretion that directors retain in reaching their governance decisions in the wake of market changes is evident from a brief comparison of Lenovo's governance experience with another of China's globalizing firms, TCL Corporation. Based in southern China's Guangdong province, TCL is an electronics manufacturer whose products include mobile phones, home appliances, and digital media. It is listed on the Hong Kong Stock Exchange as well as Shenzhen, and the government of its headquarters city of Huizhou had long been a major stockholder.

In early 2004, TCL set up a joint venture with France's Thomson Group titled TTE Corporation. Holding two-thirds of the joint venture and acquiring the RCA brand, TCL overnight became a leading global maker of color televisions. Its chief executive, Li Dongsheng, explained that "our strategic objective is to become an internationally competitive player in the global consumer electronics business." Like the Lenovo acquisition of the IBM PC division the following year, TCL's joint venture constituted a quantum leap, one of the largest globalizing moves at the time by a Chinese company.[39]

In constituting TTE's governing body, TCL pursued a path different from that of Lenovo in the wake of its IBM acquisition. It placed five directors from TCL on the TTE board and four from Thomson; appointed a Chinese national as CEO and Li Dongsheng as executive chairman; installed Chinese executives in all of the senior positions except one; included no independent or private-equity representatives on the board; and vested little decision-making discretion in the board.

After two years of operation, TTE had faltered. Upon losing RMB2.6 billion ($360 million) on its European operations in 2006, Thomson withdrew from the joint venture. TCL discontinued its branded marketing of color televisions in Europe, retreating to reselling its products under others' brand names.

TCL's foray abroad may have been premised on a flawed strategy—investment-adviser Morgan Stanley had not advocated the move and strategy-adviser BCG had even opposed it—but the relatively passive TTE board, largely in the mold of management control, may have contributed as well. In public commentary on the TTE initiative, Li Dongsheng seldom mentioned governance as a significant factor in TCL's globalization initiative. By contrast, Liu Chuanzhi frequently cited the remake of Lenovo's governance system as a critical asset for its globalization initiative. Governing boards add little when controlled by management, but when transformed into monitoring, legitimating, and partnering with management, they can add far more.[40]

Implications for Executives and Directors

The decisions of the Lenovo executives and directors leading up to the IBM PC acquisition and its aftermath point to eight implications for executives and directors of other large publicly traded companies.

1. Tailor the board to fit the evolving environment rather than a national model. Although the American governance model of widely diffused ownership and independent director-dominated boards has gained international attention in recent years, the Lenovo experience suggests that globalizing enterprises may want to create hybrids that reflect their own emerging ownership and operational realities. When functioning earlier within greater China and majority-owned by a state agency, Lenovo had created a board whose directors were largely Chinese, dominated by insiders, and only nominally independent. The postmerger board departed significantly from Chinese tradition, but did not faithfully follow the American model either. Legend Holdings remained a major shareholder—42 percent in 2007—and its representatives continued to hold two board seats, allowing them to keep a close eye on management. At the same time, three private-equity investors each acquired a seat, permitting them to protect their ownership stakes. The postmerger directors were more international and independent of management, but they also worked more closely with management.

2. Recruit board members to address the company's strategic challenges. Companies in both China and the U.S. sometimes recruit directors for their prominence in business or government. Given its new global standing, Lenovo could have readily attracted such figures, but its leadership opted instead for directors with substantive value for facilitating the postmerger integration. The three private-equity directors, reported Liu Chuanzhi, were "masters of mergers and acquisition." Lenovo had no familiarity with an international merger on the scale of the IBM operation, and these new directors brought expertise with cross-border acquisition in China and the United States. Lenovo also had scant experience with world sourcing, and here too the private-equity investors arrived with direct experience and understanding.

3. Treat the governing board as a decision-making partner. Like people everywhere, company leaders tend to credit themselves for successes and blame the environment for failures. The tendency may be especially pronounced among entrepreneurs but is also evident among executives of fast-growing companies, and one consequence is for some to view their board as formally necessary but largely ceremonial in practice. Recognizing their own inexperience in globalizing a company and integrating two firms, however, Liu Chuanzhi and Yang Yuanqing reconstituted Lenovo's board to help them achieve each, bringing on non-executive directors familiar with both and engaging them in active discussion both during and outside board meetings. When it came to identifying a new chief executive, merging the two workforces, internationalizing the supply chain, and considering other acquisitions, the board acted as an active partner with top management. Said non-executive director Shan Weijian, "every board member has been involved in the discussions," and Liu has "made us feel our contribution is valuable and value creating."

4. Invest in strengthening the board. If the board is to serve as a strategic partner, it requires an investment of time well beyond that necessitated by a legitimating board or a board controlled by management. Informed directors who trust one another and have faith in their executives constitute an essential platform, and Lenovo management worked to build it. The company adopted a rule, for instance, that all directors must attend all board meetings, which are rotated around the world, or send a predesignated alternate. No matter how demanding his schedule, chief executive William Amelio arranged a monthly dinner meeting with Liu Chuanzhi. Liu in turn frequently flew to the U.S. to meet with the American directors, especially when the board faced contentious issues.

5. *Create a device for director-executive decision making.* For companies in fast-changing markets, quarterly or even bimonthly board meetings may be too infrequent for outside directors and inside executives to jointly engage and resolve major company decisions. Drawing on Lenovo's experience, a useful device for doing so can be a strategy committee composed of a small set of top executives and non-executive directors. An operating group of this kind can provide frequent direct consultation on critical issues, as the strategy committee did for the Lenovo executive chairman, chief executive, and two outside directors. For companies with a non-executive board chair or lead director, an alternative method may be for the CEO and chair or lead director to have extended weekly if not daily consultations on major decisions as they emerge. Whatever the method, it should provide for frequent and forceful opportunities for top managers and select directors to face and resolve key issues between formal board meetings.

6. *Bring private-equity investors onto the board.* Experienced independent directors can bring much to the decisions facing a governing board, but many are time-constrained by other professional commitments. Partners of private-equity firms that have taken a significant ownership stake in a company, however, view their service on the board as strategic and are normally prepared to take

a major role in company decisions whatever the time required. Bringing one or several private-equity companies into the firm's ownership and their partners onto the company's board, as Lenovo did after acquiring the IBM personal computer division, can help to ensure that several directors are ready to play an intense role in the company's major decisions. Their value to the firm will be a function of the extent to which they bring depth experience in the critical decisions that the firm is likely to face, just as the Texas Pacific Group and General Atlantic partners brought deep familiarity with global sourcing and merger integration to Lenovo.

7. *Anticipate the governance norms of international investors.* Investment companies, hedge funds, pension systems, private-equity firms, and sovereign-wealth funds are holding increasing fractions of many companies' shares. Although large international investors bring a range of attitudes toward company governance, the quality of a firm's governing board is of increasing importance to most. Companies that are globalizing their products and services are likely to place a parallel emphasis on globalizing their ownership, as Lenovo did in the wake of its IBM PC acquisition, and that in turn will require that the globalizing firms better appreciate the governance standards of large international investors.

8. *Preemptively globalize the board.* Even if a firm is largely operating within its nation's boundaries, it may feel impelled to expand abroad when international competitors attack its home market advantage, as happened to Lenovo. Although Lenovo initiated a global remake of its board in the wake of its purchase of the IBM PC division, it may be useful to start the restructuring well ahead of international expansion, better preparing the company for its movement onto a world stage, as TCL had not. One young Chinese company, by contrast, had been rapidly building a capacity for manufacturing an alternative energy source based on innovative technologies. Anticipating that its international sales

would boom and its ownership would similarly diversify, the company chose to list itself on the New York Stock Exchange. The chief executive explained to us that he had not gone through the arduous and expensive process of doing so to secure more capital, given that his company was already amply backed by domestic investors. Rather, he listed the company in New York instead to force himself and his directors to master the norms of international governance.

Conclusion

Company leadership and governance have long been conceived as distinct domains. With the exception of the chief executive, executives and directors have often been seen as constituting different sets of people with distinct imperatives. Executives led. Directors monitored—or sometimes not even that.

We have found at Lenovo, however, that its directors came to play more of a leadership role in the wake of the international acquisition, advising and guiding executives in major company decisions and representing the company to major owners. They also played a leadership role in facilitating cross-cultural integration after the acquisition.

We have reached these conclusions by asking those in the Lenovo boardroom how they made decisions and the criteria they applied. While still serving as the owners' monitor of management, directors at Lenovo have taken on the additional roles of strategic partner and reputation enhancer. The critical driver in the Lenovo directors' shift from limited monitoring to partnering with, legitimating, and more robust monitoring of management came with its decision in 2004 to transform itself from a national maker into an international producer. That itself derived from executive recognition that the changing market for its products had made a domestic strategy doubtful and a global play promising. We have seen analogous developments in U.S. companies ranging from Boeing to Tyco, and in a host of Indian companies as well.[41]

Firms in China, India, the United States, and other major economies are increasingly reaching out of their national boundaries for similar reasons. Among the five hundred largest U.S.-listed companies, 44 percent of their revenue in 2006 derived from abroad, up from 32 percent just five years earlier.[42] Large companies in China, India, and other countries are globalizing at similar paces. Equity owners are on much the same trajectory, with institutional investors, sovereign funds, private-equity firms, and hedge funds all allocating more of their portfolios to holdings outside their home markets.

If Lenovo's experience is symptomatic of what other companies are likely to face as they globalize their operations and ownership, and we believe that it is, we can anticipate that company governance at other firms will also move toward greater engagement of directors in collaborative decision making with management. Executives and directors will ask, as one academic observer of Chinese enterprise has recently suggested, whether they "have a plan for corporate governance that will focus the firm on national competitive advantage and ultimately global advantage rather than short-term profitability in local markets."[43] As they consider or adopt such a plan, that in turn will point toward an evolving skill set for directors, with greater emphasis on director capacity to work with executives at critical choice points. It will also point toward a changing skill set for executives, with a stronger ability to work with directors expected at major decision moments and less inclination to hold directors at arm's length. Institutional investors and other major holders will be more likely as well to look for directors and executives who can collaboratively engage in the firm's most important decisions.

Understanding these changes will require an opening of what has often been viewed from the outside as the black box of company governance. Although the norm that boardroom decisions stay in the boardroom has long prevailed, we believe that the emergent norm of transparency will encourage directors and executives to reveal more about their decision making behind closed doors. If so, we should obtain a better understanding of how directors actively manage their visible hand, thereby making the traditionally unseen hand of the directors more visible.

Part V

Conclusion

15

Conventional Wisdom, Conventional Mythology, and the True Character of Board Governance

Jeffrey A. Sonnenfeld and Andrew Ward

In response to the dramatic and public meltdowns of companies at the turn of the century, such as Enron, Adelphia, and WorldCom, to name just three of the most spectacular, there has been increased attention paid to corporate governance practices. The portfolio of corrective actions has encompassed tougher prosecution, legislative reform (such as the Sarbanes-Oxley Act of 2002), new (FASB) accounting standards, elevated stock exchange listing requirements, and corporate codes of conduct. Although many of these initiatives were well intended and many were properly designed, an additional reform-branded activity, the cottage industry of governance consulting services and especially the governance rating services, offers less clear value. We contend in this chapter that much of the conventional wisdom contained in this scrutiny modeled by ratings services is overly structurally-oriented, neglects key board process issues, and fails to adequately predict firm performance or leadership integrity. We contend in this concluding chapter that instead of focusing on these checklist indicators, board observers need to focus on process and the actual character of corporate governance within the boardroom, and the caliber of leadership shared across the board members, not just on structural prescriptions.

As noted throughout this book, a board has traditionally had a three-fold role: (1) to *monitor management* and where necessary to replace underperforming management; (2) to *provide resources and connections* to the company's environment, to help bring resources and information into the organization; and (3) to *provide advice, counsel, and support* to management to facilitate an optimum strategy for the organization. Our observation is that this rush to clamp down on boards and attempt to ensure that the debacles at the turn of the century are not repeated has led to a focus that is almost exclusively on the monitoring and discipline function of the board, to the detriment of the other two, equally important, roles of the board. Furthermore, the responses of boards to engage in compliance behaviors in reaction to this increased focus has led to superficial checklisting behaviors. Although they put on a facade of "good governance," these mandates can never be more than the necessary conditions for effective governance and are never sufficient in and of themselves. As a result, many boards have descended into adopting practices that check all the right boxes, but their overall governance has, at their own admission in many cases, become less effective. This is because these window-dressing practices devour undue amounts of time, leaving little time for the advising function of the board. Further, some boards have become less functional, descending into finger-pointing when things go wrong, rather than addressing the underlying issues or conflict. Furthermore, directors are becoming increasingly, and dysfunctionally, fearful of liability issues, increasing the focus on protecting their own downside risk rather than providing effective governance. Ultimately, as the chapters in this book attest, good governance depends on the good character and leadership of the individual directors, and the board as a whole, not on mere compliance to outward signals of governance. In other words, the conventional wisdom of good governance indicators is really conventional mythology. In this concluding chapter, we seek to show the folly of this conventional wisdom, and why good governance depends on the character of the individual directors and the board that goes way beyond checklists.

Conventional Wisdom

By feeling the need to act to correct the egregious oversights that led to the scandals of the early part of the decade of the 2000s, governments, stock markets, investor bodies, and other activists created myriad indicators of good governance that they felt would protect shareholders from such failures. Ironically, looking back, many of the companies with the most devastating governance failures had already complied with many of these indicators. Nevertheless, these external parties began to require, and measure, these indicators in earnest. In fairness, to a large extent this was all they could do. They needed something that was measurable and correlated with effective governance practices. Jeffrey Sonnenfeld has previously reviewed the research to reveal that the easily measured qualities of board structure have very little, if any, correlation or predictive power in explaining a firm's financial performance, operational performance, or even outright governance performance. In fact, some scandal-ridden firms such as Enron, Computer Associates, Sunbeam, HealthSouth, and Tyco were applauded by leading governance experts immediately in advance of their egregious governance breakdowns. HealthSouth even earned a glowing 95th percentile governance assessment by the leading governance rating firm just months before five chief financial officers testified to massive fraud.[1]

In such cases, management had cynically seized the prevailing language of good governance, coopting prominent critics, but in reality continued with unsavory illegal practices. As we contend, effective governance goes beyond simplistic indicators that can be put forward as mere window dressing or checklisting, to the underlying character of the board and its members. However, as we will show, at worst, some of these nuggets of conventional wisdom can actually undermine governance effectiveness. So before we put forward an argument for the underlying character of the board, we will examine these tenets of conventional wisdom and expose the myths that exist in an overzealous pursuit of these characteristics.

Board Independence

The accumulating conventional wisdom posits that there should be no insiders on the board except the CEO, as otherwise, insiders are presumed to swing the balance of power between the board and management in favor of the management, leading to management's domination of the agenda and proceedings of the board and reducing the ability of the board to effectively monitor and control management. It is true that cronyism and interlocking directorates have been problematic. A majority of independent outsider voices on the board is not only a standard stock exchange requirement but also wise policy—as is the exclusion of insiders from compensation and audit committees.

At the same time, this independence can be taken to extremes. Defining independence is the first challenge. Someone who recently worked in management or is directly related to a top executive should be classified an "insider." However, escalating criteria now cast a suspicious eye on those who share a common educational degree and even a common religion. This is superstition bordering on bigotry.

In addition, this indicator can have perverse, unintended consequences in that this mantra overlooks the vital role of insiders to effective board functioning. In fact, having a few directors who have recently served in management or may still serve as CFO or COO helps prepare for crisis transitions and provide for more shared knowledge. The hit and run, ad hoc nature of quick visits to board meetings by management are no substitute for the stature, presence, continuity, and voice of being a genuine voting member of the board.

The presence of insiders does a number of things to the functionality of the board. First, insiders bring a depth of perspective on the company. They are inevitably involved at a deeper level of detail in the activity of the company than is the CEO. They can bring a better sense of the company's ability to execute on corporate strategy and diagnose what is currently suboptimal. They provide a great inside source of information about the company, its operations, and its environment. It is strange that governance watchdogs, who are generally concerned about the balance of power between the CEO and the board, would so strongly advocate having the board's access to information restricted to a single source, the CEO. This tighter funneling of information only puts heightened trust in the eloquence, focus, and integrity of the CEO. Thus fewer insiders on the board can actually enhance the power of the CEO relative to the board. If the board is concerned that a few management insiders will be fearful to speak freely in their CEO's presence then they have a larger problem on hand already.

The other big advantage of having some insiders on the board is in CEO succession planning. Having senior managers gain experience and comfort in the boardroom helps in the process of grooming effective successors, and also gives the outside directors more exposure to these managers so that board members can play a role in mentoring and developing these key managers and make a more informed choice of who should be the next CEO when the time comes. CEO succession can be a very disruptive event in the life of an organization, and indeed to the board itself, and smoothing this process and selecting the right candidate is one of the most important functions of the board. We therefore argue that for most companies, having more insiders than just the CEO on the board increases rather than decreases overall board effectiveness.

CEO and Chair Role Split, and Lead Director

On the whole the United States and the United Kingdom have very similar corporate governance practices, but the splitting or combining of the roles of chief executive officer and board chair is perhaps the most visible difference between the two systems, with common practice in the United Kingdom being to separate the two roles, whereas in the United States the roles have most commonly been held by the same person. As Jay Conger and Edward Lawler note in Chapter Two, in the United States pressure has been mounting for companies to split these two roles, with the argument being that such a split limits the CEO's power to control the board and allows for the board to be more independent in deciding the agenda the board follows. Indeed, the *Spencer Stuart 2007 US Board Index* shows that amongst the S&P 500 in the United States, 35 percent now have split the roles of chair and chief executive officer, up from 25 percent five years earlier.[2] Even where the roles are combined, almost all the companies (94 percent) have a designated lead or presiding director. As Chapters Two and Three illustrate, there are valid arguments on both sides of this question, with those on the side of a split role emphasizing the greater ability to monitor and restrain the power of management, while those on the side of combining the roles emphasize the benefits of unity of leadership. SpencerStuart's survey of board members points to some situations that lend themselves to splitting the roles: a new CEO, times of crisis, or alternative ownership models such as private-equity-owned companies.

However sensible such power sharing may seem to be for ensuring objective control of the board's agenda, there is no research that shows any linkage to the separation or combination of these roles and firm performance, and so this choice is better made at the individual company level driven by a company's particular situation rather than being dictated as a sign of good or poor governance. Some outside the United Kingdom have questioned the appropriateness elsewhere of the famed Cadbury Commission, which identified the chair, not the CEO, as the architect of corporate strategy. In fact, in the recent scandals at many European firms with such split roles, such as with Royal Dutch Shell and BP, the ambiguity of command may have been one contributing factor.

At the same time, there are surely transitional roles during succession events that make sense, such as at Microsoft during the transition from Bill Gates to Steve Ballmer, where this separation of roles eased the transition from an influential founder. At other times there are crises in leadership, such as at Boeing or the New York Stock Exchange, where lost faith in the credibility of the institution's leadership led to a separation of roles to reassure key constituencies.

Equity Involvement

Having some "skin in the game" is supposed to make board members more vigilant. However, the question remains, "How much is enough?" Directors are supposed to represent shareholders, and so certainly they should have some equity to be able to effectively represent the shareholder perspective. But although many governance pundits argue that directors should have a substantial portion of their net worth tied up in company stock so that they "feel the shareholders' pain" if the stock price declines, we would argue that directors can have too much stock. Most shareholders do not just own one stock, but have diversified investments. So the investment in any given company represents part of a diversified portfolio. As such, shareholders expect the company to take reasonable risks in investing their money to earn a reasonable return. Research on risk taking and risk avoidance shows that if people have too much at stake, they tend to become much more concerned about what they have to lose than what they might gain, and so become very risk averse, backing away from taking any chances. Shareholders, in seeking to make a return on their portfolios, do not want directors (or managers, for that matter) to become too risk averse, but rather to explore and exploit the market opportunity before the company. Accordingly, directors should have some reasonable equity involvement in the company to provide incentive for them to diligently represent the interests of shareholders, but they should not have so much of their net worth invested in the company that they become more risk averse than shareholders desire. That is, directors should themselves still have a well-diversified portfolio, with probably no more than a few percentage points of their net worth tied up in the stock. The practice that occasionally occurred over the past decade, of executives and even directors borrowing large sums of money, often from the company itself, to invest in company stock, thus tying a great deal of their net worth or even in excess of their net worth to the company, should be taken as a dangerous signal to other shareholders.

CEO Pay and Dismissal for Underperformance

Setting the compensation of the CEO is another important, and highly visible, function of the board, as discussed by Roger Raber in Chapter Eight. It is also perhaps the board function that in recent years has come under the most criticism. The main thrust of this criticism is that CEOs are grossly overpaid, and that this large amount of compensation is not sufficiently at risk—that is, the pay of the CEO is not tied tightly enough to the performance of the company.

We argue that companies hire CEOs, in part, to assume the symbolic responsibility for organizational performance. Furthermore, what is important about organizational performance, in relation to the CEO's responsibility, is not the absolute level of performance *per se,* but the expectations for performance placed on them by the board, shareholders, and other external constituencies. This is because performance is at least partly determined by the prevailing economic conditions that face the company, yet these important constituencies will have expectations for how the company performs in the face of these conditions. CEOs are often credited with the successes of their organizations, and, equally, blamed for organizational failures. In these days of intense scrutiny on boards, many have "itchy trigger fingers" in removing the CEO the moment performance fails to meet expectations. Thus, somewhat counterintuitively, large, high-profile organizations with long histories of success are the riskiest jobs for CEOs, because the expectations are so high. This is particularly true for organizations that have historically performed exceptionally well, but recently have stumbled. In these situations, shareholders continue to have extremely high expectations for organizational performance, but the company may need some serious fixing, which may take some time. Shareholders and boards though, expect a quick return to the expected levels of high performance, and become impatient when performance improvement is achieved only slowly.

For example, look at the Coca-Cola Company since the death of Roberto Goizueta in 1997. Under his successor, Douglas Ivestor, the company began to stumble, and made some high-profile snafus, such as the contamination that sickened some Belgian schoolchildren and conflict with European regulators in, for example, the attempted takeover of Orangina. The board stepped in and removed Ivestor, replacing him with Doug Daft. However, Daft himself also faced challenges. For example, he had to initiate the largest layoff in the company's history and was also blocked by the board in his attempt to acquire Gatorade, the biggest-selling sports drink, because the board regarded it as being too expensive. This explains why, when the company looked to replace Doug Daft with an outsider, they had so much difficulty attracting a good candidate. On the face of it, what could be a more attractive job than CEO of one of the most famous companies in the world? Yet numerous high-profile CEOs who were mentioned in the press as potential successors took themselves out of consideration. Why? Because they recognized that this was actually a very risky job. They were all CEOs in companies that were performing well. Coca-Cola was underperforming, yet shareholders and analysts continued to have extremely high expectations for performance going forward. The board was obviously diligent in demanding those high expectations be met by the executive team. This raised the bar such that these expectations could prove almost impossible to meet. In that case, the easy solution would have been to fire the outside successor as failing to meet those expectations. So as it turned out, despite the surface attractiveness of the position, virtually no amount of money would entice any of these high-profile CEOs to take on the job.

This example sheds light on one of the unintended consequences of boards being quicker to dismiss CEOs at the first sign of company performance falling short of escalating expectations. That is, this "good governance" practice exerts pressure to sharply escalate CEO pay even further than its current high levels. If boards are quicker to dismiss CEOs and use them as scapegoats, and the evidence certainly points to this being the case,[3] and increasingly turn to the outside to find replacements, then CEOs face a higher risk in taking on the job. In accordance with this increased risk, new CEOs will rationally demand higher compensation to make up for the likely shortening of their potential career. The fact that CEOs are negotiating increased compensation for this increased risk is particularly demonstrated in the exit packages they negotiate prior to joining the firm to mitigate against the risk of dismissal. As a consequence, even when they fail and the board ousts them, they walk away with huge sums, such as Robert Nardelli's $210 million exit package on leaving Home Depot. Although such "payoffs for failure" make headlines and incur the wrath of shareholders, the irony is that it is probably the "good governance" practice of a diligent board willing to replace the CEO at the first sign of underperformance, insisted on by shareholders, that is the root cause of these excessive exit packages. Counterintuitively then, boards need to "back off" from the "good" governance practice of extremely diligent monitoring and taking quick action to dismiss the CEO at the first sign of declining performance. Instead, boards need to play a more active role in providing advice and counsel on the strategy of the company, working with, and not against, the CEO in addressing any performance concerns.

Multiple Board Memberships

The new conventional wisdom dictates that directors should only be on one or two boards, as the requirements to diligently monitor management and keep abreast of the issues facing the firm take so much time that someone, particularly an active executive, couldn't be effective at performing these functions if he or she is on more than two boards. This wisdom rests on the logic that the diligent monitoring of management that the board needs to do as part of its role has to be done equally by each individual director. However, good governance for the organization doesn't reside completely in each individual director but in the board as a whole. As such, directors can fulfill different roles for the board. By taking the perspective that board members should only be on one or two boards, the board as a whole loses the capacity to fulfill the other vital roles in terms of advice to management based on members' wider experience and the connections they provide to external resources. A better approach is to look at the board holistically, rather than focusing the spotlight on each individual director. In this way, the roles of the individual directors may vary, but with the result that the board increases its overall capacity to effectively provide all three functions.

A considerable body of academic research demonstrates how innovation and best practices disseminate through the interlocks between firms created by directors. Having directors who are connected to a larger number of boards increases centrality of the firm in this corporate network, and serves to expose the firm to innovation and the practices of other firms, potentially drawing resources into the firm. Despite the implication that these individual directors may be somewhat more constrained in their monitoring role, the connections they bring to the firm and the advice they provide can be extremely valuable, without diminishing the overall monitoring capability of the board as a whole. Furthermore, taking the perspective of the network as a whole, having interconnected directors facilitates the dissemination of best practices and so should make governance stronger on average across all firms. Ideally, a board might have two or three members that sit on multiple boards across a range of industries, and others that at least have experience on other boards. The specific industries or firms to which board members are linked is of less importance than the access to specific experiences that members bring. This enables the board to have access to alternative best practices and likely experience in areas such as other circumstances of CEO succession, merger, and acquisition activity, and threats and other events that happen sporadically but are critical when they occur.

The Presence of a Past CEO

Having a former CEO remain on the board is almost universally condemned as bad governance practice. We agree that in many cases, the past CEO can be at best an uncomfortable presence and, at worst, a force to undermine the current leadership. However, even with that said, there are enough exceptions in which a former CEO has been a great positive influence to undermine the general rule. In the best circumstances, a retired CEO can play an invaluable role as a mentor and sounding board to the new CEO, as well as provide continuity in linkages to critical outside constituents. United Parcel Service (UPS) is an example of just one company that, over multiple generations of CEOs, has benefited from former CEOs retaining a place on the board and continuing to play a valuable advisory role. In UPS's case, all the CEOs and successors have been long-time UPS employees, and so the presence of retired CEOs on the board signals, as well as tangibly helps, the continuity of command represented in the transition from one CEO to the next.

Although, as noted earlier, there are times when a former CEO may retain the chairmanship to facilitate a smooth succession, this generally is a short-term arrangement. However, as in UPS's case, it is not uncommon for former CEOs to usefully remain as directors for several years after leaving the CEO role, as long as their presence continues to be a net positive for the board. A special case is that of the founder/CEO. Founders can often have a very hard time in passing the baton on to their successors without continuing to attempt to unduly interfere with their successor's management of the firm. Yet even here there are exceptions to the rule. So while we agree that this is one area where the conventional wisdom is right more often than it is wrong, there is still a good case to be made for retaining the prior CEO on the board in many instances.

Regular Meeting Attendance

Regular meeting attendance has been one of the most used markers of a conscientious director. However, though a director certainly can't be optimally effective if he or she doesn't show up to meetings, or even attend them via conference call, attendance is a necessary but not sufficient condition for effectiveness of a director. Woody Allen famously quipped, "Eighty percent of success is showing up," but the presumption for directors is that they are showing up prepared. It is actually pretty rare these days for directors to miss more than 25 percent of meetings (and thus get themselves identified for poor attendance), but it is much less clear how prepared and briefed directors are on the major issues for discussion at the board meetings. The information that flows to directors is a subject that is obviously more difficult, if not impossible, to mandate, yet is a key characteristic of an effective board. This information flow to the board includes not only formal communications and briefing materials sent out in good time before a board meeting, but also informal communications and interactions the board member has with the CEO, senior management, and other interactions with the company. Under Bernie Marcus's watch as CEO of Home Depot, board members were required to visit four stores not in their home state between every board meeting to ensure that they were in touch with associates at the store level and had a good idea of the operation of the company. This information through direct observation and interaction is invaluable to directors and is effective governance practice, as it diversifies the sources of information available to the director. If a director is directly observing problems in the firm's operations, it is hard for management to pretend in the board meeting that all is well. Each company will have its own metrics for implementing such an idea, but the principle set by the Home Depot example of board members being in touch with the frontlines of their organizations and their customers is a valuable lesson for most boards.

Board Member Skills

Like attendance, skills are a necessary but not sufficient condition for effective governance (see, for example, Chapter Six's discussion on director skills). Preparation plays a key role in transforming board member skills into effective governance. Here, the mantra is, it isn't just having the skills, it is engaging and deploying those skills, which again involves preparation and homework that lead to effective governance. So although having appropriately qualified directors on the right committees makes sense, it is again only half the story. The now classic case of Enron provides the example here. Enron's board of directors represented the finest director skill set imaginable. The list included a former

Stanford dean, who was also an accounting professor, the former CEO of an insurance company, the former CEO of an international bank, a hedge fund manager, a prominent Asian financier, and an economist who was the former head of the U.S. government's Commodity Futures Trading Commission. Scarcely could there have been a board with more financial acumen. Yet those skills were obviously not engaged sufficiently to understand the complexity of Enron's financial wizardry and detect the corruption buried within.

More recently, financial service boards ranging from the collapsed investment bank Bear Stearns to the distressed banking behemoths of Citigroup, Merrill Lynch, and Wachovia, as well as the government-sponsored financial entities of Fannie Mae and Freddie Mac, were similarly each packed with individually revered corporate leaders admired for their financial expertise and integrity. Nonetheless, collectively, the character of the board suffered through cultures and processes that suffocated good sense regarding prudent risk and regular oversight. As we will address in more detail, ideally, boards undergo an annual self-evaluation process that evaluates the effectiveness of board process. An assessment of the skill sets of the board, and the effectiveness to which those skill sets are deployed, should be a central component of this evaluation to ensure continued functioning of the board.

Board Member Age

In its most recent survey of S&P 500 boards, the executive search firm SpencerStuart reported that over the five-year period from 2001 to 2006, the percentage of boards with a mandatory retirement age increased from 58 percent to 78 percent, with most having a retirement age of seventy-two.[4] With the extra pressures, responsibilities, and time requirements placed on directors since the passage of Sarbanes-Oxley in 2002, boards may be harming themselves by placing arbitrary retirement ages on directors.

Wisdom and judgment often come with experience. Furthermore, retired leaders often have more discretionary time to prepare for their board responsibilities.

SpencerStuart also reports that since Sarbanes-Oxley, the average number of outside directorships held by active CEOs has fallen to 0.8. With an average of nine outside directors on each board, that implies that on average, eight are not current CEOs. Consequently, opportunities have been increasing for division presidents and other senior corporate executives, and this board experience serves as great training grounds for those executives as they prepare to move up to a CEO role. However, boards can greatly benefit from the continued sharing of wisdom from retired CEOs, and unnecessarily truncating this is a disservice to many boards.

Indeed, recently Coca-Cola abandoned its mandatory retirement age in order to retain highly valuable directors such as Don Keough and Warren Buffett, who continue to provide valuable input despite advancing age. Similarly, former financier William Donaldson was an especially effective reform-minded chairman of the Securities and Exchange Commission following the corporate scandals of 2001–2005. In fact, although the incumbent CEOs of the Business Roundtable in 2002 fought governance reforms, it was the counsel of prominent retired CEOs of the Conference Board who actually sounded the alarms that helped motivate business leaders, exchanges, regulators, and legislators to take the governance breakdowns seriously. Firms such as Corning Glass, Disney, Boeing, and Delta found that turning to highly skilled retirees from their boards helped them to recover from publicly criticized governance practices.

In our experience, we have known many highly experienced executives, too numerous to mention, who continue with a vitality belying their age and whose insight continues to prove extremely valuable to those firms on whose boards they serve despite being in their seventies, eighties, or even nineties. Despite many pundits putting forward the issue of the currency of the person's experience, arguing that someone who retired many years ago from an active executive role no longer understands the current business environment, we would suggest that many directors are appointed for their *general* breadth of perspective on the business community rather than for any *specific* expertise or formal role in another organization. In some industries technological change may affect the relevance of the currency of a director's expertise, but for the board as a whole, the breadth and depth of experience brought to bear by older directors provides a valuable perspective to the organization that might otherwise be lost. Having retired CEOs as outside directors may also allow these individuals with more time available to serve on multiple boards, thus adding the linkage function to resources that we discussed earlier, while still having the time needed for due attention to each directorship.

Upping the Ante for Directors

Conventional wisdom posits that the increased liability now placed on directors has made their boards more vigilant and thus more effective. However, the increased potential for personal liability now placed on directors has potentially had serious side effects in terms of the willingness of qualified directors to serve on boards. Despite the compensation paid to board members, most regard a board seat as an act of service—a means of giving back to society, rather than being in it for their own financial gain. The increased possibility of dire consequences from board service has made board seats less desirable to those very people whose service is most valuable—those who were employing their talents in this way for the public good.

The focus on liability as a means of increasing directors' vigilance also ignores the other functions of the board, and the dysfunctional aspects of many of the mantras of governance watchdogs as we have discussed earlier. Indeed, we argue that many of these items at the top of the checklists of "good governance" have actually made boards less effective because they have resulted in checklisting, self-protective behaviors, and have focused the board's attention predominantly on the monitoring and discipline functions of the board rather than the access to resources and advice functions. Furthermore, this approach to governance has reduced the pool of good directors by making the best directors more reluctant to take on board roles, which particularly hurts those companies that need them the most, those that need stronger governance. So if checklisting is ineffective, and potentially even counterproductive to good governance, how is good governance actually achieved? We contend that it comes down to the character of the board and its ability to demonstrate leadership.

The Character of the Board

Building a board of great character is both a matter of the individuals who compose the board and the group process norms the board holds. Although each individual director makes a vital contribution and can make a difference to the character of the board, ultimately it is the collective functioning of the board as a unit that provides effective corporate governance. As such, building a board is not a matter of building a model of the "ideal" director and selecting eight or ten of these ideal individuals, but instead means finding a balance of skill sets, experience, leadership, and connections across the board as a whole in order to form an ideal combination. This brings us back to some of the mythology underlying conventional wisdom that we debunked over having insiders on the board, people who hold multiple directorships, former CEOs, or older retired executives. As we demonstrated earlier, each of these categories of individuals can make a positive contribution to the board. What is more important is to focus on the character, skills, leadership, and experience of the individual, and the collective needs of the board.

Independence in Character Over Independence in Structure

The board's role as protectors of shareholder interests requires the ability to think and, if required, act independently of management. Much of the focus has been on the independence of directors in terms of their financial independence from management, but what is more important is their intellectual independence. As Bill George, former chairman and CEO of Medtronic, stated, "I continue to be amazed at the number of CEOs who want their boards to be rubber-stamp supporters rather than honest advisors. What a waste of time and talent! Ironically the loser in this kind of situation is the CEO himself or herself. Without sound advice, however, many CEOs pursue their own egos and interests, rather than operating in the best interests of the company. Or, worse yet, as they gain time in the CEO's chair, they start to think that *they* are the company. The result is decline and ultimate disaster for them, as well as their boards and shareholders."[5] This scenario can happen just as easily with structurally independent boards as it can with those packed with insiders. Where it won't happen is on a board packed with intellectually independent board members who are ready to provide advice and counsel, and, when necessary, to challenge management's strategic direction—if the board's group norms show a tolerance for candor, accountability, and trust.[6]

Quality Over Brand

Just as Harvard Business School's Rakesh Khurana detailed the fixation on a "brand name" CEO in his treatise on CEO succession, *Searching for a Corporate Savior*,[7] boards often become transfixed on "brand name" or marquee directors, and on building a "star-studded" board of well-connected and recognized directors. However, although many of these marquee directors are willing to lend their name to the board roster, what is much more important to effective governance is the quality of their contribution. Certainly many of these directors have earned their reputation through stellar board service, and continue to provide great counsel and oversight to the boards upon which they serve, but this quality of service and advice is much more valuable than the name itself. Instead of focusing on "brand names," boards should focus on individuals who bring new knowledge and networks to the board, who have a passionate interest in the business, and who are willing to learn and immerse themselves in their role. Boards need to be careful in their due diligence in selecting new directors, ensuring they select those who make positive contributions to the boards on which they sit rather than just collecting board seats as social status symbols.

Shareholder Interests Over Self-Interests

A few of those actively seeking particular board seats, even substantial shareholders in the business, are seeking those seats to pursue a particular agenda, whether social, political, or financial. Even those who have acquired a substantial stake in the company may be pursuing their own agenda rather than that of the broad set of shareholders that the board needs to represent. Although the board certainly needs to hear the concerns of multiple stakeholders, it does not need to do this from inside the boardroom through a director who is focused singularly on a particular issue or agenda. In selecting new directors, boards need to be concerned that these new directors are representing the interests of all shareholders and put the overall interests of the company first.

Norms in the Boardroom

Going beyond the selection of individuals with character and leadership capability who can make a positive contribution to the board, much of the effectiveness of the board's governance is determined by the process of the board—how the board works together—rather than at the individual director level. Roughly forty years ago, Irving Janis coined the term *groupthink* in his analysis of major foreign policy decision fiascos.[8] Janis saw such pathologies as overconfidence, stifling of dissent, obedience to authority, a righteous sense of mission, and a failure to consider contingencies as the consequence of groups of distinguished experts driven by the objective of achieving consensus and cohesion at the cost of accuracy and thoroughness.

As argued by Elise Walton in Chapter Twelve, the output of the board—effective governance—is a collective output, not an individual output. This helps explain how boards such as those at troubled leading financial institutions with badly mismanaged risk exposures, as well as boards of companies such as Enron, comprising brilliant, honest, experienced individual directors, could have performed so badly collectively.

Accordingly, boards need to have norms in place that encourage a culture of honest discussion and thorough examination of corporate strategy, rather than being a passive rubber stamp. Such norms require a climate of trust, such that even when a board member is critically challenging a proposal of management, or deliberately playing devil's advocate, these discussions are conducted knowing that everyone in the room ultimately honestly has the best interests of the organization at heart, rather than the pursuit of selfish agendas. Ultimately such a culture of open, candid discussions will test the strategies of the company in the boardroom, making them better prepared for being tested in the marketplace.

Skillfully and deliberately creating this atmosphere of trust requires a fluidity of roles amongst board members. It should not always be the same person mounting the attack on new strategic proposals, but rather different members taking the devil's advocate role on different issues. If one person becomes typecast as the dissenter on the board, without others realizing the value of the role, that person may quickly become ostracized and made peripheral to the group, ultimately perhaps effectively ousted from the board, leaving the board much more vulnerable to poor decision making through passive acceptance of untested ideas.

The atmosphere surrounding boardroom deliberations, as discussed earlier, is probably the most critical behavioral norm for effective governance. However, also very important is a norm of involvement. As we discussed in relation to the folly of focusing on regular meeting attendance as a measure of effective governance, it is really the directors' collective involvement in the organization that ensures governance effectiveness. This includes being involved with the senior managers of the organization at the levels below the CEO, so that the board can play an active role in mentoring, developing, and evaluating the next generation of leaders for the company. Sometimes this will be at the social events that surround board meetings, such as dinners and receptions; at other times it may be meeting with these executives between board meetings, for example, in gathering information for board committees. It also involves becoming familiar with the operations of the company and maintaining that familiarity—visiting facilities and meeting managers and customers to understand the core issues facing the company where it interfaces with the customer. Sometimes these will be scheduled visits for the board as a whole, but more frequently, as in the Home Depot example given earlier, it may be individual directors creating opportunities to learn more and keep in touch with the organization.

The Need for Evaluation

Boards have recently become subject to external evaluation through scrutiny from numerous governance ratings agencies and "watchdogs." Almost all boards now do an annual evaluation of the performance of the board as a whole. However, the *Spencer Stuart 2007 US Board Index* reported that just over half

(53 percent) of all boards do not assess individual director performance at all.[9] Even within the 47 percent, only about three-quarters review directors on an annual basis. Thus while boards no doubt expect annual evaluations of the senior management of the company, most do not hold their own performance to the same level of scrutiny. Although board service is indeed a service role for directors, evaluation can provide useful feedback both for the individual director and for overall board functioning, serving to uphold the overall character of the board. Chapters Five and Six provide details on how best to evaluate your board and individual directors.

Conclusion

Since the spate of corporate scandals at the turn of the twenty-first century, there has been an intense spotlight on boards of directors and their oversight role in preventing a reoccurrence of such governance failures. However, although legislation on transparency and accountability has resulted in some helpful reform, what followed was a parallel obsession regarding compliance focused on highly visible metrics that are supposed to correspond to good governance. Investors have found much of this prevailing focus on superstitious good governance practices to be disappointing in reality. Certainly many legislative reforms have been quite valuable. However, the cottage industry of good governance assessment metrics has little anchoring in predictive impact. Unfortunately, there is almost no empirical linkage between these metrics and more effective governance as might be expected in the way of improved conduct and board diligence, let alone firm performance.

Indeed, we contend that much of this conventional wisdom is actually unsubstantiated mythology—that many of the governance practices now frowned upon can actually enhance board effectiveness. Moreover, an obsessive focus on these arbitrary but easily identifiable and measurable metrics can be as misguided as using placebos as panaceas for genuine physical ailments. In short, structural board governance metrics have become circular self-serving exercises that can erode unique, honest entrepreneurial qualities of firms. Instead, what is needed is a focus on the character of the board, in terms of both the individual directors themselves and the collective functioning of the board. There are genuine preventive tasks that boards can use which do enhance collective accountability and decision making, but they defy the simplest short-term measurement. Just because something is easily measured does not justify doing so and surely does not justify mystically assigning presumed constructive impact. Much like the Heisenberg Principle in physics, the phenomena have become distorted by the measurement interventions.

Notes

Chapter One

1. Jay W. Lorsch and Robert C. Clark, "Best Practice: Leading from the Boardroom," *Harvard Business Review* 86, no. 4 (April 2008): 104.
2. "Report of the NACD Blue Ribbon Commission on Board Leadership," National Association of Corporate Directors, 2004. Available at http://www.nacdonline.org/images/BRC_boardleadership.pdf (accessed May 9, 2008); Jay A. Conger, Edward E. Lawler III, and David L. Finegold, *Corporate Boards: New Strategies for Adding Value at the Top* (San Francisco: Jossey-Bass, 2001).
3. Martin Lipton and Jay W. Lorsch, "A Modest Proposal for Improved Corporate Governance," *The Business Lawyer* 48, no. 1 (November 1992): 59; Jay W. Lorsch and Colin B. Carter, *Back to the Drawing Board: Designing Corporate Boards for a Complex World* (Boston: Harvard Business School Press, 2004).
4. Katharina Pick, "Around the Boardroom Table: Interactional Aspects of Governance," Ph.D. dissertation, Harvard Business School, 2007.
5. William C. Powers Jr., Raymond S. Troubh, and Herbert S. Winokur Jr., "Report of Investigation by the Special Investigative Committee of the Board of Directors of Enron Corp.," February 1, 2002; Deposition in Mark Newby et al., Individually and on Behalf of All Others Similarly Situated, vs. Enron Corp. et al.; The Regents of

the University of California et al., Individually and on Behalf of All Others Similarly Situated, vs. Kenneth L. Lay et al., United States District Court, Southern District of Texas, Houston Division, Civil Action No. H-01-3624 (Class Action), March 2006.

6. Dennis R. Beresford, Nicholas deB. Katzenbach, and C. B. Rogers Jr., "Report of Investigation by the Special Investigative Committee of the Board of Directors of WorldCom, Inc.," March 31, 2003; Jay W. Lorsch, "Restoring Trust at WorldCom," HBS No. 9-404-138 (Boston: Harvard Business School Publishing, 2004).
7. Lorsch and Carter, *Back to the Drawing Board*.
8. Jay W. Lorsch, "American Express (A)," HBS No. 494-093 and "American Express (B)," HBS No. 494-094 (Boston: Harvard Business School Publishing, 1994).
9. Lorsch, "American Express (A)."

Chapter Two

1. R. Romano, "Less Is More: Making Institutional Investor Activism a Valuable Mechanism of Corporate Governance," *Yale Journal of Regulation* 18, no. 2 (2001): 174–252.
2. R. C. Pozen, "Before You Split That CEO/Chair . . .", *Harvard Business Review* 84, no. 4 (April 2006): 28.
3. Pozen, "Before You Split That CEO/Chair..."
4. D. Henderson, "Redraw the Line Between the Board and the CEO," *Harvard Business Review* (March-April 1995): 160.
5. Henderson, "Redraw the Line Between the Board and the CEO," 162.
6. Henderson, "Redraw the Line," 162.
7. These responsibilities are derived from ones identified in Paul Firstenberg and Burton Malkiel, "The Twenty-First Century Boardroom: Who Will Be in Charge?" *Sloan Management Review* (Fall 1994): 31–32.
8. Firstenberg and Malkiel, "The Twenty-First Century Boardroom," 35.

Chapter Three

1. "Calls to Split CEO, Chair Roles Heat Up," *Agenda* 29 (October 2007): 1, 5.
2. R. M. Hutchins, *Great Books of the Western World. Adam Smith: An Inquiry into the Nature and Causes of the Wealth of Nations* (1776) (Chicago: Encyclopedia Britannica, 1952), 324.
3. M. A. Jacobsen, "Interested Director Transactions and the (Equivocal) Effects of Shareholder Ratification," *Delaware Journal of Corporate Law* 21 (1996): 985.
4. W. W. Bratton, "Berle and Means Reconsidered at the Century's Turn," *Journal of Corporation Law* 26 (2001): 737–770; J. C. Coffee, "The Rise of Dispersed Ownership: The Roles of Law and the State of the Separation of Ownership and Control," *Yale Law Journal* 111 (2001): 3–82; D. R. Dalton, M. A. Hitt, S. T. Certo, and C. M. Dalton, "The Fundamental Agency Problem and Its Mitigation: Independence, Equity, and the Market for Corporate Control," *The Academy of Management Annals* (New York: Routledge, 2008), 1–64; K. M. Eisenhardt, "Agency Theory: An Assessment and Review," *Academy of Management Review* 14 (1989): 57–74; M. S. Mizruchi, "Who Controls Whom? An Examination of the Relation Between Management and Board of Directors in Large American Corporations," *Academy of Management Review* 8 (1983): 426–435; and J. P. Walsh and J. K. Seward, "On the Efficiency of Internal and External Corporate Control Mechanisms," *Academy of Management Review* 15 (1990): 421–458.
5. A. A. Berle and G. C. Means, *The Modern Corporation and Private Property* (New York: MacMillan, 1932).
6. E. F. Fama, "Agency Problems and the Theory of the Firm," *Journal of Political Economy* 88 (1980): 288–307; E. F. Fama and M. C. Jensen, "Separation of Ownership and Control," *Journal of Law and Economics* 26 (1983): 301–325; E. F. Famaand and M. C. Jensen, "Agency Problems and Residual Claims," *Journal of Law and Economics* 26 (1983): 327–349; M. C. Jensen and W. F. Meckling, "Theory of the Firm: Managerial Behavior, Agency Costs,

and Ownership Structure," *Journal of Financial Economics* 3 (1976): 305–360; Mizruchi, "Who Controls Whom?"; and A. D. Chandler, *The Visible Hand: The Managerial Revolution in American Business* (Cambridge, Mass.: Harvard University Press, 1977).

7. M. Bradley and S. M. Wallenstein, "The History of Corporate Governance in the United States," in *The Accountable Corporation*, ed. M. J. Epstein and K. O. Hanson, 45–72 (Westport, Conn.: Praeger, 2006); and P. A. Gourevitch and J. Shinn, *Political Power & Corporate Control* (Princeton, N.J.: Princeton University Press, 2005).
8. Fama and Jensen, "Separation of Ownership and Control"; and Fama and Jensen, "Agency Problems and Residual Claims."
9. P. Coombes and S. C-Y. Wong, "Chairman and CEO: One Job or Two?" *McKinsey Quarterly* 2 (2004): 43–44; M. C. Jensen, "Presidential Address: The Modern Industrial Revolution, Exit and the Failure of Internal Control Systems," *Journal of Finance* 48 (1993): 831–880; M. C. Jensen, "The Modern Industrial Revolution, Exit, and the Failure of Internal Control Systems," in *Corporate Governance at the Crossroads*, ed. D. H. Chew and S. L. Gillan (New York: McGraw-Hill Irwin, 2005), 21–40; P. W. MacAvoy and I. M. Millstein, *The Recurrent Crisis in Corporate Governance* (New York: Palgrave Macmillan, 2003); and R.A.G. Monks and N. Minow, *Corporate Governance* (3rd ed.) (Malden, Mass.: Blackwell Publishing, 2004).
10. J. A. Brickley, J. L. Coles, and G. Jarrell, "Leadership Structure: Separating the CEO and Chairman of the Board," *Journal of Corporate Finance* 3 (1997): 189–220, quote 194.
11. S. Green, "Unfinished Business: Abolish the Imperial CEO," *Journal of Corporate Accounting & Finance* 15 (2004): 19–22.
12. B. R. Baliga, R. C. Moyer, and R. Rao, "CEO Duality and Firm Performance: What's the Fuss?" *Strategic Management Journal* 17 (1996): 41–53; Brickley, Coles, and Jarrell, "Leadership Structure"; C. M. Daily and D. R. Dalton, "CEO and Board Chair Roles Held Jointly or Separately: Much Ado About Nothing," *Academy of Management Executive* 11 (1997): 11–20; Dalton, Hitt, Certo, and Dalton, "Agency Theory and Its Mitigation"; W. N. Davidson,

P. Jiraporn, Y. S. Kim, and C. Nemec, "Earnings Management Following Duality-Creating Successions: Ethnostatistics, Impression Management, and Agency Theory," *Academy of Management Journal* 47 (2004): 267–275; S. Finkelstein and R. A. D'Aveni, "CEO Duality as a Double-Edged Sword: How Boards of Directors Balance Entrenchment Avoidance and Unity of Command," *Academy of Management Journal* 37 (1994): 1079–1108; J. W. Lorsch and A. Zelleke, "Should the CEO Be the Chairman?" *Sloan Management Review* 46, no. 2 (2005): 71–74; and National Association of Corporate Directors (NACD), *Report of the NACD Blue Ribbon Commission on Board Leadership* (Washington, D.C.: National Association of Corporate Directors, 2004).

13. "CEO-Chairman Split Not Giving Boost to Independence," *Agenda* (December 11, 2006): 8; "Stock Returns Lag When Former CEOs Are Chairmen, *Board Alert* (June 2005): 3–4; and J. Welch and S. Welch, "A Dangerous Division of Labor," *BusinessWeek* (November 6, 2006): 122.

14. SpencerStuart, *Spencer Stuart 2006 US Board Index* (Chicago: SpencerStuart, 2006).

15. Monks and Minow, *Corporate Governance*.

16. SpencerStuart, *Spencer Stuart 2006 US Board Index*, 9.

17. "Calls to Split CEO, Chair Roles Heat Up"; Baliga, Moyer, and Rao, "CEO Duality and Firm Performance"; B. K. Boyd, "CEO Duality and Firm Performance: A Contingency Model," *Strategic Management Journal* 16 (1995): 301–312; Brickley, Coles, and Jarrell, "Leadership Structure"; A. A. Cannella and M. Lubatkin, "Succession as a Sociopolitical Process: Internal Impediments to Outsider Selection," *Academy of Management Journal*, 36: 763–793; J. W. Coles, V. B. McWilliams, and N. Sen, "An Examination of the Relationship of Governance Mechanisms to Performance," *Journal of Management* 27 (2001): 23–50; C. M. Daily and D. R. Dalton, "The Relationship Between Governance Structure and Corporate Performance in Entrepreneurial Firms," *Journal of Business Venturing* 7 (1992): 375–386; D. R. Dalton, C. M. Daily, A. E. Ellstrand, and J. L. Johnson, "Board Composition, Leadership Structure, and

Financial Performance: Meta-Analytic Reviews and Research Agenda," *Strategic Management Journal* 19 (1998): 269–290; Dalton, Hitt, Certo, and Dalton, "Agency Theory and Its Mitigation"; O. Faleye, "Does One Hat Fit All? The Case of Corporate Leadership Structure," *Journal of Management and Governance* 11 (2007): 239–259; and E. Kang and A. Zardhoohi, "Board Leadership Structure and Firm Performance," *Corporate Governance* 13 (2005): 785–799.

18. H. Fayol, *General and Industrial Management* (London: Pitman, 1949); D. C. McCallum, "Superintendents' Report," *American Railroad Journal* 29 (1856): 225–226; M. Weber, *The Theory of Social and Economic Organization* (New York: Oxford University Press, 1947); Finkelstein and D'Aveni, "CEO Duality as a Double-Edged Sword"; and D. A. Wren, *The History of Management Thought*, 5th ed. (Hoboken, N.J.: John Wiley & Sons, 2005).
19. McCallum, "Superintendents' Report," 104.
20. Brickley, Coles, and Jarrell, "Leadership Structure."
21. D. R. Dalton, "If You Could Make One Change to the Governance System…Pull Back the 'Separating Roles' Movement," *Directors & Boards* 30, no. 1 (2005): 24.
22. Brickley, Coles, and Jarrell, "Leadership Structure"; Dalton, Hitt, Certo, and Dalton, "Agency Theory and Its Mitigation"; Lorsch and Zelleke, "Should the CEO Be the Chairman?"; J. S. Lublin, "Separating Top Posts Will Hurt CEO's Authority Some Believe," *Wall Street Journal*, January 10, 2003, c11; and P. L. Rechner and D. R. Dalton, "CEO Duality and Organizational Performance: A Longitudinal Analysis," *Strategic Management Journal* 12 (1991): 155–160.
23. Brickley, Coles, and Jarrell, "Leadership Structure"; and A. A. Alchian and H. Demsetz, "Production, Information Costs, and Economic Organization," *American Economic Review* 62 (1972): 777–795.
24. See D. R. Dalton and C. M. Dalton, "Executive Committees: The Stealth Board Body," *Directors & Boards* 30, no. 2 (2006): 44–47 for an overview of ECs and related corporate governance issues.

25. Liberum Research (2007). Available at *The Wall Street Transcript*, http://twst.com (accessed September 7, 2008); Booz Allen Hamilton, "CEO Succession 2004: The World's Most Prominent Temp Workers," 2005, available at www.boozallenhamilton.com.
26. C. Lucier, R. Schuyt, and E. Tse, "CEO 2004: The World's Most Prominent Temp Workers," *Strategy and Business* 39 (2005): 28–43.
27. D. Ciampa, "Almost Ready: How Leaders Move Up," *Harvard Business Review* (January 2005): 46–53.
28. "Nike, Inc. Names Mark Parker CEO, William D. Perez Resigns," Nike press release, January 23, 2006, available at www.nikebiz.com/media/pr/2006/01/23_perez-denson.html (accessed September 7, 2008).
29. S. Holmes, "Nike's CEO Gets the Boot," *BusinessWeek* (January 4, 2006): 13.
30. R. Fahlenbrach, B. A. Minton, and C. Pan, "The Market for Comeback CEOs," *Journal of Financial Economics* (forthcoming).
31. See D. R. Dalton and C. M. Daily, "The Enigma of the Emeritus Director," *Directors & Boards* 28, no. 1 (2003): 53–56 for a discussion of emeritus directors and related corporate governance issues.
32. "Calls to Split CEO, Chair Roles Heat Up."

Chapter Four

1. J. W. Lorsch and R. C. Clark, "Leading from the Boardroom," *Harvard Business Review* 86, no. 4 (208): 104–111.
2. Direct quotes in this chapter are taken from participants in these board meetings.
3. J. W. Lorsch and D. A. Nadler, *Report of the NACD Blue Ribbon Commission on Board Leadership* (Washington, D.C.: National Association of Corporate Directors, 2004); D. A. Nadler, B. A. Behan, and M. B. Nadler, *Building Better Boards: A Blueprint for Effective Governance* (San Francisco: Jossey-Bass, 2006).
4. J. R. Hackman, *Leading Teams: Setting the Stage for Great Performances* (Boston: Harvard Business School Press, 2002).

5. C. M. Daily, D. R. Dalton, and A. A. Cannella Jr., "Corporate Governance: Decades of Dialogue and Data," *Academy of Management Review* 28 (2003): 371–382.

6. D. P. Forbes and F. J. Milliken, "Cognition and Corporate Governance: Understanding Boards of Directors as Strategic Decision-Making Groups," *Academy of Management Review* 24 (1999): 489–505.

7. M. H. Bazerman, *Judgment in Managerial Decision Making* (Hoboken, N.J.: John Wiley & Sons, 2006).

8. G. Stasser, and W. Titus, "Pooling of Unshared Information in Group Decision-Making: Biased Information Sampling During Discussion," *Journal of Personality and Social Psychology* 48 (1985): 1467–1478.

9. Hackman, *Leading Teams;* J. R. Hackman and C. G. Morris, "Group Tasks, Group Interaction Process, and Group Performance Effectiveness: A Review and Proposed Integration," in *Advances in Experimental Social Psychology*, ed. L. Berkowitz (New York: Academic Press, 1975); and N.R.F. Maier, "Assets and Liabilities in Group Problem-Solving: The Need for an Integrative Function," *Psychological Review* 74, no. 4 (1967): 239–249.

10. J. Berger, B. P. Cohen, and M. Zelditch Jr., "Status Characteristics and Social Interaction," *American Sociological Review* 37 (1972): 241–255.

11. W. B. Swann, "Self-Verification: Bringing Social Reality into Harmony with the Self." In *Social Psychological Perspectives on the Self*, ed. J. Suls and G. Greenwald (Hillsdale, N.J.: Erlbaum, 1983).

12. J. W. Lorsch with E. MacIver, *Pawns or Potentates: The Reality of America's Corporate Boards* (Boston: Harvard Business School Press, 1989); and M. Mace, *Directors: Myth and Reality* (Cambridge, Mass.: Harvard University Press, 1971).

13. J. W. Lorsch and R. C. Clark, "Leading from the Boardroom," *Harvard Business Review* 86, no. 4 (2008): 104–111.

14. E. Stroble and J. M. Cooper, "Mentor Teachers: Coaches or Referees?" *Theory into Practice* 27, no. 3 (1988): 231–236.

15. P. R. Bernthal and C. A. Insko, "Cohesiveness Without Groupthink," *Group and Organization Studies* 18, no. 1 (1993): 66; and I. L. Janis, *Victims of Groupthink* (Boston: Houghton Mifflin, 1972).

16. D. Cartwright, "The Nature of Group Cohesiveness," in *Group Dynamics: Research and Theory*, in D. Cartwright and A. Zander (New York: Harper & Row, 1968).

17. C. B. Carter and J. W. Lorsch, *Back to the Drawing Board* (Boston: Harvard Business School Press, 2004); and Mace, *Directors*.

18. R. Myers, "The Top 10 Legal Milestones of the Last 10 Years," *Corporate Board Member* 8, no. 4 (2005): 48–62.

19. Carter and Lorsch, *Back to the Drawing Board*.

20. J. Berger, B. P. Cohen, and M. Zelditch Jr. "Status Characteristics and Social Interaction," *American Sociological Review* 37 (1972): 241–255.

21. W. B. Swann, "Self-Verification."

22. R. S. Crutchfield, "Conformity and Character," *American Psychologist* 10 (1955): 191.

23. Stasser and Titus, "Pooling of Unshared Information in Group Decision-Making."

24. R. S. Peterson and C. J. Nemeth, "Focus Versus Flexibility: Majority and Minority Influence Can Both Improve Performance," *Personality and Social Psychology Bulletin* 22, no. 1 (1996): 14–23.

25. N.R.F. Maier, "Assets and Liabilities in Group Problem-Solving: The Need for an Integrative Function," *Psychological Review* 74, no. 4 (1967): 239–249.

26. S. E. Asch, "Effects of Group Pressures Upon the Modification and Distortion of Judgments," in *Groups, Leadership, and Men*, ed. H. Guetzkow (New Brunswick, N.J.: Rutgers University Press, 1951).

27. Maier, "Assets and Liabilities in Group Problem-Solving."

28. Hackman and Morris, "Group Tasks, Group Interaction Process, and Group Performance Effectiveness."

29. K. Jehn, "Enhancing Effectiveness: An Investigation of Advantages and Disadvantages of Value-Based Intragroup Conflict," *International*

Journal of Conflict Management 5 (1994): 223–238; and K. Jehn, "A Multimethod Examination of the Benefits and Detriments of Intragroup Conflict," *Administrative Science Quarterly* 40 (1995): 256–282.

30. C.K.W. De Dreu and L. R. Weingart, "Task Versus Relationship Conflict, Team Performance, and Team Member Satisfaction: A Meta-Analysis," *Journal of Applied Psychology* 88 (2003): 741–749.
31. Janis, *Victims of Groupthink*.
32. A. V. Carron, L. N. Widmeyer, and L. R. Brawley, "The Development of an Instrument to Assess Cohesion in Sports Teams: The Group Environment Questionnaire," *Journal of Sport Psychology* 7 (1985): 244–266, quote p. 248.
33. M. Useem, *The Inner Circle: Large Corporations and the Rise of Business Political Activity in the U.S. and U.K.* (Oxford, U.K., and New York: Oxford University Press, 1984).
34. Carron, Widmeyer, and Brawley, "The Development of an Instrument," 248.
35. Carter and Lorsch, *Back to the Drawing Board;* J. A. Conger, E. E. Lawler, and D. L. Finegold, *Corporate Boards: New Strategies for Adding Value at the Top* (San Francisco: Jossey-Bass, 2001); and Lorsch with MacIver, *Pawns or Potentates*.
36. Max Weber, *Economy and Society* (Berkeley, Calif.: University of California Press, 1947).

Chapter Six

1. N. K. Chidambaran, D. Palia, and Y. Zheng, "Does Better Corporate Governance 'Cause' Better Firm Performance?" draft manuscript, March 2006, 42.
2. P. A. Gompers, J. L. Ishii, and A. Metrick, "Corporate Governance and Equity Prices," *Quarterly Journal of Economics* 118, no. 1 (2003): 107–155.
3. L. Bebchuk, A. Cohen, and A. Ferrell, "What Matters in Corporate Governance?" Working paper, 2004, Harvard Law School.

4. S. Bhagat and B. Bolton, "Corporate Governance and Firm Performance," *Journal of Corporate Finance* 14 (2008): 257.
5. J. Sonnenfeld, "Good Governance and the Misleading Myths of Bad Metrics," *Academy of Management Executive* 18, no. 1 (2004): 108–109.
6. R. Daines, I. Gow, and D. Larcker, "Rating the Ratings: How Good Are Commercial Governance Ratings?" working paper, June 26, 2008, 28–29.
7. J. Pfeffer, "Beware the Corporate Raters: Board Oversight Is a Good Thing, But the Procedures of the New Governance Firms Leave a Lot to Be Desired," CNNMoney.com, Sept. 5, 2007, p. 52. Available at http://money.cnn.com/2007/09/04/technology/Corporate_raters.biz2/index.htm (accessed September 7, 2008).
8. P. Rose, "The Corporate Governance Industry," *The Journal of Corporation Law* (Summer 2007): 887.
9. "Building an Exceptional Board," *BusinessWeek*, *Directorship*, April 29, 2008, p. 1. Available at http://www.businessweek.com/managing/content/apr2008/ca20080429_920167.htm (accessed September 7, 2008).
10. "Building an Exceptional Board," 3.
11. "Building an Exceptional Board," 1–2.
12. K. Daly, in C. Elson et al. [panel discussion], "Director Term Limits Come Up for Review," *Directors & Boards* second quarter (2008): 20.
13. "Building an Exceptional Board," 2.
14. Elson et al., "Director Term Limits," 23.
15. R. Troubh, in Elson et al., "Director Term Limits," 23.
16. Elson et al., "Director Term Limits," 18.
17. New York Stock Exchange, Listed Company Manual, "Section 303A Corporate Governance Rules, As of November 3, 2004" (New York Stock Exchange Governance Rules, approved by the SEC on November 4, 2003, as amended on November 3, 2004). Available at http://www.nyse.com/pdfs/section303A_final_rules.pdf.

18. Canadian Securities Administrators, "National Policy 58-201—Corporate Governance Guidelines" (2005) 28 OSCB 3640. Available at http://www.osc.gov.on.ca/Regulation/Rulemaking/Current/Part5/rule_20050617_58-201_corp-gov-guidelines.jsp.
19. Nexen Inc., 2008 Management Proxy Circular, "Board of Directors—Areas of Expertise," March 21, 2008, p. 23. Available at http://www.nexeninc.com/Governance/Board/AreasofExpertise.asp.

Chapter Seven

1. "After a Buyout, Fund Shops for More Women Power," Women's eNews, May 13, 2008. Available at http://womensenews.org/article.cfm?aid=3597.
2. "Women and Minorities on Fortune 100 Boards," The Alliance for Board Diversity, 9. Available at http://www.hacr.org/docLib/20080131_ABDfinalreport12208.pdf.
3. Catalyst Census, 2007. "The Bottom Line: Connecting Corporate Performance and Gender Diversity." Available at http://www.catalyst.org/publication/200/the-bottom-line-corporate-performance-and-womens-representation-on-boards.
4. T. M. Welborne, C. S. Cycyota, and C. J. Fererante, "Wall Street Reaction to Women in IPOs: An Examination of Gender Diversity in Top Management Teams," *Group & Organization Management* 32, no. 5 (October 2007): 524–547.
5. Welborne, Cycyota, and Fererante, "Wall Street Reaction to Women in IPOs," 524.
6. Welborne, Cycyota, and Fererante, "Wall Street Reaction to Women in IPOs," 543.
7. D. Cater, B. Simkins, and W. G. Simpson, "Corporate Governance, Board Diversity and Firm Value," *The Financial Review* 38 (2003): 33–53.
8. E. Erhardt, J. D. Werbel, and C. B. Shrader, "Board of Director Diversity and Firm Financial Performance," *Corporate Governance* 11, no. 2 (April 2003).

9. S. Wellington, "Women on Corporate Boards: The Challenge of Change," *Directorship*, XX, no. 11 (December 1994); entire issue.
10. Catalyst Census, 2005, "Ten Years Later: Limited Progress, Challenges Persist," 1, published March 2006. Available at http://www.catalyst.org/publication/19/2005-catalyst-census-of-women-board-directors-of-the-fortune-500.
11. I. Lang, "Foreword," Catalyst Census, 2005, "Ten Years Later: Limited Progress, Challenges Persist," 1, published March 2006. Available at http://www.catalyst.org/publication/19/2005-catalyst-census-of-women-board-directors-of-the-fortune-500.
12. Catalyst Census, 2007.
13. Catalyst Census, 2005, 3.
14. "The Double-Bind Dilemma for Women in Leadership: Damned If You Do, Doomed If You Don't," Catalyst, July 2007. Available at http://www.catalyst.org/publication/83/the-double-bind-dilemma-for-women-in-leadership-damned-if-you-do-doomed-if-you-don't (accessed August 31, 2008).
15. "The Double-Bind Dilemma for Women in Leadership."
16. S. K. Johnson, S. E. Murphy, S. Zewdie, and R. Reichard, "The Strong Sensitive Type: Effects of Gender Stereotypes and Leadership Prototypes on the Evaluation of Male and Female Leaders," *Organizational Behavior and Human Decision Processes*. Available at http://www.sciencedirect.com/science?_ob=ArticleURL&_udi=B6WP2-4RWHGTD-1&_user=945391&_rdoc=1&_fmt=&_orig=search&_sort=d&view=c&_version=1&_urlVersion=0&_userid=945391&md5=58bd34fbdf10a0936dd42baa82a4c1ed
17. Johnson, Murphy, Zewdie, and Reichard, "The Strong Sensitive Type," 55, italics added for emphasis.
18. Johnson, Murphy, Zewdie, and Reichard, "The Strong Sensitive Type," 55.
19. "The Double-Bind Dilemma for Women in Leadership," 13.
20. Catalyst Census, 2007, 8.

21. *What Directors Think: A Special Research Study 2007*, Corporate Board Member/PricewaterhouseCoopers survey, December 14, 2007. Available at www.boardmember.com/research/articles/?search=what%20directors%20think&C=668&I=1785 (accessed August 31, 2008).
22. Korn/Ferry International, 33rd Board of Directors Study for the Americas (2006 statistics). This publication is available for purchase at http://www.kornferry.com/ThoughtLeadership (accessed October 12, 2008).
23. V. W. Kramer, A. M. Konrad, and S. Erkut, *Critical Mass on Corporate Boards: Why Three or More Women Enhance Governance, Executive Summary* (Boston: Wellesley Centers for Women's Publications Office, 2006), 4.
24. G. Fabrikant, "Corner of Finance Where Women Are Climbing," *New York Times*, March 22, 2008, available at www.nytimes.com/2008/03/22/business/22women.html (accessed September 7, 2008).
25. J. A. Conger, E. E. Lawler III, and D. L. Finegold, *Corporate Boards: New Strategies for Adding Value at the Top* (San Francisco: Jossey-Bass, 2001), 53.
26. Catalyst Census, 2007.
27. H. Rubin, "Sexism," Portfolio.com. Available at http://www.portfolio.com/executives/features/2008/03/17/Sexism-in-the-Workplace?print=true (accessed October 12, 2008).
28. P. Myers, M. Nitkin, H. Colaco, P. Deyton, and I. Guertler, *Path to Leadership: Women's Experiences with and Aspirations for Board Service*, Center for Gender in Organizations (CGO) Insights, Briefing Note No. 27, March 2008, Simmons School of Management, Boston.
29. Catalyst Census, 2005, 2.
30. Catalyst Census, 2005, 2.
31. Kramer, Konrad, and Erkut, *Critical Mass on Corporate Boards*, 2.
32. Kramer, Konrad, and Erkut, *Critical Mass on Corporate Boards*, 3.

33. Kramer, Konrad, and Erkut, *Critical Mass on Corporate Boards*, 3.
34. A. H. Eagly and L. L. Carli, *Through the Labyrinth: The Truth About How Women Become Leaders* (Boston: Harvard Business School Press, 2007), 137.
35. "Higher Number of Women in the Boardroom Heralds Future Increase of Women Corporate Officers, According to Latest Catalyst Study," Press Release, New York, July 23, 2008. Available at www.catalyst.org/press-release/134/higher-number-of-women-in-the-boardroom-hyeralds-future-increase-of-women-corporate-officers-according-to-latest-catalyst-study (accessed October 12, 2008).
36. S. Seibert, M. Kraimer, and R. Liden, "A Social Capital Theory of Career Success," *Academy of Management Journal* 44, no. 2 (2001): 219–237.
37. W. Holstein, "Getting a New Director Up to Speed," *BusinessWeek*, January 24, 2008.
38. A. Burgess and P. Tharenou, "What Distinguishes Women Non-executive Directors from Executive Directors," in *Women on Corporate Boards of Directors: International Challenges and Opportunities*, ed. R. J. Burke and M. C. Mattis, pp. 253–261 (Dordrecht, The Netherlands: Kluwer Academic Publishers, 2000), 113.
39. John H. Bryan, *Directors & Boards*, Spring 1995, referenced in D.S.R. Leighton and D. H. Thain, *Making Boards Work* (New York: McGraw-Hill Ryerson, 1997), 259.
40. Catalyst Census, 2007, "Women Board Directors of the Fortune 500," Appendix I: Companies with 25 Percent or More Women Board Directors.
41. Catalyst Census, 2007.
42. "In Europe, Women Finding More Seats at the Table," *New York Times*, March 22, 2008, B4.
43. "The 50 Women to Watch 2007," *Wall Street Journal, The Journal Report*, November 19, 2007.

Chapter Eight

1. "S&P 500 CEO Pay Rises 1.3% to $8.8 Million in Equilar® Study." Press release, April 10, 2008. Available at http://www.equilar.com/press_20080410.php.
2. *Report of the NACD Blue Ribbon Commission on Executive Compensation and the Role of the Compensation Committee* (Washington, D.C.: NACD, 2003/2007).
3. Dupont Corporation Proxy Statement, 2004. Available at http://google.brand.edgar-online.com/EFX_dll/EDGARpro.dll?FetchFilingHTML1?SessionID=TElBWNCx-Eo75wh&ID=2842118&AnchorName=HH_&AnchorDistance=0&BeginHTML=%3Cb%3E%3Cfont+color%3D%22%23cc0000%22%3E&EndHTML=%3C%2Ffont%3E%3C%2Fb%3E&SearchText=%3CNEAR%2F4%3E(%22E.+B.%22%2C%22DU+PONT%22).
4. *Executive Excess* (Washington, D.C.: Institute for Policy Studies/United for a Fair Economy, August 25, 2008). Available at http://www.faireconomy.org/files/executive_excess_2008.pdf.
5. Comarco, Inc., Proxy Statement 2007. Available at http://www.secinfo.com/d14D5a.u3BQm.htm#3o51.
6. "Departing CEOs Not Receiving Increased Termination Payments at Most Companies, Watson Wyatt Survey Finds," Press release, March 20, 2008. Available at http://www.watsonwyatt.com/news/press.asp?ID=18834.
7. Comarco, Inc., Proxy Statement 2007. Available at http://www.secinfo.com/d14D5a.u3BQm.htm#3o51.
8. Text taken from Torchmark, "Compensation Committee Report on Executive Compensation," March 12, 2004. Quoted on EdgarOnline, available at http://sec.edgar-online.com/2004/03/12/0001193125-04-040610/Section15.asp (accessed September 7, 2008).
9. Text taken from 3M, "Item 3. Executive Profit Sharing Plan," March 24, 1994. Quoted on EdgarOnline, available at http://sec.edgar-online.com/1994/03/24/00/0000066740-94-000018/Section14.asp (accessed September 7, 2008).

10. *Report of the NACD Blue Ribbon Commission*.
11. *2007 Public Company Governance Survey* (Washington, D.C.: National Association of Corporate Directors, 2007).
12. Diane L. Doubleday, "A New Compass for Equitable Excecutive Pay," *Directors Monthly* (July 2007).
13. Equilar, 2007 Director Stock Ownership Guidelines Report, http://www.equilar.com/Executive_Compensation_DSOG_02_2008.php cited by Directorship.com, news item on website dated February 20, 2008, "Stock-Ownership Requirements Increasing" (directorship.com, February 20, 2008, screen 1).
14. *2007 Public Company Governance Survey*.
15 *Long-Term Value Creation: Guiding Principles for Corporations and Investors* (New York: Aspen Institute, 2007).

Chapter Nine

1. See, for example, J. W. Lorsch and R. C. Clark, "Leading from the Boardroom," *Harvard Business Review* (April 2008): 104–111.
2. The entire argument is laid out in depth in my book summarizing that research, *The CEO Within: Why Inside Outsiders Are Key to Succession Planning* (Boston: Harvard Business School Press, 2007).
3. William Fruhan, unpublished memorandum, October 1, 2007, Exhibit C. See also R. Foster and S. Kaplan, *Creative Destruction* (New York: Doubleday, 2001), 47.
4. See, for example, Y. Doz and M. Kosonen, *Fast Strategy* (U.K.: Wharton School Publishing, 2008).
5. Robert Hayes, Steven Wheelwright, and Kim Clark; Clayton Christensen.
6. J. Collins, *Good to Great* (New York: Collins Business, 2001).
7. B. Groysberg, A. N. McLean, and N. Nohria, "Are Leaders Portable?" *Harvard Business Review* (May 2006); and Bower, *The CEO Within*.
8. C. Lucier, R. Schuyt, and E. Tse, "CEO Succession 2004: The World's Most Prominent Temp Worker," *strategy + business* (Summer 2005).

9. P.-O. Karlsson, G. L. Neilson, and J. C. Webster, "CEO Succession: The Performance Paradox," *strategy + business* no. 51 (Summer 2008).
10. Kenneth Andrews, *The Concept of Corporate Strategy*, rev. ed. (Burr Ridge, Ill.: Richard D. Irwin, 1980).
11. See, for example, David Garvin, "Emerging Business Opportunities at IBM (A)," Harvard Business School case study 304075, 2004; and A. M. Kleinbaum, T. E. Stuart, and M. Tushman, "Communication (and Coordination) in the Modern Corporation," working paper, 2008.
12. Y. Doz and M. Kosonen, *Strategic Agility*.
13. Bower, *The CEO Within*, 13.
14. Society of Human Resource Mangement, "SHRM Weekly Online Poll," December 2003, results reported in S. Meisinger, "The King Is Dead, Long Live the King!" *HR Magazine* 49, no. 6 (2004).
15. J. L. Bower and S. E. Hout, "GE: The People Factory at Work," a video interview about succession, Harvard Business School video #8107, 2002.
16. Bower, *The CEO Within*, 211–212.
17. Karlsson, Neilson, and Webster, "CEO Succession."
18. R. Khurana, *In Search for the Charismatic* CEO (Cambridge, Mass.: Harvard Business School Press, 2004).
19. Khurana, *In Search for the Charismatic* CEO.
20. Booz Allen.
21. C. A. Bartlett and A. N. McLean, "The GE Talent Machine: The Making of a CEO," Harvard Business School, 9-304-049, Rev: November 3, 2006.
22. B. Vlasic and B. A. Stertz, *Taken for a Ride: How Daimler-Benz Drove Off with Chrysler* (New York: William Morrow, 2000), for example, 318–321.
23. As an aside, the high risks associated with an outsider as CEO have a good deal to do with the issue of high CEO compensation. Because most outside candidates are employed and successful at

the time they are recruited, they must be paid a premium to leave a lower-risk situation. These high-compensation packages then become part of the industry averages that compensation consultants use to counsel companies considering the pay of insiders. Despite their reservations, it is easy to see why a board that values its CEO highly would consider it unfair to pay him or her less than some new arrival to the industry with nothing but a resume. As economists tell us, the price at the margin establishes the market.

24. Karlsson, Neilson, and Webster, "CEO Succession."

Chapter Ten

1. National Association of Corporate Directors in collaboration with Oliver Wyman-Delta Organization & Leadership, *2006 NACD Public Company Governance Survey* (Washington, D.C.: Center for Board Leadership, National Association of Corporate Directors, 2006, 2007); and National Association of Corporate Directors in collaboration with Oliver Wyman-Delta Organization & Leadership, *2006 NACD Private Company Governance Survey* (Washington, D.C.: Center for Board Leadership, National Association of Corporate Directors, 2006, 2007).
2. National Association of Corporate Directors in collaboration with Oliver Wyman-Delta Organization & Leadership, *The Role of the Board in CEO Succession: A Best Practices Study*, Board Leadership Series (Washington, D.C.: National Association of Corporate Directors, 2006).
3. D. A. Nadler, B. A. Behan, and M. B. Nadler, *Building Better Boards* (San Francisco: Jossey-Bass, 2006).
4. C. Lucier, S. Wheeler, and R. Habbel, "The Era of the Inclusive Leader," *strategy + business* (Summer 2007): 42–55.
5. D. A. Nadler, "The CEO's Second Act," *Harvard Business Review* (January 2007): 66–72.
6. R. Khurana, *Searching for a Corporate Savior: The Irrational Quest for Charismatic* CEOs (Princeton, N.J.: Princeton University Press, 2002).

Chapter Twelve

1. L. Corb and T. Koller, "When to Break Up a Conglomerate: An Interview with Tyco International's CFO," *McKinsey on Strategy and Finance* 29 (Autumn 2007): 12–18.
2. CtW Investment Group, William Patterson letter to Charles Rossotti, January 16, 2008, available at http://www.ctwinvestmentgroup.com/uploads/media/CtW_Inv_Grp_to_MER_Fin_Cmte_Rossotti_Jan_16_08.pdf (accessed September 7, 2008).
3. "What Directors Think: The Corporate Board Member/PWC Special Survey," *Corporate Board Member Magazine Special Supplement*, 2007.
4. National Association of Corporate Directors, *2007 Public Company Governance Survey* (Washington, D.C.: NACD, 2007). Additional correlation analysis done by Oliver Wyman.
5. USC/Center for Effective Organizations and Heidrick and Struggles, *10th Annual Corporate Board Effectiveness Survey, 2006–2007* (Chicago: Center for Effective Organizations and Heidrick and Struggles, 2007).
6. J. Surowiecki, *The Wisdom of Crowds* (New York: Anchor Books, 2004).
7. USC/Center for Effective Organizations and Heidrick and Struggles, *10th Annual Corporate Board Effectiveness Survey*.
8. Surowiecki, *The Wisdom of Crowds*.
9. Quotes from CEOs and directors are taken from author discussions or interviews.
10. J. R. Hackman, *Leading Teams: Setting the Stage for Great Performances* (Boston: Harvard Business School Press, 2002); M. J. Conyon and S. I. Peck, "Board Size and Corporate Performance: Evidence from European Countries," *The European Journal of Finance* 4.3 (1998): 291–304; R. Adams and H. Mehran, "Corporate Performance, Board Structure, and Its Determinants in the Banking Industry," EFA 2005 Moscow Meetings, August 8, 2005, 1–12; K. Ahmed, M. Hossain, and M. B. Adams, "The Effects

of Board Composition and Board Size on the Informativeness of Annual Accounting Earnings," *Corporate Governance* 14.5 (2006): 418–431.

11. National Association of Corporate Directors, *2007 Public Company Governance Survey*.
12. SpencerStuart, *Spencer Stuart 2007 US Board Survey* (New York: SpencerStuart, 2007), www.spencerstuart.com/research/boards/1212 (accessed September 7, 2008).
13. B. Edlin, "Quality Not Quantity Needed on Boards," *Chartered Accountants Journal* (October 2005): 33–34.
14. Only 15 percent of the Russell 2000 have fewer than seven directors, and only 153 companies in the S&P 1000 have boards larger than 121, and most of these are in financial services and insurance. The largest board of 30 directors is being formed by the merger of the Chicago Mercantile Exchange with the Chicago Board of Trade.
15. K. Eichenwald, *Conspiracy of Fools* (New York: Broadway Books, 2005).
16. M. Berger and D. Pappalardo, "AT&T Merges Cable Unit with Comcast," IDG News Service and Network World Fusion, December 20, 2001, available at www.networkworld.com/news/2001/1220attcomcast.html?nw (accessed September 7, 2008).
17. For further thinking on this topic, see D. W. Anderson, S. J. Melanson, and J. Maly, "The Evolution of Corporate Governance: Power Redistribution Brings Boards to Life," *Corporate Governance* 15, no. 5 (September 2007): 780–797.
18. Staggered boards are another debatable practice. Having some minority core of continuity could help boards keep perspectives broad. However, space prevents further discussion in this chapter.
19. A. M. Isen and S. F. Simmonds, "The Effect of Feeling Good on a Helping Task That Is Incompatible with Good Mood," *Social Psychology* 41, no. 4 (December 1978): 346–349, doi:10.2307/3033588. See also F. Gino and M. E. Schweitzer, *Blinded by Anger or Feeling the Love (or Anger): How Emotions Influence Advice Taking*, Oct. 1, 2008. Available at Knowledge@Wharton.

Chapter Thirteen

1. S. A. Snook, *Friendly Fire: The Accidental Shootdown of U.S. Black Hawks Over Northern Iraq* (Princeton, N.J.: Princeton University Press, 2000).
2. B. Latane and J. M. Darley, *The Unresponsive Bystander: Why Doesn't He Help?* (New York: Appleton-Century-Crofts, 1970).
3. Although there is an occasional success story of co-CEOs, they are almost always a result of internal development and growth, and not external acquisition. For example, Bob Daly and Terry Semel at Time Warner successfully shared the top job for years; Goldman Sachs also relies on more than one person at the top to direct the firm. What's different is that such co-CEOs typically developed a working relationship that emerged over years and were not thrust together in the high-stakes, high-ego game of mergers and acquisitions.
4. Interview with Marc Porat, former chairman and CEO, General Magic, April 16, 2001.
5. D. Jeter and P. Chaney, "How Internet Companies Play Games with Their Numbers," *Bridge News* (December 7, 2000).
6. S. Stewart, "Investors Misled Over Earnings: Regulators Warn of 'Widespread Use' of Unconventional Financial Reporting," *National Post*, January 15, 2002, p. FP1.
7. M. Warner, "A Tale from the Dark Side of Silicon Valley," *Fortune*, April 13, 1998, pp. 92–96.
8. One of the two venture capitalists on the board actually did take a stand against management, but in classic fashion resigned in protest rather than staying on to fight for change.
9. C. Cooper and E. Portanger, "Flashy Clothing Site Had Good Ideas, but Financial Controls Were Lacking," *Wall Street Journal*, June 27, 2000, available at http://interactive.wsj.com/articles/SB962060900205288660.htm (accessed September 7, 2008).
10. J. Porretto, "Overbilling May Be the Next Issue to Plague WorldCom," Associated Press State and Local Wire, July 3, 2002,

http://web.lexis-nexis.com/universe/document?_m=abb9fa5e78e8a7867d1a22f68abd2932&_docnum=2&wchp=dGLbVlz-lSlAl&_md5=f829d11e83dac9a97abeb0122e171d1a.

11. T. Wallack, "WorldCom to Ante Up $8.5 Million; State Lawsuit Accused Long-Distance Phone Company of Slamming, Abusive Billing," *San Francisco Chronicle*, March 8, 2002, p. B1.
12. PlanetFeedBack is an online feedback services company that allows companies to collect and analyze customer feedback in real time.
13. PR Newswire, "PlanetFeedback Releases Consumer Data Findings on WorldCom; Thumbs Down from Consumers on Billing Practices, Customer Service and More," May 2, 2002, http://web.lexis-nexis.com/universe/document?_m=1e36d778cc6a81df16163b4eb513119a&_docnum=1&wchp=dGLbVlz-lSlAl&_md5=7407197a0f88921ba4a1b3d1a6f6e1e5.
14. Interview with John Keogh, president and COO, National Union Fire Insurance Co. of Pittsburg, Pennsylvania, October 25, 2002.
15. D. Van Natta Jr. with A. Berenson, "Enron's Collapse: The Overview; Enron's Chairman Received Warning About Accounting," *New York Times*, January 15, 2002, available at http://www.nytimes.com/2002/01/15/politics/15ENRO.html (accessed September 7, 2008).
16. Interview with John Keogh.
17. N. Machiavelli, *The Prince*, trans. and ed. M. Musa (New York: St. Martin's Press, 1946), 1514.
18. These insights owe much to a student project at Tuck by Jason Adair, Joe Bachman, Tracy Brown, Andrew McBrien, and Laura Scott.
19. D. Caruso, "For Years, Rigas Treated Adelphia Like a Family Business," Associated Press State and Local Wire, May 27, 2002, http://web.lexis-nexis.com/universe/document?_m=505b7137b8ae91c79bf40c18972ce022&_docnum=2&wchp=dGLbVtb-lSlAl&_md5=548bfe56a03943f501a9774b38980acf.
20. D. Robinson, "The Company That Lies Built," *Buffalo News*, July 28, 2002, p. B13.

21. J. Zremski, "Rigas Indictments Outlined; Founder, 4 Others Face Charges," *Buffalo News*, September 24, 2002, p. A1.
22. C. Gaither, "Top Ranks Are Thinned at Sun as No. 2 Executive Joins Exodus," *New York Times*, May 2, 2002, http://web.lexis-nexis.com/universe/document?_m=3375507b77dd541164ed807675ddea36&_docnum=23&wchp=dGLbVlz-lSlzV&_md5=5101a7d87a3f5bfc99f23794e51fc903; D. Clark, "Sun to Lay Off 11% of Workers, Posts Loss Amid Weak Revenue," *Wall Street Journal*, October 18, 2002, available at http://online.wsj.com/article/0,,SB1034789952448161308,00.html?mod=home_whats_news_us (accessed September 7, 2008).
23. D. Sanai, "M of M&C: An Interview with the Saatchi Who Talks (and Some Thoughts About the One Who Doesn't)," *The Independent*, April 12, 2000, http://www.independent.co.uk/story.jsp?story=40152.
24. P. Behr and A. Witt, "Visionary's Dream Led to Risky Business; Opaque Deals, Accounting Sleight of Hand Built an Energy Giant and Ensured Its Demise," *Washington Post*, July 28, 2002, p. A01.
25. J. Kurtzman, *Radical E: From GE to Enron—Lessons on How to Rule the Web* (Hoboken, N.J.: John Wiley & Sons, 2001).
26. H. Green, "A Web Hotshot Learns Humility," *BusinessWeek*, March 19, 2001, p. EB28–EB34.
27. C. Byron, "The Story of ImClone," *New York Post*, January 14, 2002, p. 31.
28. G. Anand, "In Waksal's Past, Repeated Ousters—at Four Prestigious Labs ImClone Founder Faced Questions About Work," *Wall Street Journal*, September 27, 2002, p. A1.
29. A study of over three hundred *Fortune* 500 companies found essentially the same result—those companies run by founders had significantly greater variability in return on assets and stock returns than companies run by non-founder "professional" executives. See R. B. Adams, H. Almeida, and D. Ferreira, "Powerful CEOs and Their Impact on Corporate Performance," working paper, Federal Reserve Bank of New York, November 27, 2002.

30. Excerpted from "Read the World, With Your Own Thinking" (November 1997), the biographical essay by Kun-Hee Lee, chairman of Samsung.
31. Interview with Barry Ridings, managing director, Lazard Freres, May 9, 2002.
32. R. Beck, "Executives Showered with Perks That Investors Often Not Told Of," Associated Press Worldstream, August 9, 2002, http://web.lexis-nexis.com/universe/document?_m=db88565efac7a7ba4c0f4852365fd01c&_docnum=3&wchp=dGLbVtb-lSlAl&_md5=7c64b82158e10446101c1e7047882ab6.
33. C. Mollenkamp, "Subprime Asset: How Money Store Inspired a Big Change in First Union's Course," *Wall Street Journal*, July 25, 2000, p. A1.
34. CMGI gave up the rights to the Patriots' new football stadium two years after acquiring them, and took a $21 million write-off. The team will now play at Gillette Stadium.
35. PSINet gave up its naming rights in early 2002, a prudent move given they were bankrupt, as did Enron (to the stadium now called Minute Maid Park).
36. Interview with Russell Lewis, president and CEO, The New York Times Co., November 6, 2002.
37. J. Doward, "Day the WorldCom World Was Turned Upside Down: The Giant's Fall," *The Observer*, June 30, 2002, Business Section, p. 4; Y. Dreazen and D. Solomon, "WorldCom Aide Conceded Flaws—Controller Said Company Was Forced to Disguise Expenses, Ignore Warnings," *Wall Street Journal*, July 16, 2002, p. A3; A. Sloan, "WorldCom's Wrong Numbers," *Newsweek*, July 8, 2002, p. 44; Economist.Com, "From Bad to Worse; WorldCom," July 1, 2002, http://web.lexis-nexis.com/universe/document?_m=6ce47e557b6f026369b64e4e4485a9ba&_docnum=1&wchp=dGLbVlz-lSlAl&_md5=0238602f6c297a03d54c1a00175c6146; and Y. Dreazen, "Push for Sales Fostered Abuses at WorldCom," *Wall Street Journal*, May 16, 2002, p. B1.
38. T. Fowler, "The Fall of Enron: A Year Ago, Enron's Crumbling Foundation Was Revealed to All When the Company Reported Its

Disastrous Third-Quarter Numbers," *Houston Chronicle*, October 20, 2002, p. A1.

39. *The American Heritage Dictionary of the English Language*, 4th ed. (New York: Houghton Mifflin, 2000).

40. A. Serwer, "The Socialite Scientist," *Fortune*, April 15, 2002, p. 152.

41. S. Schultz, "The Drug That Could Have Been," *U.S. News & World Report*, August 19, 2002, p. 23.

42. N. Deogun and S. Lipin, "Cautionary Tales: When Big Deals Turn Bad," *Wall Street Journal*, December 8, 1999, p. C1.

43. M. P. Grenier, "When Money Flows Like Wine, So Do the Memorable Quotes," *Wall Street Journal*, available at http://interactive.wsj.com/articles/SB1007395351240264440.htm (accessed September 7, 2008).

44. Grenier, "When Money Flows Like Wine."

45. N. Siggelkow, "Change in the Presence of Fit: The Rise, the Fall, and the Renaissance of Liz Claiborne," *Academy of Management Journal* 44 (2001): 838–857.

46. Interview with Stanley Gault, retired chairman and CEO, Rubbermaid, Inc., and The Goodyear Tire & Rubber Co., May 15, 2001.

47. A. Goldman, "Mattel CEO's Report Fails to Ease Investors' Doubts . . . but Barad Says the Worst Is Over," *Los Angeles Times*, October 22, 1999, p. 1.

48. R. Hof and P. Burrows, "Intel Won't Feel the Heat from This Fusion," *BusinessWeek*, November 5, 1995, p. 40.

49. Interview with Tony Galban, vice president, D&O underwriting manager, Chubb Group of Insurance Companies, June 26, 2002.

50. Interview with Tony Galban.

51. Interview with John Keogh.

52. Interview with Tony Galban.

Chapter Fourteen

1. Z. Ling, *The Lenovo Affair: The Growth of China's Computer Giant and Its Takeover of IBM-PC*, trans. M. Avery (Hoboken, N.J.: John Wiley & Sons, 2006), 354; Liu, C. "Lenovo: An Example of Globalization of Chinese Enterprises," *Journal of International Business Studies* (2007): 573–577.
2. C. I. Barnard, *The Functions of the Executive* (Cambridge, Mass.: Harvard University Press, 1968), 186.
3. A. Langley, H. Mintzberg, P. Pitcher, E. Posada, and J. Saint-Macary, "Opening Up Decision Making: The View from the Black Stool," *Organization Science* 6 (1995): 260–279.
4. M. Useem, "The Essence of Leading and Governing Is Deciding," in *Leadership and Governance from the Inside Out*, ed. R. Gandossy and J. Sonnenfeld (Hoboken, N.J.: John Wiley & Sons, 2004).
5. P. Gompers, J. Ishii, and A. Metrick, "Corporate Governance and Equity Prices," *Quarterly Journal of Economics* 118 (2003): 107–155; N. Liang and J. Li, "Board Structure and Firm Performance: An Empirical Study of China's Private Firms," *China and World Economy* 11 (2003): 51–59; E. Kang and A. Zardkoohi, "Board Leadership Structure and Firm Performance," *Corporate Governance: An International Review* 13 (2005): 785–799; T. Perry and A. Shivdasani, "Do Boards Affect Performance? Evidence from Corporate Restructuring," *Journal of Business* 78 (2005): 1403–1431; G. Chen, M. Firth, D. N. Gao, and O. Rui, "Ownership Structure, Corporate Governance, and Fraud: Evidence from China," *Journal of Corporate Finance* 12 (2006): 424–448; S. L. Gillan, "Recent Developments in Corporate Governance: An Overview," *Journal of Corporate Finance* 12 (2006): 381–402; T. Kato and C. Long, "Executive Compensation, Firm Performance, and Corporate Governance in China: Evidence from Firms Listed in the Shanghai and Shenzhen Stock Exchanges," *Economic Development & Cultural Change* 54 (2006): 945–983; and A. Yawson, "Evaluating the Characteristics of Corporate Boards Associated with Layoff Decisions," *Corporate Governance: An International Review* 14 (2006): 75–84.

6. A. Pye, "Corporate Boards, Investors and Their Relationships: Accounts of Accountability and Corporate Governing in Action," *Corporate Governance: An International Review* 9 (2001): 193.
7. J. A. Sonnenfeld, "What Makes Great Boards Great," *Harvard Business Review* (September 2002): 106–113; U.S. Senate, Permanent Subcommittee on Investigations of the Committee on Governmental Affairs, *The Role of the Board of Directors in Enron's Collapse* (Washington, D.C.: U.S. Senate, 2002); and M. Useem, "Governing Decisions in Corporate Governance," in *New Issues in Corporate Governance*, P. V. Urlacher, ed. (Hauppauge, N.Y.: Nova Science Publishers, 2008).
8. See, for instance, E. Fama and M. Jensen, "Separation of Ownership and Control," *Journal of Law and Economics* 26 (1983): 301–325.
9. Business Roundtable, *Principles of Corporate Governance* (New York: Business Roundtable, 2005), 5.
10. See, for instance, T. McNulty and A. Pettigrew, "Strategists on the Board," *Organizational Studies* 20 (1999): 47–74; C. Sundaramurthy and M. Lewis, "Control and Collaboration: Paradoxes of Governance," *Academy of Management Review* 28 (2003): 397–415; J. D. Westphal and M. K. Bednar, "Pluralistic Ignorance in Corporate Boards and Firms' Strategic Persistence in Response to Low Firm Performance," *Administrative Science Quarterly* 50 (2005): 262–298; C. B. Carter and J. W. Lorsch, *Back to the Drawing Board: Designing Corporate Boards for a Complex World* (Boston: Harvard Business School Press, 2004); R. Leblanc and J. Gillies, *Inside the Boardroom: How Boards Really Work and the Coming Revolution in Corporate Governance* (Hoboken, N.J.: John Wiley & Sons, 2005); and M. Useem, "How Well-Run Boards Make Decisions," *Harvard Business Review* (November 2006): 130–138.
11. M. Useem and A. Zelleke, "Oversight and Delegation in Corporate Governance: Deciding What the Board Should Decide," *Corporate Governance* 14 (2006): 9.
12. R. V. Aguilera and A. Cuervo-Cazurra, "Source Codes of Good Governance Worldwide: What Is the Trigger?" *Organization Studies* 25 (2004): 415–443: and C. Gabbioneta, D. Ravasi, and P. Mazzola,

"Exploring the Drivers of Corporate Reputation: A Study of Italian Securities Analysts," *Corporate Reputation Review* 10 (2007): 99–123.

13. V. Nee, S. Opeer, and S. Wong, "Developmental State and Corporate Governance in China," *Management and Organization Review* 3 (2007): 19–53.
14. X. Wu, *Conditions and Environment for Improving Corporate Governance Structure of China's Financial Enterprises* (Beijing: Zhongguo Renmin Yinhang (People's Bank of China), 2005), www.pbc.gov.cn/English; and E. C. Chang and S.M.L. Wong, "Political Control and Performance in China's Listed Firms," *Journal of Comparative Economics* 32 (2004): 617–636.
15. J. Lorsch with E. MacIver, *Pawns or Potentates: The Reality of America's Corporate Boards* (Boston: Harvard Business School Press, 1989).
16. See, for instance, D. R. Beresford, N. deB. Katzenbach, and C. B. Rogers Jr., *Report of Investigation by the Special Investigative Committee of the Board of Directors of WorldCom, Inc.*, March 31, 2003.
17. M. Useem, *Investor Capitalism: How Money Managers Are Changing the Face of Corporate America* (New York: Basic Books/HarperCollins, 1996).
18. Research Center, Shanghai Stock Exchange, *China Corporate Governance Report 2004: Independence and Effectiveness of Boards of Directors* (Shanghai: Fudan University Press, 2004).
19. Research Center, Shanghai Stock Exchange, *China Corporate Governance Report 2004*.
20. J. F. Xue, *Ownership Structure, Corporate Governance and Corporate Performance*, Ph.D. dissertation, Shanghai University of Finance and Economics, 2001.
21. M. W. Meyer and X. Lu, "Managing Indefinite Boundaries: The Strategy and Structure of a Chinese Business Firm," *Management and Organization Review* 1 (2005): 57–86.
22. See, for instance, M. Fong, "Chinese Refrigerator Maker Finds U.S. Chilly," *Wall Street Journal*, March 18, 2008, p. B1.

23. Liu, "Lenovo: An Example of Globalization of Chinese Enterprises."
24. Ling, *The Lenovo Affair;* and Liu, "Lenovo: An Example of Globalization of Chinese Enterprises."
25. Ling, *The Lenovo Affair*, 354, 366.
26. M. Useem, N. Liang, and J. Wan, "Lenovo Chairman Liu Chuanzhi: 'We Have Decided to Refocus on PCs,'" *Knowledge@Wharton*, September 8, 2004, http://knowledge.wharton.upenn.edu/article.cfm?articleid=1035; and M. Useem, *The Go Point: When It's Time to Decide* (New York: Crown Business/Random House, 2006).
27. B. G. Glaser and A. L. Strauss, *Discovery of Grounded Theory: Strategies for Qualitative Research* (Hawthorne, N.Y.: Aldine de Gruyter, 1967).
28. M. Ma, "Newsmaker Q&A: Lenovo's 'Unique Opportunity,' CFO Mary Ma Says after the IBM PC Deal," *BusinessWeek*, December 8, 2004.
29. Institutional Shareholder Services, *Governance Ratings on Lenovo*, personal communication, December 21, 2007.
30. International Data Corporation, *PC Shipments Worldwide, by Vendor, 2004 & 2005*, www.eMarketer.com (accessed December 19, 2007).
31. D. Primack, "Lenovo Gives TPG, General Atlantic a China Presence," *Buyouts*, March 6, 2006; and V. Feng, and P. Anderson, "General Atlantic Shares Secrets of its Success in China: INSEAD's Phillip Anderson Interviews Vince Feng of General Atlantic," 2007. Available at http://generalatlantic.com/uploads/0000/0015/General_Atlantic_Shares_Secrets.pdf.
32. W. J. Amelio, "View from the Top," *Financial Times*, August 3, 2007.
33. J. Engen, "Inside the Board of the Chinese Company That Bought IBM's PC Business," *Corporate Board Member* (May-June 2005): 2; and J. Engen, "Lessons from Lenovo," *Corporate Board Member* (September-October 2006).
34. Liu, "Lenovo: An Example of Globalization of Chinese Enterprises," 577.
35. W. Niu and M. Li, "Yang Yuanqing Proves Lenovo to the World," *China Entrepreneurs*, November, 2007 (in Chinese).

36. RateFinancials Inc, *NYSE-Traded Chinese Companies Have Poor Earnings Quality and Inadequate Governance* (New York: RateFinancials, 2007), www.ratefinancials.com; Heidrick and Struggles, with Fudan University's School of Management, "Benchmarking Corporate Governance in China," *Corporate Board Member* (2007); J. Allen, "The Race Changes: Rankings and Results," CG *Watch* (2007); S.Y.L. Regional Cheung and H. Jang, "Scorecard on Corporate Governance in East Asia," Center for International Governance Innovation, 2006 (www.cigionline.org); Institutional Shareholder Services, *2006 Global Institutional Investor Study. Corporate Governance: From Compliance Obligation to Business Imperative* (Rockville, Md.: Institutional Shareholder Services, 2007); N. Liang (ed.), *Corporate Governance: American Experience and Chinese Practices* (Beijing: People's University Press, 2000); C. Lin, "Corporatisation and Corporate Governance in China's Economic Transition," *Economics of Planning* 34 (2001): 5–35; and Y. Su, D. Xu, and P. H. Phan, "Principal-Principal Conflict in the Governance of the Chinese Public Corporation," *Management and Organization Review* 4 (2008): 17–38.

37. W. J. Amelio, "Worldsource or Perish," *Forbes*, August 17, 2007.

38. Niu and Li, "Yang Yuanqing Proves Lenovo to the World."

39. M. Useem, J. Spector, and N. Liang, "TCL's Dongsheng Li: 'We Should Control and Own Our Brands,'" *Knowledge@Wharton*, June 1, 2005, available at http://knowledge.wharton.upenn.edu/article.cfm?articleid=1168 (accessed September 7, 2008).

40. C. Ouyang, "Liu Chuanzhi: What Did Lenovo Get from IBM PC Acquisition." *Economics and Finance*, December 12, 2007 (in Chinese).

41. P. Cappelli, H. Singh, J. V. Singh, and M. Useem, "The DNA of Indian Business Leadership: The Governance, Management, and Leadership of Indian Firms," presented at the National Human Resource Development Network Conference, Kolkata, India, November, 2007.

42. Standard and Poor's, "Foreign Sales by U.S. Companies on the Rise," Standard and Poor's, July 9, 2007.

43. M. W. Meyer, "China's Second Economic Transition: Building National Markets," *Management and Organization Review*, 2008: 11; CLSA and Asian Corporate Governance Association, *Report*, September 17, 2007; Lenovo, Annual Reports, 2001, 2002, 2003, 2004, 2005, 2006, and 2007; and G. Wei, "Ownership Structure, Corporate Governance and Company Performance in China," *Asia Pacific Business Review* 13 (2007): 519–545.

Chapter Fifteen

1. J. A. Sonnenfeld, "Good Governance and the Misleading Myths of Bad Metrics," *Academy of Management Executive* 18 (2004): 101–113.
2. SpencerStuart, *Spencer Stuart 2007 US Board Index* (New York: Spencer Stuart, 2007), www.spencerstuart.com/research/boards/1212 (accessed September 7, 2008).
3. For instance, the *Spencer Stuart 2007 US Board Index* (note 2) shows that average CEO tenure continues to decline, and its annual examination of CEO turnover in the S&P 500 shows that fewer CEOs are retiring from their positions, as opposed to leaving for other reasons such as resignations or dismissals, than they were prior to the passage of the Sarbanes-Oxley Act in 2002.
4. SpencerStuart, *Spencer Stuart 2007 US Board Index*.
5. W. W. George, "Wither Governance: Process or People?" in *Leadership and Governance from the Inside Out*, ed. R. Gandossy and J. Sonnenfeld (Hoboken, N.J.: John Wiley & Sons, 2004), 113.
6. J. Sonnenfeld, "What Makes Great Boards Great," *Harvard Business Review* 80, no. 9 (September 2002): 106–113.
7. R. Khurana, *Searching for a Corporate Savior: The Irrational Quest for Charismatic CEOs* (Princeton, N.J.: Princeton University Press, 2002).
8. I. Janis, *Victims of Groupthink: A Psychological Study of Foreign-Policy Decisions and Fiascoes* (Boston: Houghton Mifflin, 1972).
9. SpencerStuart, *Spencer Stuart 2007 US Board Index*.

Index

A

R

S